United States Edition

2022 Year C

Workbook for Lectors, Gospel Readers, and Proclaimers of the Word®

Catherine Cory

Elizabeth Nagel

Peter O'Leary

Stephen S. Wilbricht, csc

LTP

LITURGY
TRAINING
PUBLICATIONS

CONTENTS

WORKBOOK FOR LECTORS, GOSPEL READERS, AND PROCLAIMERS OF THE WORD® 2022, United States Edition © 2021 Archdiocese of Chicago. All rights reserved.

Liturgy Training Publications, 3949 South Racine Avenue, Chicago, IL 60609, 800-933-1800, fax: 800-933-7094, orders@ltp.org, www.LTP.org.

Cover art: Barbara Simcoe

(continues on next page)

Ordinary Time

This book was edited
by Victoria M. Tufano.
Christian Rocha was
the production editor,
Anna Manhart was the designer,
and Kari Nicholls was the
production artist.

Printed in the United States
of America

ISBN: 978-1-61671-624-0

WL22

In accordance with c. 827,
permission to publish was
granted on April 6, 2021, by
Most Rev. Robert Casey, Vicar
General of the Archdiocese of
Chicago. Permission to publish
is an official declaration of
ecclesiastical authority that
the material is free from doctrinal
and moral error. No legal
responsibility is assumed by
the grant of this permission.

MESSAGE AND PROCLAMATION

According to the *Catechism of the Catholic Church*, the liturgy is an "action" of the *whole Christ*, one that recapitulates the eternal drama in which "the Spirit and the Church enable us to participate whenever we celebrate the mystery of salvation in the sacraments" (1139). It is a celebration of the whole community: participative, connective, and joyful. Crucial to the celebration is the Liturgy of the Word, through which the Holy Spirit awakens faith, offering signs—in the lectionary and the book of the Gospels; in procession, incense, and candles; and in the place of proclamation at the ambo—and instruction—through the proclamation itself of the Word of God to the faithfully assembled. As the *Catechism* puts it, "The Spirit makes present and communicates the Father's work, fulfilled by the beloved Son" (1155).

To read the Word of God is an act of proclamation. What is being proclaimed? The faith itself. *Kerygma* is the Greek word for proclamation; it appears multiple times in the New Testament, in St. Paul's letters and in the Acts of the Apostles, for instance, to refer to both the act and the content of proclaiming the good news. In Paul's first letter to the Corinthians, he confesses, "When I came to you, brothers and sisters, *proclaiming* the mystery of God, I did not come with sublimity of words or of wisdom. For I resolved to know nothing while I was with you except Jesus Christ, and him crucified. I came to you in weakness and fear and much trembling, and my message and my *proclamation* were not with persuasive words of wisdom, but with a demonstration of spirit and power, so that your faith might rest not on human wisdom but on the power of God" (1 Corinthians 2:1–5; emphasis added). St. Paul doesn't want to be persuasive; rather, he wants his proclamation to reflect the spirit of God's power that fills him. When you proclaim, you reflect this spirit of the power of God.

In his apostolic exhortation *Evangelii gaudium*, Pope Francis insists that evangelization relies on a deeper understanding of proclamation. Francis refers to proclamation (he calls it *kerygma*, using the Greek term) as the "first announcement," whose essential confidence brings us deeper into the mystery of faith. (It is first because it is primary.) Francis is thinking of the importance of instruction when he writes, "All Christian formation consists of entering more deeply into the kerygma, which is reflected in and constantly illumines the work of catechesis, thereby enabling us to understand more fully the significance of every subject which the latter treats" (165). But this catechesis, which means simply a ministry of the word (catechesis, which

> The word of God constantly proclaimed in the Liturgy is always a living and effective word through the power of the Holy Spirit. It expresses the Father's love that never fails in its effectiveness toward us.

means instruction, comes from the Greek word *katechein*, which means "echo"), has an instructive social element you involve yourself in whenever you attend Mass and whenever you participate as a proclaimer of the Word. Francis insists, "The kerygma has a clear social content: at the very heart of the Gospel is life in community and engagement with others" (177). Engagement with the community and deepening your life in that community are precisely what you accomplish as a lector, Gospel reader, and proclaimer of the Word.

Alpha and Omega

"I am the Alpha and the Omega." Thus says the Lord in the Revelation to John. Twice, in fact, in the opening chapter and in the twenty-second. It's one of the most potent and memorable phrases in all of the New Testament. Among its many interpretations and purposes, it might usefully serve as a motto for all proclaimers of the Word in the Church: lectors, deacons, and priests. One way to paraphrase this claim is that God is saying, "I am the alphabet."

Language, of course, is the medium you use as a lector, the instrument you play. Effective proclaiming is like effective piano playing. As every music teacher knows, some students are no good at playing the piano because they don't practice and don't have a good feel for the instrument. Other students are pretty good because they practice and have learned how to read music and to play the notes in the proper order. A few students are superb because they combine the discipline of practice with an intimate and immediately audible feel for the instrument, combining voicing, pauses, skill, and poise. Proclamation involves a similar skill set. Practice is important, but so is developing as good a feel for language—your instrument—as you can.

How do we develop a feel for language? One of the main ways that meaning is conveyed when modern English is spoken is through the interplay of syntax (the order of words in a sentence or phrase) and stress (the emphasis in speech that falls on one part of a word or phrase over another). Poetry is the literary form most attentive to syntax and stress. Poetry in English is qualitative, which means that it relies on the repetition of strong stresses in words to convey its patterns and meanings. This is called meter.

Scripture is organized by book, chapter, and verse. This system of organization is modern, coming into use in the sixteenth century. It was first used in English when the *Geneva Bible* was published in 1560. Verses refer, in the main, to sentences, since most of Scripture is written in prose. Some verses are poetic verse, including especially the Psalms but also the prophetic books in the Old Testament. Nevertheless, because the use and study of verse in English involve descriptive terminology, it is helpful to think about proclaiming the Word as a lector, deacon, or priest in terms of reading poetry aloud.

There are five basic metrical units in English, the names for which are all borrowed from Greek. A metrical unit is a pattern of stressed (DA) and unstressed (da) syllables. The five basic units, with examples of words that follow each pattern, are

iamb—da-DA (Detroit);

trochee—DA-da (London);

anapest—da-da-DA (Tennessee);

dactyl—DA-da-da (Arkansas);

and spondee—DA-DA (New York).

There are other meters, of course, but it's useful to have a sense of these five basic units when you are reading anything aloud, including Scripture, much of which, even in English translation, comes through as poetry.

You will note that the two longest of these metrical units have only three syllables. This means, practically speaking, that every two or three syllables, when you read something aloud, there should be a stress, an emphasis. Identifying these stresses does not exaggerate the sound of the phrase; instead, it enhances the phrase, highlighting its natural expressiveness.

Consider again "I am the Alpha and the Omega." This statement, one of the boldest of all in the New Testament, doesn't require any exaggeration or intensification on your part beyond identifying where the stresses in this statement lie. First, in the personal pronoun. Second, in the first syllable of Alpha. And third, in the second syllable of Omega. You could write the statement out this way, using capital letters to emphasize the stresses:

I am the ALpha and the oMEGa.

That captures the stresses. However, it doesn't entirely capture the most effective pace for proclaiming this statement.

Thinking about metrical units in English, you can identify where the pauses in this statement might usefully lie. The pauses in your speaking set

---

It is necessary that those who exercise the ministry of reader . . . be truly suited and carefully prepared, so that the faithful may develop a warm and living love for Sacred Scripture from listening to the sacred readings.

---

the pace. Every two or three syllables, when speaking aloud, there is an opportunity for a pause, even if it's only a slight hesitation that allows you to enhance the stresses. We can use this symbol | to indicate pauses, however slight, and rewrite the statement from Revelation this way:

I | am the ALpha | and | the oMEGa.

An alternative reading would eliminate the third pause:

I | am the ALpha | and the oMEGa.

In the first version, the line has four beats:

1) I; 2) am the ALpha; 3) and; 4) the oMEGa.

The second version has three beats:

1) I; 2) am the ALpha; 3) and the oMEGa.

In the first version, the third pause, after "and," allows you to emphasize the parallel being drawn between the beginning and the end in the Lord's statement. In the second version, you speed ever so noticeably quicker to Omega, which is the word in the verse imbuing it with ominous power.

The Sacred Scriptures, above all in their liturgical proclamation, are the source of life and strength.

Both versions are effective. Both, if you speak them aloud (as practice), can be suited to your speaking style. And both possible readings reinforce one of the most helpful strategies for effective proclaiming: read slowly enough that stresses and emphases can be heard by the congregation. A good rule of thumb, easy to remember, when reading anything aloud is:

Read twice as loud and at half the pace that you normally speak.

Most lectors will be reading into a microphone, which means you need not increase your volume in the way you would without a microphone. However, the rule of thumb above can serve as a reminder that you are reading in front of an audience, your congregation, and the more clearly you proclaim, the more likely it is that they will pay attention. Like a teacher coming into a classroom and raising their voice above the level of the din or a coach blowing a whistle to get the attention of the team, you can command the attention of your congregation by the pitch and volume of your voice. Don't be afraid to use it.

Likewise, read slowly. Depending on the architecture of your church, it's likely that your amplified voice will echo. Reading slowly allows your words to be heard and absorbed, rather than reflected and distorted.

Similarly, the more clearly you read, while paying attention to where the stresses lie in the passage from Scripture you are reading, the more intelligible and available your proclaiming will be. You do not need to act out any of the phrases by changing the pitch of your voice or feigning emotion. Scripture already contains all the drama and power required for its proper expression. You need merely to voice it.

"Less is more" might be a useful axiom for proclaiming, but you don't want to excuse yourself from the work of proclaiming, which requires your presence for maximum effect. Your presence includes your voice, which allows you to announce the Word of God, but also your attention, which shows you where the stresses and emphases in the passage you are proclaiming lie. Simone Weil, the twentieth-century activist and mystic, wrote, "Absolutely unmixed attention is prayer." The attention you bring to your proclaiming enables you then to pray the Word of God with your congregation.

Readings Old and New

The Liturgy of the Word typically consists of a reading from the Old Testament, a reading from the New Testament (often one of the letters of Paul), and a reading from the Gospels. In the case of Year C, which this workbook covers, almost all of the Gospel readings, with exceptions on some of the feasts, come from Luke.

Gospel readings during Ordinary Time tend to go more or less in order. In Year C, they start from early in Luke and work towards the Gospel's end. Readings on feast days, as well as during the seasons of Advent, Christmas, Lent, and Easter, are selected specifically for those Sundays and don't necessarily follow a sequential order. The first reading—again, typically from the Old Testament—is selected to harmonize with the Gospel reading.

The second reading—again, often from one of the letters of Paul, but not always—is more deliberately instructive. Usually, from week to week at Sunday Mass, you will notice that one Sunday's second reading picks up where the previous week's left off.

Each of these parts of Scripture can be proclaimed differently, with subtle but valuable effects. First readings tend to be more poetic than second readings. You can effectively infuse your first reading with forms of poetic attention, being mindful especially of pauses, but also of some of the other rhetorical features that make Scripture so rich. These include

> *anaphora*, which is the use of the repetition of a word or phrase;
>
> *parallel structure*, in which an entire phrase is repeated with slight variation;
>
> *the imperative voice*, in which the speaker commands the audience to do something, usually to *listen*, to hear, and to *heed*; and
>
> *the power of questions*, in which the speaker asks forceful questions not necessarily easy or comfortable to answer.

Each of these rhetorical features serves to enhance the power of the words and phrases in the reading.

Consider the first reading for the Twenty-Second Sunday in Ordinary Time, from the third chapter of Sirach. This reading concerns advice, provided in the second person, for how best to behave. It's fairly short:

> My child, conduct your affairs with humility,
>   and you will be loved more than a giver of gifts.
> Humble yourself the more, the greater you are,
>   and you will find favor with God.
> What is too sublime for you, seek not,
>   into things beyond your stretch search not.
> The mind of a sage appreciates proverbs,
>   and an attentive ear is the joy of the wise.
> Water quenches a flaming fire
>   and alms atone for sins.
>   (Sirach 3:17–18, 20, 28–29)

The whole reading relies on repeated parallel structures in which a claim is made in the first line and then advanced or completed in the indented line immediately following. So, "conduct your affairs with humility" is followed by its completion, "and you will be loved more than a giver of gifts." Furthermore, each parallel is enhanced by the anaphora of the word *and*, which begins every indented line. In addition, as is often the case in an exhortatory reading, the imperative voice is used, which augments the urgency of the advice being given. Recognizing these

patterns can show you how best to proclaim these verses and where to lay the emphasis.

The Gospel for the Twenty-Second Sunday in Ordinary Time comes from a stretch of Luke's Gospel in which Jesus is actively preaching in parables as a way to instruct his listeners. In this case, it's a para-

---

God's word shows us what we should hope for with such a longing that in this changing world our hearts will be set on the place where our true joys lie.

---

ble giving advice to guests at a dinner party where they should sit (Hint: Not at the best seat at the table). Likewise, he gives advice to the host of a dinner party about whom to invite (Hint: Not the fanciest people you know but rather the lowliest). The first and Gospel readings in this way directly reinforce each other.

The second reading for the Twenty-Second Sunday in Ordinary Time offers a reading from the Letter to the Hebrews, a potent, exhortatory reading constructed in two parts. In the first part, in vivid language, the Hebrews are told what they have *not* done. In the second part, in equally vivid language, the Hebrews are told what they *have* done. The reading relies on repeated uses of the word *and* to drive home its point: to praise the Hebrews for the quality of their faith. Readings from the previous two Sundays are also drawn from Hebrews, a short run that this reading concludes.

Where the first reading is often poetic, the second reading is typically instructive. It's also almost always a shorter reading. You should proclaim it as instruction. Read slowly, take your time presenting its argument, and emphasize its point, which will come in the last sentence or two of the reading.

First and second readings always conclude with the phrase "The Word of the Lord." Try to pause a moment before you read this conclusion. Likewise, don't rush through the phrase. It will blur, sounding like "Word Lord." Instead, break the phrase into two units, reading it like this: The WORD | of the LORD.

It's effective to pause for two or three beats after you say this before stepping away from the ambo.

Preparation and Execution

It helps to practice. You should read through your assigned reading at least a few times, once silently to yourself to get its sense and two or three times aloud to get a feel for its rhythm and pace, as well as any unusual words, names, or place names. (The marginal pronunciation guides will help you with these.)

If you are assigned to proclaim the first reading, read the Gospel for that week as well. They will be connected in thematic ways. If you are assigned to proclaim the second reading, take a look at the previous week's second reading as well as the following week's to see where the second reading is coming from and where it is going. This will give you some context for the insights it contains.

For many of us, our main experience reading aloud comes from reading to children. Proclaiming Scripture is something different. When you practice reading aloud, it's better to read in as straightforward a way as possible than it is to try to dramatize your reading through inflection, pitch, or voicing in the way you might if you were reading something to a child. Scripture is unusually powerful in its expressiveness, symbolism, and language. If you read in a steady, evenly pitched, and articulate voice, its power will come through your reading. You will be during Mass the instrument of its power.

For many people, it can be a little intimidating to stand before a congregation and proclaim. You might find it helpful to place one of your index fingers in the margin of the lectionary to remind you of your place. You might also find it helpful to place your other hand on the ambo to steady yourself. This has the effect of giving you the appearance of an open posture.

As you read, try to look up from time to time and make eye contact. Choose faces in different places of the assembled congregation to focus on when you look up, sometimes close by, sometimes farther back, and sometimes from one side to the other. This simple gesture has an inclusive effect; you are not merely reading to the congregation, you are reading for it and with it. If you use your index finger to keep your place in the lectionary, you will not worry about getting lost whenever you look up.

That said, you are not performing. You don't need to smile unnecessarily, you don't need to emote beyond what the words themselves suggest, and you don't need somehow to exemplify the words in your comportment or your presentation. The words of Scripture are utterly endowed with power. You are the instrument to voice that power. A sincere and plainspoken proclamation will invariably convey that power to your fellow congregants.

For the purposes of your proclaiming, you can usefully consider readings falling into three general forms: *narrative*, *didactic*, and *exhortatory*. (These designations are taken from Douglas Leal, author of *Stop Reading and Start Proclaiming!* and an author for *Workbook* in previous years.)

A *narrative* reading tells a story, containing a plot. It moves from point to point and typically comes to a conclusion. Many of these stories, because of their repetition in the liturgy but also because of their importance to Christian thought, are very familiar. Take some pleasure in that familiarity while also encouraging your assembly to listen to the whole story, including all of its setup and context, which you can do by focusing on the pace of the story and its rhythm as accented in its language.

A *didactic* reading offers instruction, often leading to a specific point of teaching or faith. Paul's letters are typically didactic. He is trying to instruct members of the early Church on how to behave and what to believe. So much of what Paul writes is new to these communities, and therefore confusing. Paul's tone sometimes betrays his exasperation. He wants these followers to understand! When you read a didactic reading, imagine yourself not as the letter's writer (whether Paul or James or John or Peter, for instance) but as the recipient of that letter. Put yourself in the shoes of its hearer, which is exactly what you and your congregation are.

An *exhortatory* reading is one that makes an urgent appeal. (It comes from the word *exhort*, which comes from *ex-*, an intensifier, plus *hortari*, "to urge," and means to thoroughly urge or encourage.) Many of the writings from the prophets in the Old Testament are exhortatory, urging their listeners to change their lives or to prepare themselves for some divinely mandated change. Likewise, the Gospels contain exhortations when Jesus is preaching and even when he is talking to his disciples. An exhortatory reading is like God directly addressing us. When you proclaim an exhortatory reading, treat it as though it is intended for you personally. Imagine you are hearing it for the first time.

Participation

For inspiration, consider these words by Pierre Teilhard de Chardin, from *The Divine Milieu*, his "essay on the interior life."

> We may, perhaps, imagine that the Creation was finished long ago. But that would be quite wrong. It continues still more magnificently, and in the highest zones of the world. *Omnis creatura adhuc ingemescit et parturit.* And we serve to complete it, even by the humblest work of our hands. That is, ultimately, the meaning and value of our acts. Owing to the inter-relation between matter, soul, and Christ, we lead part of the being which He desires back to God *in whatever we do.* With each one of our *works,* we labor—atomically, but no less really—to build the Pleroma; that is to say, to bring to Christ a little fulfillment.

The Church is nourished spiritually at the twofold table of God's word and of the Eucharist: from the one it grows in wisdom and from the other in holiness.

For Teilhard, "Pleroma" means the mysterious fullness of creation. The Latin phrase *omnis creatura adhuc ingemescit et parturit,* refers to Romans 8:22, "all creation is groaning in labor pains until now." We are still in the process of creation; whenever you participate in the Mass, you are adding to that work. And whenever you proclaim at Mass, you are helping, by the humblest work of your voice, to bring to Christ a little fulfillment.

Boxed quotations throughout this article are from the introduction to the *Lectionary for Mass.*

Peter O'Leary

The Authors

Catherine Cory is associate professor of theology at the University of St. Thomas in St. Paul, MN. She holds a doctorate in New Testament studies with sub-specialties in Old Testament and early Church. Her research interests are in the Gospel of John and Revelation. She has edited and/or authored several books including *The Christian Theological Tradition, A Voyage through the New Testament,* and *Revelation* for the New Collegeville Bible Commentary series. In addition to her academic teaching at the undergraduate and graduate level, she enjoys doing adult education presentations at local parishes.

Elizabeth M. Nagel is a professor emerita of biblical exegesis at the University of Saint Mary of the Lake / Mundelein Seminary and a retired president of its Pontifical Faculty of Theology. She earned the licentiate (SSL) and doctorate (SSD) in Sacred Scripture at the Pontifical Biblical Institute and is the author of *Be a Blessing: A Spring of Refreshment on the Road of Daily Life* and a contributor to the *Paulist Biblical Commentary* (2018).

Peter O'Leary studied religion and literature at the Divinity School of the University of Chicago, where he received his doctorate. He has written several books of poetry, most recently, *Earth Is Best,* as well as two books of literary criticism, most recently *Thick and Dazzling Darkness: Religious Poetry in a Secular Age.* He teaches at the School of the Art Institute of Chicago and at the University of Chicago. He lives with his family in Oak Park, Illinois.

Stephen S. Wilbricht, CSC, is associate professor in the Religious Studies and Theology Department at Stonehill College in Easton, MA. He holds a doctorate in sacred theology from the Catholic University of America in Washington, DC, and has served in two parishes in the Southwest. He is the author of several books, including *Baptismal Ecclesiology and the Order of Christian Funerals* (LTP, 2018), *The Role of the Priest in Christian Initiation* (LTP, 2017), and *Rehearsing God's Just Kingdom: The Eucharistic Vision of Mark Searle* (Liturgical Press, 2013). He is also a team member for LTP's *Catechumeneon.*

The authors' initials appear at the end of the Scripture commentaries.

An Option to Consider

The third edition of *The Roman Missal* encourages ministers of the Word to chant the introduction and conclusion to the readings ("A reading from . . . "; "The word of the Lord"). For those parishes wishing to use these chants, they are demonstrated in audio files that may be accessed either through the QR codes given here (with a smartphone) or through the URL indicated beneath the code. This URL is case sensitive, so be careful to distinguish between the letter l (lowercase L) and the numeral 1.

The first QR code contains the tones for the first reading in both a male and a female voice.

http://bit.ly/l2mjeG

The second QR code contains the tones for the second reading in both a male and a female voice.

http://bit.ly/krwEYy

The third QR code contains the simple tone for the Gospel.

http://bit.ly/iZZvSg

The fourth QR code contains the solemn tone for the Gospel.

http://bit.ly/lwf6Hh

A fuller explanation of this new practice, along with musical notation for the chants, is provided in a downloadable PDF file found at http://www.ltp.org /t-productsupplements.aspx. Once you arrive at this web page, scroll until you find the image of the cover of *Workbook*, click on it, and the PDF file will appear.

Recommended Works

Find a list of recommended reading and assistance in considering and implementing chanted introductions and conclusions to the readings in downloadable PDF files at http://www.ltp.org/products/details /WL22.

Pronunciation Key

bait = bayt	thin = thin
cat = kat	vision = VIZH*n
sang = sang	ship = ship
father = FAH-ther	sir = ser
care = kayr	gloat = gloht
paw = paw	cot = kot
jar = jahr	noise = noyz
easy = EE-zee	poison = POY-z*n
her = her	plow = plow
let = let	although = ahl-THOH
queen = kween	church = cherch
delude = deh-LOOD	fun = fuhn
when = hwen	fur = fer
ice = īs	flute = floot
if = if	foot = foot
finesse = fih-NES	

Shorter Readings

In the Scripture readings reproduced in this book, shorter readings are indicated by brackets and a citation given at the end of the reading.

FIRST SUNDAY OF ADVENT

Jeremiah = jayr-uh-MĪ-uh

An exhortatory reading. This reading defines the anticipatory mindset that characterizes Advent.
Equal emphasis on "those" and "that."

Steady rhythm from "do" to "right" to "just" to "land."

For meditation and context:

LECTIONARY #3

READING I   Jeremiah 33:14–16

A reading from the Book of the Prophet Jeremiah

The **days** are **coming**, says the L ORD ,
   when I will **fulfill** the **promise**
   I **made** to the **house** of **Israel** and **Judah.**
In **those** days, in **that** time,
   I will raise **up** for David a **just shoot**;
   he shall **do** what is **right** and **just** in the **land.**
In those days **Judah** shall be **safe**
   and **Jerusalem** shall dwell **secure**;
   this is what they shall **call** her:
"The L ORD our **justice.**"

RESPONSORIAL PSALM   Psalm 25:4–5, 8–9, 10, 14 (1b)

R. To you, O Lord, I lift my soul.

Your ways, O L ORD , make known to me;
   teach me your paths,
guide me in your truth and teach me,
   for you are God my savior,
   and for you I wait all the day.

Good and upright is the L ORD ;
   thus he shows sinners the way.
He guides the humble to justice,
   and teaches the humble his way.

All the paths of the L ORD are kindness
   and constancy
   toward those who keep his covenant
   and his decrees.
The friendship of the L ORD is with those
   who fear him,
   and his covenant, for their instruction.

TO KEEP IN MIND

The responsorial psalm "has great liturgical and pastoral importance, since it fosters meditation on the Word of God," the *General Instruction of the Roman Missal* says. Pray it as you prepare.

READING I On this first Sunday of Advent, the first reading comes from the Book of Jeremiah, who was a prophet during the siege of Jerusalem by the Babylonians in the latter part of the sixth century BC. In this extremely dark time in Judah's history, all seemed lost, and it appeared that God had turned away from the chosen people. Yet Jeremiah has a message of hope for all who await the coming reign of God, which will be manifested in the birth of a messiah from the line of David.

In this reading, the prophet announces the emergence of a shoot or sprout from David's line. This allusion to an orchard or vineyard is a metaphor for kingship: this sprout will act with justice over the land. Justice or righteousness are attributes usually given to God; this sprout from David's line mirrors an essential characteristic of God. Those to whom we proclaim this reading might be reminded of the prophecy that Nathan made to David: from his line would come an everlasting king who would be like

a son to God and to whom God would be like his father (2 Samuel 7:8–17). Notice, also, the assignment of a new name to Jerusalem: "The Lord our Justice." God's justice or righteousness consists of judgment against Judah's sins, of course, but also mercy, and the mercy of God is evident in today's reading.

Thessalonians = thes-uh-LOH-nee-uhnz

An exhortatory reading in which Paul challenges the members of the early Church in Thessalonica to improve themselves.

Even emphasis on "blameless" and "holiness."

Stress both "conduct" and "conducting."

READING II   1 Thessalonians 3:12—4:2

A reading from the first Letter of Saint Paul to the Thessalonians

Brothers and **sisters**:
May the **Lord** make you **increase** and **abound** in **love**
  for one **another** and for **all**,
  just as we **have** for **you**,
  so as to **strengthen** your **hearts**,
  to be **blameless** in **holiness** before our **God** and **Father**
  at the **coming** of our Lord **Jesus** with **all** his **holy** ones. Amen.

Finally, brothers and sisters,
  we earnestly **ask** and **exhort** you in the Lord **Jesus** that,
  as you **received** from us
  how you should **conduct** yourselves to **please** God
  —and as you are **conducting** yourselves—
  you **do** so even **more**.
For you **know** what **instructions** we **gave** you
    through the Lord **Jesus**.

READING II Today's reading from Paul's communication with the Christian community in Thessalonica also anticipates the future manifestation of God's reign. Paul has been encouraging the community not to lose hope over the delay of the return of Christ in glory at the end time. He also tells them how they ought to live in this "between time," which he does in the form of a prayer. He asks that they love one another so that they might strengthen each other and be ready to present themselves as pure and holy before God and the messiah-king, when he returns in glory at the end time. We who still await the return of Christ should heed Paul's advice and live in the "between time" with love for one another so we can one day reign with Christ forever.

GOSPEL The Gospel for today follows easily from the first two readings on the theme of God's justice and the coming messiah, but it focuses more specifically on how the believers will recognize the coming Day of the Lord. As Luke tells the story, Jesus and his disciples were in the precincts of the Jerusalem Temple, and Jesus made a prophecy about the destruction of the Temple. His disciples then asked when this terrible thing would happen. Jesus answered by talking about signs of the end time, typical of apocalyptic literature of the time: first there will be wars, earthquakes, and cosmic phenomena, and people will be running to hide from the anticipated disaster. But then he describes "the Son of Man coming in a cloud with power and great glory" (Luke 21:27) to rescue the believers. And what should the believer do? Stand tall with your heads high, Jesus says, because your

GOSPEL   Luke 21:25–28, 34–36

A reading from the holy Gospel according to Luke

Jesus said to his disciples:
"There will be **signs** in the **sun**, the **moon**, and the **stars**,
    and on earth **nations** will be in **dismay**,
      perplexed by the **roaring** of the **sea** and the **waves**.
People will die of **fright**
    in **anticipation** of what is **coming** upon the **world**,
    for the **powers** of the **heavens** will be **shaken**.
And then they will **see** the Son of **Man**
    coming in a **cloud** with **power** and great **glory**.
But when these **signs** begin to **happen**,
    stand **erect** and raise your **heads**
    because your **redemption** is at **hand**.

"Beware that your **hearts** do not become **drowsy**
    from **carousing** and **drunkenness**
    and the **anxieties** of daily **life**,
    and that **day** catch you by **surprise** like a **trap**.
For that **day** will assault **everyone**
    who **lives** on the **face** of the **earth**.
Be **vigilant** at all **times**
    and **pray** that you have the **strength**
    to **escape** the **tribulations** that are **imminent**
    and to **stand** before the **Son** of **Man**."

An exhortatory reading thrumming with apocalyptic anticipation. Be forceful. These exhortations, especially in the second half, are colored with teaching, offered in the imperative.

Note how the signs are heavenly, things seen in the heavens.

This verse marks a slight shift in the kind of attention to be paid.

carousing = kuh-ROW-zing

The core of the reading: "Be vigilant."

tribulations = trih-byoo-LAY-shuhnz
imminent = IM-uh-nuhnt

---

redemption is at hand. What a beautiful promise of hope and sign of confidence!

In the Gospels, the title "Son of Man" is one that Jesus uses of himself, but biblical scholars have long been puzzled over its precise origin and original meaning. One theory is that it is simply a way for Jesus to talk about himself, the human Jesus, in the third person, but clearly something more significant than that is intended here. The book of Daniel contains a number of visions purportedly given to Daniel, a member of the Jewish aristocracy in Jerusalem, who was taken into captivity during the Babylonian Exile. In one particular vision, he describes seeing God's court convened in heaven and the beast and its arrogant horn—symbols of the empire that was persecuting the Jews of that time—being destroyed in God's burning fires. As the vision continues, Daniel saw "One like a Son of Man," that is, someone who resembled a human being, coming from the heavenly realm on a cloud and appearing before the Ancient of Days, who is God. The idea of someone riding on a cloud will sound strange to us today, but ancient peoples believed that the clouds were sky vehicles used to transport angels and spirits throughout the cosmos.

Who is this "One like a Son of Man"? The prophet does not tell us directly. In the interpretation that follows this vision, however, "One like a Son of Man" is equated with "the holy ones of the Most High, whose kingship shall be an everlasting kingship and whom all dominions shall serve and obey" (Daniel 7:27). In other words, Daniel's "One like a Son of Man" is a symbol for the holy ones who will participate in the coming reign of God. Will we choose to be among them? C.C.

DECEMBER 5, 2021

SECOND SUNDAY OF ADVENT

LECTIONARY #6

READING I   Baruch 5:1–9

A reading from the Book of the Prophet Baruch

Jerusalem, take off your **robe** of **mourning** and **misery**;
  put on the **splendor** of **glory** from **God** forever:
Wrapped in the **cloak** of **justice** from **God**,
  bear on your head the **mitre**
  that **displays** the **glory** of the eternal **name**.
For God will **show** all the **earth** your **splendor**:
  you will be **named** by God **forever**
  the **peace** of justice, the **glory** of God's **worship**.

Up, Jerusalem! **stand** upon the **heights**;
  look to the **east** and **see** your **children**
gathered from the **east** and the **west**
  at the **word** of the **Holy One**,
  rejoicing that they are **remembered** by God.
Led away on **foot** by their **enemies** they **left** you:
  but **God** will bring them **back** to **you**
  borne **aloft** in glory as on royal **thrones**.
For **God** has commanded
  that every lofty **mountain** be made **low**,
and that the age-old **depths** and **gorges**
  be **filled** to level **ground**,
  that **Israel** may advance **secure** in the glory of **God**.
The **forests** and **every fragrant kind** of tree
  have overshadowed **Israel** at God's **command**;

Baruch = buh-ROOK

An exhortatory reading replete with rich imagery and forceful expressions. No need to overplay these elements. Pay attention to the rhythms of the reading and they will come through.

Emphases on the first words in these lines: "Wrapped" and "bear."

Emphasis on "Up," but don't over-dramatize this by shouting.

TO KEEP IN MIND
Read the Scripture passage and its commentary in *Workbook*. Then read it from your Bible, including what comes before and after it, so that you understand the context.

Even emphasis on "every fragrant kind."

READING I Today's first reading is taken from the book of Baruch. According to Josephus, the first-century AD Jewish historian, Baruch was part of the Jewish aristocracy of Jerusalem and the manager of King Zedekiah's household. Later he became a scribe for the prophet Jeremiah, and both witnessed the destruction of Jerusalem and the deportation of its people in the Babylonian Exile in the late sixth century BC. However, the book of Baruch, which is a collection of prayers, poems, and prophetic speeches, was prob-

ably written over a longer period of time by a variety of authors.

In this segment of the book, the prophet is speaking to personified Jerusalem to comfort her in what appears to be a mourning ceremony. Perhaps we could think of her as "sitting *shiva*." Among our Jewish brothers and sisters, "sitting *shiva*" is a seven-day rite of mourning in the home of the bereaved, which starts immediately after the funeral. Sometimes the family members and close friends sit on low stools to symbolize how they are "brought

low" by the loss of their loved one, as others come to comfort them.

But Baruch urges Jerusalem to throw off her garments of grief and put on the garment of the splendor of glory and the cloak of God's justice so that all may see that her period of mourning is finished. The miter, or turban, that she is given to wear recalls the one that was prescribed for the priest Aaron. It had a gold plate in the form of a seal that read "Holy to the Lord" (Exodus 28:36–37). She is also given a new name: "the peace of justice and the glory of

4

for **God** is leading **Israel** in **joy**
   by the **light** of his **glory**,
   with his **mercy** and **justice** for **company**.

For meditation and context:

RESPONSORIAL PSALM   Psalm 126:1–2, 2–3, 4–5, 6 (3)

R. The Lord has done great things for us; we are filled with joy.

When the LORD brought back the captives
      of Zion,
   we were like men dreaming.
Then our mouth was filled with laughter,
   and our tongue with rejoicing.

Then they said among the nations,
   "The LORD has done great things
      for them."
The LORD has done great things for us;
   we are glad indeed.

Restore our fortunes, O LORD,
   like the torrents in the southern desert.
Those who sow in tears
   shall reap rejoicing.

Although they go forth weeping,
   carrying the seed to be sown,
they shall come back rejoicing,
   carrying their sheaves.

Philippians = fih-LIP-ee-uhnz

READING II   Philippians 1:4–6, 8–11

A reading from the Letter of Saint Paul to the Philippians

An exhortatory reading in which St. Paul is trying to encourage the members of the early Church at Philippi. Adopt an encouraging tone in your proclamation.

Brothers and **sisters**:
I pray always with **joy** in my every prayer for **all** of you,
   because of your **partnership** for the **gospel**
   from the **first day** until **now**.
I am **confident** of this,
   that the **one** who began a **good work** in you
   will **continue** to **complete** it
   until the **day** of Christ **Jesus**.

Emphasis on "confident." This word conveys St. Paul's hope for the recipients of this letter.

God is my **witness**,
   how I long for **all** of you with the **affection** of Christ **Jesus**.
And **this** is my **prayer**:
   that your **love** may increase **ever** more and **more**
   in **knowledge** and every **kind** of **perception**,
   to **discern** what is of **value**,
   so that you may be **pure** and **blameless** for the day of **Christ,** »

Emphasis on "this": St. Paul's prayer is that the Philippians' love will increase.

discern = dih-SERN

God's worship." How radiant is Lady Jerusalem adorned in splendor! Further, Baruch tells Jerusalem to stand tall and look toward Babylon in the east to see her children rejoicing as they make their way toward her from across the lands. And who is leading the caravan? It is none other than God accompanied by God's personified justice and mercy! Can you imagine Lady Jerusalem's sense of relief and amazement?

READING II This reading from Paul's Letter to the Philippians introduces the themes of the letter, but it

also gives us some hints about Paul's relationship to the community of faith. Clearly, Paul loves them! He prays in thanksgiving for the partnership (Greek *koinonia*, meaning "community" or "joint participation") that he shares with them.

Paul is writing to this community from prison (Philippians 1:12–13), which explains his longing for them with "the affection of Christ Jesus." After all, Christ's suffering was an act of love, too. The Greek word that is translated here as "affection" is associated with the bowels or intestines. Ancient peoples believed that this was the

seat of a person's strongest emotions, like love and hate. Thus, we should think of this affection not as simple fondness but as zealous love. Paul urges the community to continue to grow in *agape* love, the kind of love that knows no bounds and that expects nothing in return. It is the kind of love that will make them pure and blameless, when Christ returns in glory. The phrase "fruit of righteousness" describes the active response of Christian believers to the gift of right relationship with God. Elsewhere, Paul calls it "faith working through love" (Galatians 5:6).

filled with the fruit of **righteousness**
that **comes** through **Jesus Christ**
for the **glory** and **praise** of **God**.

GOSPEL Luke 3:1–6

A reading from the holy Gospel according to Luke

In the **fifteenth** year of the **reign** of Tiberius Caesar,
    when **Pontius Pilate** was **governor** of Judea,
    and **Herod** was **tetrarch** of **Galilee**,
    and his brother **Philip tetrarch** of the **region**
        of **Ituraea** and **Trachonitis**,
    and **Lysanias** was **tetrarch** of **Abilene**,
    during the **high priesthood** of **Annas** and **Caiaphas**,
    the **word** of **God** came to **John** the son of **Zechariah**
        in the **desert**.
John went throughout the **whole region** of the **Jordan**,
    proclaiming a **baptism** of **repentance** for the **forgiveness**
        of **sins**,
    as it is **written** in the **book** of the **words** of the prophet **Isaiah**:
    *A **voice** of one crying **out** in the **desert**:*
    *"**Prepare** the way of the **Lord**,*
        *make **straight** his **paths**.*
    *Every **valley** shall be **filled***
        *and every **mountain** and **hill** shall be made **low**.*
    *The **winding roads** shall be made **straight**,*
        *and the **rough ways** made **smooth**,*
    *and all **flesh** shall see the **salvation** of **God**."*

Tiberius = tī-BEER-ee-uhs
Caesar = SEE-zehr

A narrative reading that concludes with the quotation of a prophetic exhortation. Hearing this proclamation, your congregation is drawn back into prophetic foretime.

Take some time to practice the unusual place and personal names in these verses. There's a list below.

Note the pace of this line: even emphasis on "John went" and "whole region."

Modulate your voice slightly in pitch to signal the words of Isaiah.

Pontius = PON-shuhs
Pilate = PĪ-luht
Judea = joo-DEE-uh or joo-DAY-uh
Ituraea = ih-too-REE-ah
Tetrarch = TET-rahrk
Trachonitis = trak-uh-NĪ-tihs
Lysanias = lī-SAY-nee-uhs
Annas = AN-uhs
Caiaphas = KAY-uh-fuhs or KĪ-uh-fuhs

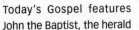 Today's Gospel features John the Baptist, the herald of the coming kingdom or reign of God. Luke introduces him by providing a historical setting for his story in a very long, elegantly constructed sentence that extends from the beginning to the end of the first paragraph of our reading. Luke wants the reader to know that this is an important turning point in the Gospel.

While the presentation of John as the baptizer is found in all four Gospels, Luke includes two interesting details about John's mission. First, he notes that John traveled throughout the region or surrounding neighborhood of the Jordan River with his proclamation. In other words, he was a traveling preacher. Second, we learn that his message included a baptism of repentance for the forgiveness of sin. The Greek word *baptisma* means "immersion" or "submersion," but we should not confuse it with Christian baptism, which will come later. Rather, this is a purification ritual that has deep roots within Judaism; it signifies one's desire to be put right with one another and the world. The Greek word *metanoia*, which is translated as "repen-

tance," appears several times in Luke's Gospel, and it means "a change of mind." The Greek word for forgiveness means "a release from bondage."

Finally, John the Baptist's mission as one who models how we ought to prepare for the coming reign of God is emphasized by Luke's inclusion of Isaiah 40:3–5, which is a prophecy about an exodus from bondage. Now it is our own exodus from the bondage of sin, and we live in hope of seeing the salvation of God. C.C.

THE IMMACULATE CONCEPTION OF THE BLESSED VIRGIN MARY

LECTIONARY #689

READING I   Genesis 3:9–15, 20

A reading from the Book of Genesis

This reading contains some of the conclusion of one of the foundational narratives of our faith. Because it is a very familiar story, slow your recitation slightly to emphasize its richness.

After the man, **Adam**, had **eaten** of the **tree**,
 the Lord God **called** to the man and **asked** him,
  "Where are you?"
He answered, "I **heard** you in the **garden**;
 but I was **afraid**, because I was **naked**,
 so I **hid myself.**"
Then he asked, "Who **told** you that you were **naked**?
You have **eaten**, then,
 from the **tree** of which I had **forbidden** you to **eat**!"

The shifting of blame from Adam to Eve and then from Eve to the serpent is crucial to the reading's drama. You can locate this shift in the repetition of the word "woman."

The man replied, "The **woman** whom you **put here** with me—
 she **gave me fruit** from the **tree**, and so I **ate** it."
The Lord God then asked the **woman**,
 "Why did you **do** such a **thing**?"
The woman answered, "The **serpent tricked me** into it,
 so I **ate** it."

Here, the scorn is heaped on the serpent. The punishment God metes out is as cruel as it is deserved.

Then the Lord God said to the **serpent**:
 "**Because** you have done this, you shall be **banned**
  from all the **animals**
  and from all the **wild creatures**;
 on your **belly** shall you **crawl**,
  and **dirt** shall you **eat**
  all the **days** of your **life**. »

READING I   The Solemnity of the Immaculate Conception is a frequently misunderstood feast. Briefly, it celebrates the teaching that Mary, the mother of Jesus, was preserved free from the effects of original sin at the moment of her conception, when the soul animated the body, and that she was further protected from sin during her lifetime, so that she could be a fitting host for the incarnate Christ. From earliest times, the traditions of the Church professed the holiness of Mary. Already in the seventh century AD, there was a feast of the Conception of Mary, but

it was not universally observed. There was not, as yet, an official doctrine of Mary's sinlessness, even though theologians of the Eastern Churches had been talking about it as early as the fifth century AD. Finally, on December 8, 1854, Pope Pius IX issued a public declaration entitled *Ineffabilis Deus* and made its teaching about Mary's sinlessness from the moment of her conception an official doctrine of the Catholic Church.

Among the many images and metaphors used over the centuries to describe Mary, the mother of Jesus, one of the earliest and the one that is most consistent

with this feast is Mary, the new Eve. The parallel is obvious if we think about Adam and Eve before the fall, when they did not yet know sin or evil. This was Mary's state of being throughout her life.

Today's first reading describes the consequences of Adam and Eve's sin and God's promise to humanity of future redemption. A really smart snake told Eve that eating from the tree of the knowledge of good and evil would make them wise like God, but instead, by eating from the forbidden tree, the pair learned evil. God appeared in the garden, prepared to take an evening walk

enmity = EN-mih-tee = mutual hatred

> I will put **enmity** between **you** and the **woman**,
>   and between your **offspring** and hers;
> he will **strike** at your **head**,
>   while you **strike** at his **heel**."

The reading ends with Eve being named. The shift from "woman" to "Eve" feels significant. Convey this in your reading.

> The man called his wife **Eve**,
>   because she became the **mother** of **all** the **living**.

For meditation and context:

RESPONSORIAL PSALM   Psalm 98:1, 2–3ab, 3cd–4 (1)

R. Sing to the Lord a new song, for he has done marvelous deeds.

Sing to the LORD a new song,
    for he has done wondrous deeds;
His right hand has won victory for him,
    his holy arm.

The LORD has made his salvation known:
    in the sight of the nations he has revealed
        his justice.
He has remembered his kindness and
    his faithfulness
toward the house of Israel.

All the ends of the earth have seen
    the salvation by our God.
Sing joyfully to the LORD, all you lands;
    break into song; sing praise.

Ephesians = ee-FEE-zhuhnz

READING II   Ephesians 1:3–6, 11–12

A reading from the Letter of Saint Paul to the Ephesians

Brothers and sisters:

Blessed = BLES-uhd
Blessed = blesd

An exhortatory reading. Notice the three divisions: "Blessed be the God and Father . . . ," "In love he destined us . . . ," and "In him we were also chosen." Use these divisions to organize your reading.

> **Blessed** be the **God** and **Father** of our **Lord** Jesus Christ,
>   who has **blessed** us in Christ
>   with every **spiritual blessing** in the **heavens**,
>   as he chose us **in him**, before the **foundation** of the **world**,
>   to be **holy** and without **blemish** before him.
> In **love** he **destined us** for **adoption** to himself
>   through **Jesus** Christ,
>   in **accord** with the **favor** of his will,
>   for the **praise** of the **glory** of his **grace**
>   that he **granted** us in the **beloved**.

Slight emphasis on "praise," "glory," and "grace."

with Adam and Eve, but they are nowhere to be found. When God called to them, Adam replied that he had been hiding because he was naked. Having lost his innocence, shame entered into humanity's relationship with God. When God asked how they knew about their nakedness, Adam responded by blaming Eve. Eve, in turn, blamed the crafty serpent for tricking her into eating from the tree. Thus, deception and blame further hindered humanity's relationship with God.

The consequences of Adam and Eve's sin continue to be manifest as the story

unfolds. No longer can they live in the garden, because only goodness and well-being are allowed there. Before they are made to leave the garden, God makes clothing to protect them from the cruelties of life. Women will suffer in childbirth and be required to submit to their husbands, and men will have to work hard for a living. This is an etiology, a story that explains the origin of things.

But all is not lost. God promised that the woman would bear an offspring who will eventually crush the head of that crafty serpent. As the story ends, we learn that

Adam names his wife Eve, "the mother of the living." Thus, Eve is a type—a pattern or blueprint of a greater reality—of Mary and her offspring, Jesus, who will defeat evil and redeem humanity of their sin.

READING II   Our second reading begins with a formula of blessing that is commonly found in early Jewish and Christian prayers of the time. It then enumerates some of the reasons why God should be blessed: for God's many gifts of spiritual blessings, for having chosen us to be holy and spotless before God, for destining us to

This is Paul's point.

In **him** we were also **chosen**,
    destined in accord with the **purpose** of the One
    who **accomplishes** all things according to the **intention**
        of his **will**,
    so that we might **exist** for the **praise** of his **glory**,
    we who **first hoped** in Christ.

You are assuring the assembly of this first hope.

GOSPEL   Luke 1:26–38

A reading from the holy Gospel according to Luke

A narrative reading of one of the most solemn passages in the Gospels, which is also one of the most frequently depicted by artists through the centuries. It's very easy to visualize as a result. Treat it like a pageant.

The **angel Gabriel** was **sent** from God
    to a **town** of **Galilee** called **Nazareth**,
    to a **virgin betrothed** to a man named **Joseph**,
    of the **house** of David,
    and the **virgin's name** was Mary.
And coming to her, he said,
    "**Hail**, **full** of **grace**! The **Lord** is with **you**."

Because these words are so familiar from prayer, they can have a new life in the context of this reading.

But she was **greatly troubled** at what was **said**
    and **pondered** what sort of **greeting** this might be.
Then the **angel** said to her,
    "**Do not** be **afraid**, Mary,
    for you have found **favor** with God.
Behold, you will **conceive** in your womb and **bear** a son,
    and you shall **name him** Jesus.
He will be **great** and will be called **Son** of the **Most High**,
    and the **Lord God** will give him the **throne** of David his **father**,
    and he will **rule over** the house of **Jacob forever**,

"Most High" and "no end" share a rhythmical and thematic echo.

    and of his **Kingdom** there will be **no end**."
But **Mary** said to the **angel**,
    "How can this **be**,
    since I have **no relations** with a **man**?" »

---

become part of God's family through the agency of Jesus Christ. Biblical scholars are not certain whether the phrase "in love" refers to humanity and its relationship to God (in the previous sentence) or to God's motivation for choosing to include humanity in God's family (in the following sentence). The translation used in our lectionary prefers the latter. Regardless, the Greek word used for love is *agape*, the kind of love that is God-given in the sense that it is boundless and with no strings attached. Notice also that the author of this letter describes Jesus as God's beloved, a form of the same

root word, *agape*. And none of this is by our merit. Rather, it is according to God's will and plan that we exist to praise God. Amen, alleluia!

GOSPEL   Today's Gospel is a familiar one to most of us. It is the story of the Annunciation, in which the angel Gabriel tells Mary that she will conceive by the Holy Spirit and bear a son, who is to be called Jesus. The setting for this story is Nazareth, a mostly Jewish town in Galilee. Although it is extremely difficult to gauge the population of ancient cities,

archeologists estimate that it was a relatively small town. It could have had as many as 1,200 inhabitants, but it more likely had as few as 500. Mary is engaged to a man named Joseph.

According to ancient Near Eastern cultural practice, girls were engaged to be married as soon as it was clear that they would make it to adulthood, perhaps as young as twelve or thirteen years of age. Because of high mortality rates, it was not uncommon for a woman to be married a second or even a third time, but clearly Mary is very young, since she is twice described

And the **angel** said to her in **reply**,
 "The Holy Spirit will **come upon** you,
 and the **power** of the **Most High** will over**shadow** you.
Therefore the **child** to be **born**
 will be called **holy**, the **Son** of **God**.
And **behold**, Elizabeth, your relative,
 has **also conceived** a son in her old age,
 and this is the **sixth month** for her who was called **barren**;
 for **nothing** will be **impossible** for God."
Mary said, "**Behold**, I am the **handmaid** of the **Lord**.
May it be **done** to **me** according to **your word**."
Then the **angel departed** from her.

This is the good news that Gabriel delivers to Mary.

And Mary's declaration defines the role of all believers, including the Church.

as a virgin. Most likely, this was an arranged marriage. Mary and Joseph might have known about each other before marriage, but they would not have been dating or anything of the sort. Among first-century Jews, betrothal was a serious commitment; canceling an engagement required a writ of divorce.

As the story unfolds, we learn that Mary was visited by an angel and was troubled by his greeting. He called her "Graced One," which means "encircled by favor." The angel reiterates his greeting by telling

her that she need not be afraid because she has found favor with God. After being told that she would bear a son, and after the angel explains the mission and destiny of this child, Mary asks "How can this be?" One might be tempted to think that this question amounts to a refusal to cooperate with God's will, but that is far from the truth. She is neither ignorant nor naïve. She is well aware of where babies come from and of her virginal state. But having received the angel's response, and with little confirmation except for the announcement that her

cousin, who had been barren, would soon deliver a child, she said, "Yes, God's will be done!" Her free and full obedience is what earns Mary the title "the New Eve." C.C.

THIRD SUNDAY OF ADVENT

LECTIONARY #9

Zephaniah = zef-uh-NĪ-uh

An exhortatory reading of high-hearted encouragement.

Slight extra emphasis on "against" to distinguish it from "judgment."

Emphasis on "not" and "discouraged." This line speaks directly to your assembly.

Slight extra emphasis on "because."

TO KEEP IN MIND
Pause after you announce the book of the Bible at the beginning of the reading. Pause again after the reading, before you proclaim the concluding statement ("The Word of the Lord" or "The Gospel of the Lord").

READING I   Zephaniah 3:14–18a

A reading from the Book of the Prophet Zephaniah

> **Shout** for **joy**, O **daughter Zion**!
>   Sing **joyfully**, O **Israel**!
> Be **glad** and **exult** with all your **heart**,
>   O **daughter** Jerusalem!
> The LORD has removed the **judgment against** you,
>   he has turned **away** your **enemies**;
> the King of **Israel**, the LORD, is in your **midst**,
>   you have no **further** misfortune to **fear**.
> On that **day**, it shall be **said** to Jerusalem:
>   Fear **not**, O **Zion**, be not **discouraged**!
> The LORD, your **God**, is in your **midst**,
>   a mighty **savior**;
> he will **rejoice** over you with **gladness**,
>   and **renew** you in his **love**,
> he will sing **joyfully because** of you,
>   as one **sings** at **festivals**.

READING I The Third Sunday of Advent is traditionally celebrated as Gaudete ("rejoice") Sunday. In the liturgy for this day, which is at the midpoint of Advent, the theme is joy and gladness as we anticipate the celebration of Christ's coming.

In today's first reading, we hear from the prophet Zephaniah, who preached during the reign of King Josiah (ruled 640–609 BC) of Judah. It was a time of political turmoil, when Assyria's power was beginning to wane and Egypt, which was allied with Assyria, was trying to keep its empire from collapsing. Babylon was quickly moving in to fill the power vacuum, and there sat tiny Judah in the middle. In the first part of this book, Zephaniah writes a lot about the Day of the Lord, meaning judgment day. He rails against Judah for its idol worship, and he delivers several oracles or threats against nations that were traditional enemies of Judah.

However, in the last part of the book, which includes today's reading, Zephaniah's oracles of doom become powerful and consoling words of hope and promise, especially for Jerusalem, also known as Zion or Daughter Zion. The prophet delivers a call to joy by saying that Jerusalem should rejoice as God rejoices over its people and showers love upon them. Jerusalem no longer needs to be discouraged or afraid, because God, her savior, has vanquished its enemies. Moreover, twice in this short reading, Zephaniah declares that God dwells (present tense) among the chosen people. If we let this reality truly sink into our consciousness, we can do nothing else but be overwhelmed with joy.

11

For meditation and context:

RESPONSORIAL PSALM   Isaiah 12:2–3, 4, 5–6 (6)

R. Cry out with joy and gladness: for among you is the great and Holy One of Israel.

God indeed is my savior;
  I am confident and unafraid.
My strength and my courage is the LORD,
  and he has been my savior.
With joy you will draw water
  at the fountain of salvation.

Give thanks to the LORD, acclaim his name;
  among the nations make known his deeds,
  proclaim how exalted is his name.

Sing praise to the LORD for his glorious
    achievement;
  let this be known throughout all
    the earth.
Shout with exultation, O city of Zion,
  for great in your midst
  is the Holy One of Israel!

Philippians = fih-LIP-ee-uhnz

READING II   Philippians 4:4–7

A reading from the Letter of Saint Paul to the Philippians

An exhortation. St. Paul is being encouraging.

The emphasis here is on "Rejoice," which St. Paul repeats.

Proclaim this line slowly and clearly.

"Thanksgiving" informs the "prayer" and "petition."

Brothers and **sisters**:
Rejoice in the Lord **always**.
I shall say it again: **rejoice**!
Your **kindness** should be **known** to **all**.
The **Lord** is **near**.
Have no **anxiety** at all, but in **everything**,
  by **prayer** and **petition**, with **thanksgiving**,
  make your **requests** known to **God**.
Then the **peace** of **God** that **surpasses** all **understanding**
  will guard your **hearts** and **minds** in Christ **Jesus**.

READING II   Today's second reading continues the theme of rejoicing. In fact, it is one of the central themes of Paul's Letter to the Philippians. Nowhere does Paul actually define what he means by joy and rejoicing, but it is not equivalent to happiness, contentment, pleasure, or satisfaction. He exhorts the Christian community to rejoice, even as he sits in prison, not knowing whether he will be killed or released to continue his ministry (Philippians 1:18; see 1:13, 20). He also writes about his joy for the community, while he praises

them for steadfastness in their faith in the face of persecution (Philippians 1:25). In other words, for Paul, joy is closely related to suffering as Christ suffered.

Here, in the closing exhortations of this letter, Paul urges the community to "rejoice in the Lord always," acting with great kindness and without fear and praying with confidence, because the Lord is near. And what shall be our reward? God's peace that "surpasses all understanding." Whether this phrase means a peace "too great for our minds to comprehend" or a

peace that "accomplishes more than we can imagine" is not clear. Regardless, it is worthy of our deep and abiding joy.

GOSPEL   Today's Gospel is a continuation of the Gospel reading for the Second Sunday of Advent, in which John the Baptist is presented as a traveling preacher who offered a baptism of repentance for the forgiveness of sin. Today we see John acting as a mentor for those who want to participate in the coming reign of God. The other Gospels have nothing that

GOSPEL   Luke 3:10–18

A reading from the holy Gospel according to Luke

The **crowds** asked John the **Baptist**,
  "What should we **do**?"
He said to them in **reply**,
  "Whoever has **two cloaks**
  should **share** with the person who has **none**.
And whoever has **food** should do **likewise**."
Even **tax** collectors came to be **baptized** and they **said** to him,
  "**Teacher**, what should we **do**?"
He **answered** them,
  "**Stop collecting more** than **what** is **prescribed**."
Soldiers also asked him,
  "And what is it that **we** should do?"
He told them,
  "Do not practice **extortion**,
  do not falsely accuse **anyone**,
  and be **satisfied** with your **wages**."

Now the **people** were **filled** with **expectation**,
  and **all** were **asking** in their **hearts**
  whether **John** might be the **Christ**.
John answered them all, saying,
  "I am **baptizing** you with **water**,
  but one **mightier** than I is **coming**.
I am not **worthy** to loosen the **thongs** of his **sandals**.
He will **baptize** you with the Holy **Spirit** and **fire**.
His **winnowing** fan is in his **hand** to clear his **threshing** floor
  and to gather the **wheat** into his **barn**,
  but the **chaff** he will **burn** with **unquenchable fire**."
Exhorting them in many other ways,
  he preached good **news** to the **people**.

A narrative reading that concludes with a grand exhortation. You are speaking to underscore the anticipations of the Advent season.

This reading consists of advice John the Baptist provides in response to questions he is asked. The advice he offers forms the moral core of Church teachings. The first advice is about charity.

The second advice is about not imposing unnecessary hardships on others.

extortion = ehk-STOHR-shuhn

The third advice is about not cheating or lying.

John the Baptist concludes with this exhortation about the one who is to come. Emphasis on "Holy Spirit" and "fire."

winnowing = WIN-oh-wihng

exhorting = ehg-ZOHRT-ing

---

parallels this. It is important to recognize this because, when we examine the unique features of a Gospel, we can deduce something about the Gospel writer's theology.

The refrain that runs through today's Gospel is "What then should we do?" and there are two things we should observe about the text. First, who is asking for John's advice? Luke identifies three groups: the crowds, the tax collectors, and the soldiers. Jewish religious authorities looked down on the crowds as ignorant and uneducated about Jewish law. The tax collectors were considered to be corrupt because they made their living by charging more than the Roman authorities demanded and keeping the rest for themselves. The soldiers were likely Jewish militia belonging to Herod Antipas, and they were hated because their job was to enforce Roman rule on their own people. Notice that all three groups belonged to the marginalized when compared to the religious authorities of early Judaism.

Second, what kind of advice does John give to those who want to see "the salvation of God" (Luke 3:6)? To anyone who has two cloaks, share! For the poor, especially, a cloak was a necessity of life; it not only kept a person warm and dry when they were outside, but it also served as bedding at night. To the tax collector, do not cheat by taking more than what is due. To the soldier, do not extort the population or falsely charge people with crimes. It is no wonder that the people questioned whether John was the messiah, because Jesus would soon teach the same things—justice and mercy—on behalf of the poor and marginalized of society. C.C.

FOURTH SUNDAY
OF ADVENT

Micah = MĪ-kuh

An exhortatory reading of an emphatic promise for the people made by God. Ephrathah = EF-ruh-thuh

Emphasis on "you," as above in the second line of the reading.

Emphasis on "Therefore," at which point the mood of the reading elevates even more into the positive.

TO KEEP IN MIND

The words in bold are suggestions for ways to express the meaning of the reading. Consider using them as you practice the reading, then choose to stress them or to find your own way of proclaiming.

Equal emphasis on "reach," "ends," and "earth"; likewise, on "peace." Don't swallow this last word of the reading.

LECTIONARY #12

READING I   Micah 5:1–4a

A reading from the Book of the Prophet Micah

> **Thus** says the LORD:
> **You**, Bethlehem-Ephrathah,
>   too **small** to be among the **clans** of **Judah**,
> from **you** shall come **forth** for **me**
>   **one** who is to be **ruler** in **Israel**;
> whose **origin** is from of **old**,
>   from **ancient times**.
> **Therefore** the **Lord** will give them up, until the **time**
>   when **she** who is to give **birth** has **borne**,
> and the **rest** of his **kindred** shall **return**
>   to the **children** of **Israel**.
> He shall stand **firm** and shepherd his **flock**
>   by the **strength** of the ,
>   in the majestic name of the LORD, his **God**;
> and they shall **remain**, for **now** his greatness
>   shall **reach** to the **ends** of the **earth**;
> he shall be **peace**.

READING I Although little is known about the life of the prophet Micah, his writings suggest that his ministry was directed toward the southern kingdom of Judah during and after the Assyrian conquest of the northern kingdom of Israel in 722 BC. Like most prophetic books, Micah is composed of oracles, or prophecies, of doom and oracles of promise. Today's reading is an example of an oracle of promise, but this one is especially noteworthy because early Christians saw it as a prophecy about the birth of Jesus.

The oracle of promise that composes today's first reading is preceded by another powerful oracle about Daughter Zion, which is Jerusalem personified. It promises that God's house will be established on the highest mountain—Jerusalem is on a mountain —and that swords will be beaten into plowshares, meaning that there will be no more war. On that day, the prophet declares, the lame, the weak, and the outcasts will be restored. But the prophet, speaking for God, also asks why Jerusalem cries out as if in labor. Is it because you have no king? Is it because you are besieged by your enemies?

This is the context for today's first reading. The prophet issues God's promise that a ruler for Israel will come from Bethlehem, which was the hometown of Jesse and his son David, but this is not a new prophecy. The prophet says that the promise of a ruler for Israel has its origin in ancient times. Although Jerusalem's children will continue to suffer for a short time— this is the meaning of "the Lord will give them up"—Daughter Zion will soon be ready to give birth. Her child will become king by God's authority, and Jerusalem's inhabitants will return to her. Further, we

For meditation and context:

RESPONSORIAL PSALM   Psalm 80:2–3, 15–16, 18–19 (4)

R. Lord, make us turn to you; let us see your face and we shall be saved.

O shepherd of Israel, hearken,
  from your throne upon the cherubim,
    shine forth.
Rouse your power,
  and come to save us.

Once again, O LORD of hosts,
  look down from heaven, and see;
take care of this vine,
  and protect what your right hand
    has planted,
  the son of man whom you yourself
    made strong.

May your help be with the man of your
    right hand,
  with the son of man whom you yourself
    made strong.
Then we will no more withdraw from you;
  give us new life, and we will call upon
    your name.

Hebrews = HEE-brooz

A didactic reading that follows an effective rabbinical strategy of citing from Scripture and then pulling it apart to interpret its meaning, to be concluded by a final claim.

This first part of the reading consists of the quotation. Which, as it happens, includes a quotation within a quotation. Proclaim slowly and confidently so this element is clear.

holocausts =
HAHL-uh-kawsts *or* HOH-luh-kawsts
The second part of the reading begins with and consists mostly of the act of pulling apart the quotation in the first part. Proclaim these verses like they are evidence.

With "By this 'will,'" the final claim. Emphasis on "consecrated."

READING II   Hebrews 10:5–10

A reading from the Letter to the Hebrews

Brothers and **sisters**:
When **Christ** came into the **world**, he said:
  "**Sacrifice** and **offering** you did **not** desire,
    but a **body** you **prepared** for me;
  in **holocausts** and **sin offerings** you took no **delight**.
  Then I said, 'As is **written** of me in the **scroll**,
  behold, I come to **do** your **will**, O **God**.'"

First he says, "**Sacrifices** and **offerings**,
  holocausts and **sin** offerings,
  you neither **desired** nor **delighted** in."
These are offered **according** to the law.
Then he says, "**Behold**, I **come** to do your **will**."
He takes away the **first** to establish the **second**.
By this "**will**," we have been **consecrated**
  through the **offering** of the body of Jesus **Christ** once for **all**.

---

are told, this king will be a shepherd of the people. This imagery was often used in early Judaism to refer to a good and just king. Moreover, this king will be peace. The prophet does not say he will bring peace, but rather he will be peace! What does it mean to be peace?

READING II Today's second reading comes from the Letter to the Hebrews. We do not know the author of this letter, but it appears to have been a Jewish Christian writing in approximately AD 80–90. Also, although we call this docu-

ment a letter, it does not follow the pattern of a letter. It is more like a homily, designed to encourage people to hold fast to the Gospel and to warn against apostasy, abandoning the faith. In making his case, the author uses arguments that we might call "from the lesser to the greater." If something can be demonstrated to be true in a small matter, then it must be even more true when it concerns a greater matter that is similar to the first.

  This reading picks up the second half of a "lesser to greater" argument that began with a statement about how Jewish

Law was a foreshadowing of greater things to come (Hebrews 10:1). Next, the author suggests that the sacrifice offered on Yom Kippur, the day of atonement, was not fully effective because it had to be repeated each year. While you might argue with the author's logic, the point he wants to make is that Christ's once-for-all sacrifice makes other sacrifices unnecessary (Hebrews 10:2). Using quotations from the Old Testament, the author provides evidence that sacrifices and sin offerings were required by Jewish Law, but, in Christ, we experience the real, more perfect sacrifice. Because

GOSPEL   Luke 1:39–45

A reading from the holy Gospel according to Luke

A narrative reading of sublime beauty.

Mary set out
   and **traveled** to the **hill** country in **haste**
   to a town of **Judah**,
   where she **entered** the house of **Zechariah**
   and greeted **Elizabeth**.

Zechariah = zek-uh-RĪ-uh

When **Elizabeth** heard Mary's **greeting**,
   the **infant** leaped in her **womb**,
   and **Elizabeth**, **filled** with the Holy **Spirit**,
   cried **out** in a loud **voice** and said,

This is a reading of a sign and the wonder that arises from it. The infant, John the Baptist, leaping in the womb is the sign.

   "**Blessed** are you among **women**,
   and **blessed** is the **fruit** of your **womb**.

These words form the basis of one of our most cherished prayers. They express the wonder of Elizabeth.

And **how** does this **happen** to me,
   that the **mother** of my **Lord** should come to **me**?
For at the **moment** the **sound** of your **greeting** reached my **ears**,
   the **infant** in my **womb** leaped for **joy**.

A crucial repetition of the sign of the child leaping in the womb.

blessed = BLE-s*d

Repetition of "Blessed," which extends our understanding of Mary's sanctity.

Blessed are you who **believed**
   that what was **spoken** to you by the **Lord**
   would be **fulfilled**."

Christ does the will of the Father in all things, his sacrifice of obedience, which reaches its zenith in his crucifixion, surpasses the Law.

GOSPEL   Today's Gospel is a familiar one for many of us. The story of the visitation of Mary to her cousin Elizabeth during her pregnancy is told only in Luke's Gospel. It comes after the parallel stories of the angel Gabriel's announcement to Zechariah, husband of Elizabeth, concerning the birth of John the Baptist and his announcement to Mary, betrothed to Joseph, concerning the virginal conception and birth of Jesus. We know that Luke's presentation of Mary and Elizabeth's encounter is not intended to be a strictly historical account, because it would have been incomprehensible for a young pregnant girl, living in first-century Palestine, to undertake a journey of several days on foot and by herself. Instead, we should think of this story as a theological statement about the blessings God bestowed on humanity through these two women. Consider the sacrifice that Mary made in allowing herself to participate in God's gracious plan to bring salvation to the world. Think about how Elizabeth, empowered by the Holy Spirit, was able to discern that her unborn baby would be the precursor of Jesus, when he "leaped for joy" in her womb. Such are the fruits of the Holy Spirit. C.C.

THE NATIVITY OF THE LORD (CHRISTMAS): VIGIL

LECTIONARY #13

READING I   Isaiah 62:1–5

A reading from the Book of the Prophet Isaiah

For **Zion's** sake I will **not** be **silent**,
    for **Jerusalem's** sake I will **not** be **quiet**,
until her **vindication shines forth** like the **dawn**
    and her **victory** like a burning **torch**.

Nations shall **behold** your **vindication**,
    and all the **kings** your **glory**;
you shall be **called** by a new **name**
    pronounced by the **mouth** of the LORD.
You shall be a **glorious crown** in the **hand** of the LORD,
    a **royal diadem** held by your God.
No more shall people call you "**Forsaken**,"
    or your land "**Desolate**,"
but you shall be called "**My Delight**,"
    and your land "**Espoused**."
For the LORD **delights** in you
    and makes your land his **spouse**.
As a young man marries a **virgin**,
    your **Builder** shall **marry** you;
and as a **bridegroom rejoices** in his **bride**
    so shall your God rejoice in **you**.

Sidebar notes (left column):

Isaiah = ī-ZAY-uh

An exhortatory reading. Notice the repetitions of the phrase "you shall." Pace your readings with each expression of "you shall" (or its variations) as a marker.

Notice the sound carried from "Zion's" to "silent" to "quiet."

diadem = DĪ-uh-dem

Give extra emphasis to each of these four names.

Even emphasis on all the words in this last line, with extra added on "you."

There are options for today's readings. Contact your parish staff to learn which readings will be used.

READING I   If you have ever had the opportunity of watching a sunrise over the desert, you can appreciate the imagery that is used in the opening verses of today's first reading. The relatively clean air and the lack of humidity make the longer wavelengths of light—the oranges and reds—appear much more intense, and the horizon can look like it is on fire. Consider this scenario as a backdrop for our reflection on this reading from the prophet Isaiah.

At the opening of this oracle, the prophet speaks in God's name, saying that he refuses to keep silent any longer. This part of Isaiah is thought to have been written after the Babylonian Exile, when a remnant of God's people had begun to return to Judea. In an earlier part of Isaiah, the prophet describes God as saying, with reference to the Exile, "For a long time I have kept silent" (Isaiah 42:14). In other words, God has decided that it is time to act on Lady Jerusalem's behalf, and God will not stop until her salvation and vindication, or righteousness, shine like a brilliant sunrise in the desert or a flaming torch for all the nations to see.

What will Lady Jerusalem's vindication be like? The shame of her devastation under the Babylonians will be lifted, she will be given a new name, and she will be like a bride to God. The imagery is especially rich and evocative. Lady Jerusalem will be like a glorious crown in God's hand. In other words, metaphorically speaking, God will "wear her on his head" as a symbol of his kingship. The Hebrew word *tipharah*, which

For meditation and context:

RESPONSORIAL PSALM   Psalm 89:4–5, 16–17, 27, 29 (2a)

R. For ever I will sing the goodness of the Lord.

I have made a covenant with my chosen one,
    I have sworn to David my servant:
forever will I confirm your posterity
    and establish your throne for
        all generations.

Blessed the people who know the
        joyful shout;
    in the light of your countenance, O LORD,
        they walk.

At your name they rejoice all the day,
    and through your justice they are exalted.

He shall say of me, "You are my father,
    my God, the rock, my savior."
Forever I will maintain my kindness
        toward him,
    and my covenant with him stands firm.

READING II   Acts of the Apostles 13:16–17, 22–25

A reading from the Acts of the Apostles

When **Paul** reached Antioch in Pisidia and entered the synagogue,
    he stood up, motioned with his hand, and said,
    "**Fellow Israelites** and you others who are **God-fearing**, **listen**.
The God of this people **Israel** chose our **ancestors**
    and exalted the people during their **sojourn** in the land
        of Egypt.
With **uplifted arm** he led them **out** of it.
Then he removed **Saul** and raised up **David** as king;
    of him he testified,
    'I have found **David**, son of **Jesse**, a man after my own **heart**;
    he will carry out my **every** wish.'
From this man's descendants **God**, according to his **promise**,
    has brought to Israel a **savior**, **Jesus**.
John heralded his coming by proclaiming a **baptism** of **repentance**
    to **all** the people of Israel;
    and as John was completing his course, he would say,
    'What do you suppose that I **am**? I **am not he**.
Behold, one is coming **after** me;
    I am not **worthy** to unfasten the **sandals** of his **feet**.'"

Antioch = AN-tee-ahk
Pisidia = pih-SID-ee-uh
sojourn = SOH-jern (exile)
A didactic reading that sets up a prophetic succession, beginning with the Israelites in the desert and moving from David to John the Baptist, and finally to Jesus.

Though Paul is speaking in this reading, he is quoting the words of his predecessors. You can modulate your voice slightly to suggest this shift.

Paul concludes with John the Baptist's memorable phrase about Jesus. A slight emphasis on "sandals" and "feet" will remind the assembly whose words these are.

---

is here translated as "glorious," can refer to a woman's extreme beauty or her exalted status. In Exodus 28:2, it is used to describe the vestments of the high priest Aaron, brother of Moses.

God will also give Lady Jerusalem a new name. In the ancient world, the act of naming was seen as a way to exert authority over another or to claim him or her as one's own. Her old names, Forsaken and Desolate, reflect a time when the Israelites broke covenant with God. Thus, God restores relationship with the chosen people by giving Lady Jerusalem the name "My Delight is

in her" and by calling her land "Espoused." With Israel's purity and innocence restored, she can be called God's bride once again. This is cause for great rejoicing!

READING II The second reading for this vigil is from the Acts of the Apostles. According to Luke, when Saul and Barnabas were in Antioch in Syria, they were commissioned by the community, at the prompting of the Holy Spirit, to set out on a missionary journey to do the work to which the Spirit called them (Acts 13:2–3). Thus, Saul and Barnabas arrived in Antioch

of Pisidia (in southern Turkey today), after a stop at Perga in Pamphylia. These two cities were approximately 100 miles apart and accessible only through a mountainous passage, so this trip must have been extremely arduous.

On the Sabbath after they arrived, Saul and Barnabas attended synagogue services, and after the readings from the Law and Prophets, the synagogue officials asked them to speak. By the way, some synagogues continue this practice today when visitors join the congregation for Sabbath prayers. Saul—known as Paul from this

A whopper of a reading. Much of it is didactic before it shifts into a narrative. The first part of this reading is a performative, rhythmical incantation, one unusual name leading to the next. It goes from Abraham to David; from David to the Babylonian exile; from the Babylonian exile to Jesus. It's a folding screen with two hinges, each panel of the screen exactly the same size, and the image of Jesus' birth appears on its front.

Genealogy = jee-nee-OL-uh-jee
Judah = JOO-duh
Perez = PAYR-ez
Zerah = ZEE-rah
Tamar = TAY-mahr
Hezron = HEZ-ruhn
Ram = ram
Amminadab = uh-MIN-uh-dab
Nahshon = NAH-shon
Salmon = SAL-muhn
Boaz = BOH-az
Rahab = RAY-hab
Obed = OH-bed
Jesse = JES-ee

Uriah = yoo-RI-uh
Rehoboam = ree-huh-BOH-uhm
Abijah = uh-BĪ-juh
Asaph = AY-saf
Jehoshaphat = jeh-HOH-shuh-fat
Joram = JOHR-uhm
Uzziah = yuh-Zī-uh
Jotham = JOH-thuhm
Ahaz = AY-haz
Hezekiah = hez-eh-Kī-uh

GOSPEL   Matthew 1:1–25

A reading from the holy Gospel according to Matthew

The book of the **genealogy** of **Jesus Christ**,
    the son of David, the son of Abraham.

Abraham became the father of **Isaac**,
    Isaac the father of **Jacob**,
    Jacob the father of **Judah** and his **brothers**.
Judah became the father of **Perez** and **Zerah**,
    whose mother was **Tamar**.
Perez became the father of **Hezron**,
    Hezron the father of **Ram**,
    Ram the father of **Amminadab**.
Amminadab became the father of **Nahshon**,
    Nahshon the father of **Salmon**,
    Salmon the father of **Boaz**,
    whose mother was **Rahab**.
Boaz became the father of **Obed**,
    whose mother was **Ruth**.
Obed became the father of **Jesse**,
    Jesse the father of **David** the **king**.

David became the father of **Solomon**,
    whose **mother** had been the wife of **Uriah**.
Solomon became the father of **Rehoboam**,
    Rehoboam the father of **Abijah**,
    Abijah the father of **Asaph**.
Asaph became the father of **Jehoshaphat**,
    Jehoshaphat the father of **Joram**,
    Joram the father of **Uzziah**.
Uzziah became the father of **Jotham**,
    Jotham the father of **Ahaz**,
    Ahaz the father of **Hezekiah**. »

point onward—rose and addressed the community, waving his hands in a gesture of inclusion. Imagine Paul saying something like "You all gathered here, Jews and Gentiles who seek God, *you* are God's chosen ones." Having garnered their attention, he begins a beautiful summary retelling of Israel's salvation history. For the sake of brevity and focus, the lectionary omits a few verses of the biblical text and jumps from the Exodus to the reign of King David. Paul describes David as a man after God's own heart and as the one from whom God would bring forth a savior, whose name was

Jesus. Further, he tells the story of John the Baptist (see Luke 3:3–6) to confirm that, while some might have thought John was the messiah, he clearly was not.

Was Paul's catechesis well received? By some it was, but as the text that follows today's reading reveals, things went very badly on the following Sabbath, when massive crowds came to hear Paul's teaching. The religious authorities responded with jealousy and fierce attacks on Paul and his message. Eventually Paul and Barnabas were run out of town, but Paul apparently

saw this as confirmation that his mission was intended for the Gentiles.

GOSPEL On this vigil of the Nativity of the Lord, the lectionary presents us with a long form and a short form of today's Gospel. The long form includes the genealogy of Jesus as told by the author of the Gospel of Matthew. Ancient genealogies were not entirely historical, because there were no birth or death certificates to verify every detail. But genealogies were very important, because they identified one's place in the

Manasseh = muh-NAS-uh
Amos = AY-m*s
Josiah = joh-SĪ-uh
Jechoniah = jek-oh-NĪ-uh

Shealtiel = shee-AL-tee-uhl
Zerubbabel = zuh-ROOB-uh-b*l
Abiud = uh-BĪ-uhd
Eliakim = ee-LĪ-uh-kim
Azor = AY-sohr
Zadok = ZAD-uhk
Achim = AH-kim
Eliud = ee-LĪ-uhd
Eleazar = el-ee-AY-zer
Matthan = MATH-uhn

Hezekiah became the father of **Manasseh**,
   Manasseh the father of **Amos**,
   Amos the father of **Josiah**.
Josiah became the father of **Jechoniah** and his **brothers**
   at the time of the Babylonian **exile**.

After the Babylonian exile,
   Jechoniah became the father of **Shealtiel**,
   Shealtiel the father of **Zerubbabel**,
   Zerubbabel the father of **Abiud**.
Abiud became the father of **Eliakim**,
   Eliakim the father of **Azor**,
   Azor the father of **Zadok**.
Zadok became the father of **Achim**,
   Achim the father of **Eliud**,
   Eliud the father of **Eleazar**.
Eleazar became the father of **Matthan**,
   Matthan the father of **Jacob**,
   Jacob the father of **Joseph**, the husband of **Mary**.
Of her was born **Jesus** who is called the **Christ**.

Thus the total number of **generations**
   from **Abraham** to **David**
   is **fourteen** generations;
   from **David** to the Babylonian **exile**,
   fourteen generations;
   from the Babylonian **exile** to the **Christ**,
   fourteen generations.

[Now **this** is how the **birth** of Jesus **Christ** came about.
When his mother **Mary** was betrothed to **Joseph**,
   but before they **lived** together,
   she was found with **child** through the Holy **Spirit**.
Joseph her **husband**, since he was a **righteous man**,
   yet unwilling to expose her to **shame**,
   decided to **divorce** her quietly.

Now that Jesus' genealogy has been established, the story of his birth can be told. The focus is Joseph, the second-to-last name in the genealogy. Attune the dynamics of your reading to the figure of Joseph, with whom the assembly is meant to identify.

world, which was essential in an honor/shame culture.

This particular genealogy is organized into three groups of fourteen generations. Abraham is the starting point, which is appropriate because Israel's salvation story starts with Abraham. The second group of fourteen generations begins with David, lauded by some as the greatest king of Israel. The third group begins with the Babylonian Exile, which was the low point of Israel's history, when the Jerusalem Temple was destroyed, the king was deposed, and many of the inhabitants of Judea were sent into exile. It concludes with "Joseph, the husband of Mary. Of her was born Jesus who is called the Christ," which confirms Jesus' identity as a descendant of David but also hints at what will be an unusual conception through the power of the Holy Spirit.

And what about this mysterious number fourteen? Very likely it represents a bit of rabbinic *gematria*, which was a way of interpreting the Scriptures or related events by computing the numerical value of the letters that make up certain words (each Hebrew letter also has a number value). In this case, fourteen is David's number. The transliteration of his Hebrew name is *dvd*, and the numbers associated with these Hebrew letters are four for *d* and six for *v*. When you add up the numbers associated with *dvd*, you get fourteen. Thus, this genealogy, with its three-part organization, shows that Jesus as messiah king is much greater than David, who had been lauded as the greatest king of Israel.

Immediately after the presentation of Jesus' genealogy, the Gospel writer begins to tell the story of Jesus' birth. It is a story fraught with troubles. We learn that Mary and Joseph are engaged to be married.

When the angel says here Joseph's name, it is a summons. Read it that way.

Such was his intention when, **behold**,
   the **angel** of the Lord appeared to him in a **dream** and said,
   "**Joseph**, son of David,
   do not be afraid to take Mary your wife into your **home**.
For it is **through** the Holy Spirit
   that this child has been **conceived in her**.
She will bear a **son** and you are to name him **Jesus**,
   because he will **save** his people from their **sins**."
All this took place to **fulfill**
   what the Lord had said through the **prophet**:
      *Behold, the **virgin** shall conceive and bear a **son**,*
         *and they shall name him **Emmanuel**,*
   which means "**God** is **with** us."

Joseph awaking is what happens to the assembly at this moment.

When Joseph **awoke**,
   he **did** as the angel of the Lord had **commanded** him
   and took his **wife** into his **home**.
He had no **relations** with her until she bore a **son**,
   and he **named** him **Jesus**.]

[Shorter: Matthew 1:18–25 (see brackets)]

Given marriage practices of this time, Mary might have been about twelve years of age. We tend to think of Joseph as much older, because of the non-canonical Gospel of James, which describes him as a widower with grown children, but otherwise he might have been only fourteen or fifteen years old. Their marriage was not yet consummated but the engagement was binding, and breaking an engagement was a significant occasion for shame. Thus, Joseph decided to divorce Mary quietly to avoid publicly shaming her family, demonstrating that, whatever his age, Joseph was a righteous and kind man.

But then Joseph received a message from an angel in a dream. The angel told him that he need not be afraid to take Mary as his wife, because the child in her womb had been conceived by the Holy Spirit and not by rape or any wrongdoing on her part. Yes, sadly, women in the ancient Near East were considered blameworthy if they were raped. The narrator of the Gospel adds that this happened to fulfill the prophetic words of Isaiah 7:13 about a virgin or young girl giving birth to a son, who would be named Emmanuel or "God is with us." What wondrous joy! But just to ensure that there was no confusion about the child's paternity, the narrator adds that the marriage was not consummated until after the child was born. C.C.

THE NATIVITY OF THE LORD (CHRISTMAS): NIGHT

LECTIONARY #14

READING I   Isaiah 9:1–6

A reading from the Book of the Prophet Isaiah

The people who walked in **darkness**
    have **seen** a great **light**;
upon those who dwelt in the **land of gloom**
    a **light** has **shone**.
You have **brought** them abundant **joy**
    and **great rejoicing**,
as they **rejoice** before you as at the **harvest**,
    as people make **merry** when dividing **spoils**.
For the **yoke** that burdened them,
    the **pole** on their shoulder,
and the **rod** of their taskmaster
    you have **smashed**, as on the day of **Midian**.
For every **boot** that **tramped** in **battle**,
    every **cloak rolled** in **blood**,
    will be **burned** as fuel for flames.
For a child is born to us, a **son** is given us;
    upon his shoulder **dominion** rests.
They name him **Wonder-Counselor**, **God-Hero**,
    Father-Forever, **Prince** of **Peace**.
His dominion is **vast**
    and **forever** peaceful,
from David's **throne**, and over his **kingdom**,
    which he **confirms** and **sustains**

Sidebar notes (left margin):

Isaiah = ī-ZAY-uh

An exhortatory reading, one of great joy and mystery. Read with emphasis on the contrasts between light and gloom, battle and peace.

Take note here of the yoke, the pole, and the rod. These lines express parallel images in parallel constructions.

Midian = MID-ee-uhn

These names are the heart of this reading. Give them due emphasis.

There are options for today's readings. Contact your parish staff to learn which readings will be used.

READING I Although there is much that we do not fully understand about this reading, some biblical scholars think it might be a thanksgiving poem or a hymn celebrating the king's coronation and accession to his throne. Others think this oracle is concerned with the birth of a future king.

In the first part of this oracle, the prophet is speaking about God. Light is fre-quently used as a symbol for God's presence on behalf of the chosen. The "land of gloom" is a metaphor for the Israelites' oppression under foreign rulers, and the verses that follow emphasize the severity of Israel's oppression. Three times in succes-sive lines of text, the prophet calls attention to devices of forced labor—the yoke, the pole, and the rod—that would otherwise be used to harness animals. But this text also includes a strong portrayal of God as a war-rior who destroys enemies in a flash "as on the day of Midian" (Isaiah 9:4). Midian was a son of Abraham by a later marriage whose descendants became the Midianites (Genesis 25:1–2). Midian means "place of judgment." Apparently, Isaiah associated it with a great battle of good over evil.

The second part of this oracle contains a profoundly visionary description of the as-yet-unborn child from the line of David who will lead Israel according to the will of God. He will be Wonder-Counselor insofar as he will have no need for advice-givers who might lead him astray from what is good and right. He will be God-Hero, other-wise translated "mightiest God" or "God warrior," and he will be Father-Forever, who

Give each of the pairs in these three lines—confirms and sustains; judgment and justice; now and forever—equal emphasis.

by **judgment** and **justice**,
   both **now** and **forever**.
The **zeal** of the LORD of **hosts** will **do** this!

For meditation and context:

RESPONSORIAL PSALM   Psalm 96:1–2, 2–3, 11–12, 13 (Luke 2:11)

R. Today is born our Savior, Christ the Lord.

Sing to the LORD a new song;
   sing to the LORD, all you lands.
Sing to the LORD; bless his name.

Announce his salvation, day after day.
   Tell his glory among the nations;
   among all peoples, his wondrous deeds.

Let the heavens be glad and the earth rejoice;
   let the sea and what fills it resound;
   let the plains be joyful and all that is
      in them!
Then shall all the trees of the forest exult.

They shall exult before the LORD,
   for he comes;
   for he comes to rule the earth.
He shall rule the world with justice
   and the peoples with his constancy.

Titus = TĪ-tuhs

An exhortatory reading, all in one long sentence, broken into three parts, beginning with "The grace of God," continuing with "the appearance of the glory," concluding with "who gave himself for us." Pace your reading accordingly.

Equal emphasis on these three adverbs.

Read the phrase "eager to do what is good" as a Christmas wish.

A narrative reading, divided into two parts. The first part tells the story of the census, moving Joseph and Mary from Nazareth to Bethlehem where Jesus will be born. The second part shifts to the shepherds visited by the angel of the Lord. Two vivid Christian images come from this reading: the manger

READING II   Titus 2:11–14

A reading from the Letter of Saint Paul to Titus

Beloved:
The **grace** of God has appeared, saving **all**
   and training us to reject **godless ways** and **worldly desires**
   and to live **temperately**, **justly**, and **devoutly** in this age,
   as we await the blessed **hope**,
   the **appearance** of the **glory** of our great **God**
   and **savior** Jesus Christ,
   who gave himself for us to **deliver** us from all **lawlessness**
   and to **cleanse** for himself a **people** as his own,
   eager to do what is **good**.

GOSPEL   Luke 2:1–14

A reading from the holy Gospel according to Luke

In those days a **decree** went out from Caesar Augustus
   that the **whole world** should be **enrolled**. ≫

will as a father caring for his own. Finally, the title "Prince of Peace" is a reference to the quality of good kingship: there will be peace in the land forever. This is the messiah for whom the people of Israel hoped.

READING II Titus was the overseer (Greek *episkopon*, also translated as "bishop") of several early Christian Churches on the island of Crete. The purpose of this letter is to instruct Church leaders in managing the good order of their faith communities, in being of good conscience, and in warning against false

doctrine. Here, the author of this letter is explaining the reason for the believing community to live a good and moral life, not just now but also for our future destiny. It is because of the saving grace that God has already bestowed on all human beings!

Twice in this very short text, the author uses the words "appeared" and "appearance." Assuming that there is a parallel between the phrases that contain "appear" and "appearance," we might be able to understand "the grace of God" and "the great glory of our God and savior" as descriptors of Jesus Christ. Notice also how

the author of this letter understands Jesus' death as the way we are redeemed or bought back from sinful ways to be eager to do good. In other words, our acknowledgment of Jesus' sacrifice on our behalf, which is the grace of God, should prompt us to live justly, temperately, and with devotion to God.

GOSPEL Luke tells us that Caesar Augustus ordered a census during the reign of Quirinius, governor of Syria (AD 6–12), but this conflicts with what Matthew's Gospel says about the date of

of the Nativity and the heavenly host with the angel proclaiming glory to God, witnessed by the shepherds watching over their flocks. Both images come alive in this reading.

Caesar Augustus = SEE-zer aw-GUHS-tuhs
Quirinius = kwih-RIN-ee-uhs
Judea = joo-DEE-uh

Place emphasis on these lines by slowing your pace just slightly to draw attention to the image.

In this line, each word should have almost equal emphasis.

This was the **first** enrollment,
    when Quirinius was governor of Syria.
So **all went** to be **enrolled**, **each** to his own **town**.
And **Joseph too** went up from **Galilee** from the town
        of **Nazareth**
    to **Judea**, to the city of **David** that is called **Bethlehem**,
    because he was of the **house** and **family** of David,
    to be **enrolled** with **Mary**, his betrothed, who was with child.
While they were there,
    the time came for **her** to have her **child**,
    and she gave birth to her **firstborn son**.
She wrapped him in swaddling **clothes** and
        laid him in a **manger**,
    because there was **no room** for them in the inn.

Now there were **shepherds** in that **region** living in the fields
    and **keeping** the **night watch** over their flock.
The **angel** of the Lord appeared to them
    and the **glory** of the Lord **shone** around them,
    and they were **struck** with great **fear**.
The angel **said** to them,
    "**Do not be afraid**;
    for **behold**, I proclaim to you **good news** of **great joy**
    that will be for **all** the people.
For today in the city of **David**
    a **savior** has been **born** for you who is **Christ** and **Lord**.
And **this** will be a **sign** for you:
    you will find an **infant wrapped** in swaddling clothes
    and **lying** in a **manger**."
And **suddenly** there was a multitude of the heavenly host with
        the angel,
    praising God and saying:
    "**Glory** to God in the **highest**
        and on **earth peace** to those on whom his **favor** rests."

Jesus' birth, which is usually given as 6–4 BC. Should we be concerned about the historical reliability of this story? Not really. Luke apparently knew the tradition about Jesus being born in Bethlehem, and he needed an explanation for why Mary and Joseph ventured out on a trip of approximately ninety miles so late in her pregnancy. In any case, the theological message is what is most important. Mary's child will be born in Bethlehem, the home of his Davidic ancestry.

Other details indicate an important theme in Luke's Gospel: just as God is on the side of the poor and disenfranchised, so

was Jesus, even in his birth. The swaddling clothes remind us that Jesus was treated as an ordinary baby of the time; swaddling quiets a baby and allows the child to fall asleep quickly and safely. There was no place in an inn for the Holy Family to stay. Often, first-century inns consisted of an extra place to lie down in someone's home. But people also kept their animals within the confines of their tiny housing complexes, thus, a manger served as a bed for the baby Jesus.

Unlike Matthew's Gospel, where magi were the first to visit, Luke's Gospel says

that shepherds are invited to come and see the newborn infant, the Messiah and Lord. Shepherds were an essential part of the Palestinian economy, but their place in society was quite low. Also, shepherds would have been considered ritually unclean because they regularly dealt with feces, dead animals, and other prohibited items. Who is this Jesus who dwells among the poor and outcast? Listen to the angels! Their song is a proclamation of the peace that rains down upon the earth when God's kingship is fully realized. C.C.

THE NATIVITY OF THE LORD (CHRISTMAS): DAWN

LECTIONARY #15

READING I   Isaiah 62:11–12

A reading from the Book of the Prophet Isaiah

> **See**, the LORD **proclaims**
>   to the ends of the earth:
> **say** to daughter Zion,
>   your **savior** comes!
> Here is his reward with him,
>   his **recompense before** him.
> They shall be **called** the holy **people**,
>   the **redeemed** of the LORD,
> and you shall be called "**Frequented**,"
>   a **city** that is not **forsaken**.

RESPONSORIAL PSALM   Psalm 97:1, 6, 11–12

R. A light will shine on us this day: the Lord is born for us.

The LORD is king; let the earth rejoice;
   let the many isles be glad.
The heavens proclaim his justice,
   and all peoples see his glory.

Light dawns for the just;
   and gladness, for the upright of heart.
Be glad in the LORD, you just,
   and give thanks to his holy name.

READING II   Titus 3:4–7

A reading from the Letter of Saint Paul to Titus

Beloved:
When the **kindness** and generous **love**
   of **God** our savior appeared, »

There are options for today's readings. Contact your parish staff to learn which readings will be used.

READING I The first reading for this dawn celebration of the Nativity of the Lord is from the part of the book of Isaiah that is thought to have been written after the Babylonian Exile, when a remnant of God's people had begun to return to Judea. It was a time of cautious hopefulness mixed with the challenges of rebuilding a land and culture destroyed by the Babylonians. These few verses make up the closing summary of an oracle that was read during the celebration of the vigil of the Nativity.

Here, God declares to the entire world in so many words, "Tell Lady Jerusalem that your savior comes!" While this language is metaphorical, since God does not speak as humans speak, can you imagine the reverberation of God's cry across the land and the joy of those eagerly awaiting their salvation, when the savior comes with the wages of his work? When their salvation comes, God will give both the city and its people new names, which represent a reversal of their destinies. Jerusalem, which was once desolate and forsaken, is now called "'Frequented,' a city that is not forsaken." The people who were once "not my people" are now God's "holy people, the redeemed of the Lord." Thus, the savior brings transformation to all God's people.

READING II The second reading is from the Letter to Titus, a companion of Paul in his mission work and the overseer (Greek *episkopon*, also translated as "bishop") of several early Christian Churches on the island of Crete.

not **because** of any righteous deeds we had done
    but because of his mercy,
he **saved us** through the **bath** of rebirth
    and **renewal** by the Holy **Spirit**,
whom he **richly poured** out on **us**
    through **Jesus** Christ our **savior**,
so that we might be **justified** by his **grace**
    and become **heirs** in **hope** of eternal **life**.

GOSPEL   Luke 2:15–20

A reading from the holy Gospel according to Luke

When the **angels** went away from them to **heaven**,
    the **shepherds** said to one another,
    "Let us **go**, then, to **Bethlehem**
    to **see this thing** that has taken place,
    which the **Lord** has made **known** to us."
So they went in **haste** and found **Mary** and **Joseph**,
    and the **infant lying** in the manger.
When they **saw** this,
    they made **known** the message
    that had been **told them** about this child.
All who heard it were **amazed**
    by what had been **told** them by the **shepherds**.
And **Mary** kept all these things,
    reflecting on them in her **heart**.
Then the **shepherds** returned,
    glorifying and **praising** God
    for **all** they had **heard** and **seen**,
    just as it had been **told** to them.

The rhythm of this line provides this reading with its reverberant note, so allow yourself to slow slightly as you come to this conclusion.

A short narrative reading that concludes the Nativity story. While the focus is on the infant Jesus lying in the manger, the eyes through which we see him are those of the shepherds. The shepherds modeled Christian devotion from the beginning of our faith.

manger = MAYN-jer

Amazement is the primary emotion of this story.

The shepherds' glorifying and praising are to be our own.

This reading is an extension of the second reading for the night celebration of the Nativity of the Lord. It continues the theme of the saving grace, or favor, that God has already bestowed on humanity. It also continues to use the word "appearing" to refer to the coming of the savior. Notice in this reading the attributes that are associated with the coming savior. They are kindness, which can also be translated as moral goodness and integrity, and love of humanity, which can also be translated as benevolence or fondness for humanity. So rich in meaning, these attributes deserve our contemplation during this holy season. The "bath of rebirth" is a reference to baptism, which the author of this letter understands to be comparable to Paul's teaching about the "new creation" (see 2 Corinthians 5:17).

GOSPEL The Gospel continues Luke's story of the shepherds who come to visit the newborn baby Jesus. The angels who had come to the shepherds in the fields near Bethlehem to announce the birth of the messiah and to sing their beautiful song of peace on earth are now gone, and the shepherds go to Bethlehem to find everything as the angels said. Their immediate response is to tell the good news. Finally, Luke adds a touching note concerning Mary. This young girl could not have known what lay ahead for her and for her son. But Luke says that she treasured all these things and pondered them in her heart. In what sense is she a disciple of Jesus? Pray that we can follow her example. C.C.

THE NATIVITY OF THE LORD (CHRISTMAS): DAY

LECTIONARY #16

READING I   Isaiah 52:7–10

A reading from the Book of the Prophet Isaiah

How **beautiful** upon the **mountains**
    are the **feet** of him who **brings glad tidings**,
announcing **peace**, bearing good **news**,
    announcing **salvation**, and saying to Zion,
    "Your **God** is **King!**"

Hark! Your sentinels **raise** a cry,
    together they **shout** for **joy**,
for they see **directly**, before their **eyes**,
    the LORD restoring Zion.
Break out together in song,
    O ruins of Jerusalem!
For the LORD comforts his **people**,
    he **redeems** Jerusalem.
The LORD has bared his holy arm
    in the **sight** of all the **nations**;
all the **ends** of the **earth** will **behold**
    the **salvation** of our **God**.

Isaiah = ī-ZAY-uh

An exhortatory reading of great joy. In reading this, you are bringing glad tidings to the assembly.

"Hark" is a word with rich Christmas associations. Allow it to resonate in your reading.

TO KEEP IN MIND
Pause to break up separate thoughts, set apart significant statements, or indicate major shifts. Never pause in the middle of a thought. Your primary guide for pauses is punctuation.

Allow "salvation" to resonate here. This word is the key to the whole reading.

There are options for today's readings. Contact your parish staff to learn which readings will be used.

READING I   Today's first reading is taken from the second part of the book of Isaiah, which was written during the Babylonian Exile. Even in this extremely dark period of Israel's history, the prophet found cause for rejoicing, as is evident in this oracle. In the first part of this oracle, which is not included in today's reading, the prophet shouts, "Wake up! Wake up! Sit up and dust yourself off!" as he tries to rouse personified Zion/Jerusalem from her sad stupor. Further, he tells Zion to remove the bonds that held her down and put on her glorious garments, because God is coming to redeem her people and rescue them from their enemies.

This is where the lectionary reading begins. The prophet speaks of a herald who announces peace and the good news of Zion's salvation. Peace is the measure of a good and just king who cares for his people. Thus, the prophet proclaims, "Your God is King!" The Hebrew word *shalom* means completeness, welfare, health, soundness of body, or prosperity. This is a beautiful thing, indeed! The prophet continues, telling Lady Jerusalem to listen to the watchmen stationed on the ruined walls of the city. Imagine this scene, if you can! The watchmen are shouting and crying out for joy because they see God leading the exiles back to the city with their own eyes. Even the ruined city joins in the song of joy! God's bared, holy arm is a symbol of power. By the power of God, peace and salvation now reign over all God's people. What a sight for sore eyes!

For meditation and context:

RESPONSORIAL PSALM   Psalm 98:1, 2–3, 3–4, 5–6 (3c)

R. All the ends of the earth have seen the saving power of God.

Sing to the LORD a new song,
    for he has done wondrous deeds;
his right hand has won victory for him,
    his holy arm.

The LORD has made his salvation known:
    in the sight of the nations he has revealed
      his justice.
He has remembered his kindness and his
    faithfulness
    toward the house of Israel.

All the ends of the earth have seen
    the salvation by our God.
Sing joyfully to the LORD, all you lands;
    break into song; sing praise.

Sing praise to the LORD with the harp,
    with the harp and melodious song.
With trumpets and the sound of the horn
    sing joyfully before the King, the LORD.

READING II   Hebrews 1:1–6

A didactic reading of poetic and argumentative power about the nature and glory of Christ. The reading consists of a long and poetic setup that yields to an argumentative call-and-response. Allow the setup to gather tension in your reading that the call-and-response releases.

refulgence = ree-FUHL-j*nts = radiance or brilliance

"Universe," "refulgence," and "glory": This is celestial language to characterize the Son.

The call-and-response is like a small theater piece.

A reading from the Letter to the Hebrews

Brothers and sisters:
In times **past**, God **spoke** in **partial** and **various** ways
    to our **ancestors** through the **prophets**;
    in these **last days**, he has **spoken to us** through the **Son**,
    whom he **made heir** of all **things**
    and through **whom** he created the **universe**,
      who is the **refulgence** of his **glory**,
        the very **imprint** of his **being**,
    and who **sustains all things** by his **mighty** word.
    When he had **accomplished** purification from sins,
    he **took** his **seat** at the right **hand** of the **Majesty** on high,
    as **far superior** to the angels
    as the **name** he has **inherited** is more **excellent** than theirs.

For to which of the angels did God ever say:
    You are my son; this day I have begotten *you*?

READING II   The Letter to the Hebrews is more properly called a homily or a theological treatise than a letter. Most of its arguments use a construction that we might call "from the lesser to the greater." If something can be demonstrated to be true in a small matter, then it must be even more true in a greater matter that is similar to the first. Here, the author is comparing Jesus Christ, the Son, to the angels of heaven. The angels are great, but the Son is greater than the angels. The author uses quotations from the Old Testament to make his point. Only three are included in this lectionary reading, but there are seven altogether. In the ancient world, seven was understood to be a symbol of perfection or fullness.

This reading opens with a beautifully constructed "then and now" comparison statement focused on God's revelation. Notice who is the agent of God's revelation in both cases. Then, the agents were Israel's ancestors and prophets. Now there is one agent, God's Son, who is described in exactly seven phrases. Two of these descriptors are especially noteworthy. First, the Son is the "refulgence" of God's glory. The

Greek word translated here as "refulgence" can also be translated as "radiance," "reflection," or "reflected brightness." Thus, the glory that belongs to God belongs to God's Son.

Second, the Son is "the very imprint" of God's being. The Greek word translated here as "imprint" is related to engraving and, therefore, suggests a mark or figure stamped upon the Son, which is an exact representation of God. And what is the mark or stamp? It is God's being! The Greek word translated as "being" is *hupostasis*, meaning "substance" or "actual existence"

Or **again**:

*I will be a **father** to him, and he shall be a **son** to me?*
And **again**, when he **leads** the firstborn into the **world**, he says:
*Let **all** the angels of God **worship** him.*

GOSPEL   John 1:1–18

An exhortatory reading that is one of the pillars of Christian theology. The emphases in the opening verses are crucial to that theology.

A reading from the holy Gospel according to John

[In the **beginning** was the **Word**,
    and the **Word** was with **God**,
    and the Word **was** God.
He **was** in the beginning **with** God.
All things came to be **through** him,
    and **without him nothing** came to be.
What came to be **through him** was **life**,
    and **this life** was the **light** of the human **race**;
    the light **shines** in the **darkness**,
    and the **darkness** has not overcome it.]
A man named **John** was sent from God.
He came for **testimony**, to testify to the **light**,
    so that all might believe **through him**.
He was **not** the light,
    but came to **testify to** the light.
[The **true light**, which enlightens **everyone**,
    was **coming** into the world.
  He was **in** the world,
    and the **world** came to be **through** him,
    but the **world** did not **know** him.
  He **came** to what was his **own**,
    but his **own people** did not **accept** him. »

Linger a little at the contrast between light and darkness.

This passage about John links his testimony with the light.

---

of God. This same word is used by early Church theologians to describe the three-in-oneness of God.

 GOSPEL   The lectionary presents us with a reading taken from the prologue of John's Gospel. Prologues can serve different purposes. Sometimes they give us insight into the reason why the author wrote his or her book. Sometimes they give us the backstory that led up to the topic to be addressed in the book. Sometimes they offer a synopsis of the entire book, as in the case of this Gospel reading.

Much of John's prologue is written in the style of poetry. The first part uses a particular literary device called chain verse. This is where the last word of the first line is repeated at the start of the second line and so forth. Chain verse can be difficult to recognize when translated, but this unpolished translation of the first lines might be a helpful way to see the beauty of this poetry and the care with which it was composed.

In the beginning was the *Word*
And the *Word* was (turned) toward God
And (what) God was the *Word* was.
  He [sic. the *Word*] was in the beginning with God.

The first part of this prologue has strong echoes of the Genesis creation story with its references to darkness and light. It also recalls the wisdom traditions of the Bible, in which personified Wisdom is described as being with God in the beginning and acting as God's helper in the act of creation (see Proverbs 8, Wisdom 6–9). This is one of the biblical texts that theologians of the early Church used to develop its doctrine of the divinity and pre-existence of the Son of God.

The second poetic section focuses on the incarnation (literally, enfleshment) of the Son of God. Regarding the "true light,"

The Word becoming flesh is the heart of this reading.

But to those who **did** accept him
 he gave **power** to become **children** of God,
 to those who **believe** in his **name**,
 who were born **not** by natural generation
 nor by **human choice** nor by a man's **decision**
 but of **God**.
  And the **Word** became **flesh**
  and made his **dwelling among** us,
  and we **saw** his **glory**,
  the **glory** as of the **Father's only** Son,
  full of **grace** and **truth**.]

And once again, John testifies. His testimony yields revelation. Give proper emphasis to the word "revealed" at the end of the reading.

John **testified** to him and **cried out**, saying,
 "This was **he** of **whom** I **said**,
 'The one who is coming **after** me ranks **ahead** of me
 because he existed **before** me.'"
From his **fullness** we have **all** received,
 grace in place of **grace**,
 because while the **law** was given through **Moses**,
 grace and **truth** came through Jesus **Christ**.
No one has ever **seen** God.
The only **Son**, God, who is at the Father's side,
 has **revealed** him.

[Shorter: John 1:1–5, 9–14 (see brackets)]

the Greek word *aléthinos* is not about truth versus falsehood or good versus bad. Rather, it means "real" or "genuine" as opposed to "counterfeit." This genuine light came into the world, John says, and the world did not recognize him, nor would it accept him. John continues, saying that the Word became flesh, or took on a body and human nature. The Word made his dwelling among us! Other meanings for the Greek word "to dwell" are "to pitch one's tent" or "to set up one's tabernacle." And we looked up or contemplated his glory as God's only begotten. And who is the "we"

here? It refers to those who believe or accept the Word and are given power to become God's children.

The longer form of this reading includes two short sections of prose, both of which focus on John the Baptist. We learn that John was sent from God to testify or be a witness to the Word, which is the true light of the world. The Baptizer makes it clear that he is not the light but only that he witnesses to the light. "Witness" is an interesting concept in this context. Prophets testify to the word of God in their prophecies. People testify in a court of law. But here in

John's Gospel it also means to put oneself on the line to stand with or trust in Jesus as the revelation of God. In John's Gospel, there is no sitting on the fence. You must decide! C.C.

THE HOLY FAMILY OF JESUS, MARY, AND JOSEPH

LECTIONARY #17

READING I   1 Samuel 1:20–22, 24–28

A narrative reading that suggests the ambience of prophetic times long past. Hannah's offering of Samuel anticipates the Holy Family's sacrifice with Christ.

Elkanah = el-KAY-nah

The narrative effectively repeats the central point: Hannah will offer up Samuel to the priesthood three times. This portion of the reading sets up those repetitions. In your proclamation, move slowly and clearly through this portion of the reading to make the relationships clear.

Hannah's speech is the first repetition. Emphasis on "perpetual nazirite."

nazirite = NAZ-uh-right
ephah = EE-fah
Shiloh = SHī-loh

The second repetition, this time in narrative form. Make the details—"an ephah of flour"—clear.

Eli = EE-lī

A reading from the first Book of Samuel

In **those** days Hannah **conceived**,
   and at the **end** of her **term** bore a **son**
  whom she called **Samuel**, since she had asked the LORD
   for him.
The next time her husband **Elkanah** was going **up**
  with the **rest** of his **household**
  to offer the customary **sacrifice** to the LORD
   and to **fulfill** his **vows**,
  Hannah did not **go**, explaining to her **husband**,
  "**Once** the child is **weaned**,
  I will take him to **appear** before the LORD
  and to **remain** there **forever**;
  I will **offer** him as a **perpetual nazirite**."

Once **Samuel** was **weaned**, Hannah brought him **up** with her,
  along with a **three-year-old bull**,
  an **ephah** of **flour**, and a **skin** of **wine**,
  and **presented** him at the **temple** of the LORD in **Shiloh**.
After the boy's **father** had sacrificed the young **bull**,
  Hannah, his **mother**, approached **Eli** and said:
  "**Pardon**, my lord! »

There are options for today's readings. Contact your parish staff to learn which readings will be used.

READING I   **Samuel.** The lectionary provides two options for the first reading on this feast of the Holy Family. The first, from the First Book of Samuel, tells the story of Hannah's dedication of her child, Samuel, to God. Hannah was already old when she gave birth to her first and only son. Her husband, Elkanah, loved her, but his other wife, Peninnah, treated her horribly because she had many sons and daughters, whereas Hannah had been barren throughout her marriage.

One evening after a ritual meal, on one of the family's annual trips to the temple in Shiloh, Hannah entered the temple alone, not realizing that Eli, the priest of the temple, was sitting nearby. Distraught over Peninnah's constant torments, she wept bitterly and prayed desperately to God for a son. She promised that she would dedicate him to God, if God would grant her petition. Eli was watching but, not being able to hear, he thought she was drunk, and he scolded her for making such a spectacle of herself. She stood her ground and explained that she was not drunk. Instead, she was expressing her deep sorrow to God over her plight in life. Eli responded with a blessing and a wish that God would hear her prayer.

When Hannah's son was born, she named him Samuel, meaning "God heard." When it was time for the family to make their annual trip to the temple, Hannah remained behind, saying that she would wait until she could take her son to be dedicated in the temple. Thus, perhaps as young as three, Samuel is taken to Shiloh and is dedicated as a nazirite. The book of

As you **live**, my lord,
   I am the **woman** who stood near you **here**,
     praying to the LORD.
I **prayed** for this child, and the LORD **granted** my **request**.
Now **I**, in turn, give **him** to the LORD;
   as **long** as he **lives**, he shall be **dedicated** to the LORD."
Hannah left **Samuel there**.

Or:

READING I   Sirach 3:2–6, 12–14

A reading from the Book of Sirach

God sets a father in **honor** over his children;
   a mother's **authority** he **confirms** over her sons.
Whoever **honors** his father **atones** for sins,
   and **preserves** himself from them.
When he **prays**, he is **heard**;
   he stores up **riches** who reveres his **mother**.
Whoever **honors** his father is **gladdened** by children,
   and, when he **prays**, is **heard**.
Whoever **reveres** his father will live a **long life**;
   he who **obeys** his father brings **comfort** to his mother.

My son, take **care** of your father when he is old;
   grieve him **not** as **long** as he lives.
Even if his **mind** fail, be **considerate** of him;
   revile him not all the **days** of his **life**;
kindness to a father will not be **forgotten**,
   firmly planted against the **debt** of your sins
   —a **house** raised in justice to **you**.

The third repetition, once again in the form of Hannah's speech. Emphasis on "I" and "him."

Sirach = SEER-ak; SĪ-ruhk

A didactic reading in which each set of phrases offers advice.

Note the parallels established by the repetition of the word "whoever." The word "and" serves a similar purpose. Each of these teachings is meant to be equal.

The advice in the second section, beginning here, is more familial, the words of a father to his son. You can proclaim it in this spirit.

TO KEEP IN MIND
Be careful not to swallow your words. Articulate carefully, especially at the end of lines.

Numbers describes the Nazirite vow in three parts: abstaining from wine and any food that involves grapes; not cutting their hair until after their vow is complete; not coming into contact with a corpse. All this is to say that Samuel, son of Elkanah and Hannah, is "holy to the Lord" (Numbers 6:1–8).

Sirach. Another option for today's first reading is from the book of Sirach, one of the wisdom books of the Bible, which consists mostly of poems, proverbs, pithy sayings about right living, hymns of praise and prayers of petition. This reading is excerpted from a longer section that focuses on the

respect that children owe their parents (Sirach 3:1–16). The gist of this teaching is that those who honor their parents, even in their old age, will enjoy many blessings from God, including forgiveness of sin and a long and satisfying life. We should remember, as well, that the command to honor one's father and mother is the first of the Ten Commandments focused on what it means to love our neighbors (Exodus 20:12). Of course, family life is often not as idyllic as this reading suggests, but that does not mean we can discount this teaching. How do we honor our parents and make our

families holy in the midst of the messiness of life?

READING II   **1 John.** As with the first reading, the lectionary provides two options for the second reading. The first, from the first letter of John, is part of a larger section that focuses on God's love as the primary attribute that makes us children of God (1 John 3:1–24). The letter itself is heavily influenced by the Gospel of John, and some of the vocabulary that we find here is also found in the Gospel of John. For example, the prologue of John's

For meditation and context:

RESPONSORIAL PSALM   Psalm 84:2–3, 5–6, 9–10 (see 5a)

R. Blessed are they who dwell in your house, O Lord.

How lovely is your dwelling place,
    O Lord of hosts!
    My soul yearns and pines for the courts
        of the Lord.
My heart and my flesh cry out for the
        living God.

Happy they who dwell in your house!
    Continually they praise you.
Happy the men whose strength you are!
    Their hearts are set upon the pilgrimage.

O Lord of hosts, hear our prayer;
    hearken, O God of Jacob!
O God, behold our shield,
    and look upon the face of your anointed.

Or:

For meditation and context:

RESPONSORIAL PSALM   Psalm 128:1–2, 3, 4–5 (1)

R. Blessed are those who fear the Lord and walk in his ways.

Blessed is everyone who fears the Lord,
    who walks in his ways!
For you shall eat the fruit of your handiwork;
    blessed shall you be, and favored.

Your wife shall be like a fruitful vine
    in the recesses of your home;
your children like olive plants
    around your table.

Behold, thus is the man blessed
    who fears the Lord.
The Lord bless you from Zion:
    may you see the prosperity of Jerusalem
    all the days of your life.

READING II   1 John 3:1–2, 21–24

A reading from the first Letter of Saint John

Beloved:
See what love the **Father** has **bestowed** on us
    that we may be **called** the **children** of **God**.
And so we **are**.
The **reason** the world does not **know** us
    is that it did **not** know **him**. »

A didactic reading that gathers its power from the three repetitions of the word "Beloved."
Beloved = bee-LUHV-uhd

Emphasis on "are."

Note the shift here from "know" to "*not know him*."

Gospel describes the Word coming into the world and the world not knowing him (John 1:10), but those who did accept him were given "power to become children of God" (John 1:12). The letter writer emphasizes that *now* we are children of God in order to highlight an even greater gift that will come to us at a later time: we will be like God! Similarly, the Gospel writer describes Jesus as praying to the Father in the hours before his arrest and crucifixion, that we might be with him and see the glory that the Father gave him before the beginning of creation (John 17:24).

The remainder of this reading focuses on the confidence we ought to have in God, because we keep God's commandments. And God's commandments are clear: believe in his Son and love one another with the love that God has for us. Again, the language is very similar to that of the Gospel of John, when Jesus says to his disciples, "This is my commandment: love one another as I love you" (John 15:12) and "If you keep my commandments, you will remain in my love, just as I have kept my Father's commandments and remain in his love" (John 15:10). Finally, the author of the

First Letter of John exhorts us to keep God's commandments so that we can remain in God and God in us. And how will we know that God remains in us? Through the Holy Spirit! The word translated here as "remain" can also be translated as "abide" or "dwell in." May you know with great confidence that, as a child of God, you dwell in God and God in you!

Colossians. Another option for today's second reading is from the Letter to the Colossians. It is part of a lengthy section of ethical teachings, which includes two lists of vices to avoid (Colossians 3:5–10),

And here note the shift of emphasis from "know" to "revealed."

This is the third repetition of "Beloved." Proclaim this word as if to someone familiar.

"Commandment" here provides a core Christian doctrine: believing in Christ and loving each other. Give "this" extra emphasis.

Colossians = kuh-LOSH-uhnz

A didactic reading that speaks of the virtues of building community.
Beloved = bee-LUHV-uhd
Each of these qualities is worthwhile, deserving emphasis.

This passage concludes with a note of thanksgiving, a feeling to guide the community as it builds.

Beloved, we are **God's** children now;
　　what we shall **be** has not yet been **revealed**.
We do **know** that when it is **revealed** we shall be **like** him,
　　for we shall **see** him as he **is**.

Beloved, if our **hearts** do not **condemn** us,
　　we have **confidence** in God and **receive** from him
　　　　whatever we **ask**,
　　because we **keep** his commandments and **do** what
　　　　pleases him.
And his **commandment** is **this**:
　　we should **believe** in the name of his Son, **Jesus Christ**,
　　and **love** one another **just** as he **commanded** us.
Those who **keep** his commandments **remain** in him,
　　and **he** in **them**,
　　and the way we **know** that he **remains** in us
　　is from the **Spirit** he **gave** us.

Or:

READING II   Colossians 3:12–21

A reading from the Letter of Saint Paul to the Colossians

[Brothers and sisters:
Put on, as God's chosen ones, **holy** and **beloved**,
　　heartfelt **compassion**, **kindness**, **humility**, **gentleness**,
　　　　and **patience**,
　　bearing with one another and forgiving one another,
　　if one has a **grievance** against another;
　　as the **Lord** has forgiven **you**, so must you also do.
And over **all these** put on **love**,
　　that is, the **bond** of perfection.
And let the **peace** of Christ control your **hearts**,
　　the **peace** into which you were also **called** in one body.
And be **thankful**.

a list of virtues to emulate (Colossians 3:11–17), and a household code (Colossians 3:18–4:1), all of which is fairly typical of first-century philosophical teachings focused on right living. The phrase "Put on, as God's chosen ones" suggests a baptismal formula, in which those who wish to be a follower of Jesus are invited to clothe themselves in Christ (Galatians 3:27). The virtues that we must emulate are compassion, kindness, humility, gentleness, patience, forgiveness, and, most of all, love.

The household code that follows immediately after this list of virtues can be problematic and even offensive to modern readers. But, to be clear, this household code does not mean that husbands have a right to oppress or dominate their wives, even though that was allowed in patriarchal cultures of the first-century Mediterranean world. Rather, in light of the aforementioned virtues, families that are baptized into Christ should emulate the Holy Family, acting toward one another in Christian love. The Greek word is *agape*, indicating a

gracious and generous love that expects nothing in return. It is the word most often used of God's love.

GOSPEL Today's Gospel has some resonances with the story of Elkanah and Hannah's annual trips to the temple in Shiloh. The difference is that here Mary and Joseph are described as making annual visits to the Temple in Jerusalem. Samuel, who would become the last of the judges and first of the prophets of Israel, was brought to the Shiloh temple presum-

Let the word of Christ **dwell** in you richly,
   as in all wisdom you **teach** and **admonish** one another,
   singing **psalms**, **hymns**, and spiritual **songs**
   with **gratitude** in your hearts to God.
And whatever you **do**, in **word** or in **deed**,
   do **everything** in the name of the Lord **Jesus**,
   giving **thanks** to God the Father **through** him.]

Wives, be **subordinate** to your husbands,
   as is proper in the Lord.
Husbands, love your **wives**,
   and avoid any **bitterness** toward them.
Children, obey your **parents** in everything,
   for this is **pleasing** to the Lord.
Fathers, do not **provoke** your children,
   so they may not become **discouraged**.

[Shorter: Colossians 3:12–17 (see brackets)]

GOSPEL   Luke 2:41–52

A reading from the holy Gospel according to Luke

Each year **Jesus' parents** went to **Jerusalem** for the **feast**
   of **Passover**,
   and when he was **twelve years old**,
   they went up according to festival **custom**.
After they had **completed** its days, as they were **returning**,
   the boy **Jesus** remained **behind** in **Jerusalem**,
   but his **parents** did not **know** it.
Thinking that he was in the **caravan**,
   they **journeyed** for a **day**
   and **looked** for him among their **relatives** and **acquaintances**,
   but not **finding** him,
   they **returned** to **Jerusalem** to **look** for him. »

A challenging passage to proclaim: it reinforces codes of conduct common to Greco-Roman society but which Paul typically disdains. (Most scholars of early Christianity regard these verses as added later by someone other than the original author, likely a scribe.) Probably best to read this in a neutral tone.

A very familiar narrative reading, almost like a small but intensely dramatic play. Because its contents are so spectacular (imagine parents leaving behind a child and not noticing for over a day), resist the temptation to dramatize your proclamation. The drama will come through when you proclaim this passage evenly.

Nearly even stresses on all the words of this line, with a little extra on "custom."

Here the story intensifies. You can quicken your pace slightly.

Added emphasis on "look."

---

ably at a young age. In this story, Jesus accompanies his parents to Jerusalem for the Passover feast, suggesting that they are devout Jews fulfilling their obligation of pilgrimage, and he decides to stay in the Temple, unbeknownst to his parents.

At the end of the Passover feast, either seven or eight days in length, Luke tells us that the Holy Family joined a caravan destined for Nazareth. Walking distance would have been about sixty-five miles, amounting to a journey of several days. Luke notes that Jesus was twelve at the time. We

might think of him as just a boy, but males were married by eighteen, at least, and often by fifteen. This helps to explain why Mary and Joseph were unaware of his absence at first. If you have late adolescent children, you know how hard it is to keep track of them!

Luke illustrates the anxiety that filled Mary and Joseph's hearts, when they realized that their son was not with the caravan. Luke says that they looked for Jesus among their friends and family for a full day before leaving the caravan to return to

Jerusalem. Traveling alone was dangerous business, especially at night, because they would be easy prey for robbers and troublemakers. After three days of searching, they finally found him in the Jerusalem Temple, listening to the teachers and asking questions of them. The teachers were amazed, also translated as "beside themselves in wonderment," over Jesus. But his parents were astonished, also translated as "struck with shock and panic," so much so that Mary blurted out, "Child, why have you done this to us?" Can you feel their pain?

At this point, when Jesus' parents rediscover him, slow your pace slightly.

These well-known words appear to be the core of this reading. Emphasis on "know" and "be."

Perhaps more likely, Mary keeping these things in her heart is the core of this reading. She's having to come to terms with her son's divinity. It's something entirely mysterious to her.

After **three days** they found him in the **temple**,
    sitting in the **midst** of the **teachers**,
    listening to them and asking them **questions**,
    and **all** who heard him were **astounded**
    at his **understanding** and his **answers**.
When his **parents** saw him,
    they were **astonished**,
    and his mother **said** to him,
    "**Son**, why have you **done** this to us?
Your **father** and I have been **looking** for you with great **anxiety**."
And he **said** to them,
    "Why were you **looking** for me?
Did you not **know** that I must **be** in my Father's house?"
But they did **not understand** what he **said** to them.
He went **down** with them and came to **Nazareth**,
    and was **obedient** to them;
    and his **mother** kept all these **things** in her heart.
And Jesus advanced in **wisdom** and **age** and **favor**
    before **God** and **man**.

PRAYERFUL READING, OR *LECTIO DIVINA*

1. *Lectio:* Read a Scripture passage aloud slowly. Notice what phrase captures your attention and be attentive to its meaning. Silent pause.

2. *Meditatio:* Read the passage aloud slowly again, reflecting on the passage, allowing God to speak to you through it. Silent pause.

3. *Oratio:* Read it aloud slowly a third time, allowing it to be your prayer or response to God's gift of insight to you. Silent pause.

4. *Contemplatio:* Read it aloud slowly a fourth time, now resting in God's Word.

In response, Jesus questions why they were even looking for him and gives an answer that we might take as rude and disrespectful. "Did you not know that I must be in my Father's house [or about my Father's business]?" The Greek word translated here as "must" carries the notion of divine necessity. Thus, in these first words attributed to Jesus in Luke's Gospel, Jesus' identity is revealed. Even as he goes home, obedient to his parents, the reader of this Gospel knows that Jesus is compelled by divine necessity toward a life of obedience to his heavenly Father. Of course, his parents did not understand. Would you have understood?

Luke's story of the finding of Jesus in the Temple differs considerably from the medieval and Renaissance paintings of the Holy Family, in which Jesus is portrayed as a perfectly composed mini-adult, Mary and Joseph look serene and well-rested, and everyone is immaculately dressed. But Luke's story is much more realistic and more relatable for everyone who is trying to raise a family in challenging times. C.C.

MARY, THE HOLY MOTHER OF GOD

LECTIONARY #18

READING I   Numbers 6:22–27

A reading from the Book of Numbers

The LORD said to **Moses**:
  "**Speak** to Aaron and his sons and **tell** them:
  This is how you shall bless the Israelites.
Say to them:
   The LORD bless you and **keep** you!
   The LORD let his face **shine** upon
      you, and be **gracious** to you!
   The LORD look upon you **kindly** and
      give you **peace**!
So shall they **invoke** my name upon the **Israelites**,
   and I will **bless** them."

A didactic reading, built on advice that God gives to Moses. The verbs "speak," "say," and "invoke" are crucial, as are repetitions of "The Lord." Use these repetitions to guide your proclamation.

Note how the word "bless" is repeated.

Note how "bless" echoes in "peace."

For meditation and context:

RESPONSORIAL PSALM   Psalm 67:2–3, 5, 6, 8 (2a)

R. May God bless us in his mercy.

May God have pity on us and bless us;
   may he let his face shine upon us.
So may your way be known upon earth;
   among all nations, your salvation.

May the nations be glad and exult
   because you rule the peoples in equity;
   the nations on the earth you guide.

May the peoples praise you, O God;
   may all the peoples praise you!
May God bless us,
   and may all the ends of the earth fear him!

READING I   On the Solemnity of Mary the Holy Mother of God, we celebrate Mary's role in the mystery of salvation effected through Jesus' incarnation, death, and resurrection. This day is also celebrated as the World Day of Peace, which was first established by Pope Paul VI in 1968. Our first reading is particularly appropriate on this day. It is sometimes called the priestly blessing, because the blessing was given to Aaron, the priest and brother of Moses, to bestow on the children of Israel. The image of God's face shining upon the people is a metaphor for

God's presence. The phrase translated here as "The Lord look upon you kindly" can also be translated as "The Lord raise his face toward you." It is the opposite of the biblical concept of God hiding his face, when Israel felt abandoned by God.

READING II   Today's reading from the Letter to the Galatians is a part of a much longer argument that Paul makes concerning justification by faith. The mostly Gentile Christian communities of Galatia were apparently influenced by some Jewish Christian missionaries who

taught that justification, or right relationship with God, came through obedience of Jewish law. Paul argues that only God can restore humanity to its right relationship with God, and God does so as a free gift through the agency of Jesus Christ in his death and resurrection.

To illustrate this point, Paul uses several metaphors, including the one in this reading, which contrasts the situation of a slave with that of an adopted child of God. The slave represents those who think that obedience to the Law will make them right with God. The minor child, Paul says, is no

A didactic reading in which Paul connects the members of the early church in Galatia directly to Jesus. He does so in three sentences, introduced by "when," "as," and "so." In short order, he builds his argument and then concludes it.

READING II   Galatians 4:4–7

A reading from the Letter of Saint Paul to the Galatians

Brothers and sisters:
When the **fullness** of time had come, God sent his Son,
    born of a woman, **born** under the law,
    to ransom those **under** the law,
    so that we might **receive** adoption as sons.
As **proof** that you are **sons**,
    God sent the **Spirit** of his Son into our hearts,
    crying out, "**Abba**, Father!"
So you are **no longer** a slave but a **son**,
    and if a **son** then also an **heir**, **through** God.

The conclusion of Paul's argument, that we are no longer slaves but sons and heirs of God, is truly radical. It deserves some astonishment and emphasis.

GOSPEL   Luke 2:16–21

A reading from the holy Gospel according to Luke

The **shepherds** went in haste to **Bethlehem** and found **Mary**
        and **Joseph**,
    and the infant **lying** in the manger.
When they **saw** this,
    they made **known** the message
    that had been **told** them about this child.
All who heard it were **amazed**
    by what had been **told** them by the **shepherds**.
And **Mary** kept all these things,
    reflecting on them in her **heart**.
Then the **shepherds** returned,
    glorifying and **praising** God
    for **all** they had **heard** and seen,
    just as it had been **told** to them.

When eight days were **completed** for his circumcision,
    he was named **Jesus**, the name **given** him by the **angel**
    before he was **conceived** in the **womb**.

A short narrative reading that concludes the Nativity story. While the focus is on the infant Jesus lying in the manger, the eyes through which we see him are those of the shepherds. The shepherds modeled Christian devotion from the beginning of our faith.

Amazement is the primary emotion of this story.

The shepherds' glorifying and praising are to be our own.

different, because he is under the control of another. But in the fullness of time or at the appropriate time, God sent Jesus, born of Mary, to ransom humanity from its slavery and make them adoptive sons and daughters and heirs of God. The Greek word translated here as "ransom" means "to pay the price to recover someone from the power of another," much as one might pay the price to free a slave from the master.

GOSPEL Today's Gospel presents a tender story about some shepherds from the pastures around Bethlehem who come to see the wondrous sight that the angels announced to them. They find Mary and Joseph with their newborn baby, who was lying in a hay trough, or manger. Perhaps they were staying in a home that had a place for animals, or maybe they were sharing an open-air space where travelers would stop to rest their animals. When the shepherds saw the Holy Family just as the angels described, they spread the news all around, and everyone was in wonder about what they heard. Mary treasured all these things, keeping them close to her heart. This is also a strange story. Why would God choose these marginalized folks to be proclaimers of the good news? How does this story speak to our world today? C.C.

THE EPIPHANY OF THE LORD

LECTIONARY #20

READING I   Isaiah 60:1–6

Isaiah = ī-ZAY-uh

An exhortatory reading filled with rich and poetic images and phrases. Radiance, light, gift giving, and praise guide this prophetic passage. Let these words guide your reading.

A reading from the Book of the Prophet Isaiah

Rise up in splendor, Jerusalem! Your **light** has **come**,
    the **glory** of the **Lord shines** upon you.
See, **darkness** covers the earth,
    and **thick clouds cover** the peoples;
but upon **you** the Lord **shines**,
    and **over** you appears his **glory**.
Nations shall walk by your **light**,
    and **kings** by your shining **radiance**.
Raise your eyes and **look** about;
    they all **gather** and **come** to you:
your **sons come** from **afar**,
    and your **daughters** in the **arms** of their **nurses**.

This passage is addressed to Jerusalem, but because it is written in the second person, it allows you to speak directly to the assembly. "Raise your eyes and look about. . . . "

Then you shall be **radiant** at what you **see**,
    your **heart** shall **throb** and over**flow**,
for the **riches** of the sea shall be **emptied** out before you,
    the **wealth** of nations shall be **brought** to you.
Caravans of **camels** shall **fill** you,
    dromedaries from **Midian** and **Ephah**;
all from **Sheba** shall come
    bearing **gold** and **frankincense**,
    and **proclaiming** the **praises** of the Lord.

dromedaries = DROM-eh-dayr-ees = single-humped camels
Midian= MID-ee-uhn
Ephah = EE-fuh
The camels and the gifts they carry prefigure the magi. Present this passage as a prelude to the Epiphany story.

READING I   The Solemnity of the Epiphany of the Lord is a celebration of the manifestation of divinity. Our first reading comes from the part of the book of Isaiah written after the return of Judean exiles from Babylon. This was a tumultuous time for the returnees as they struggled to reestablish themselves in a land devastated by their oppressors while living among peoples who did not welcome their return. Here the prophet conveys a message of hope and delight to Zion, or personified Jerusalem, encouraging her people to recognize their new reality. God's

glory is described as light dawning on a world once covered in darkness, and God's people are described as bright or radiant in God's reflected glory, so much so that they will be a beacon of light to the Gentiles. Nations will bring abundance of wealth back to Jerusalem, and kings bearing gold and frankincense will honor Zion, as her exiled children continue their return from Babylon. The awe and excitement embodied by this poem is palpable! But note especially the beautiful promise made to Jerusalem: "your heart shall throb and overflow" (Isaiah 60:5). The Hebrew word *lebab*, translated here as

"heart," refers to the inner self, including the mind and will. God's promise is for us as well. May our hearts swell with joy at the realization of God's glory.

READING II   Today's reading from the Letter to the Ephesians celebrates the revelation or manifestation of God's ongoing plan of salvation. The author reminds his Gentile readers of the stewardship or administration of God's grace that was given to Paul for their benefit. The Greek word is *oikonomia*, referring to the oversight or management of someone

For meditation and context:

RESPONSORIAL PSALM   Psalm 72:1–2, 7–8, 10–11, 12–13 (11)

R. Lord, every nation on earth will adore you.

O God, with your judgment endow the king,
    and with your justice, the king's son;
he shall govern your people with justice
    and your afflicted ones with judgment.

Justice shall flower in his days,
    and profound peace, till the moon
        be no more.
May he rule from sea to sea,
    and from the River to the ends of
        the earth.

The kings of Tarshish and the Isles shall
        offer gifts;
    the kings of Arabia and Seba shall
        bring tribute.
All kings shall pay him homage,
    all nations shall serve him.

For he shall rescue the poor when
        he cries out,
    and the afflicted when he has no one
        to help him.
He shall have pity for the lowly and the poor;
    the lives of the poor he shall save.

Ephesians = ee-FEE-zhuhnz

A didactic reading in which Paul emphatically includes the Gentile members of the early church in Ephesus into the community of believers. It's in two long sentences, emphasizing revelation and the Gospel respectively.

READING II   Ephesians 3:2–3a, 5–6

A reading from the Letter of Saint Paul to the Ephesians

Brothers and sisters:
You have **heard** of the **stewardship** of God's **grace**
    that was given to me for your **benefit**,
    namely, that the **mystery** was made known to me by **revelation**.
It was not made known to **people** in other **generations**
    as it has **now** been revealed
    to his **holy apostles** and **prophets** by the **Spirit**:
    that the **Gentiles** are **coheirs**, **members** of the **same** body,
    and **copartners** in the **promise** in Christ **Jesus** through
        the **gospel**.

Emphasize "Gentiles," "coheirs," "members," and "copartners" as part of the "same body."

A narrative reading that tells a rich and mysterious story, one that includes astrology and betrayal, providing a vivid context for the world into which Jesus was born.

The arrival of the magi sets the scene. Their desire to pay homage to the newborn king prepares the way for our own worship.

GOSPEL   Matthew 2:1–12

A reading from the holy Gospel according to Matthew

When **Jesus** was born in **Bethlehem** of **Judea**,
    in the **days** of King **Herod**,
    behold, **magi** from the **east** arrived in Jerusalem, saying,
    "**Where** is the newborn **king** of the **Jews**?

---

else's property. This grace, or free gift of God, which was not made known in previous generations but is now revealed through the apostles and prophets, is the mystery of Christ, that is, God's hidden purpose or intention for humanity. What is this mystery? Notice how the author of this letter keeps us in suspense until the very end of today's reading. It is that God's plan for salvation includes the Gentiles as joint heirs, joint members, and joint partakers with the Jewish people in the Gospel, or good news, of Jesus Christ. What an awesome mystery, indeed!

GOSPEL Today's Gospel story is familiar to most Christians, and it is the scriptural basis for the feast of the Epiphany. Unfortunately, we often misremember the biblical story and sometimes fail to recognize its more troubling side. The people whom Matthew says come from the East were magi, not kings. The early Christian writer Tertullian (AD 155–220) was apparently the first to suggest that they were kings. But magi (singular, *magus*) describes a category of scholars who engaged in dream interpretation, astrology, and predictions of the future. Matthew

does not tell us how many magi there were or their names. Those things are added to the tradition much later, probably because Matthew was so spare with the details.

As Matthew tells the story, these magi observed a star that was believed to signal the birth of a king "at its rising," and they had come to worship him. Not knowing exactly where to find him, they were in danger of falling into a trap. When they entered Jerusalem asking for information about the newborn king of the Jews, their inquiry reached the ears of Herod the Great. Herod asked his own advisors about

homage = HOM-ij

Herod's trouble represents doubt and deception, which the subsequent verses elaborate.

TO KEEP IN MIND
As you prepare your proclamation, make choices about what emotions need to be expressed. Some choices are evident from the text, but some are harder to discern. Understanding the context of the Scripture passage will help you decide.

Pause slightly after "stopped."

prostrated = PROS-tray-t*d

Awe and wonder authenticate the magi and their prophetic visions. Their gifts are utterly precious. And their dream of warning is impossible to ignore. Don't sell their departure short. It's what makes this passage so vivid.

We saw his **star** at its **rising**
and have **come** to do him **homage**."
When King Herod heard this,
he was greatly **troubled**,
and **all Jerusalem** with him.
Assembling all the chief priests and the scribes of the people,
he **inquired** of them **where** the Christ was to be **born**.
They said to him, "In **Bethlehem** of **Judea**,
for **thus** it has been **written** through the **prophet**:
And **you**, **Bethlehem**, land of **Judah**,
are by **no means least** among the **rulers** of Judah;
since from **you** shall **come** a **ruler**,
who is to **shepherd** my people **Israel**."
Then **Herod** called the magi **secretly**
and ascertained from them the **time** of the star's **appearance**.
He sent them to Bethlehem and said,
"**Go** and search **diligently** for the **child**.
When you have **found** him, bring me **word**,
that **I too may go** and do him homage."
After their **audience** with the king they set out.
And **behold**, the **star** that they had seen at its rising
preceded them,
until it **came** and **stopped over** the place where the **child was**.
They were **overjoyed** at seeing the star,
and on entering the house
they saw the child with **Mary** his mother.
They **prostrated** themselves and did him **homage**.
Then they **opened** their treasures
and offered him gifts of **gold**, **frankincense**, and **myrrh**.
And having been **warned** in a **dream** not to **return** to Herod,
they **departed** for their country by **another** way.

where this king was to be born, and they told him "Bethlehem," because of the prophetic words of Micah, "from you shall come a ruler, who is to shepherd my people Israel" (Matthew 2:6; see Micah 5:2). Bethlehem was David's hometown, and shepherding was a metaphor for kingship (see 2 Samuel 5:2).

The gifts of gold and frankincense that the magi bring to the child Jesus are fit for a king, as the first reading suggests, but myrrh was also used as a painkiller and in burial. Further, if bringing a symbol of suffering and death to a tiny baby were not troubling enough, Matthew tells us about Herod's request that the magi return to him after they find the child. For thirty-two years, Herod oppressed the people of Palestine at the expense of his massive building projects. He was greedy for power and diligent about putting down anyone who might oppose him. Clearly, his motive in the case of this baby was not to pay his respects! The story that follows the visit of the magi is the escape of Joseph, Mary, and the baby to Egypt and Herod's slaughter of the babies in Bethlehem (Matthew 2:13–18). C.C.

THE BAPTISM OF THE LORD

LECTIONARY #21

Isaiah = ī-ZAY-uh

A didactic reading spoken in a voice of wisdom and care.

READING I   Isaiah 40:1–5, 9–11

A reading from the Book of the Prophet Isaiah

> **Comfort**, give **comfort** to my **people**,
>   says your **God**.
> Speak **tenderly** to **Jerusalem**, and **proclaim** to her
>   that her **service** is at an **end**,
>   her **guilt** is **expiated**;
> **indeed**, she has **received** from the **hand** of the LORD
>   **double** for all her **sins**.
>
>   A **voice** cries **out**:
> In the **desert** prepare the **way** of the LORD!
>   Make **straight** in the **wasteland** a **highway** for our **God**!
> Every **valley** shall be filled **in**,
>   every **mountain** and **hill** shall be made **low**;
> the rugged **land** shall be made a **plain**,
>   the rough **country**, a broad **valley**.
> Then the **glory** of the LORD shall be **revealed**,
>   and all **people** shall see it **together**;
>   for the **mouth** of the LORD has **spoken**.
>
> **Go up on** to a high **mountain**,
>   **Zion**, **herald** of glad **tidings**;
> cry **out** at the top of your **voice**,
>   **Jerusalem**, **herald** of good **news**!

The voice that cries out speaks words of familiarity and power. Treat this passage like the recitation of a poem. Note how each verse concludes with a stress.

TO KEEP IN MIND
Smile when you share good news. Nonverbal cues like a smile help the assembly understand the reading.

"Go up on": each word receives the same stress.

There are options for today's readings. Contact your parish staff to learn which readings will be used.

READING I   **Isaiah 40.** This reading the opening of Second Isaiah (Isaiah 40–55), written during the Babylonian Exile, when the morale of the Judeans was shattered by the loss of the Jerusalem Temple, the deportation of the people, and the termination of their king. They had suffered greatly for their failure to keep covenant with God, even thinking that God had abandoned them entirely.

Now the prophet proclaims God's word to the heavenly assembly, "Comfort, give comfort to my people." Israel is described as "my people," which indicates that God has not abandoned the covenant. Further, "Jerusalem" is personified here; the prophet is not addressing an inanimate city but rather the people who inhabit it. In the phrase "Speak to the heart of Jerusalem," the Hebrew word is *leb*, which refers to the heart, mind, or inner self of the people. Ancient Israelites would have understood the heart to be the seat of reasoning. Hence, God is telling the heavenly assembly

to convince Israel that God has not abandoned Israel, that God recognizes the enormity of their sorrow for their unfaithfulness, and that they are now purified of their sin.

Then a member of the heavenly assembly speaks out, "In the wilderness prepare the way of the Lord!" Thus, God will take the lead in a new exodus, clearing the way for Israel to return from slavery in Babylon to the soon-to-be restored Jerusalem. There the "glory of the Lord," or the divine presence, will reside, not only for God's people but for all humankind. Finally, Jerusalem, also known as Zion, is told to

"Here" is repeated three times before the
end of this passage. Give each expression
of "here" a little added emphasis.

Fear **not** to cry **out**
    and say to the **cities** of **Judah**:
      Here is your **God**!
Here comes with **power**
    the Lord **GOD**,
    who **rules** by his strong **arm**;
here is his **reward** with **him**,
    his **recompense before** him.
Like a **shepherd** he feeds his **flock**;
    in his **arms** he gathers the **lambs**,
carrying them in his **bosom**,
    and **leading** the ewes with **care**.

Or:

READING I   Isaiah 42:1–4, 6–7

Isaiah = ī-ZAY-uh

A reading from the Book of the Prophet Isaiah

An exhortatory reading in which the
Lord identifies his servant, characterizing
his virtues in terms of his humility and
preparedness, followed by a passage in
which the Lord shifts from talking about his
chosen servant in the third person ("he")
to the second person ("you"), which allows
you to direct your proclamation to the
gathered assembly. Take advantage of this
shift in pronouns.

Thus says the LORD:
Here is my **servant** whom I uphold,
    my **chosen one** with whom I am **pleased**,
upon whom I have **put** my spirit;
    he shall bring forth **justice** to the **nations**,
not crying **out**, not **shouting**,
    not making his **voice heard** in the **street**.
A bruised reed he shall not break,
    and a **smoldering wick** he shall not **quench**,
until he establishes **justice** on the **earth**;
    the **coastlands** will wait for his **teaching**. »

Even stresses on the words in this line,
which present a compelling image. A bruised
reed is easy to break; why isn't the chosen
servant breaking the reed?

climb a high mountain—the city itself is seated on seven mountain peaks—and shout the good news, "Here comes with power the Lord God." Note the beautiful pastoral image of God feeding his flock, carrying lambs in his bosom or at his chest, and gently leading the pregnant ewes as they make their way toward Jerusalem. There is no greater consolation!

Isaiah 42. This reading is also from Second Isaiah. Again, God is speaking, most likely to the heavenly assembly. Much of the first part of this reading is organized as a poem with couplets in which the first and second lines of the couplet repeat themselves. Occasionally, a couplet in the second line completes the idea presented in the first line.

Notice how God announces the servant: he is upheld by God, God's chosen one, and the one in whom God is pleased. We are never told his name, nor do we know if the servant represents an individual or a group of people. One clue can be found in the prophet's words about the servant being endowed with God's spirit. Elsewhere in the book of Isaiah, something similar is said of the messiah who was to

come from David's line: "The spirit of the Lord shall rest upon him" (Isaiah 11:2).

The servant's mission, is to bring justice not only to the Jewish people but also to the whole world. Moreover, it is a mission that will be accomplished quietly, with care and with perseverance. Yes, there is such a thing as strength in restraint.

In the last part of today's reading, God is still speaking, but now the servant is being addressed directly in what could be described as a commissioning or a call to ministry. The phrase translated here as "for justice" can also be translated as "in

I, the LORD, have **called** you for the **victory** of justice,
    I have **grasped you** by the hand;
I **formed** you, and set you
        as a **covenant** of the people,
        a **light** for the nations,
    to open the **eyes** of the **blind**,
        to bring out **prisoners** from **confinement**,
        and from the **dungeon**, those who live in **darkness**.

Emphasize "grasped you" and "formed you."

The passage ends with images of dire things the Lord will use "you" to correct.

For meditation and context:

RESPONSORIAL PSALM   Psalm 104:1b–2, 3–4, 24–25, 27–28, 29–30 (1)

R. O bless the Lord, my soul.

O LORD, my God, you are great indeed!
    You are clothed with majesty and glory,
robed in light as with a cloak.
    You have spread out the heavens
        like a tent-cloth.

You have constructed your palace upon
        the waters.
    You make the clouds your chariot;
you travel on the wings of the wind.
    You make the winds your messengers,
and flaming fire your ministers.

How manifold are your works, O LORD!
    In wisdom you have wrought them all—
the earth is full of your creatures;
    the sea also, great and wide,
in which are schools without number
    of living things both small and great.

They look to you to give them food in
        due time.
    When you give it to them, they gather it;
when you open your hand, they are filled
        with good things.

If you take away their breath, they perish and
        return to the dust.
    When you send forth your spirit,
        they are created,
and you renew the face of the earth.

Or:

For meditation and context:

RESPONSORIAL PSALM   Psalm 29:1–2, 3–4, 3, 9–10 (11b)

R. The Lord will bless his people with peace.

Give to the LORD, you sons of God,
    give to the LORD glory and praise,
give to the LORD the glory due his name;
    adore the LORD in holy attire.

The voice of the LORD is over the waters,
    the LORD, over vast waters.
The voice of the LORD is mighty;
    the voice of the LORD is majestic.

The God of glory thunders,
    and in his temple all say, "Glory!"
The LORD is enthroned above the flood;
    the LORD is enthroned as king forever.

TO KEEP IN MIND
The responsorial psalm "has great liturgical and pastoral importance, since it fosters meditation on the Word of God," the *General Instruction of the Roman* Missal says. Pray it as you prepare.

---

righteousness" or even as "in the victory of justice." Notice, also, that the servant is described as both a covenant (a treaty or agreement) and a light to the nations with the goal of healing blindness and breaking the bonds of imprisonment.

READING II | **Titus.** We also have two choices for the second reading. The first option is from the Letter to Titus. The context for this reading is a household code, which is a teaching on right behavior within a family and in the family's interactions with other parts of society.

Although they are common in some of the New Testament letters, we see them in philosophical writings of earlier times, as well. The underlying principle was that the family is a microcosm of the larger society, and strong families make for strong societies.

What is different about household codes in the New Testament letters is their rationale. After addressing older men and women, younger men, and slaves about how they should behave, the author of this letter goes on to say that God's grace (free gift) has appeared to teach all humanity how "to live temperately, justly, and devoutly in

this age" as we await the return of the risen Christ in the glory of God. The Greek word *epiphaino*, which is translated here as "appeared," can also mean "to become visible" or "to show oneself," which further suggests that God's grace is not a thing that we are given but rather a being whose mission is from God. This is where we get our English word "epiphany."

Thus, the Christian believer's rationale for right behavior should be Jesus himself, who redeemed us, that is, bought us back, from lawlessness and purified us as his own. The author of this letter goes on to

Titus = TĪ-tuhs

A didactic reading whose notes are reassurance and hope.
Beloved = bee-LUHV-uhd

There is a rhythmical parallel between "godless ways" and "worldly desires."
blessed = BLES-uhd
This passage includes words and phrases of liturgical familiarity; try to proclaim them as words to be found in a letter addressed to an intimate.

Emphasis on "not."

The "bath of rebirth" signals baptism.

READING II   Titus 2:11–14; 3:4–7

A reading from the Letter of Saint Paul to Titus

Beloved:
The **grace** of **God** has **appeared**, saving **all**
   and **training** us to reject **godless ways** and **worldly desires**
   and to live **temperately**, **justly**, and **devoutly** in this age,
   as we **await** the blessed **hope**,
   the **appearance** of the **glory** of our great **God**
   and **savior** Jesus **Christ**,
   who **gave himself** for us to deliver us from **all lawlessness**
   and to **cleanse** for **himself** a **people** as his **own**,
   eager to do what is **good**.

   When the **kindness** and generous **love**
      of **God** our **savior appeared**,
   not because of any righteous **deeds** we had **done**
      but because of his **mercy**,
   he **saved** us through the **bath** of **rebirth**
      and **renewal** by the Holy **Spirit**,
   whom he **richly** poured **out** on **us**
      through Jesus **Christ** our **savior**,
   so that we might be **justified** by his **grace**
      and become **heirs** in **hope** of eternal **life**.

Or:

READING II   Acts 10:34–38

A reading from the Acts of the Apostles

Peter proceeded to speak to those gathered
   in the **house** of Cornelius, saying:
"In **truth**, I see that **God** shows no **partiality**. »

An exhortatory reading in a narrative context, spoken by Peter to some early apostles of Jesus. This reading expresses ancient convictions of the earliest members of the faith.

describe Jesus as God's kindness and love, which comes to us through baptism and the Holy Spirit. What a beautiful image. The Greek word here used for "kindness" can also mean integrity and moral goodness, and the Greek word "love" means love for humankind or benevolence.

Acts of the Apostles. Our second choice on this feast is from the Acts of the Apostles. It is part of a conversation that Peter has with a Roman centurion named Cornelius at his home. Why is this noteworthy? Remember that Peter was a Jew. Jews adhered to a more restrictive diet than their Gentile neighbors, and ordinarily they would not enter a Gentile's home. Although Peter and Cornelius had not met before, Cornelius had received a vision of an angel telling him to send for Peter (Acts 10:3–8). In the meantime, Peter received a threefold vision of a large sheet coming down from heaven filled with all kinds of animals, birds, and reptiles (Acts 10:11–16). When he was told to slaughter and eat them, he refused, because not all of the creatures were kosher, or approved for Jews to eat. But the voice from heaven was again heard to say, "What God has made clean, you are not to call profane" (Acts 10:15). Thus, Peter concluded that God was giving permission for him to interact with Gentiles, and he willingly accompanied Cornelius' servants when they came to get him.

Peter's speech begins with a formula that we see elsewhere in sacred Scripture, "God shows no partiality" (see Deuteronomy 10:17–18; Sirach 35:15–16; Romans 2:11). In this Gentile context and spoken by a Jew, the message is truly radical: our God does not play favorites but rather is a respecter of all people. Peter wants everyone to know that Israel's salvation story reaches its

"Peace," "Christ," and "Lord" express a unified vision of things.

Even emphasis on the words of this line.

Even emphasis here as well, characterizing Jesus' powers.

Rather, in every nation whoever fears him and acts **uprightly**
    is **acceptable** to him.
You know the **word** that he sent to the **Israelites**
    as he proclaimed **peace** through Jesus **Christ**,
        who is **Lord** of all,
    what has **happened** all over **Judea**,
    beginning in Galilee after the **baptism**
    that John preached,
    how God **anointed** Jesus of Nazareth
    with the **Holy Spirit** and **power**.
He went about doing **good**
    and healing all those oppressed by the devil,
    for **God** was **with** him."

GOSPEL   Luke 3:15–16, 21–22

A narrative reading in which the ritual of baptism manifests the anticipation to be felt for the coming of Jesus.

Note the parallel of John to Jesus. Even emphasis on both names.

Here, John begins to develop the contrast between himself and Jesus in a passage of lucid imagery.

A reading from the holy Gospel according to Luke

The **people** were **filled** with **expectation**,
    and **all** were **asking** in their **hearts**
    whether **John** might be the **Christ**.
John answered them all, saying,
    "I am **baptizing** you with **water**,
    but one **mightier** than **I** is **coming**.
I am not **worthy** to loosen the **thongs** of his **sandals**.
He will **baptize** you with the Holy **Spirit** and **fire**."

After all the **people** had been **baptized**
    and **Jesus** also had been **baptized** and was **praying**,
    heaven was opened and the Holy **Spirit** descended **upon** him
    in bodily **form** like a **dove**.
And a **voice** came from **heaven**,
    "**You** are my beloved **Son**;
    with **you** I am well **pleased**."

These words of the voice from heaven represent mysterious confirmation and solace.

fullness in Jesus Christ, the bringer of peace. Notice also how Luke alludes to the story of the baptism of Jesus in this speech; he was anointed by the Holy Spirit and with power, and God was with him.

 Prior to the opening of this reading, John is preaching repentance for the forgiveness of sins (Luke 3:3). We are told that crowds are coming to John in the wilderness seeking this forgiveness, and he gives them advice about how

to demonstrate repentance: share what you have and be ethical in business and law.

John's message made many in the crowds excited, and *all* were thinking that he might be the messiah or the "anointed" of God. Therefore, John addresses *all*. Such a small word, but it is so important here. It indicates that the message of repentance for the forgiveness of sin is intended for Jews and Gentiles, tax collectors and soldiers, for everyone!

Luke continues, "After *all* the people had been baptized." Luke presents Jesus as submitting to this baptism, very likely as a way of affirming the continuity between John's ministry and Jesus' ministry to follow. More important is the mention of Jesus at prayer. This is a common theme in Luke's Gospel. Everything Jesus does or says in his ministry is marked by prayer. Here, Jesus' prayer opens the way for the outpouring of the Holy Spirit and elicits a heaven-sent affirmation that God takes great pleasure in his beloved Son. C.C.

SECOND SUNDAY IN ORDINARY TIME

LECTIONARY #66

READING I Isaiah 62:1–5

A reading from the Book of the Prophet Isaiah

For **Zion's** sake I will **not** be **silent**,
  for **Jerusalem's** sake I will **not** be **quiet**,
her **vindication** shines **forth** like the **dawn**
  and her **victory** like a burning **torch**.

Nations shall **behold** your **vindication**,
  and all the **kings** your **glory**;
you shall be **called** by a new **name**
  pronounced by the **mouth** of the LORD.
You shall be a **glorious crown** in the **hand** of the LORD,
  a royal **diadem held** by your **God**.
No **more** shall people call you "**Forsaken**,"
  or your land "**Desolate**,"
but you shall be **called** "My **Delight**,"
  and your **land** "**Espoused**."
For the LORD **delights** in **you**
  and makes your **land** his **spouse**.
As a **young man** marries a **virgin**,
  your **Builder** shall marry **you**;
and as a **bridegroom** rejoices in his **bride**
  so shall your **God** rejoice in **you**.

Isaiah = ī-ZAY-uh

An exhortatory reading of rousing and rhythmical affirmation. Don't overdo it; the language in this reading is potent. The second-person address of the reading makes the reading more direct.

vindication = vihn-dih-KAY-shuhn

"Vindication" is repeated from above; it's a crucial term in the reading.

diadem = DĪ-uh-dem
Slight pause between "diadem" and "held."

espoused = ehs-POWSD

Likewise, a slight pause between "land" and "Espoused."

READING I Today's first reading comes from the third part of Isaiah, which is thought to have been written after the Babylonian Exile, when a remnant of God's people had begun to return to Judea. The silence to which the prophet refers is the period of the exile, when the people feared that God had abandoned them. But God has decided that now it is time to act on Lady Jerusalem's behalf, and God will not stop until her salvation and vindication, or righteousness, shine like a brilliant sunrise in the desert or a flaming torch for all the nations to see.

What does the prophet say about Lady Jerusalem's vindication? The shame of her devastation under the Babylonians will be lifted. The imagery is especially rich and evocative. We are told that Lady Jerusalem will be like a glorious crown in God's hand. Thus, metaphorically speaking, God will "wear her on his head" as a symbol of his kingship. The Hebrew word *tipharah*, which is here translated as "glorious," can refer to a woman's extreme beauty or her exalted status. In Exodus 28:2, it is used to describe the vestments of the high priest Aaron, brother of Moses.

God will also give Lady Jerusalem a new name. In the ancient world, the act of naming was about exerting authority over another or claiming him or her as one's own. Her old names, Forsaken and Desolate, reflect a time when the Israelites broke covenant with God. Thus, God restores relationship with the chosen people by giving Lady Jerusalem the name "My Delight is in her" and by calling her land "Espoused." With Israel's purity and innocence restored, she can be called God's bride once again. This is cause for great rejoicing!

For meditation and context:

RESPONSORIAL PSALM   Psalm 96:1–2, 2–3, 7–8, 9–10 (3)

R. Proclaim his marvelous deeds to all the nations.

Sing to the LORD a new song;
 sing to the LORD, all you lands.
Sing to the LORD; bless his name.

Announce his salvation, day after day.
Tell his glory among the nations;
 among all peoples, his wondrous deeds.

Give to the LORD, you families of nations,
 give to the LORD glory and praise;
 give to the LORD the glory due his name!

Worship the LORD in holy attire.
 Tremble before him, all the earth;
Say among the nations: The LORD is king.
 He governs the peoples with equity.

Corinthians = kohr-IN-thee-uhnz

An exhortatory reading that enumerates in vivid language the gifts of the Holy Spirit that continue to be given in the Church even to this day.

"Different kinds," "different forms," and "different workings": these are counterpoised by "the same Spirit," "the same Lord," and "the same God."

Slight emphasis on "each."

The rhythm of the presentation of these gifts follows a pattern that builds through this passage. "To one," "to another," and so on. Emphasize "another" followed by the gift itself, "faith," "healing," "deeds," "prophecy," and so on.

prophecy (noun) = PROF-uh-see

discernment = dih-SERN-m*nt

Shift the emphasis to "one" and "all."

READING II   1 Corinthians 12:4–11

A reading from the first Letter of Saint Paul to the Corinthians

Brothers and **sisters:**
There are **different kinds** of spiritual **gifts** but the same **Spirit**;
 there are **different forms** of **service** but the same **Lord**;
 there are **different workings** but the same **God**
 who produces **all** of them in **everyone**.
To **each** individual the **manifestation** of the Spirit
 is **given** for some **benefit**.
To **one** is given through the **Spirit** the **expression** of **wisdom**;
 to **another**, the expression of **knowledge** according
  to the same **Spirit**;
 to **another, faith** by the same **Spirit**;
 to **another**, gifts of **healing** by the one **Spirit**;
 to **another**, mighty **deeds**;
 to **another**, **prophecy**;
 to **another**, **discernment** of **spirits**;
 to **another**, **varieties** of **tongues**;
 to **another**, **interpretation** of **tongues**.
But **one** and the same **Spirit** produces **all** of these,
 distributing them **individually** to each **person** as he **wishes**.

READING II This reading from Paul's First Letter to the Corinthians does not have obvious connections to today's first reading or the Gospel, but that should not surprise us, because the lectionary is set up in such a way as to expose us to as much of Sacred Scripture as possible during a three-year cycle. Now and for the next several weeks, our second reading will come from the First Letter to the Corinthians.

First-century Corinth was a bustling trade city with a diverse population. The Christian community itself was quite diverse, as well, and some of its members thought of themselves as better or more enlightened than others, in part because they possessed spiritual gifts such as prophecy and *glossolalia,* or speaking in tongues. As an antidote to the Corinthian community's jealousy and infighting over spiritual gifts, Paul teaches them that these gifts are gifts of the Holy Spirit. They possess these gifts not because *they* (the members) are special but because these gifts come from the one Spirit who binds all of their ministries together for the good of the community. This is a message for all of us. In the genuine community of faith, there should be no bickering over who has the greater gifts and who is most important. Whatever spiritual gift we have been given should be at the service of the one Lord Jesus Christ.

A narrative reading with the inherent drama of a short play. This reading records Jesus' earliest miracle (in terms of his life story). The drama has less to do with the miracle itself than it does with Jesus' interaction with Mary.

Give due emphasis to "mother."

Don't overdo "Woman," even though the word is crucial to this passage.

There is an iambic rhythm to this line you might emphasize.

This line contains two emphatic sets of words, each with equal stresses: "six stone water jars" and "Jewish ceremonial washings."

The drama of this passage fixes on this line.

There is a lot of information conveyed in this description of the headwaiter. Read it in such a way that the twists and turns of the tale are clear to your assembly.

The rhythms in this line help to bring the passage to its conclusion. Equal stresses on "did this."

GOSPEL John 2:1–11

A reading from the holy Gospel according to John

There was a **wedding** at **Cana** in **Galilee**,
  and the **mother** of **Jesus** was **there**.
Jesus and his **disciples** were **also** invited to the wedding.
When the **wine** ran **short**,
  the mother of **Jesus said** to him,
  "They **have** no **wine**."
And Jesus said to her,
  "**Woman**, how does your **concern** affect **me**?
My **hour** has **not** yet **come**."
His **mother** said to the **servers**,
  "Do **whatever** he **tells** you."
Now there were **six stone water jars** there for **Jewish**
    ceremonial washings,
  each holding **twenty** to **thirty** gallons.
Jesus told them,
  "**Fill** the **jars** with **water**."
So they **filled** them to the **brim**.
Then he told them,
  "**Draw** some **out now** and **take** it to the **headwaiter**."
So they **took** it.
And when the **headwaiter** tasted the **water** that had
    become **wine**,
  without **knowing** where it **came** from
  —although the **servers** who had drawn the water **knew**—,
  the **headwaiter** called the **bridegroom** and **said** to him,
  "**Everyone** serves good wine **first**,
  and then when people have drunk **freely**, an **inferior** one;
  but **you** have kept the **good** wine until **now**."
Jesus **did this** as the **beginning** of his **signs** at **Cana** in **Galilee**
  and **so** revealed his **glory**,
  and his **disciples** began to **believe** in him.

GOSPEL Like the first reading, today's Gospel takes up the marriage theme and in somewhat the same way, surprisingly. A typical miracle story has three parts: description of need, the miracle worker's word or deed, and evidence that the miracle took place. Here, the need is a source of great embarrassment and humiliation for the families of the bride and groom. They have run out of wine! Jesus' mother is more involved than the ordinary guest. Perhaps this wedding involves someone from within their family. She suggests that Jesus might fix the prob-

lem, and he answers in rather harsh language, "Woman, how does your concern affect me?"

But the story does not end there. Without fanfare, Jesus tells the waiters to fill the water jars reserved for Jewish ritual washings, but he does nothing more. As he serves what is now wine, the headwaiter thinks only that the couple or their families had made an odd choice in waiting to serve their best wine until their guests were well imbibed. Each of these jars would have held 20 to 30 gallons of water, making this a secret but bountiful miracle! But wine is

the blood of the grape and, in such superabundance, it would make people think of the messianic banquet that will accompany the future manifestation of God's reign (see Isaiah 25:6, Joel 2:24–26). Thus, when Jesus says, "My hour has not yet come," he is telling his mother that the time for him to shed his blood is not yet, but, when he has completed the work that the Father has given him to do, his glory will be revealed and God's people will enjoy a celebration that knows no bounds. C.C.

THIRD SUNDAY IN ORDINARY TIME

Nehemiah = nee-huh-MĪ-uh

Ezra = EZ-ruh

A narrative reading of intertwining complexity that concludes with a rousing exhortation. Allow the narrative to build towards the conclusion, which offers enticing encouragement.

Ezra the priest is the focus of this reading. Each time his name is uttered, some of the action described in the reading shifts. Use these mentions of the name Ezra to locate your proclamation and to ensure that your assembly is following.

The third mention of Ezra.

LECTIONARY #69

READING I   Nehemiah 8:2–4a, 5–6, 8–10

A reading from the Book of Nehemiah

Ezra the priest brought the **law** before the **assembly**,
    which consisted of **men**, **women**,
    and those **children** old enough to **understand**.
Standing at one end of the open place that was before
        the **Water Gate**,
    he read **out** of the book from **daybreak** till **midday**,
    in the **presence** of the **men**, the **women**,
    and those **children** old enough to **understand**;
    and all the people listened **attentively** to the book of the **law**.
Ezra the scribe stood on a wooden **platform**
    that had been **made** for the **occasion**.
He opened the **scroll**
    so that all the people might **see it**
    —for he was standing **higher up** than any of the **people**—;
    and, as he **opened** it, **all** the people **rose**.
Ezra blessed the LORD, the great **God**,
    and all the **people**, their hands raised **high**, answered,
    "**Amen, amen!**"
Then they bowed **down** and **prostrated** themselves
        before the LORD,
    their **faces** to the **ground**.

 READING I In academic circles, the books of Ezra and Nehemiah are often treated together, and for much of their history they were parts of the same book. Modern biblical scholars have tried to construct a chronological arrangement of the narratives, but these efforts have not been too successful, because of historical discrepancies that appear to place Ezra and Nehemiah in different time periods, while parts of the biblical text place them in the same time period and same location. In spite of these problems, we are able to put together a brief biography of these two characters, Ezra and Nehemiah, who appear together in today's first reading.

Nehemiah was living in exile under the Persian king Artaxerxes in the fifth century BC and serving as a cupbearer in the king's court. This is around the time when another Persian king, Cyrus the Great, was rising to power, eventually conquering the Babylonian empire in 539 BC. With permission from King Cyrus, some of the Judeans who had been displaced in the Babylonian Exile were returning to Jerusalem, but the place was in ruins. When Nehemiah learned of their sad plight, he asked to go to Jerusalem and rebuild its city walls. He ended up staying there for twelve years to serve as governor of Judea.

The second character mentioned in today's reading, Ezra, was a Jewish priest and scribe living in Babylon during the time of King Artaxerxes—it might not be the same Artexerxes as in the Nehemiah story—when he was directed to lead a group of exiles back to Jerusalem and to teach God's law to those who did not know it. Thus, Ezra's story has some similarities with the story of Moses and the giving of the law during the Exodus. According to some tra-

The fourth mention of Ezra. Here Ezra is doing what you as lector and proclaimer are doing: reading plainly from the book so that it might be understood.

Levites = LEE-vīts

Ezra read **plainly** from the book of the **law** of **God**,
  interpreting it so that **all** could **understand** what was **read**.
Then **Nehemiah**, that is, His **Excellency**, and **Ezra**
  the priest-scribe
  and the **Levites** who were instructing the **people**
  said to **all** the people:
"**Today** is **holy** to the LORD your **God**.
Do not be **sad**, and do not **weep**"—
  for all the people were **weeping** as they heard the **words**
  of the **law**.

Here is the core of the concluding exhortation. Emphasize "rich foods" and "sweet drinks."

He said **further**: "**Go**, eat **rich foods** and drink **sweet drinks**,
  and allot **portions** to **those** who had **nothing** prepared;
  for **today** is **holy** to our LORD.
Do not be **saddened** this day,
  for **rejoicing** in the LORD must be your **strength**!"

For meditation and context:

RESPONSORIAL PSALM   Psalm 19:8, 9, 10, 15 (see John 6:63c)

R. Your words, Lord, are Spirit and life.

The law of the LORD is perfect,
  refreshing the soul;
the decree of the LORD is trustworthy,
  giving wisdom to the simple.

The precepts of the LORD are right,
  rejoicing the heart;
the command of the LORD is clear,
  enlightening the eye.

The fear of the LORD is pure,
  enduring forever;
the ordinances of the LORD are true,
  all of them just.

Let the words of my mouth and the thought
  of my heart
  find favor before you,
O LORD, my rock and my redeemer.

ditions, Ezra was a descendant of the last High Priest of the first Temple in Jerusalem (Ezra 7:1; see 1 Kings 25:18) and a relative of the first High Priest of the second Temple. The first Temple was destroyed in 586 BC by the Babylonians. The second Temple was in place by about 516 BC.

This is where our lectionary reading begins. The Jews who returned to Jerusalem after the Exile are gathered in an assembly to hear Ezra read and explain the book of the law. The book to which the author is referring is likely the five books of the Torah, also called the Pentateuch, the first

five books of what Christians call the Old Testament. We know that this was a formal occasion because they built a special platform on which Ezra could stand. He presented the scroll for all to see, and he led the group in a prayer of blessing. Ezra read the book of the law to the people from dawn to midday. It should have been a glorious event, but the people were weeping! Perhaps it was because they were not previously aware of the high standards to which they were expected to live, and the new reality was too much to bear. But Nehemiah and the others who have been

helping instruct the people say, "Today is holy to the Lord your God. Do not be sad, and do not weep!" Perhaps you have had a similar experience of wrestling with something that causes you great pain, while knowing that somehow or in some way it is also cause for rejoicing.

READING II   Today's reading from Paul's first letter to the Corinthians is a continuation of last Sunday's reading, which focused on spiritual gifts— a source of contention in the Corinthian community —and the reminder that all spiritual gifts

Corinthians = kohr-IN-thee-uhnz

A didactic reading of great complexity and subtlety. In this letter, St. Paul is developing a powerful argument first about the body and its components as a way of understanding the purposes of God, and second about the various roles different people can play in the early Church. Proclaim this reading with confidence and authority at a slow and even pace to allow its potent ideas time to develop in the imaginations of those in your assembly. Even stresses on "so also Christ."

Here begins the repeated use of the word "body," whose use and meaning shift subtly to the end of the reading.

TO KEEP IN MIND

When you proclaim of the Word you participate in catechizing the faithful and those coming to faith. Understand what you proclaim so those hearing you may also understand.

With "Indeed," St. Paul begins to readjust his argument. You can signal this with a slight shift in your tone or by speeding up your reading slightly.

READING II   1 Corinthians 12:12–30

A reading from the first Letter of Saint Paul to the Corinthians

[Brothers and sisters:
As a **body** is **one** though it **has** many **parts**,
  and all the **parts** of the **body**, though **many**, are **one body**,
  so also Christ.
For in **one Spirit** we were all **baptized** into one **body**,
  whether **Jews** or **Greeks, slaves** or **free** persons,
  and we were **all given** to **drink** of one **Spirit**. »

Now the **body** is not a single **part**, but **many**.]
If a **foot** should **say**,
  "Because I am not a **hand** I do not belong to the **body**,"
  it does not for this **reason** belong any **less** to the **body**.
Or if an **ear** should say,
  "Because I am not an **eye** I do not belong to the **body**,"
  it does not for this **reason** belong any **less** to the **body**.
If the whole **body** were an **eye**, where would the **hearing** be?
If the whole body were **hearing**, where would the sense
    of **smell** be?
But as it **is**, **God** placed the **parts**,
  each **one** of them, in the **body** as he **intended**.
If they were **all** one part, where would the **body** be?
But as it is, there are many parts, yet one **body**.
The **eye** cannot say to the **hand**, "I do not **need** you,"
  nor again the **head** to the **feet**, "I do not **need** you."
Indeed, the parts of the body that seem to be **weaker**
  are all the more **necessary**,
  and those **parts** of the **body** that we consider less **honorable**
  we **surround** with greater **honor**,
  and our **less** presentable parts are treated with
    greater **propriety**,
  whereas our **more** presentable parts do not **need** this.

---

come from the one Holy Spirit and are not a measure of their status in the community. Here again Paul addresses divisions in the community by using the metaphor of the human body. He likens the Corinthian community to the body of Christ, with each of them being members, or parts, of Christ's body. Whatever their differences, they cannot deny that they share a common existence in Christ Jesus. Further, the reference to the community as having one Spirit to drink means that the Holy Spirit resides within the community.

Paul goes on to emphasize the necessity of the body's unity in diversity in two ways. First, no part of the body can declare itself separate from the rest of the body. How true! An ear separated from the body becomes nothing more than a piece of rotted flesh. Second, each part of the body needs the other parts of the body to function. He ends this middle section of today's reading with a powerful and poignant statement about the quality of communal life that Christians ought to share: "If one part suffers, all the parts suffer with it; if

one part is honored, all the parts share its joy" (1 Corinthians 12:26).

In the last part of this reading, Paul returns to a theme with which he began: "Now you are Christ's body and individually parts of it" (1 Corinthians 12:27; see 12:14). Notice how he enumerates and ranks three spiritual gifts—apostles, prophets, and teachers—and the rest he places in a simple list. We can assume that the enumerated gifts are most important in Paul's mind because they represent the ministries of evangelization. Of the three, the role of the Christian prophet might be the least

Note the shifts from "one" to "all."

But **God** has so constructed the **body**
as to give greater **honor** to a part that is **without** it,
so that there may be no **division** in the body,
but that the **parts** may have the same concern
for one **another**.
If **one** part suffers, **all** the parts suffer **with** it;
if **one** part is honored, **all** the parts **share** its joy.

Now [**you** are Christ's **body**, and individually **parts** of it.]
Some people God has designated in the **church**
to be, **first**, **apostles**; **second**, **prophets**; **third**, **teachers**;
then, **mighty deeds**;
then **gifts** of healing, **assistance**, **administration**,
and **varieties** of tongues.
Are **all** apostles? Are **all** prophets? Are **all** teachers?
Do **all** work mighty **deeds**? Do **all** have gifts of **healing**?
Do **all** speak in **tongues**? Do **all** interpret?

[Shorter: 1 Corinthians 12:12–14, 27 (see brackets)]

Here, St. Paul begins to talk about the different roles. Give each one of them its due.

Don't overplay the questions that conclude this reading. Let them accumulate and ring out.

GOSPEL   Luke 1:1–4, 4:14–21

A reading from the holy Gospel according to Luke

Since **many** have undertaken to compile a **narrative**
of the **events**
that have been fulfilled **among** us,
just as **those** who were eyewitnesses from the **beginning**
and **ministers** of the word have handed them **down** to us,
I **too** have **decided**,
after **investigating** everything accurately **anew**,
to write it **down** in an orderly **sequence** for you,
most excellent **Theophilus**,
so that you may **realize** the **certainty** of the **teachings**
you have **received**. »

A narrative reading with exhortatory passages built into it, one that splices the opening of St. Luke's Gospel to a later passage that asserts Jesus' prophetic mastery.

The stresses in "most excellent Theophilus" are almost even.
Theophilus = thee-AWF-uh-luhs

obvious to us, but Paul considers the prophet to be a voice of encouragement and instruction for the building up of the community (see 1 Corinthians 14:3). The last spiritual gift in this list, varieties of tongues, is rather controversial for Paul. Although he has the gift himself, he says that speaking in tongues and interpreting tongues must always go together, because someone speaking in tongues without someone to interpret does nothing for the building up of the community (1 Corinthians 14:18–19).

GOSPEL Today's Gospel consists of the prologue of Luke's Gospel and his account of Jesus' first public teaching in the synagogue at Nazareth. Like the first and second readings, it is all about proclaiming God's Word. In the prologue, Luke addresses someone called Theophilus, a "lover of God," and tells him that he is about to embark on something that others have done before him, that is, to write a narrative of all that Jesus said and did among the people, but he will do it somewhat differently. He reassures Theophilus and his associates that he has done his homework, examining the other Gospels—we do not know which ones—and talked to eyewitnesses of the Jesus story, so that they can know with certainty the teachings they have received (Luke 1:4).

What are these teachings? Luke describes them in a story about Jesus returning to his hometown of Nazareth and attending synagogue on a Sabbath. If you attend a synagogue service even today, you will observe that important guests who are known to the worshipping community are invited to do one of the Torah readings or give a brief homily, or both. Likewise, in

Here we shift to chapter 4 of St. Luke's Gospel, which depicts Jesus' prophetic fulfillment.

synagogues = SIN-uh-gogs

This passage from Isaiah should feel as though it is speaking directly about Jesus.

Don't rush over "Rolling up the scroll," which depicts symbolically the fulfillment of Isaiah's prophecy in Christ himself.

Jesus returned to **Galilee** in the **power** of the **Spirit**,
    and **news** of him spread throughout the whole **region**.
He **taught** in their **synagogues** and was **praised** by all.

He came to **Nazareth**, where he had grown **up**,
    and went **according** to his **custom**
    into the **synagogue** on the **sabbath day**.
He stood up to **read** and was handed a **scroll** of
    the **prophet Isaiah**.
He **unrolled** the **scroll** and found the **passage** where
    it was **written**:
        The **Spirit** of the **Lord** is **upon** me,
            because he has **anointed** me
            to bring **glad tidings** to the **poor**.
        He has **sent** me to proclaim **liberty** to **captives**
            and **recovery** of **sight** to the **blind**,
            to let the **oppressed** go **free**,
            and to proclaim a **year** acceptable to the **Lord**.
Rolling up the **scroll**, he handed it **back** to the attendant
    and sat **down**,
    and the **eyes** of **all** in the **synagogue** looked intently at him.
He said to them,
    "**Today** this **Scripture** passage is **fulfilled** in your **hearing**."

the first century AD, Jesus is invited to do the reading. He reads from the prophet Isaiah, "The Spirit of the Lord is upon me, because he has anointed me" (Luke 4:18; see Isaiah 42:6–7). His homily is extremely brief. As everyone is watching and listening for his words, he says, "Today this Scripture passage is fulfilled in your hearing" (Luke 4:21). This is what Jesus came to do and to teach: that the poor will know the good news, the captives will be rescued, the blind will see, and the oppressed will be freed.

Such is the year of the Lord's favor. In the tradition of the Jubilee Year, it is a precursor of the coming kingdom of God that Jesus inaugurates this day. C.C.

FOURTH SUNDAY IN ORDINARY TIME

LECTIONARY #72

Jeremiah = jayr-uh-MĪ-uh

An exhortatory reading in which God speaks through the prophet Jeremiah to fortify the will of the people.

gird = gerd
Take note of the unusual syntax: "But do you gird . . . "

The repetition of "crushed" speaks to God's protective claims in this passage.

Note how the stresses fall on the prepositions in these lines: "against," "over," and "with."

READING I Jeremiah 1:4–5, 17–19

A reading from the Book of the Prophet Jeremiah

The **word** of the LORD came to me, **saying**:
  Before I **formed** you in the womb I **knew** you,
    before you were **born** I **dedicated** you,
    a **prophet** to the **nations** I **appointed** you.

But do you **gird** your **loins**;
    stand **up** and **tell** them
    all that I **command** you.
  Be not **crushed** on their account,
    as though I would leave you **crushed before** them;
  for it is **I** this **day**
    who have **made** you a **fortified city**,
  a **pillar** of iron, a **wall** of brass,
    against the **whole land**:
  against **Judah's kings** and **princes**,
    against its **priests** and **people**.
  They will fight **against** you but not prevail **over** you,
    for I am **with you** to **deliver** you, says the LORD.

READING I Following upon last Sunday's readings that celebrated the work of the ministers of God's Word, today's readings make clear the cost of this ministry to those who respond to God's call.

Among the prophetic writings, Jeremiah is perhaps the most striking example of the cost of proclaiming God's Word. Jeremiah had a very long history as a prophet, starting in the time of King Josiah (reigned 640–609 BC) in Judea, through the time of King Jehoiakim (609–597 BC), to the end of King Zedekiah's reign (c. 597–586 BC),

and into the period of the Babylonian Exile (Jeremiah 1:1–3). This first reading begins with God speaking to Jeremiah in very intimate terms about how he was called and chosen even before he was born.

What the lectionary leaves out is Jeremiah's protest, "Ah, Lord God!" . . . I do not know how to speak. I am too young!" (Jeremiah 1:6). Can you imagine Jeremiah's terror? But God is not to be deterred, telling Jeremiah that he will indeed go where God wants him to go and that God will be with him to deliver him. "To deliver him from what?" you might ask. God will deliver him

from the pain and insults of preaching God's Word to those who do not want to hear of the disaster that is about to befall them for their unfaithfulness to God's covenant. If Jeremiah was not scared before, surely he is now!

Returning to the lectionary reading, God tells Jeremiah to gird his loins, stand tall, and say to the people exactly what God tells him to speak. The phrase "gird your loins," means something like "Get ready to do battle immediately!" God also warns Jeremiah about breaking down—the Hebrew word can be translated as "shattered" or

For meditation and context:

RESPONSORIAL PSALM   Psalm 71:1–2, 3–4, 5–6, 15, 17 (see 15ab)

R. I will sing of your salvation.

In you, O LORD, I take refuge;
   let me never be put to shame.
In your justice rescue me, and deliver me;
   incline your ear to me, and save me.

Be my rock of refuge,
   a stronghold to give me safety,
   for you are my rock and my fortress.
O my God, rescue me from the hand of the
   wicked.

For you are my hope, O Lord;
   my trust, O God, from my youth.
On you I depend from birth;
   from my mother's womb you are my
   strength.

My mouth shall declare your justice,
   day by day your salvation.
O God, you have taught me from my youth,
   and till the present I proclaim your
   wondrous deeds.

Corinthians = kohr-IN-thee-uhnz

A richly expressive exhortatory reading of unusual lyric beauty. Despite its familiarity (as a reading frequently included in weddings), the conclusive claims made about love in this passage deserve to be repeated frequently.

Even emphasis on "greatest spiritual gifts" and "still more excellent."

Love is the focus of this passage, which is set up by the use of "if" in three different phrases. These "ifs" build St. Paul's argument.

prophecy (noun) = PROF-uh-see

Love remains the focus of this passage, more often indicated by the pronoun "it." Treat the word with the same reverence as you would give to "love."

READING II   1 Corinthians 12:31 — 13:13

A reading from the first Letter of Saint Paul to the Corinthians

[**Brothers** and **sisters**:]
Strive **eagerly** for the **greatest spiritual gifts**.
But I shall **show** you a **still more excellent** way.

If I speak in **human** and angelic **tongues**,
   but do **not** have **love**,
   I am a resounding **gong** or a clashing **cymbal**.
And if I have the gift of **prophecy**,
   and comprehend all **mysteries** and all **knowledge**;
   if I have all **faith** so as to move **mountains**,
   but do not have **love**, I am **nothing**.
If I give away **everything** I **own**,
   and if I hand my **body over** so that I may **boast**,
   but do not have **love**, I gain **nothing**.

[Love is **patient**, love is **kind**.
It is not **jealous**, it is not **pompous**,
   it is not **inflated**, it is not **rude**,
   it does not **seek** its own **interests**,

"dismayed"—in front of the religious and civil leaders of Jerusalem and the people of Judea. At the same time, God tells him that he has made Jeremiah into "a fortified city, a pillar of iron, a wall of brass" (Jeremiah 1:17). In other words, he is already impenetrable and fully prepared to encounter his opponents in battle.

READING II Today's second reading is a continuation of last Sunday's second reading, and it is a familiar one to many of us. It is a poem-like teaching on what Paul understands to be the

greatest of the spiritual gifts and what we know today as one of the cardinal virtues, namely, love. The Greek word *agapēn* is used throughout. It refers to the kind of love that is completely generous and giving of the self without expectation of return.

This reading has three parts. The first part (1 Corinthians 13:1–3) picks up on the spiritual gifts mentioned in 1 Corinthians 12 and treats them in reverse order, from the least to most important for the ministry of the word of God: *glossolalia* (speaking in tongues), prophecy, knowledge, and faith. None of these gifts matter, Paul says, if one

does not have love. Neither does it matter if you give away all that you have or allow your body to be burned—ancients thought it was the most horrible way to die—if one does not have love.

The second part of this reading (1 Corinthians 13:4–7) consists of a description of the attributes of personified love: this is what love does and does not do! Count up the adjectives and verbs in this section. Although it is not as obvious in the English translation, because most are translated as adjectives, but the Greek text has fifteen verbs! What does this mean

it is not **quick-tempered**, it does not **brood** over **injury**,
it does not **rejoice** over **wrongdoing**
    but **rejoices** with the **truth**.
It **bears** all things, **believes** all things,
    hopes all things, **endures** all things.

Love never fails.
If there are **prophecies**, they will be brought to **nothing**;
    if **tongues**, they will **cease**;
    if **knowledge**, it will be brought to **nothing**.
For we **know** partially and we **prophesy** partially,
    but when the **perfect** comes, the **partial** will pass **away**.
When I was a **child**, I used to **talk** as a child,
    think as a child, **reason** as a child;
    when I became a **man**, I **put aside childish things**.
At present we see **indistinctly**, as in a **mirror**,
    but then **face** to **face**.
At **present** I know **partially**;
    then I shall know **fully**, as **I** am fully **known**.
So **faith, hope, love** remain, **these three**;
    but the **greatest** of **these** is **love**.]

[Shorter: 1 Corinthians 13:4–13 (see brackets)]

GOSPEL   Luke 4:21–30

A reading from the holy Gospel according to Luke

Jesus began **speaking** in the **synagogue**, saying:
    "**Today** this Scripture passage is **fulfilled** in your **hearing**."
And **all** spoke **highly** of him
    and were **amazed** at the gracious **words** that **came**
        from his **mouth**.
They also asked, "Isn't **this** the son of **Joseph**?" »

Sidebar notes:

Even emphasis: "Love never fails."

prophesy (verb) = PROF-uh-sī
Notice that "prophesy" is pronounced differently than "prophecy."

Even emphasis on "put aside childish things."

Many of the words in these final lines carry equal weight. Since "love" is the last word spoken, you don't need to overemphasize it.

A complex narrative reading about Jesus' early ministry that sets the stage for why he wasn't actively preaching in Nazareth, his native place. Though narrative, the reading involves Jesus accusing the people of Nazareth of bad faith, to which they respond with rage. There are a lot of volatile emotions at work in this passage. Stress "this."

---

about the nature of *agape* love? This is not passive or complacent love. No, it is always about action on behalf of the other.

The third and concluding section of this reading (1 Corinthians 13:8–13) is a comparison of "now," the time in which the Corinthian community was living, and a future reality. In this future, they no longer are fighting with one another and putting their own interests above others. In this future, they no longer act as "infants in Christ" (see 1 Corinthians 3:1), and they can know and be known fully. In this future, faith, hope, and, love are the only gifts that

matter to them. What about us? Can we say that faith, hope, and love are the only things that matter to us?

GOSPEL Today's Gospel follows on last Sunday's Gospel. Jesus identified himself as the fulfillment of Isaiah's prophecy about the poor knowing the good news, the captives being rescued, the blind being able to see, and the oppressed being allowed to go free. What an arrogant thing for Jesus to say, especially in his hometown, where everyone thinks they know him! Who does he think

he is? This is the sense in which the people's response, "Isn't this the son of Joseph?" is intended. But the Lukan Jesus does not back down. Instead, he brings their criticism into the light of day and challenges them with a proverb and a rebuttal of his own. The proverb was likely a familiar one to Luke's audience. It means something like, "Take care of your own business before accusing others," and, in this case, "We dare you to show us what people say you've been doing in Capernaum."

Jesus' rebuttal, "no prophet is accepted in his own native place," is a not-so-subtle

From "He said" through "Syrian," Jesus is speaking to those gathered in Nazareth at the synagogue to hear him. There are quotations nested in his speech, as well as a complex historical anecdote, that need to be comprehensible in order to understand the people's reaction. Proclaim slowly and at an even pace.

Capernaum = kuh-PER-nee-*m *or* kuh-PER-nay-*m *or* kuh-PER-n*m

famine = FAM-ihn

Here, the tone shifts, describing the anger of the people.

Jesus' ability to depart undetected suggests something of his coming into supernatural powers.

He said to them, "**Surely** you will **quote** me this **proverb**,
  '**Physician**, **cure** yourself,' and **say**,
    'Do **here** in your native **place**
    the **things** that we **heard** were done in **Capernaum**.'"
And he said, "**Amen**, I say to **you**,
  no **prophet** is accepted in his **own native place**.
Indeed, I tell you,
  there were many **widows** in Israel in the **days** of **Elijah**
    when the **sky** was closed for **three** and a half **years**
    and a severe **famine** spread over the entire **land**.
It was to **none** of these that **Elijah** was **sent**,
  but **only** to a **widow** in Zarephath in the land of **Sidon**.
Again, there were many **lepers** in **Israel**
  during the **time** of Elisha the **prophet**;
    yet not **one** of them was **cleansed**, but only **Naaman**
      the **Syrian**."
When the **people** in the synagogue **heard** this,
  they were all **filled** with **fury**.
They **rose** up, drove him **out** of the town,
  and **led** him to the brow of the **hill**
    on which their **town** had been **built**,
    to **hurl** him down **headlong**.
But **Jesus** passed through the **midst** of them and went **away**.

accusation concerning their lack of faith. He follows this rebuttal with two stories. One is about Elijah, a prophet and miracle worker who lived in the northern kingdom of Israel in the ninth century BC. Jesus notes that Israel was suffering a terrible drought for a long time, but God did not intervene. Instead, God sent Elijah to a starving and penniless widow from a Phoenician city north of Israel, who, because of her kindness to Elijah, was left with a never-ending jar of flour and jug of oil (1 Kings 17:9–18). The second story is about Elisha, Elijah's successor, who was also a prophet and miracle worker. Jesus says that there were many lepers in Israel during Elisha's time, but he healed only Naaman, the commander of the army of the king of Aram, in what is Syria today (2 Kings 5:1–19).

What a fury Jesus unleashed! These people were enraged that he would suggest that God cares about people who were not God's people by covenant. How dare he! But, like Jeremiah in our first reading, God enveloped him with protection so that he was able to slip away from the angry crowd, even as they were about to throw him off a cliff! C.C.

FIFTH SUNDAY IN ORDINARY TIME

LECTIONARY #75

READING I   Isaiah 6:1–2a, 3–8

A reading from the Book of the Prophet Isaiah

In the **year** King **Uzziah** died,
  I saw the Lord seated on a **high** and lofty **throne**,
  with the **train** of his garment filling the **temple**.
Seraphim were stationed **above**.

They cried **one** to the **other**,
  "**Holy, holy, holy** is the LORD of **hosts**!
All the **earth** is **filled** with his **glory**!"
At the **sound** of that **cry**, the **frame** of the door **shook**
  and the **house** was filled with **smoke**.

Then I said, "**Woe** is me, I am **doomed**!
For I am a **man** of unclean **lips**,
  living among a **people** of unclean **lips**;
  yet my **eyes** have seen the **King**, the LORD of **hosts**!"
Then one of the seraphim **flew** to me,
  holding an **ember** that he had **taken** with **tongs**
    from the **altar**.

He touched my **mouth** with it, and **said**,
  "**See**, **now** that this has **touched** your **lips**,
  your **wickedness** is **removed**, your **sin purged**."

Then I heard the **voice** of the Lord saying,
  "**Whom** shall I **send**? **Who** will **go** for us?"
"**Here** I am," I said; "**send me**!"

Isaiah = ī-ZAY-uh
A narrative reading with exhortative and lyrical powers on display. Isaiah is describing the moment of his prophetic selection, using an authoritative language incorporated into our very liturgy.
Uzziah = uh-ZĪ-uh

Though the text states "cried out," you need not raise your voice here. The words "Holy, holy, holy" are drenched in solemnity. They are a part of the Trisagion, a central liturgical hymn of Eastern Christians, and of our own acclamation after the preface of the Eucharistic Prayer.

Don't overdo this statement; read it plainly and clearly.

> **TO KEEP IN MIND**
> Pause to break up separate thoughts, set apart significant statements, or indicate major shifts. Never pause in the middle of a thought. Your primary guide for pauses is punctuation.

Slight pause between "See" and "now."

purged = perjd
Even stresses on "sin" and "purged."

Equal emphasis on "Here" and "me."

READING I The readings for this Fifth Sunday in Ordinary Time continue the focus on the call to be ministers of God's word that we heard on the previous two Sundays. Last Sunday's first reading was the narrative of Jeremiah's call to be God's prophet. This Sunday's reading recounts the call of Isaiah. Biblical call narratives were important because they provided authenticity to the prophet's teaching and credibility to his ministry. Even if someone was unhappy with the prophet's message, they had to accept that it was the word of God.

Isaiah describes his call by first situating it in the year of King Uzziah's death (792 BC). A master builder and powerful military leader, King Uzziah reigned for five decades as king of Judah, but eventually pride got the best of him. In his later years, he suffered from a disfiguring skin disease for usurping the role of the high priest and offering incense in the Temple (2 Chronicles 26:1–19). It is striking, therefore, that God appears in Isaiah's vision as a mighty and sovereign king seated on a heavenly throne, filling the entire space of the heavenly temple with his garments, and attended by sera-phim, angels whose job it was to guard God's throne. So much for Uzziah's arrogance! The song of the seraphim, "Holy, holy, holy is the Lord of hosts!" is similar to the heavenly worship that takes place in the book of Revelation (see Revelation 4:8). The smoke and shaking of the earth are further signs that Isaiah is experiencing a theophany, a manifestation of God.

While we can appreciate Isaiah's response to the vision even today, in the ancient world people believed that humans could not survive a direct encounter with God (see Exodus 33:20). This is why he says,

For meditation and context:

RESPONSORIAL PSALM   Psalm 138:1–2, 2–3, 4–5, 7–8 (1c)

R. In the sight of the angels I will sing your praises, Lord.

I will give thanks to you, O LORD, with all
    my heart,
    for you have heard the words of my mouth;
    in the presence of the angels I will sing
    your praise;
I will worship at your holy temple
    and give thanks to your name.

Because of your kindness and your truth;
    for you have made great above all things
    your name and your promise.
When I called, you answered me;
    you built up strength within me.

All the kings of the earth shall give thanks to
    you, O LORD,
    when they hear the words of your mouth;
and they shall sing of the ways of the LORD:
    "Great is the glory of the LORD."

Your right hand saves me.
    The LORD will complete what he has done
    for me;
your kindness, O LORD, endures forever;
    forsake not the work of your hands.

Corinthians = kohr-IN-thee-uhnz

A didactic reading in which St. Paul makes claims about what to believe and his own worthiness as an apostle. This letter to the Corinthians suggests that it is in answer to a dispute he is having with some of the other leadership in the early Church. He seems at pains to distinguish himself from that leadership and also to point out that he is working harder than anybody else. Emphasis on "saved."

Here, St. Paul begins to record the basic tenets about Christ that form our core beliefs.

READING II   1 Corinthians 15:1–11

A reading from the first Letter of Saint Paul to the Corinthians

I am **reminding** you, [**brothers** and **sisters**,]
    of the **gospel** I **preached** to you,
    which you **indeed received** and in which you **also stand**.
Through it you are **also** being **saved**,
    if you hold **fast** to the **word** I **preached** to you,
    unless you **believed** in vain.
For [I handed **on** to you as of **first** importance
        what I also **received**:
    that **Christ died** for our sins in **accordance**
        with the **Scriptures**;
    that he was **buried**;
    that he was **raised** on the third **day**
        in **accordance** with the **Scriptures**;
    that he **appeared** to **Cephas**, **then** to the **Twelve**.
After that, Christ **appeared** to more
        than **five hundred brothers** at **once**,
    most of whom are still **living**,
    though **some** have fallen **asleep**.

Emphasis on "living," which provides a sense of proof to the Corinthians.

"Woe is me, I am doomed!" He fears that he is going to die! Biblical scholars are still undecided about what Isaiah meant when he said, "I am a man of unclean lips," but a likely explanation is that Isaiah thought he should say something but that he had no words that were worthy of expressing the manifest glory of God. Since Isaiah expressed his human limitations in terms of unclean lips, the detail about the angel purifying his lips with fire is a way of saying that God will transcend Isaiah's human limitations to prepare him for the task to which he is being called. Therefore, when God

says, "Whom shall I send?" Isaiah is able to say, "Send me!" Do we trust that God will ready us for the ministry of the Word?

READING II   The second reading is a continuation of the previous Sundays' readings from the First Letter to the Corinthians. Here, however, the topic is different. Rather than talking about spiritual gifts, Paul is teaching about resurrection of the dead. Apparently, the Corinthian community willingly professes Jesus raised from the dead, but they do not accept the

notion that Christians will be raised from the dead, at least not bodily.

Paul provides a preface to his teaching on resurrection of the body that functions a lot like Isaiah's call narrative. He asserts that his call to ministry is genuine and his words have credibility by reiterating a creed that expresses belief in the redemptive death of Jesus, his resurrection, and then a list of appearances of the risen Christ. In Paul's mind, these multiple appearances are important evidence that Jesus was raised bodily. It would not be possible for this many people to be imagining a ghost!

Emphasis on "Last." St. Paul wants to distinguish himself from all the others in a curious combination of humility and pride.

persecuted = PER-suh-kyoo-t*d
Stress "am" both times.

Emphasis on "harder."

After **that** he appeared to **James**,
　　then to all the **apostles**.
Last of all, as to one born **abnormally**,
　　he appeared to **me**.]
For I am the **least** of the **apostles**,
　　not **fit** to be **called** an apostle,
　　because I **persecuted** the **church** of **God**.
But by the **grace** of God I **am** what I **am**,
　　and his **grace** to **me** has **not** been **ineffective**.
Indeed, I have toiled **harder** than **all** of them;
　　not **I**, however, but the **grace** of God that is **with** me.
[**Therefore**, whether it be **I** or **they**,
　　so we **preach** and so you **believed**.]

[Shorter: 1 Corinthians 15:3–8, 11 (see brackets)]

GOSPEL　Luke 5:1–11

A narrative reading presenting St. Luke's version of the call of the disciples.

Gennesaret = geh-NES-uh-reht

Nearly even stresses on the words in this line.

You can proclaim these words of St. Peter in a slightly wearied tone. (But don't overdo it.)

A reading from the holy Gospel according to Luke

While the **crowd** was pressing in on **Jesus** and **listening**
　　to the word of **God**,
　　he was **standing** by the Lake of **Gennesaret**.
He saw **two boats** there alongside the **lake**;
　　the **fishermen** had **disembarked** and were **washing** their **nets**.
Getting into one of the **boats**, the one belonging to **Simon**,
　　he **asked** him to put out a short **distance** from the **shore**.
Then he sat **down** and taught the **crowds** from the **boat**.
After he had finished **speaking**, he said to **Simon**,
　　"**Put out** into deep **water** and **lower** your **nets** for a **catch**."
Simon said in reply,
　　"**Master**, we have worked **hard** all night and have
　　　　caught **nothing**,
　　but at your **command** I will lower the **nets**." ≫

Some of the witnesses are still alive, Paul says, hinting that they could ask *them*, if they will not accept Paul's word.

Notice the very deferential way in which Paul inserts himself into this creed. He, too, experienced the risen Christ, and as a consequence he was called to be the apostle to the Gentiles (see Acts 9:1–19). But like others before him, he has learned that the call to ministry is never easy. Paul describes himself as prematurely born or as immature at birth in the sense that he is not equal to the apostles who were with Jesus before his death and resurrection, but he insists that he is an apostle, nonetheless. Most likely Paul is thinking about some incident involving the Corinthian community that caused him to go off on a little tirade in 1 Corinthians 9:1–12. The word apostle means "one who is sent."

GOSPEL　Today's Gospel is also a call narrative, and an especially beautiful one. It reminds us that our call to ministry, like Simon Peter's, can come when least expected and in the very ordinariness of life. In last Sunday's Gospel, after Jesus escaped his detractors in Nazareth, who were infuriated by his suggestion that God could care about Gentiles as much as Jews, he spent time in and around Capernaum healing people and attracting large crowds of people.

Thus, this story begins with Jesus pressed up against the Sea of Gennesaret, also known as the Sea of Galilee, by the crowds who wanted to hear him teach. When he saw boats anchored near the shore and fishermen cleaning and mending their nets—not an unusual scene—he got into one of the boats and asked the owner to push out from the shore a short distance.

The emphasis is on the fish. A lot of fish!

When they had **done** this, they caught a **great number** of **fish**
  and their **nets** were **tearing**.
They **signaled** to their partners in the other boat
  to come to **help** them.
They **came** and **filled** both **boats**
  so that the boats were in danger of **sinking**.
When Simon Peter saw this, he **fell** at the **knees**
    of Jesus and said,
  "**Depart** from me, Lord, for **I** am a **sinful man**."
For **astonishment** at the catch of **fish** they had **made seized** him
  and all those **with** him,
  and **likewise** James and John, the sons of Zebedee,
  who were **partners** of Simon.
Jesus said to Simon, "**Do not** be **afraid**;
  from **now on** you will be catching **men**."
When they brought their **boats** to the **shore**,
  they left **everything** and **followed** him.

Parallel emphasis on "Do not" and "now on."

The conclusion of this passage, narratively and vocationally, remains extraordinary. Who is prepared to leave everything and to follow Christ?

But when Jesus asked Simon to go out into deep water and lower their nets, Simon protested at first. Fishermen typically fished at night so they would have fresh fish to sell in the morning, but they had no luck that night, and they were bone tired. Simon admits as much to Jesus, but then relents and lets down his nets.

Before long, Simon and his companions had filled two boats to the point of sinking. Being experienced fishermen, they had to know what a stunning catch this was, but Simon Peter likely sensed something more. He fell at Jesus' feet and tells Jesus that he is not worthy to be in Jesus' presence. This detail should remind us of Isaiah's reaction when he encountered God on his heavenly throne. And then comes the call to ministry. "Do not be afraid; from now on you will be catching men." C.C.

SIXTH SUNDAY IN ORDINARY TIME

LECTIONARY #78

READING I   Jeremiah 17:5–8

Jeremiah = jayr-uh-MĪ-uh

An exhortatory reading in which the prophet Jeremiah channels the voice of the Lord.

The reading is divided between describing those who are cursed, followed by those who are blessed. To begin, emphasize "cursed," "trusts," and "human beings."

Blessed = BLE-s*d

Here the reading shifts. Emphasize "blessed," "trusts," and "the Lord."

> **TO KEEP IN MIND**
> If you are assigned to proclaim the first reading, read the Gospel for that week as well. They are connected in thematic ways.

A reading from the Book of the Prophet Jeremiah

Thus says the LORD:
  Cursed is the one who **trusts** in human **beings**,
    who seeks his **strength** in **flesh**,
    whose **heart** turns away from the LORD.
  He is like a **barren bush** in the **desert**
    that enjoys no **change** of **season**,
  but stands in a **lava waste**,
    a **salt** and empty **earth**.
  Blessed is the one who **trusts** in the LORD,
    whose **hope** is the LORD.
  He is like a **tree planted beside** the **waters**
    that **stretches** out its **roots** to the **stream**:
  It fears not the **heat** when it **comes**;
    its **leaves** stay **green**;
  in the **year** of drought it shows no **distress**,
    but **still** bears **fruit**.

READING I Today's reading from the Book of Jeremiah is the first of a small collection of wisdom sayings, which can be described as clever proverbs about human behavior or human experience. This one is characterized as a blessing and a curse. Ancient peoples understood that, as a blessing was spoken, it was already being bestowed on its intended recipient. Likewise, as a curse was spoken, watch out! It was already taking effect!

Additionally, this wisdom saying is an example of Hebrew poetry, which uses thought rhyme rather than sound rhyme. Here we have a combination of antithetical parallelism, where the second or subsequent lines contrast the thought of the first; synthetic parallelism, where the second line finishes the thought of the first line; and synonymous parallelism, where the second or subsequent lines repeat the thought of the first. Antithetical parallelism is evident in the phrases "Cursed is the one who trusts in human beings" and "Blessed is the one who trusts in the Lord." Synthetic parallelism can be seen in the phrases "He is like a barren bush in the desert" and "that enjoys no change of season." See if you can find other examples of synthetic and synonymous parallelism.

While we will never know who composed this bit of poetry or their motive for doing so, we can appreciate that its complex parallelisms help us to slow down and contemplate its truth: God is our refuge always and our only hope in times of trouble.

READING II In his First Letter to the Corinthians, Paul devotes an entire chapter to his teaching about

For meditation and context:

RESPONSORIAL PSALM   Psalm 1:1–2, 3, 4, 6 (40:5a)

R. Blessed are they who hope in the Lord.

Blessed the man who follows not
    the counsel of the wicked,
nor walks in the way of sinners,
    nor sits in the company of the insolent,
but delights in the law of the LORD
    and meditates on his law day and night.

He is like a tree
    planted near running water,
that yields its fruit in due season,
    and whose leaves never fade.
Whatever he does, prospers.

Not so the wicked, not so;
    they are like chaff which the
        wind drives away.
For the LORD watches over the way
    of the just,
    but the way of the wicked vanishes.

Corinthians = kohr-IN-thee-uhnz

A didactic reading that relies on the logic of an if/then argument.

The first "if." Each of these "if" elements allows for the argument to build.

The second and third "if" elements.
Take note of the repetitions of "raised."
Here is the "then" that succeeds the "ifs."
One final "if"; even emphasis on "this life only."

pitiable = PIT-ee-uh-b*l

Parallel emphasis between "Christ/dead" and "firstfruits/asleep."

READING II   1 Corinthians 15:12, 16–20

A reading from the first Letter of Saint Paul to the Corinthians

Brothers and **sisters**:
If **Christ** is **preached** as **raised** from the **dead**,
    how can **some** among you say there is no **resurrection**
        of the **dead**?
If the **dead** are not **raised**, neither has Christ been **raised**,
    and if **Christ** has not been **raised**, your **faith** is **vain**;
    you are **still** in your **sins**.
Then **those** who have fallen asleep in Christ have perished.
If for **this life only** we have hoped in **Christ**,
    we are the most **pitiable** people of **all**.

But now **Christ** has been raised from the **dead**,
    the **firstfruits** of those who have fallen **asleep**.

---

resurrection of the dead. As we noted in last Sunday's second reading, he begins with a creed or statement of belief in Jesus' death and resurrection (1 Corinthians 15:3–11). In today's reading, Paul begins to reveal the problem that he wants to address: Everyone in this community acknowledges Jesus' death and resurrection, but some deny the possibility of their own resurrection from the dead.

This is the core of Paul's argument: "If the dead are not raised, neither has Christ been raised," and he articulates four very serious consequences of the community's faulty thinking. First, their faith is vain. The Greek word translated as "vain" means "devoid of force, truth or result." Second, they are still in their sins, meaning that their baptism and incorporation into the Christian community did not transform them, as they claimed. Apparently, some members of this community called themselves "spiritual people" as a result of their baptism—an attribution which Paul did not accept (1 Corinthians 3:1). Third, Christians who had died would not enjoy salvation; they are forever lost. Finally, if their hope in Christ is limited to this life only, Paul says, they are the most miserable or pitiable of all humanity. Can it be any worse?

Paul counters these views with full conviction: "Christ has been raised from the dead." Further, he calls the risen Christ the firstfruits of the deceased. The term "firstfruits" describes the first and best of the produce of the land, which was offered in sacrifice to God, thereby consecrating the whole harvest to God. Let us join with Paul in celebrating this wondrous mystery that is also our destiny.

A narrative reading with a strong exhortatory component. Jesus is preaching, and the contents of his sermon offer praise and blame. The reading situates Jesus geographically in his ministry then proceeds to four beatitudes, followed by an exhortation to rejoice, and then concluded with four "woes," clearly meant to parallel the beatitudes he begins with. It's a cunning and effective presentation of Jesus' message of the importance of taking care of the poor and the disenfranchised.

Here the beatitudes begin. Emphases on those being blessed.
Blessed = BLE-s*d

Here is the exhortation. The focus is on the just treatment of prophets.

Here the "woes" begin. Emphasis on the contrasts to the beatitudes, for instance, poor/rich, hungry/satisfied, and so forth.

GOSPEL   Luke 6:17, 20–26

A reading from the holy Gospel according to Luke

Jesus came down with the **Twelve**
    and **stood** on a stretch of **level ground**
    with a **great crowd** of his **disciples**
    and a **large number** of the **people**
    from **all Judea** and **Jerusalem**
    and the **coastal** region of **Tyre** and **Sidon**.
And raising his **eyes** toward his **disciples** he said:
    "**Blessed** are **you** who are **poor**,
        for the **kingdom** of **God** is **yours**.
    Blessed are **you** who are now **hungry**,
        for **you** will be **satisfied**.
    Blessed are **you** who are now **weeping**,
        for you will **laugh**.
    Blessed are **you** when people **hate** you,
        and when they **exclude** and **insult** you,
        and denounce your **name** as **evil**
        on **account** of the **Son** of **Man**.
Rejoice and **leap** for **joy** on that day!
Behold, your **reward** will be **great** in **heaven**.
For their **ancestors** treated the **prophets** in the same **way**.
    But **woe** to **you** who are **rich**,
        for you have **received** your consolation.
    Woe to **you** who are **filled now**,
        for you will be **hungry**.
    Woe to you who **laugh** now,
        for you will **grieve** and **weep**.
    Woe to you when all speak well of you,
        for their **ancestors** treated the **false prophets** in this **way**."

GOSPEL   Today's Gospel is taken from Luke's Sermon on the Plain (Luke 6:20–49). Its counterpart is Matthew's Sermon on the Mount (Matthew 5:1–7:27). These two sermons are similar in some respects, but Luke's version gives less attention to Jewish law and practice and has a greater focus on social justice and being merciful as God is merciful.

Like our first reading, this segment of the Sermon on the Plain is structured as a collection of blessings. Jesus calls blessed the poor, the hungry, those who weep and mourn, and those who are judged and hated on account of the Son of Man, a title by which he identifies himself. Unlike the first reading, which follows the blessings with curses, this part of the sermon delivers a series of "woes," warnings of extreme caution to those who are rich and well fed and those who laugh in joy and satisfaction as people heap praise on them. For both groups, the context is the coming reign of God, when God's power is fully manifested against the forces of evil in the world.

Notice, too, how these two groups are associated with true and false prophets. True prophets trust in God and speak God's truth regardless of the consequences; false prophets deceive themselves and others about their calling and about the words they speak. This Gospel should give us pause to reflect on where we stand. Do we take up our calling to be true prophets or do we close ourselves to the word of God and, in effect, become false prophets? C.C.

SEVENTH SUNDAY
IN ORDINARY TIME

LECTIONARY #81

READING I   1 Samuel 26:2, 7–9, 12–13, 22–23

A narrative reading with a rich and dramatic story that demonstrates David's essential righteousness.

Ziph = zif

Abishai = uh-Bī-shī

A reading from the first Book of Samuel

In those days, **Saul** went down to the desert of **Ziph**
  with **three thousand** picked men of **Israel**,
  to search for **David** in the **desert** of **Ziph**.
So **David** and **Abishai** went among Saul's **soldiers** by **night**
  and found **Saul lying asleep** within the **barricade**,
  with his **spear** thrust into the **ground** at his **head**
  and **Abner** and his **men** sleeping **around** him.

The drama begins here when Abishai urges David to allow him to murder Saul. Make clear the difference between the speakers.

Abishai whispered to **David**:
  "**God** has delivered your **enemy** into your **grasp** this day.
Let me **nail** him to the **ground** with one **thrust** of the **spear**;
  I will not **need** a second **thrust**!"

> ### TO KEEP IN MIND
> Pay attention to the pace of your reading. Varying the pace gives listeners clues to the meaning of the text. The most common error for proclaimers new to the ministry is speaking too fast.

But **David** said to **Abishai**, "**Do not harm** him,
  for **who** can lay **hands** on the LORD's **anointed**
    and remain **unpunished**?"
So **David** took the **spear** and the **water jug** from their **place** at
    Saul's **head**,

Slight pause between "anyone's" and "seeing."

  and they got **away** without **anyone's seeing** or **knowing**
    or **awakening**.
All remained **asleep**,

The motif of supernatural sleep pervades Scripture. Emphasis on "deep slumber."

  because the LORD had put them into a **deep slumber**.

Going **across** to an opposite **slope**,
  David **stood** on a remote **hilltop**

Ner = nuhr

  at a great **distance** from **Abner**, son of **Ner**, and the **troops**.

READING I Today's first reading recalls one of several stories about political and military conflicts between David and Saul. Although Saul was the king of Israel at the time, he had lost favor with God because of his failure to carry out God's command against the Amalekites, one of Israel's fiercest enemies. Just as Samuel, the last of the judges and first of the prophets, had secretly anointed Saul to be king of Israel (1 Samuel 9:1—10:16), later he secretly anointed David to take Saul's place (1 Samuel 16:1–13). In subse-

quent chapters of 1 Samuel, we see David gradually rise to power while Saul steadily experiences losses within his family and loses control of his kingdom.

In this lectionary reading, we see Saul pausing in his battle with the Philistines to pursue David and his men in the wilderness of Ziph. Can you sense the excitement that this war story is supposed to engender? Saul has 3,000 warriors with him, while David has only 600, but, when night comes, David and Abishai, one of his military leaders, are able to enter Saul's encampment

without waking a single soldier, even those who were supposed to be guarding Saul while he slept. After a whispered conversation about why Abishai should not kill Saul on the spot, they depart without drawing attention and taking only Saul's spear and water jug. How unnerving!

This story is supposed to demonstrate David's high moral character. There are other stories that demonstrate otherwise, but here, even though Saul was trying to kill him, David would not raise a hand against the king, because he was God's anointed

With "here," David declares his righteousness. Emphasis on "harm" and "anointed."

He said: "**Here** is the king's **spear**.
Let an **attendant** come over to **get** it.
The LORD will reward each **man** for his **justice** and **faithfulness**.
Today, though the LORD delivered you into my **grasp**,
  I would not **harm** the LORD's **anointed**."

For meditation and context:

RESPONSORIAL PSALM   Psalm 103:1–2, 3–4, 8, 10, 12–13 (8a)

R. The Lord is kind and merciful.

Bless the LORD, O my soul;
  all my being, bless his holy name.
Bless the LORD, O my soul,
  forget not all his benefits.

He pardons all your iniquities,
  heals all your ills.
He redeems your life from destruction,
  crowns you with kindness
    and compassion.

Merciful and gracious is the LORD,
  slow to anger and abounding in kindness.
Not according to our sins does
    he deal with us,
  nor does he requite us according to
    our crimes.

As far as the east is from the west,
  so far has he put our transgressions
    from us.
As a father has compassion on his children,
  so the LORD has compassion on those who
    fear him.

Corinthians = kohr-IN-thee-uhnz
A mysterious didactic reading that is part of a larger argument St. Paul makes to the members of the early Church in Corinth about resurrection. The question is: Which body is resurrected? Here, St. Paul makes a distinction between the earthy and the spiritual, to help develop his argument. Allow for the distinction between "spiritual" and "natural" by proclaiming these lines in a neutral, declarative tone. St. Paul's argument is subtle; you can't force it by shifting your intonation.

READING II   1 Corinthians 15:45–49

A reading from the first Letter of Saint Paul to the Corinthians

Brothers and **sisters**:
It is written, *The* **first** *man,* **Adam**, *became a* **living being**,
  the last **Adam** a life-giving **spirit**.
But the **spiritual** was not **first**;
  rather the **natural** and then the **spiritual**.
The **first** man was from the **earth**, **earthly**;
  the **second** man, from **heaven**.
As was the **earthly** one, so **also** are the **earthly**,
  and **as** is the **heavenly** one, so **also** are the **heavenly**.
Just as we have borne the **image** of the **earthly** one,
  we shall **also** bear the **image** of the **heavenly** one.

The conclusion of this reading relies on parallels, which you can emphasize subtly: image/earthly; image/heavenly.

and only God had the right to decide his fate. The storyteller also reveals the measure of God's favor toward the leadership of Israel. God favors those who show justice toward others and faithfulness to God.

READING II   Today's second reading is a continuation of Paul's teaching on resurrection of the dead, which we first encountered two Sundays ago. Finally, in today's reading, Paul raises a very practical question that underlies this theological treatise: "How are the dead raised? With

what kind of body will they come back?" (1 Corinthians 15:35). Anyone living in the first-century Mediterranean world knew how quickly the body decays after death, so resurrecting that same body was unthinkable.

Paul addresses this question—with what kind of body will we come back?—by offering a commentary on a sentence from the second creation story in Genesis: "Then the Lord God formed the man out of the dust of the ground and blew into his nostrils the breath of life, and the man became

a living being" (Genesis 2:7). Notice how he distinguishes the "first man, Adam" from the "second man, from heaven," while maintaining the connection between the two. The "first man" is likened to the man formed out of the dust of the earth, with a physical body. The "second man" is likened to Adam being brought to life by the breath/spirit of God. Paul concludes with a powerful expression of faith: As we bear the image of Christ on earth, so will we bear the image of the risen Christ in heaven.

GOSPEL   Luke 6:27–38

A reading from Luke

Jesus said to his **disciples**:
"To **you** who **hear** I say,
　　love your enemies, do **good** to those who **hate** you,
　　bless those who **curse** you, **pray** for those who **mistreat** you.
To the **person** who strikes you on **one** cheek,
　　offer the **other one** as **well**,
　　and from the **person** who takes your **cloak**,
　　do not withhold even your **tunic**.
Give to **everyone** who asks of you,
　　and from the one who **takes** what is **yours** do **not** demand
　　　　it **back**.
Do to **others** as you would have them **do** to **you**.
For if you **love** those who **love** you,
　　what **credit** is that to **you**?
Even **sinners** love those who **love** them.
And if you do **good** to those who do **good** to you,
　　what **credit** is that to **you**?
Even **sinners** do the **same**.
If you lend **money** to those from whom you expect **repayment**,
　　what **credit** is that to **you**?
Even **sinners** lend to **sinners**,
　　and get **back** the same **amount**.
But rather, **love** your enemies and do **good** to them,
　　and **lend** expecting nothing **back**;
　　then your **reward** will be **great**
　　and you will be **children** of the **Most High**,
　　for he himself is **kind** to the **ungrateful** and the **wicked**.
Be **merciful**, just as your **Father** is merciful.

A didactic reading into which are compressed several essential teachings, in what amounts to the ethics he expects of those who would follow him. Emphasize "you" and "hear." "Love your enemies": the core teaching.

Nearly even stress on the words in this line. Tunic = TOO-nihk

Here begins a series of teachings about how to be better. Jesus emphasizes them with claims that begin "even sinners." He is using these examples to set up how he expects his followers to behave.

At "But rather," Jesus declares how you can be better. Each of these is as necessary as it is challenging: love your enemies, lend without expecting a return, and so forth.

GOSPEL　Today's Gospel is a continuation of Luke's Sermon on the Plain. Some biblical commentators say that this section is an attempt to contemporize or concretize the blessings and woes, which we reflected upon last Sunday. They say this because of a parallel between the fourth beatitude/blessing, "Blessed are you when people hate you" (Luke 6:22), and the opening of today's reading, "Love your enemies, do good to those who hate you." We know how hard it can be to love our enemies, but it can be even harder to appreciate how radical it would have sounded to early Christians of the Mediterranean world. In an honor/shame culture, to allow someone to slap you was a source of shame. To restore your honor, you were expected to fight back, so turning the other cheek was a source of even more dishonor.

The social system of the ancient world operated on a kind of reciprocity agreement, lending only to those who can pay you back and repaying a good deed with a similar good deed. This is the kind of behavior that was expected! But Luke portrays Jesus as saying that his disciples should do the opposite. If someone takes your overgarment, you should give him your undergarment, too. If you lend money, do not expect to get it back. All of this countercultural activity is summed up in a simple imperative: "Be merciful, just as your Father is merciful." When we act in this radical way and forget about self-protections, God will give us such superabundance that we will

Note the repetitions that conclude this passage, which you should emphasize: judging/judged; condemning/condemned; forgive/forgiven; give/given; and measure/measure.

"Stop **judging** and you will not be **judged**.
Stop **condemning** and you will not be **condemned**.
Forgive and you will be **forgiven**.
Give, and gifts will be **given** to you;
    a good **measure**, packed **together**, shaken **down**,
        and **overflowing**,
    will be **poured** into your **lap**.
For the **measure** with which you **measure**
    will in **return** be measured out to **you**."

not be able to contain it. The Greek word translated here as "lap" can mean "bosom" or "chest," and it can refer to the folds of one's garments, which people used to carry things. C.C.

EIGHTH SUNDAY
IN ORDINARY TIME

LECTIONARY #84

READING I   Sirach 27:4–7

A reading from the Book of Sirach

When a **sieve** is **shaken**, the **husks** appear;
  so do one's **faults** when one **speaks**.
As the **test** of what the potter **molds** is in the **furnace**,
  so in **tribulation** is the **test** of the **just**.
The **fruit** of a tree shows the **care** it has **had**;
  so **too** does one's **speech** disclose the **bent** of one's **mind**.
Praise **no one** before he **speaks**,
  for it is **then** that people are **tested**.

Sirach = SEER-ak *or* SĪ-ruhk

A short, potent exhortatory reading that consists almost entirely of a metaphor presented by way of comparison. Proclaim evenly and slowly so that its message can be absorbed.

sieve = siv

tribulation = trih-byoo-LAY-shuhn

"Test" is the crucial word in the reading. Emphasize the word slightly in this line and the next.

Slight extra emphasis on "tested."

For meditation and context:

RESPONSORIAL PSALM   Psalm 92:2–3, 13–14, 15–16 (see 2a)

R. Lord, it is good to give thanks to you.

It is good to give thanks to the LORD,
  to sing praise to your name, Most High,
to proclaim your kindness at dawn
  and your faithfulness throughout
    the night.

The just one shall flourish like the palm tree,
  like a cedar of Lebanon shall he grow.
They that are planted in the house of
  the LORD
  shall flourish in the courts of our God.

They shall bear fruit even in old age;
  vigorous and sturdy shall they be,
declaring how just is the LORD,
  my rock, in whom there is no wrong.

READING I The Book of Sirach belongs to the collection of wisdom books of the Bible. Among Catholics and several Eastern-rite Churches, this book is also categorized as deuterocanonical. The word "deuterocanonical" means "second canon," and the word "canon" refers to the list of religious writings that are considered authoritative for faith. Our Protestant brothers and sisters call these books "apocryphal," meaning "secret" or "obscure," and they do not consider them to be officially part of the Bible.

Today's first reading consists of several proverbs that provide advice about how we might assess the quality of a person. It is preceded by several proverbs about the dangers of engaging in commerce, and it is followed by advice about how to live a righteous life. This section, which is centered on speech, uses imagery that is both familiar and rich in meaning. A sieve or strainer that was used for separating good from bad is often a metaphor for judgment (see Amos 9:9; Isaiah 30:28; Luke 22:31). A potter's creation that is tested in the kiln can also be a metaphor for judgment. Well made, it will become stronger in the kiln; poorly made, it will break or explode. Similarly, a tree that is well cared for will produce good fruit, but a neglected tree will produce inferior fruit. By comparison, the true nature of a person will be revealed in their speech. Thus, a wise person will wait until people speak before praising them.

Corinthians = kohr-IN-thee-uhnz

A didactic reading of lyrically powerful subtlety and complexity. As is often the case, St. Paul uses a few key words to advance his argument and to allow it to resonate.

corruptible = kohr-RUPT-uh-b*l
incorruptibility = ihn-koh-ruhp-tuh-BIL-ih-tee
Emphasis on "this." Notice the parallel between corruptible/incorruptibility; mortal/immortality.

The rhythm in these lines is important, especially in the repetition of "death."

St. Paul concludes here with an exhortation. It is offered as hopeful advice.

READING II   1 Corinthians 15:54–58

A reading from the first Letter of Saint Paul to the Corinthians

Brothers and **sisters**:
When **this** which is **corruptible clothes** itself
    with **incorruptibility**
  and **this** which is **mortal clothes** itself with **immortality**,
  then the **word** that is **written** shall come **about**:
  Death is *swallowed up in victory.*
    Where, O death, is your victory?
    Where, O death, is your sting?
The **sting** of **death** is **sin**,
  and the **power** of **sin** is the **law**.
But **thanks** be to **God** who gives us the **victory**
  through our **Lord** Jesus **Christ**.

Therefore, my **beloved brothers** and **sisters**,
  be **firm**, **steadfast**, **always fully devoted** to the **work**
    of the **Lord**,
  knowing that in the **Lord** your **labor** is not in **vain**.

A didactic reading in which Jesus relies on images of wood to make his points, two of which make up this reading.

The first point contrasts the splinter with the wooden beam. So emphatic is Jesus about this point that he repeats it *entirely* a second time before including it in a command a third time. Your assembly will have an opportunity to understand what Jesus means as a result of these repetitions.

GOSPEL   Luke 6:39–45

A reading from the holy Gospel according to Luke

Jesus told his **disciples** a **parable**,
  "Can a **blind person** guide a **blind person**?
Will not **both** fall into a **pit**?
No disciple is **superior** to the **teacher**;
  but when **fully trained**,
    every disciple will be like his **teacher**.
Why do you notice the **splinter** in your **brother's eye**,
  but **do not perceive** the wooden **beam** in your **own**? »

READING II | Our second reading comes from the final section of Paul's teaching on resurrection from the dead in his First Letter to the Corinthians, continuing from the previous three Sundays' readings. In the first section, Paul recalled a credal statement about the death and resurrection of Jesus and his many post-resurrection appearances. In the second section, he highlighted the consequences of refusing to believe in resurrection of the dead. The third section addressed the question of the nature of the resurrected body. In this last section, Paul makes a proclamation of faith concerning the transformation that we will experience at death, when this physical body, which is subject to decay, takes on an immortal body.

Building toward his climax, Paul alludes to two Scripture texts. The first is Isaiah 25:8, "[God] will destroy death forever." The second is Hosea 13:14, in which the prophet conveys God's words against Ephraim, saying, "Shall I deliver them from the power of Sheol? shall I redeem them from death? Where are your plagues, O death! where is your sting, Sheol!" In Jewish cosmology, Sheol was understood to be a place under the earth where the spirits of the dead reside in a state of quasi-existence. Finally, he asserts in dramatic fashion that our victory over sin and death comes through Jesus Christ, which is a gift to all who are steadfast in their commitment to the work of the Lord. Amen! Alleluia!

Here begins Jesus' second point, which contrasts a good tree to a rotten one. Emphasize the contrast between "good" and "rotten."
hypocrite = HIP-uh-kriht

The reading concludes with a final, related contrast between "good" and "evil." Subtle emphasis on both "good" and "evil."

How can you **say** to your **brother**,
  'Brother, let me remove that **splinter** in your **eye**,'
  when you do not even **notice** the wooden **beam** in your
    own eye?
You **hypocrite**! **Remove** the wooden **beam** from your eye **first**;
  then you will see **clearly**
  to remove the **splinter** in your **brother's eye**.

"A **good tree** does not **bear** rotten **fruit**,
  nor does a **rotten** tree bear good **fruit**.
For every **tree** is **known** by its **own fruit**.
For **people** do not pick **figs** from **thornbushes**,
  nor do they gather **grapes** from **brambles**.
A **good person** out of the **store** of **goodness** in his **heart**
    produces **good**,
  but an **evil person** out of a **store** of **evil** produces **evil**;
  for from the **fullness** of the **heart** the mouth **speaks**."

PRAYERFUL READING, OR *LECTIO DIVINA*

1. *Lectio:* Read a Scripture passage aloud slowly. Notice what phrase captures your attention and be attentive to its meaning. Silent pause.

2. *Meditatio:* Read the passage aloud slowly again, reflecting on the passage, allowing God to speak to you through it. Silent pause.

3. *Oratio:* Read it aloud slowly a third time, allowing it to be your prayer or response to God's gift of insight to you. Silent pause.

4. *Contemplatio:* Read it aloud slowly a fourth time, now resting in God's Word.

GOSPEL   Today's Gospel is the conclusion of Luke's Sermon on the Plain, which we began to explore two Sundays ago. It consists of three brief parables or sayings, but, in order to interpret these sayings well, we first need to examine their literary context. In the verses that immediately precede these sayings, the Lukan Jesus gives his disciples this advice: "Stop judging and you will not be judged. . . . Forgive and you will be forgiven. . . . Give and gifts will be given to you" (Luke 6:37–38). Further, in the larger context of the sermon, we are being called to be vulnerable in the face of shame and violence, to give without expecting a return, and to love our enemies. We are also called to be merciful as God is merciful.

What, then, is the message of the saying about the blind leading the blind? What is the meaning of the saying about the disciples who will never be superior to their teacher? What is the significance of the saying about the guy who is preoccupied about the splinter in his neighbor's eye, while walking around with a plank in his own eye? All three sayings have a similar message that is made apparent in the teaching about a good tree that produces good fruit. As our first reading reminds us, what people say and do reveals what is in their hearts. The fruit we produce is evidence of the disposition and intentions of our inner selves. We should strive, therefore, to be fully committed disciples of Jesus who are eager to turn our inner arrogance and judgment into openness and humility before the One who can teach us to act with love and mercy from "the store of goodness" in our hearts. C.C.

ASH WEDNESDAY

LECTIONARY #219

READING I   Joel 2:12–18

A reading from the Book of the Prophet Joel

Even **now**, says the LORD,
　　return to me with your **whole heart**,
　　with **fasting**, and **weeping**, and **mourning**;
Rend your **hearts**, not your **garments**,
　　and **return** to the LORD, your **God**.
For **gracious** and **merciful** is **he**,
　　slow to anger, **rich** in kindness,
　　and **relenting** in punishment.
Perhaps he will **again** relent
　　and leave **behind** him a **blessing**,
Offerings and **libations**
　　for the LORD, your **God**.

Blow the trumpet in **Zion**!
　　proclaim a fast,
　　call an assembly;
Gather the people,
　　notify the congregation;
Assemble the elders,
　　gather the children
　　and the **infants** at the breast;
Let the **bridegroom** quit his **room**
　　and the **bride** her **chamber**. »

Joel = JOH-*l
rend = tear

An exhortatory reading in which Joel in his role as prophet becomes the mouthpiece for the Lord; it is as if God is addressing the people directly in this reading. Proclaim this reading like Joel himself, letting your voice be the instrument for this highly charged and poetic language to come to life. No need to exaggerate or emote; the language is filled to the brim with feeling. Proclaim with a sure and steady voice and that vibrancy will come through.

libations = li-BAY-shuhnz
This reading makes use of frequent parallels. Give the words in pairs emphasis: "hearts" and "garments"; "gracious" and "merciful"; "slow" and "rich"; "offerings" and "libations."

The energy picks up with a series of imperative verb forms. These words are highly charged—God is telling the assembly directly what to do. "Blow," "proclaim," "call," "gather," "notify," "assemble," "let."

READING I On Ash Wednesday, the beginning of the season of Lent, we hear from the prophet Joel. Little is known about the author of this book or the time in which it was written, though the majority view of biblical scholars is that it was written sometime after the Babylonian Exile and the rebuilding of the Jerusalem Temple but before the destruction of Tyre and Sidon by Alexander the Great's armies (c. 515–343 BC). The first parts of the book appear to have been written as a response to a drought and plagues of locusts that hit the countryside around Jerusalem. The later parts of the book are more eschatological in tone, suggesting an end-time encounter between God and Israel.

Today's reading comes from the first parts of the Book of Joel. The author begins with a description of the devastation caused by locust swarms and the drought that accompanied them. The prophet is beside himself with alarm as he sees the day turn to night because of the armies of insects in the sky and the land turn to a desert wasteland. Animals are starving and the grain of the field is gone. The trees with their fruits are destroyed and the vines have dried up. The prophet calls to the farmers and vinedressers, the elders and the priests of the temple to wake up, pray to God and proclaim a fast so that God will intervene on their behalf.

God speaks through the prophet and calls the people to conversion of heart through acts of repentance and mourning inwardly, not simply outwardly, so that God will relent in his punishment upon them. Today, we would not necessarily think of

Between the **porch** and the **altar**
    let the **priests**, the **ministers** of the L ORD, **weep**,
And say, "**Spare**, O L ORD, your **people**,
    and make **not** your **heritage** a **reproach**,
    with the **nations** ruling **over** them!
Why should they **say** among the **peoples**,
    '**Where** is their **God**?' "

Then the L ORD was stirred to **concern** for his **land**
    and took **pity** on his **people**.

Allow for a slight pause between the question and the final expression in the reading.

For meditation and context:

RESPONSORIAL PSALM   Psalm 51:3–4, 5–6ab, 12–13, 14 and 17 (3a)

R. Be merciful, O Lord, for we have sinned.

Have mercy on me, O God, in your goodness;
    in the greatness of your compassion wipe
        out my offense.
Thoroughly wash me from my guilt
    and of my sin cleanse me.

For I acknowledge my offense,
    and my sin is before me always:
"Against you only have I sinned,
    and done what is evil in your sight."

A clean heart create for me, O God,
    and a steadfast spirit renew within me.
Cast me not out from your presence,
    and your Holy Spirit take not from me.

Give me back the joy of your salvation,
    and a willing spirit sustain in me.
O Lord, open my lips,
    and my mouth shall proclaim your praise.

READING II   2 Corinthians 5:20—6:2

A reading from the second Letter of Saint Paul to the Corinthians

Brothers and **sisters**:
We are **ambassadors** for **Christ**,
    as if **God** were appealing **through** us.
We **implore** you on behalf of **Christ**,
    be **reconciled** to God.
For **our** sake he made him to **be** sin who did not **know** sin,
    so that we might become the **righteousness** of **God** in **him**.

Corinthians = kohr-IN-thee-uhnz
An exhortatory reading in which Paul seeks to impress upon the members of the early Church at Corinth the importance of reconciliation with God in preparation to receive God.
ambassadors =
am-BAS-uh-dehrs or am-BAS-uh-dohrs

The phrasing in this statement, "he made him to be sin," is a little peculiar. Practice it a few times and sound it out. It's not an expression we commonly use in relation to sin. "Be" is paralleled with "know." Emphasize those two words to anchor your proclamation.

natural disasters as God's punishment, but the prophetic books tend to follow a long-established pattern: (1) Israel sins; (2) God punishes; (3) Israel repents; (4) God relents and restores Israel. Although it is difficult to recognize in English translation, the author of this book includes a delightful play on the Hebrew verb *shub*, which means "to turn back or return." At the beginning of today's reading, God first invites the people to "return" to him, and then the prophet calls the people to "return" to God. Finally, the prophet says wistfully, "Perhaps God will return [verb, *shub*] and relent."

Notice how the prophet gives us a list of attributes of God: "gracious and merciful, slow to anger, rich in kindness, and relenting in punishment." This same formula can be found in Jonah 4:2, but similar formulas are found throughout the Old Testament. Notice, also, how the words "elders" and "infants at the breast" encompass all of humanity. Finally, notice how the prophet announces the completion of the four-stage pattern: "Then the Lord was stirred to concern for his land and took pity on his people." Concern is a stronger word than it may seem. It means something like "zealous,"

suggesting that God was roused to passion for the land and its people.

READING II The theme of our second reading, the ministry of reconciliation, is very appropriate for Ash Wednesday. Paul calls himself and his coworkers "ambassadors" for Christ. But in what sense? In the verses that immediately precede this reading, Paul says that God is the one who initiates reconciliation, bringing God and humanity together again, while Christ is the agent of reconciliation, through his sacrificial offering on our behalf. Paul's

Working **together**, then,
   we **appeal** to you not to **receive** the grace of God in **vain**.
For he **says**:

   *In an acceptable time **I heard** you,*
      *and on the day of salvation **I helped** you.*

Behold, **now** is a **very acceptable time**;
   behold, **now** is the **day** of **salvation**.

GOSPEL   Matthew 6:1–6, 16–18

A reading from the holy Gospel according to Matthew

Jesus said to his disciples:
   "Take **care** not to **perform** righteous deeds
   in order that people may **see** them;
   otherwise, you will have **no** recompense from
      your heavenly Father.
When you give **alms**,
   do **not** blow a **trumpet** before you,
   as the **hypocrites** do in the **synagogues** and in the **streets**
   to win the **praise** of others.
Amen, I say to you,
   they have **received** their **reward**.
But when **you** give alms,
   do not let your **left** hand know what your **right** is doing,
   so that your **almsgiving** may be **secret**.
And your **Father** who sees in secret will **repay** you. »

The exhortation of the reading resolves in Paul's use of the word "acceptable." In its first appearance, you do not need to emphasize it. When it reappears, be sure to give it extra emphasis.

A didactic reading in which Jesus provides advice for how to approach the practices of almsgiving, prayer, and fasting. Each section of advice is constructed very similarly, creating parallel expressions. Don't let them become formulaic in your proclamation. Each of these practices is important to Jesus for bringing us closer to God.

Almsgiving comes first.

hypocrites = HIP-uh-krihts
synagogues = SIN-uh-gogs

Emphasis on "left," "right," "secret," "Father," and "repay."

role is to convey the message of reconciliation to others. He and his coworkers serve as mediators of God's gift of reconciliation to the world. Thus, on behalf of Christ, Paul pleads with the recipients of his letter to be reconciled to God, so that they might become the righteousness of God. And what does it mean to become the righteousness of God? Perhaps Joel gives us the answer: God is "gracious and merciful, slow to anger, rich in kindness, and relenting in punishment" (Joel 2:13). If we are to be ministers of reconciliation, then our task is to be the righteousness of God for others,

that is, to demonstrate how God understands God's right relationship with humanity. Are you ready?

GOSPEL | Our Gospel for today is from Matthew's Sermon on the Mount. This discourse is longer than Luke's Sermon on the Plain (which was proclaimed over the last three Sundays) in part because it contains some elements that are consistent with Jewish piety and practice, which Luke does not have. One example is its teaching on prayer, fasting, and almsgiving. We should not forget that the very first Jesus

followers were Jews who believed Jesus to be the long-awaited messiah.

Matthew portrays Jesus as beginning with a general warning about not performing righteous deeds for the purpose of letting others see your righteousness. You will not receive a reward from God, he says, because you will have already received your reward. The Greek word translated here as "take heed" can also be translated as "beware" or "be attentive." Almsgiving, or charity, was and still is highly prized in Judaism. In Hebrew the word is *tzedakah*, which has the same root as "righteousness."

Next comes prayer. The wording is very similar to that in the almsgiving section. Emphasis on "inner," "secret," "Father," "secret," and "repay."

"When you **pray**,
     do **not** be like the **hypocrites**,
     who love to **stand** and **pray** in the **synagogues**
          and on street corners
     so that **others** may **see** them.
Amen, **I** say to you,
     they have **received** their **reward**.
But when **you** pray, **go** to your inner **room**,
     close the door, and **pray** to your **Father** in **secret**.
And your **Father** who sees in **secret** will **repay** you.

And finally comes fasting. Once again, similar wording. This time, emphasis on "head," "face," "appear," "Father," "hidden," and "repay."

"When you **fast**,
     do not look **gloomy** like the **hypocrites**.
They **neglect** their **appearance**,
     so that they may **appear** to others to be **fasting**.
Amen, I say to you, they have **received** their **reward**.
But when you **fast**,
     anoint your **head** and wash your **face**,
     so that you may not **appear** to be **fasting**,
     except to your **Father** who is **hidden**.
And your **Father** who sees what is **hidden** will **repay** you."

Jesus' words do not change the obligation to perform acts of charity, but his teaching is all about motivation and intentionality. Remarkably, the twelfth-century Jewish scholar and interpreter of Talmud, Moses Maimonides, outlined eight stages of *tzedakah*. The second-highest stage is when the giver and recipient do not know each other. The highest is when you help support a person before they become dependent on others for the necessities of life. The biblical reason given for charity work is that God "executes justice for the orphan and the widow, and loves the resident alien, giving them food and clothing" (Deuteronomy 10:18).

The tone of Jesus' teaching on fasting is similar to that of almsgiving. It is all about motivation and intentionality. Fasting has a very long history in religious movements of all kinds. It was done to express repentance or mourning. It prepared a person for encounter with the divine. It was also done to ask the gods to intercede on the people's behalf in time of trouble. If it is done so that others see that you are fasting, then you have already received your reward. But God rewards what is hidden. What will your "hidden" fasting and almsgiving consist of during this Lenten season? C.C.

FIRST SUNDAY OF LENT

LECTIONARY #24

READING I   Deuteronomy 26:4–10

A reading from the Book of Deuteronomy

Moses spoke to the **people**, saying:
   "The **priest** shall **receive** the basket from **you**
   and shall **set** it in **front** of the **altar** of the LORD, your God.
Then you shall **declare** before the LORD, your God,
   'My **father** was a wandering **Aramean**
   who went **down** to Egypt with a small **household**
   and **lived** there as an **alien**.
But **there** he became a **nation**
   great, strong, and **numerous**.
When the **Egyptians maltreated** and **oppressed** us,
   imposing **hard labor upon** us,
   we **cried** to the LORD, the **God** of our **fathers**,
   and he **heard** our **cry**
   and **saw** our **affliction**, our **toil**, and our **oppression**.
He brought us out of **Egypt**
   with his **strong hand** and outstretched **arm**,
   with terrifying **power**, with **signs** and **wonders**;
   and bringing us into this **country**,
   he **gave** us this **land** flowing with **milk** and **honey**.
Therefore, I have now brought you the **firstfruits**
   of the **products** of the **soil**
   which **you**, O LORD, have **given** me.'
And having **set** them before the **Lord**, your **God**,
   you shall bow **down** in his **presence**."

Deuteronomy = doo-ter-AH-nuh-mee *or* dyoo-ter-AH-nuh-mee

A narrative reading that concludes with an exhortation. Most of the reading consists of a long quotation within a quotation. A slight change in tone at the conclusion will signal this to your assembly. (See below.)

Aramean = ayr-uh-MEE-uhn

Even emphasis on "great, strong, and numerous"

Slight pause between "labor" and "upon."

> **TO KEEP IN MIND**
> Use the pitch and volume of your voice to gain the attention of the assembly.

"Therefore" the long quotation to a close and begins the concluding exhortation. Slow down slightly.

This last sentence reinforces the exhortation, bringing it to its conclusion. Emphasis on "down."

READING I The first reading for this First Sunday of Lent is taken from the Book of Deuteronomy, specifically the part known as the Deuteronomy Law Code. This begins at chapter 12 with the words "These are the statutes and ordinances which you must be careful to observe in the land which the Lord, the God of your ancestors, has given you to possess, throughout the time you live on its soil," and it extends through Deuteronomy 26:15, concluding with a recommitment to the covenant that God made with Moses and the Israelites at Sinai (Deuteronomy 26:16–19).

It covers a wide range of topics such as the establishment of a single sanctuary in the land and the feasts and sacrifices to be associated with this place, as well as food regulations; tithing; limits on slavery; rules for the king, priests, and prophets; penalties for infractions against others; and marriage, divorce, and adultery rules.

This section of the Deuteronomy Law Code focuses on the offering of the firstfruits that God's chosen were supposed to make when they entered the promised land after the Exodus. It is later commemorated in the Jewish feast of *Shavuot*, also known

as the Feast of Weeks or Pentecost, which is a harvest festival and celebration of the giving of the Law at Sinai. The firstfruits of the harvest typically included wheat, barley, wine, figs, pomegranates, olive oil, and dates, all harvested from the land of Israel. After handing the basket of firstfruits to the priest in charge, the Law Code prescribed that the people make a declaration in God's presence of their journey from slavery in Egypt to freedom. The firstfruits are evidence that they have indeed arrived and now dwell in the promised land.

For meditation and context:

RESPONSORIAL PSALM Psalm 91:1–2, 10–11, 12–13, 14–15 (see 15b)

R. Be with me, Lord, when I am in trouble.

You who dwell in the shelter of the
    Most High,
  who abide in the shadow of the Almighty,
say to the LORD, "My refuge and fortress,
  my God in whom I trust."

No evil shall befall you,
  nor affliction come near your tent,
for to his angels he has given command
    about you,
  that they guard you in all your ways.

Upon their hands they shall bear you up,
  lest you dash your foot against a stone.
You shall tread upon the asp and the viper;
  you shall trample down the lion and
    the dragon.

Because he clings to me, I will deliver him;
  I will set him on high because he
    acknowledges my name.
He shall call upon me, and I will answer him;
  I will be with him in distress;
I will deliver him and glorify him.

READING II Romans 10:8–13

A reading from the Letter of Saint Paul to the Romans

Brothers and **sisters**:
What does **Scripture** say?
  The **word** *is* **near** *you,*
    in your **mouth** *and in your* **heart**
  —that is, the word of **faith** that we **preach**—,
for, if you **confess** with your mouth that **Jesus** is **Lord**
and **believe** in your **heart** that God **raised** him from the **dead**,
you will be **saved**.
For one **believes** with the **heart** and so is **justified**,
  and one **confesses** with the **mouth** and so is **saved**.
For the **Scripture** says,
  No one who **believes** *in him will be put to* **shame**.
For there is no **distinction** between **Jew** and **Greek**;
  the same **Lord** is Lord of **all**,
  enriching **all** who call **upon** him.
For **"everyone** who **calls** on the **name** of the **Lord** will be **saved**."

A didactic reading that develops its argument through a series of simple repetitions.

Here St. Paul introduces two key terms: the "mouth" and the "heart."

Notice the repetitions of "heart" then "mouth." Emphasize both words.

This reading concludes with an emphatic rhythm.

READING II Our second reading, from Paul's Letter to the Romans, discusses the nature of righteousness that comes from faith. It is part of an interlude in a long diatribe that extends from Romans 9:1 through Romans 11:36. A diatribe is a literary form in which the writer delivers a long speech designed to persuade his audience of a particular position on a topic by conducting a fictional debate with an imagined opponent. The topic that Paul is discussing is the role of his Jewish brothers and sisters in God's plan of salvation. In the interlude, or pause, in the debate (Romans 9:30—10:16), Paul stops to reflect on the paradox created by the fact that the Gentiles who did not pursue righteousness and who do not know the Law are justified by faith, while the Jews who know the Law cannot be justified by the Law.

Paul explains his answer to this paradox using two Scripture texts that he attributes to Moses. The first, which precedes today's reading, comes from the Book of Leviticus, where Moses speaks to the people on God's behalf: "Keep, then, my statutes and decrees, for the person who carries them out will find life through them.

I am the Lord" (Leviticus 18:5). But Paul changes its meaning ever so slightly by making it about righteousness or justification through obedience to Jewish law. The second Scripture to which Paul alludes is from Deuteronomy: "For this command which I am giving you today is not too wondrous or remote for you. It is not in the heavens, that you should say, 'Who will go up to the heavens to get it for us and tell us of it, that we may do it?' Nor is it across the sea, that you should say, 'Who will cross the sea to get it for us and tell us of it, that we may do it?' No, it is something very near

GOSPEL Luke 4:1–13

A reading from the holy Gospel according to Luke

Filled with the Holy **Spirit**, **Jesus** returned from the **Jordan**
    and was **led** by the **Spirit** into the **desert** for forty days,
    to be **tempted** by the **devil**.
He ate **nothing** during those days,
    and when they were **over** he was **hungry**.
The devil **said** to him,
    "If **you** are the Son of **God**,
    command this stone to become **bread**."
Jesus **answered** him,
    "It is written, *One* **does not live** *on* **bread** *alone*."
Then he took him **up** and **showed** him
    all the **kingdoms** of the **world** in a single **instant**.
The devil **said** to him,
    "I shall give to you **all** this **power** and **glory**;
    for it has been handed **over** to me,
    and I may **give** it to whomever I **wish**.
All **this** will be **yours**, if you worship **me**."
Jesus **said** to him in **reply**,
    "It is written:
    You shall **worship** *the* **Lord**, *your* **God**,
        and **him alone** *shall you* **serve**."
Then he led him to **Jerusalem**,
    made him **stand** on the parapet of the **temple**,
        and **said** to him, »

A narrative reading that reads almost like a short play whose two characters are sparring for victory. No need, however, to spice it up in your proclamation. The writing itself provides clear signals about the story being told.

"He" refers to the devil; "him" refers to Jesus.

Paired emphasis on "yours" and "me."

Again, "he" refers to the devil; "him" refers to Jesus.
parapet = PAYR-uh-peht

to you, in your mouth and in your heart, to do it" (Deuteronomy 30:11–14).

But again, Paul deftly alters the meaning of Deuteronomy 30:11–14 by applying this quotation to Christ, who came down to be one of us, descended into death and was raised, not by our efforts, but by God's free gift to humanity. While righteousness that comes through obedience to Jewish Law is hard work and is never assured, this kind of righteousness, justification by faith, has already been freely given by God to all of humanity. We merely have to accept the gift.

Two more Scripture quotations round out Paul's explanation. The first is from Isaiah 28:16, in which the prophet is talking about God laying a cornerstone in Zion such that "whoever puts faith in it shall not waver." The second is from Joel 3:5, where the prophet speaks about the "Day of the Lord," when God will preserve Zion as a remnant and "everyone who calls upon the name of the Lord will escape harm."

Although Paul does not say this in so many words, he seems to suggest that the cornerstone and remnant is Christ, who

saves us from harm. Thus, justification and salvation are not an issue of Jews versus Gentiles; these are God's gifts to all of humanity.

GOSPEL The Gospel for this First Sunday in Lent depicts Jesus having his own desert experience. Luke's version of the story is similar to Matthew's but with a few key differences. For example, Luke's mention of Jesus being "filled with the Holy Spirit" and returning from the Jordan is a reminder of the baptism

"If **you** are the Son of **God**,
throw yourself **down** from here, for it is written:
    *He will **command** his angels **concerning** you, to **guard** you,*
and:
    *With their **hands** they will **support** you,*
    *lest you **dash** your **foot** against a **stone**."*
Jesus said to him in reply,
    "It also says,
    *You **shall not** put the Lord, your **God**, to the **test**."*
When the ***devil*** had finished every ***temptation***,
    he **departed** from **him** for a **time**.

The narrative concludes with parallel statements. First, the devil makes a challenge and then quotes Scripture. In response, Jesus quotes Scripture. Jesus is clearly defeating the devil at his own game. Note the rhythm of the last verse. Emphasis on "departed," "him," and "time."

scene, in which a heavenly voice proclaimed, "You are my beloved Son; with you I am well pleased" (Luke 3:22).

The forty days in the wilderness is intended as a reminder of the forty-year sojourn of the Israelites in the Exodus. The Greek word *diabolos*, translated here as "the devil," means a slanderer or a false accuser, whose intention is to trip someone up and cause them to sin. Jesus is hungry after fasting for such a long time, so the devil tempts him into using his powers to turn stones to bread, but Jesus quotes Deuteronomy 8:3 about humans not living by bread alone. Next, the devil tempts him to usurp political power, but Jesus quotes Deuteronomy 6:13 about worshipping God alone. Finally, the devil transports Jesus to Jerusalem and tempts him to prove that he is God's Son by throwing himself off the pinnacle of the temple. And how bold can he get? The devil even quotes Scripture in defense of his proposal (Psalm 91:11–12)! Jesus answers with another quotation from Deuteronomy 6:16: "You shall not put the Lord, your God, to the test."

You would think that the devil would slink away in defeat at this point, and he does for a time, but the narrator tells us that he will be back. It is appropriate, then, that this third temptation takes place in Jerusalem, where Jesus will suffer and die. C.C.

SECOND SUNDAY OF LENT

LECTIONARY #27

READING I Genesis 15:5–12, 17–18

A reading from the Book of Genesis

The Lord **God** took **Abram** outside and **said**,
    "Look **up** at the **sky** and **count** the **stars**, if you can.
Just **so**," he added, "shall your **descendants** be."
Abram put his **faith** in the L ORD,
    who **credited** it to him as an act of **righteousness**.

He then said to him,
    "**I** am the L ORD who brought you from **Ur** of the **Chaldeans**
    to give you this **land** as a **possession**."
"O **Lord** G OD," he asked,
    "**how** am I to **know** that I shall **possess** it?"
He answered him,
    "**Bring** me a three-year-old **heifer**, a three-year-old **she-goat**,
    a three-year-old **ram**, a **turtledove**, and a young **pigeon**."
Abram brought him **all** these, split them in **two**,
    and **placed** each half **opposite** the other;
    but the **birds** he did **not** cut **up**.
Birds of **prey** swooped down on the **carcasses**,
    but Abram stayed **with** them.
As the **sun** was about to **set**, a **trance** fell upon Abram,
    and a **deep**, terrifying **darkness enveloped** him.

When the sun had **set** and it was **dark**,
    there appeared a **smoking fire pot** and a **flaming torch**,
    which passed **between** those **pieces**. »

Genesis = JEN-uh-sihs

Abram = AY-br*m
A narrative reading of great and mysterious power. At its center is a sacrificial ritual and a dream vision. It reads like a great myth.

Chaldeans = kal-DEE-uhnz or kahl-DEE-uhnz

The sacrifice is voiced by God in the imperative. It reads like a cross between a recipe and a spell. Slow your pace slightly as you proclaim this portion.

carcasses = KAHR-kuhs-iz

Enveloped = ehn-VEL-uhpd
Emphasis on "trance"; slight pause between "darkness" and "enveloped."

READING I Even as we are beginning to immerse ourselves more deeply in the fasting and penitence of the Lenten season, today's readings remind us that Lent is not an end in itself. Rather, for Christians it carries a promise of renewed life in Christ.

Today's first reading is an edited account of God's promise to Abram of land, descendants, and a blessing. In Genesis 17:1–22, his name will be changed to Abraham. In the section preceding this lectionary reading, the narrator describes how

Abram received a vision of God telling him that his reward will be very great. But Abram complains to God that the thing he wants most, offspring of his own, is far out of reach. This is the context for God's promise that Abram will have descendants as numerous as the stars in the sky.

God also promises that Abram will possess the land, but how will Abram know that God's promise is sure? God directs Abram to prepare a covenant sacrifice and puts him into a deep trance, from which he sees a "smoking fire pot and a flaming

torch" passing between the carcasses of the sacrificial offering. Jeremiah 34:17–24 describes a similar covenant ritual, in which the party passing through the split carcasses declares that their fate would be like these animals, if they break the covenant. Thus, God, who is represented by the fire pot and the fire, is putting his integrity on the line, essentially declaring, "May I be split in two if I break covenant with Abram!"

It was on **that** occasion that the LORD made a **covenant**
    with Abram,
    saying: "To your **descendants** I give this **land**,
from the **Wadi** of Egypt to the Great **River**, the **Euphrates**."

The reading concludes with a varied repetition of the covenant that begins it. It's meant as a reward. Let your tone reflect that.

For meditation and context:

RESPONSORIAL PSALM   Psalm 27:1, 7–8, 8–9, 13–14 (1a)

R. The Lord is my light and my salvation.

The LORD is my light and my salvation;
    whom should I fear?
The LORD is my life's refuge;
    of whom should I be afraid?

Hear, O LORD, the sound of my call;
    have pity on me, and answer me.
Of you my heart speaks; you my
    glance seeks.

Your presence, O LORD, I seek.
    Hide not your face from me;
do not in anger repel your servant.
    You are my helper: cast me not off.

I believe that I shall see the bounty
    of the LORD
    in the land of the living.
Wait for the LORD with courage;
    be stouthearted, and wait for the LORD.

READING II   Philippians 3:17—4:1

A reading from the Letter of Saint Paul to the Philippians

Join with others in being **imitators** of me, [**brothers** and **sisters**,]
    and observe **those** who thus **conduct** themselves
    according to the model you have in **us**.
For **many**, as I have often **told** you
    and now **tell** you even in **tears**,
    conduct themselves as **enemies** of the cross of **Christ**.
Their **end** is **destruction**.
Their **God** is their **stomach**;
    their **glory** is in their "**shame**."
Their minds are **occupied** with earthly **things**.
But [our **citizenship** is in **heaven**,
    and **from** it we also await a **savior**, the **Lord** Jesus Christ.
He will **change** our lowly **body**
    to **conform** with his glorified body
    by the **power** that **enables** him also
    to bring **all things** into **subjection** to **himself**.

Philippians = fih-LIP-ee-uhnz

A didactic reading that follows a complex argument beginning with an urgent request, followed by an accusation, and then a shift toward a correction and a conclusion. Treat your reading in these four parts. The urgent request begins with "Join."

Repetition of the word "their" signals the nature of the accusation: enemies of the cross are behaving badly.

"But" signals the correction. Brighten your tone here slightly.

READING II | In today's second reading, Paul encourages the community to be imitators of himself and to use him as a model of the life of the baptized. To modern ears, this talk sounds arrogant and self-aggrandizing, but, in the context of this letter, clearly it is not. Earlier, he tells his readers that everything he once considered a gain or an accomplishment is rubbish, if he might gain Christ (Philippians 3:8). But Paul does not mean that he somehow earned a relationship with Christ. Instead, he says that Christ had taken possession of *him* (Philippians 3:12). Imagine how our day-

to-day lives would be transformed if we could say the same. Paul also knows that he has not yet fully arrived, so he presses forward, reaching for the prize that is life with the resurrected Christ.

This is what Paul means when he urges the community to imitate him. This is also what Paul means when he says that our citizenship is in heaven. Although we have not yet fully arrived, it is our destiny. We should, therefore, be exercising the duties of citizenship in the coming reign of God even now. And when that time comes for the full realization of God's reign, our

earthly bodies will be transformed into the likeness of Christ's resurrected body. This future reality Paul contrasts with the fate of the people whom he describes as "enemies of the cross of Christ." And who are these "enemies of the cross of Christ"? Most likely they were Jewish-Christian missionaries who believed that Gentiles could not be Jesus followers unless they first became Jews. But Paul stands firm: adherence to Jewish law effectively nullifies the cross of Christ. For us, too. We cannot know the joy of the resurrection without first going to the cross.

"Therefore" signals the conclusion, which exhorts the Philippians—and, by extension, your assembly—to "stand firm."

Therefore, my **brothers** and **sisters**,
    whom I **love** and **long** for, my **joy** and **crown**,
    in **this way** stand **firm** in the **Lord**.]

[Shorter: Philippians 3:20—4:1 (see brackets)]

GOSPEL   Luke 9:28b–36

A reading from the holy Gospel according to Luke

A narrative reading depicting one of the great transformative events in the Gospels, the Transfiguration, a scene of great strangeness and power.

The change begins immediately. No need to overdo it; the language is well suited to describing it.
Elijah = ee-LĪ-juh

Even emphasis.

Allow your tone to capture some of Peter's ignorance about what he is witnessing.

Proclaim these words in an even, clear tone.

Jesus took **Peter**, **John**, and **James**
    and went **up** the **mountain** to **pray**.
While he was **praying** his face changed in **appearance**
    and his **clothing** became dazzling **white**.
And **behold, two men** were conversing with him, **Moses**
        and **Elijah**,
    who **appeared** in **glory** and **spoke** of his **exodus**
    that he was going to **accomplish** in **Jerusalem**.
Peter and his companions had been overcome by **sleep**,
    but **becoming fully awake**,
    they **saw** his glory and the **two men** standing **with** him.
As they were about to **part** from him, Peter said to **Jesus**,
    "**Master**, it is **good** that we are **here**;
    let us make **three tents**,
    one for **you**, one for **Moses**, and one for **Elijah**."
But he did not **know** what he was **saying**.
While he was **still speaking**,
    a **cloud** came and cast a **shadow** over them,
    and they became **frightened** when they entered the **cloud**.
Then from the cloud came a **voice** that said,
    "**This** is my chosen **Son**; **listen** to him."
After the **voice** had **spoken**, **Jesus** was found **alone**.
They fell **silent** and did **not** at that time
    tell **anyone** what they had **seen**.

GOSPEL Today's Gospel gives us yet another powerful image of a future hope of life in Christ. It is the story of Jesus' transfiguration. Because Luke introduces this story with the phrase "About eight days after he said this," we can assume that he wants us to view the transfiguration in light of Jesus' prediction of his death and resurrection and his teaching on the cost of discipleship (Luke 9:23–27) that appears immediately prior to this one.

This transfiguration scene is a theophany, a manifestation of God, as is evidenced by the mountain setting, the deep sleep that falls upon the disciples, and the voice from a cloud. The detail about Moses, the great lawgiver, and Elijah, God's prophet, appearing in glory suggests the heavenly realm. Likewise, Jesus' altered face and his now glistening white clothing evoke the sense of a heavenly reality. It is also a prefiguring of Jesus' resurrected state.

Luke tells us that the heavenly trio are talking about Jesus' exodus that will take place in Jerusalem. Of course, this is a reference to Jesus' arrest, crucifixion, and death. But poor Peter does not understand. When he and the others are aroused from their slumber, he asks about building some tents for the heavenly trio, presumably because he wants to hang out and enjoy this glorious event. But this is not God's plan. Instead, the voice from heaven declares, "This is my chosen Son; listen to him." Yes, listen to him! C.C.

THIRD SUNDAY OF LENT

LECTIONARY #30

READING I   Exodus 3:1–8a, 13–15

Exodus = EK-suh-duhs

Midian = MID-ee-uhn
Horeb = HOHR-eb

A narrative reading that recounts one of the most vivid, imaginative scenes in the Old Testament in which God speaks directly to Moses in the form of a burning bush. This story is as familiar as it is dramatic. Proclaim it evenly and with confidence.

A reading from the Book of Exodus

Moses was tending the **flock** of his father-in-law **Jethro**,
    the priest of **Midian**.
Leading the **flock** across the **desert**, he came to **Horeb**,
    the mountain of **God**.
There an angel of the LORD appeared to Moses in **fire**
    flaming out of a **bush**.
As he looked **on**, he was surprised to see that the **bush**,
    though on **fire**, was not **consumed**.
So Moses **decided**,
    "I must go **over** to **look** at this remarkable **sight**,
    and **see** why the bush is not **burned**."

Avoid the desire to overly dramatize this passage. You need not change your tone or raise your voice when proclaiming "Moses! Moses!" or "Come no nearer!" Let the rich language of the passage convey the drama.

When the LORD saw him coming **over** to look at it more **closely**,
    God called out to him from the **bush**, "**Moses! Moses!**"
He answered, "**Here** I am."
God said, "**Come** no **nearer**!
Remove the **sandals** from your **feet**,
    for the **place** where you **stand** is **holy ground.**
I am the **God** of your **fathers**," he continued,
    "the God of **Abraham**, the God of **Isaac**, the God of **Jacob.**"
Moses hid his **face**, for he was **afraid** to look at **God**.

There are options for today's readings. Contact your parish staff to learn which readings will be used.

READING I   The readings for this Third Sunday of Lent are a reminder that God is there for us in times of trouble, but they also serve as a warning that we should not be complacent. An attitude of repentance or conversion of heart is always appropriate before God and one another.

In the first reading, we hear the story of Moses' first encounter with the God of Abraham, Isaac, and Jacob. Moses, a child of Hebrew slaves in Egypt, was raised in the house of the pharaoh. He ran from Egypt to avoid punishment after he killed an Egyptian who was abusing a slave. Thus we find him in the wilderness of Midian near Mount Horeb, which is also called Sinai in some of the biblical traditions, tending sheep for his father-in-law. Mountaintops were traditionally understood to be places where God's presence could be felt. Likewise, fire was thought to represent the presence of God. When Moses steps closer to observe the bush that was not consumed by the fire, he might not have been surprised by the voice coming from the bush. Note his immediate response to God's call: "Here I am." Then the fear of a direct encounter with the God of his ancestors overtook him, and he hid his face.

This will not be the only indicator of human frailty that we find in the Moses story. When God tells Moses that he has heard the cries of his people and has come down to rescue them, he sends Moses to deliver them from their slave holders. (This part is left out of the lectionary reading, probably for the sake of brevity.) Moses responds, "Who am I that I should go to

Adjust your tone slightly here. God is expressing sympathy for the Israelites and offering to rescue them from the Egyptians.

But the LORD said,
   "I have **witnessed** the **affliction** of my **people** in **Egypt**
   and have **heard** their **cry** of **complaint**
      against their **slave** drivers,
   so I know **well** what they are **suffering**.
   Therefore I have come **down** to **rescue** them
      from the **hands** of the **Egyptians**
      and **lead** them out of that **land** into a **good** and **spacious** land,
   a land **flowing** with **milk** and **honey**."

Moses said to **God**, "But when I **go** to the **Israelites**
   and **say** to them, 'The **God** of your **fathers** has **sent** me to **you**,'
   if they **ask** me, 'What is his **name**?' what am I to **tell** them?"

Note the rhythm of this line: "I AM who AM."

God replied, "**I am** who **am**."

Even emphasis on "I AM."

Then he **added**, "**This** is what you shall tell the Israelites:
   I AM sent **me** to **you**."

God spoke **further** to **Moses**, "**Thus** shall you say
      to the **Israelites**:
   The **LORD**, the **God** of your **fathers**,
   the God of **Abraham**, the God of **Isaac**, the God of **Jacob**,
   has **sent** me to **you**.

   "**This** is my **name forever**;
      thus am I to be **remembered** through **all** generations."

For meditation and context:

RESPONSORIAL PSALM   Psalm 103:1–2, 3–4, 6–7, 8, 11 (8a)

R. The Lord is kind and merciful.

Bless the LORD, O my soul;
   and all my being, bless his holy name.
Bless the LORD, O my soul,
   and forget not all his benefits.

He pardons all your iniquities,
   heals all your ills.
He redeems your life from destruction,
   crowns you with kindness
      and compassion.

The LORD secures justice
   and the rights of all the oppressed.
He has made known his ways to Moses,
   and his deeds to the children of Israel.

Merciful and gracious is the LORD,
   slow to anger and abounding in kindness.
For as the heavens are high above the earth,
   so surpassing is his kindness toward those
      who fear him.

Pharaoh and bring the Israelites out of Egypt?" (Exodus 3:11). Clearly, Moses thinks he is not up to the task! Picking up the lectionary reading: Moses expresses his hesitancy to take on this monumental task by asking God to tell him God's name, in case the people ask. God's answer is hard to discern. The translation here is "I am who am," but some biblical scholars have suggested that it means something like "I will be with you" or "I am the one who creates." While we may never solve this dilemma, we know that the Hebrew word *hayah* is some form

of the verb "to be." Perhaps we can think of God as Beingness itself.

Two more times in Moses' first encounter with God, we see his frailty. The first is in Exodus 4:1–9, when he expresses his fear that the people will not believe him. The second is in Exodus 4:10–17, when Moses says that he is not an eloquent speaker and that someone else should be sent in his place. In response to this excuse, God gives him Aaron, his kin, to speak on his behalf, but, be warned! God does not relent!

READING II   Our second reading, from the First Letter to the Corinthians, is Paul's reflection on another part of the Moses story, namely the Israelites' time in the wilderness during the Exodus. His warning to the Corinthian community is that, just as God's chosen people in the wilderness became overconfident and suffered for their sin, they too can fall victim to overconfidence. To grasp the significance of Paul's interpretation fully, it helps to know the Exodus story. As the Israelites escaped Egypt, God led them

Corinthians = kohr-IN-thee-uhnz

A didactic reading in which St. Paul instructs the Corinthians about the bad example their ancestors set for them. Note the ways that Paul builds to his conclusion.

Note the parallels between eating and drinking, which help Paul build his argument.

Emphasis on "examples" and "us." Paul wants to be clear that ancestral failures did not please God.

"Therefore" concludes Paul's argument. His message is stern. Proclaim accordingly.

READING II   1 Corinthians 10:1–6, 10–12

A reading from the first Letter of Saint Paul to the Corinthians

I do **not** want you to be **unaware**, **brothers** and **sisters**,
   that our **ancestors** were all under the **cloud**
   and all **passed** through the **sea**,
   and **all** of them were **baptized** into **Moses**
   in the **cloud** and in the **sea**.
All **ate** the same spiritual **food**,
   and all **drank** the same spiritual **drink**,
   for they **drank** from a spiritual **rock** that **followed** them,
   and the **rock** was the **Christ**.
Yet **God** was not **pleased** with **most** of them,
   for they were struck **down** in the **desert**.

These things happened as **examples** for **us**,
   so that we might not **desire** evil things, as **they** did.
Do not **grumble** as some of them did,
   and suffered **death** by the **destroyer**.
These things happened to them as an **example**,
   and they have been written **down** as a **warning** to **us**,
   upon **whom** the **end** of the **ages** has **come**.
Therefore, whoever **thinks** he is standing **secure**
   should take **care** not to **fall**.

toward the Red Sea by a column of cloud during the day and a column of fire by night (Exodus 13:17–22). When they got to the sea, God told Moses to raise his arms over the sea. Then God directed a strong wind to split the water so that the Israelites could pass on dry land (Exodus 14:10–22). When the people complained about having no food in the wilderness, God gave them manna from the heavens to eat (Exodus 16:4–18). When they had nothing to drink, God gave them water from a rock (Exodus 17:1–7). Notice how Paul interprets the passing through the Red Sea as baptism

and the rock from which the Israelites were given water as Christ.

Yet, when Moses was delayed in his return from the mountain where he had received God's Law, the people assumed that he was not returning. They decided to make an image of a god—the golden calf—to lead them the rest of the way through the wilderness (Exodus 32:1–11). Needless to say, neither God nor Moses was pleased, and the people involved in the rebellion suffered for their sin. Paul says that the consequences that the Israelites suffered in the wilderness are examples

(Greek *tupos*) so that the community will not desire these evil things. When it comes to biblical interpretation, a type is an Old Testament person or event that is a pattern or example of the more perfect New Testament person or event.

GOSPEL   Today's Gospel reading also focuses on the need for repentance. It is part of a series of teachings in Luke's Gospel that Jesus delivers to his disciples as they make their way to Jerusalem, where he will be arrested and put to death. It begins with a report about

GOSPEL   Luke 13:1–9

A reading from the holy Gospel according to Luke

Some **people** told **Jesus** about the **Galileans**
  whose **blood Pilate** had **mingled** with the **blood**
    of their **sacrifices**.
Jesus **said** to them in **reply**,
  "Do you **think** that because these Galileans **suffered**
    in this **way**
  they were **greater sinners** than all other **Galileans**?
By no **means**!
But I **tell** you, if you do not **repent**,
  you will all **perish** as **they** did!
Or those **eighteen people** who were **killed**
  when the **tower** at **Siloam fell** on them—
  do you **think** they were more **guilty**
  than everyone else who **lived** in **Jerusalem**?
By no **means**!
But I **tell** you, if you do not **repent**,
  you will all **perish** as **they** did!"

And he **told** them this **parable**:
  "There **once** was a **person** who had a **fig** tree **planted**
    in his **orchard**,
  and when he **came** in search of **fruit** on it but found **none**,
  he said to the **gardener**,
  'For **three years** now I have **come** in search of **fruit**
    on this **fig** tree
  but have found **none**.
So cut it **down**.
Why should it **exhaust** the **soil**?'
He said to him in reply,
  '**Sir**, **leave** it for this year **also**,
  and I shall **cultivate** the ground around it and **fertilize** it;
  it may bear **fruit** in the **future**.
If **not** you can cut it **down**.'"

Galileans = gal-ih-LEE-uhn
A narrative reading that concludes with a vivid parable, giving the whole a didactic quality.

"By no means!" The phrase is connected to sin in Jesus' teaching. He will repeat the phrase below but with a different tone.

Siloam = sih-LOH-uhm
Slight pause between "Siloam" and "fell."

Repetition of "By no means!" This time the phrase means almost the opposite of what it meant the first time Jesus used it.

The person's question is a practical one. Give it a straightforward proclamation.

The gardener's response is even more practical. Give it that weight when you proclaim it.

some Galileans who had been humiliated in death by Pontius Pilate, who mixed their blood with the blood of sacrifices to pagan deities. We have no additional evidence that this event took place, but traditional thinking at the time was that bad things happened to bad people. Therefore, if these Galileans suffered such a terrible ending, they must have been terribly bad. But the Lukan Jesus dispels that view by saying, "By no means!" At the same time, he uses this as a warning to those who do not repent, and he uses it again after the reference to the people who were killed when the tower in Siloam fell on them. This is another story that is unique to Luke.

Following these warnings about repenting before it is too late, the Lukan Jesus delivers a parable about a fig tree in a vineyard. Matthew and Mark have parables about a fig tree that Jesus curses because it has no fruit, just as the Temple is judged to be no longer fruitful (Matthew 21:19; Luke 11:13). This parable is different. Jesus describes a vineyard owner who has been patiently waiting for three years for fruit from his fig tree. The reasonable thing would be to remove it, so that something more productive can be planted in its place. Instead, the owner is convinced to let the person tending the tree give it some extra attention in the hope that it will bear fruit next season. The message of the parable: God is a God of second chances for those who are willing to repent. C.C.

THIRD SUNDAY OF LENT, YEAR A

LECTIONARY #28

READING I   Exodus 17:3–7

Exodus = EK-suh-duhs

A narrative reading which is essentially a dialogue involving the Israelites, Moses, and the Lord. It is inherently dramatic; you need mainly emphasize when the different speakers begin to speak.

Moses is exasperated here.

The words of the Lord are meant to placate Moses' exasperation. But they are also instructions. Read them in this spirit.

Horeb = HOHR-eb

Massah = MAS-uh
Meribah = MAYR-ih-bah

The passage concludes with a naming of the place where this happened, but in the form of a question. The question does not shed the most generous light on the Israelites. Be sure to give emphasis to the word "not."

A reading from the Book of Exodus

In **those** days, in their **thirst** for **water**,
    the people **grumbled** against **Moses**,
    saying, "**Why** did you ever make us leave **Egypt**?
Was it just to have us **die** here of thirst
    with our **children** and our **livestock**?"
So **Moses** cried out to the LORD,
    "What shall I **do** with this **people**?
A little more and they will **stone** me!"
The LORD answered Moses,
    "Go over **there** in front of the **people**,
    along with some of the **elders of Israel**,
    holding in your **hand**, as you go,
    the **staff** with which you **struck** the river.
I will be **standing** there in front of you on the **rock** in Horeb.
Strike the **rock**, and the **water** will flow **from** it
    for the **people** to **drink**."
This Moses did, in the presence of the elders of Israel.
The place was called **Massah** and **Meribah**,
    because the **Israelites** quarreled there
    and **tested** the LORD, saying,
    "Is the **LORD** in our **midst** or **not**?"

There are options for today's readings. Contact your parish staff to learn which readings will be used.

READING I   Water plays an important role in the Exodus story. One can rightly surmise that water symbolizes freedom for the Israelites in the context of their liberation from Egyptian captivity and in their developing relationship with God throughout the desert. Recall the birth of Moses and his release from Pharaoh's clutches, as his mother hides him in a papyrus basket and sets him afloat down the Nile River (Exodus 2:1–10). The water of the Nile comes into play again when the adult Moses confronts Pharaoh with the Ten Plagues, the first being the turning of the water into blood (Exodus 7:14–25). Certainly, the most dramatic mention of water in Exodus takes place when Moses parts the Red Sea, allowing the Israelites to pass through to safety and escape the pursuit of the Egyptians one last time (Exodus 14:15–31). Surely, as Moses progressed in his understanding of God's choosing him as the shepherd of the Israelites with the job of molding them into God's Chosen People, he had to be struck by the powerful role water would play in their prolonged pilgrim journey.

In today's reading from Exodus, the Israelites have moved beyond the marshy region of the Red Sea into the arid desert of sin. In the previous chapter, chapter 16, which takes place two weeks after they had departed from Egypt, the Israelites began to grumble against Moses and Aaron when they started to run out of food and became hungry. How very quickly they abandoned a sense of awe and gratitude for God's might in releasing them from bondage. Instead,

For meditation and context:

RESPONSORIAL PSALM   Psalm 95:1–2, 6–7, 8–9 (8)

R. If today you hear his voice, harden not your hearts.

Come, let us sing joyfully to the LORD;
   let us acclaim the Rock of our salvation.
Let us come into his presence with
      thanksgiving;
   let us joyfully sing psalms to him.

Come, let us bow down in worship;
   let us kneel before the LORD who made us.
For he is our God,
   and we are the people he shepherds, the
      flock he guides.

Oh, that today you would hear his voice:
   "Harden not your hearts as at Meribah,
      as in the day of Massah in the desert,
where your fathers tempted me;
   they tested me though they had seen
      my works."

TO KEEP IN MIND

On the Third, Fourth and Fifth Sundays of Lent, the readings from Year A are used when the Scrutinies—prayers for purification and strength—are celebrated with the elect, those who will be baptized at the Easter Vigil.

READING II   Romans 5:1–2, 5–8

A reading from the Letter of Saint Paul to the Romans

Brothers and sisters:
Since we have been **justified** by faith,
   we have **peace** with God through our **Lord** Jesus Christ,
   through whom we have gained **access** by faith
   to this **grace** in which we **stand**,
   and we **boast** in hope of the **glory** of God.

And **hope** does **not** disappoint,
   because the **love** of God has been **poured out** into our hearts
   through the **Holy Spirit** who has been **given** to us.
For **Christ**, while we were still **helpless**,
   died at the appointed time for the **ungodly**.
Indeed, only with **difficulty** does one **die** for a just **person**,
   though perhaps for a **good person** one might even find **courage**
      to die.
But **God proves** his **love** for us
   in that while we were **still sinners** Christ **died** for us.

An exhortatory reading in which Paul provides a clear sense of how faith progresses from the proof of God's love evident in Christ's death. As is often true in Paul's letters, he gets right to the point. You should allow yourself to read this passage in the same spirit.

The tone shifts slightly here, especially at "disappoint." Despite the difficulty of what Christ accomplished, his success means victory, giving us hope.

The words in this line should have almost equal emphasis, especially "proves," "love," and "us."

---

they complained profusely: "If only we had died at the Lord's hand in the land of Egypt, as we sat by our kettles of meat and ate our fill of bread!" (Exodus 16:3). God responds by providing manna for them to eat.

   In today's passage, the Israelites are raising their complaint to Moses yet again. Thirst has consumed them, and they cry out in desperation. In what appears to be exasperation, Moses cries out to God for help: "What shall I do with this people?" (Exodus 17:4). The Lord displays no hint of losing heart with the Israelites; instead he patiently explains to Moses what he can do

to alleviate their thirst. Just as he did at the Red Sea, Moses is to use his staff to strike a rock from which water will flow to quench the people's thirst.

   Today's reading contains a theme that runs throughout the Book of Exodus. Even though God proves himself faithful in providing for the needs of his people, their fidelity is weak; they are easily distracted from God's providence. However, this ultimately provides the means for God to display his greatest show of might, bestowing the gift of mercy in abundance (Exodus 34:6–7). God's mercy may be likened to a stream of flowing

water that never runs dry and always makes possible the flourishing of new life.

READING II Paul beautifully states that "the love of God has been poured out into our hearts." This is grace. Grace may be defined simply as presence. Thus, God's presence resides in our hearts through the working of the Holy Spirit. Paul's way of describing grace here suggests that it is given by God in abundance and is not earned or merited.

   Scripture is full of stories of people throughout the ages turning away from this

Samaria = suh-MAYR-ee-uh
Sychar = SĪ-kahr

A lengthy reading with a rich narrative progression. The focus of this reading is on the transformation of the Samaritan woman, who presents herself to Jesus as a skeptic but becomes a true believer by the end of the reading. Her conversion is presented in slight contrast to the work of Jesus' disciples, who themselves are skeptical of the Samaritan woman, mostly out of prejudice. Allow the rich social and spiritual realities of this passage to resonate in your proclamation.

At this point the dialogue between Jesus and the Samaritan woman begins. Distinguish between their words by slightly adjusting the pitch of your voice for each speaker.
Samaritan = suh-MAYR-uh-tuhn

The rhythm of this line is emphatic. Notice the stresses.

cistern = SIS-tern

These words of Jesus are the core of his exchange with the Samaritan woman.

GOSPEL   John 4:5–42

A reading from the holy Gospel according to John

[Jesus came to a town of **Samaria** called Sychar,
    near the **plot** of land that **Jacob** had given to his son **Joseph**.
Jacob's well was **there**.
Jesus, tired from his **journey**, sat down there at the **well**.
It was about **noon**.

A woman of **Samaria** came to draw **water**.
Jesus said to her,
    "**Give me** a **drink**."
His disciples had gone into the **town** to buy **food**.
The Samaritan woman **said** to him,
    "How can **you**, a **Jew**, ask **me**, a **Samaritan woman**, for a **drink**?"
—For Jews use **nothing** in common with **Samaritans**.—
Jesus answered and said to her,
    "If you **knew** the gift of **God**
    and who is **saying** to you, 'Give me a **drink**,'
    you would have **asked** him
    and he would have **given** you living **water**."
The woman **said** to him,
    "**Sir**, you do not even have a **bucket** and the cistern is **deep**;
    where then can you **get** this **living** water?
Are you **greater** than our father **Jacob**,
    who **gave** us this cistern and **drank** from it **himself**
    with his **children** and his **flocks**?"
Jesus answered and said to her,
    "Everyone who **drinks** this water will be **thirsty** again;
    but whoever drinks the water **I** shall give will **never** thirst;
    the water **I** shall give will **become** in him
    a spring of water **welling up** to eternal life."
The woman **said** to him,
    "Sir, **give** me this **water**, so that I may **not** be thirsty
    or have to keep **coming** here to draw **water**."]

gift. God approaches people with love and mercy, and still there are those who reject God's grace. Paul reminds his hearers that we were once like this: "we were still helpless." Those who choose to dwell apart from God are indeed "helpless," but the gift of Christ's sacrifice for all sinners overturns this situation. Christ's death continues to manifest God pouring himself out for the reconciliation and peace of all the world.

Such a free gift of justification cannot be chosen or enacted by anyone; this act must come from God alone. Thus, Paul suggests that our only means of boasting, or of claiming anything on our own, is to "hope

in the glory of God." Our realization of the overflowing of grace into our world is through hope: never rejecting God's abundance of love and trusting that no situation of despair will end in defeat. God's love conquers all. As Paul writes: "hope does not disappoint." Hope is thus the true hallmark of Christian faith. Like the grace of God, which flows freely and overflows like a torrent, hope continues even in the face of darkness and sin. The sacrifice of Christ has produced the outpouring of grace into the human heart; there is nothing that can contain our boasting in that hope which endures forever.

GOSPEL The fourth chapter of John's Gospel is designed around baptismal imagery. It is not just the "living water" that Jesus speaks of that makes this chapter baptismal in nature; it is also the encounter between Jesus and the Samaritan woman in general: his invitation to her personally to come to faith and the call to deepen that faith in worship make this a grace-filled moment of initiation into God's kingdom. While it is not Jesus' intention to baptize the Samaritan woman, the actions of this encounter are undeniably immersion into a faithful following of his mission.

Jesus said to her,
  "Go **call** your husband and come **back**."
The woman answered and said to him,
  "I do not **have** a husband."
Jesus answered her,
  "You are **right** in saying, 'I **do not** have a **husband**.'
For you have had **five** husbands,
  and the one you have **now** is **not** your husband.
What you have **said** is **true**."
The woman said to him,
  ["**Sir**, I can see that you are a **prophet**.
Our **ancestors worshiped** on this mountain;
  but you people say that the place to worship is in **Jerusalem**."
Jesus said to her,
  "**Believe** me, woman, the **hour** is coming
  when you will **worship** the Father
  neither on this **mountain** nor in **Jerusalem**.
You people **worship** what you do not **understand**;
  we worship **what** we understand,
  because **salvation** is from the **Jews**.
But the hour is coming, and is **now** here,
  when **true worshipers** will worship the Father in **Spirit**
    and **truth**;
  and indeed the Father **seeks** such people to **worship** him.
God is **Spirit**, and those who **worship** him
  must **worship** in Spirit and **truth**."
The woman said to him,
  "I **know** that the Messiah is **coming**, the one called the **Christ**;
  when he **comes**, he will tell us **everything**."
Jesus said to her,
  "I am **he**, the the one (who is) **speaking** with you."]

At that moment his **disciples** returned,
  and were **amazed** that he was talking with a **woman**,
  but still no one said, "What are you looking for?"
  or "Why are you talking with her?" »

With these words, the Samaritan woman's skepticism shifts into belief.

And here, Jesus reveals himself as the Messiah. Emphasize "he" and "speaking" to express the revelation.
The return of the disciples reinforces the "problem" of Jesus interacting with a Samaritan woman (something Jewish custom ordinarily forbad); it also marks a slight excursion, because the disciples want Jesus to eat while he has a lesson he wants to convey to them.

It is important to recognize where and when this conversation takes place. First, Samaria is located between Galilee and Judea. The Samaritans were considered unorthodox by the Jews, strangers to the law, and thus unclean. It was unwarranted for Jews to interact with Samaritans. Second, the exchange takes at a well, one that is believed to have been the property of Jacob's family. Wells were considered sacred places where the divine was known to break into the human domain. Finally, the encounter takes place in the noonday sun. Women usually drew water in the early morning, before the heat of the day; John the Evangelist seems to suggest that this woman is unafraid of exposing herself to the heat as well as to the light of the truth.

When Jesus encounters the woman, he is alone; his disciples have gone into town to buy supplies. Jesus breaks the silence by instructing the woman, "Give me a drink." When she questions his command, due to gender differences and religious law, he offers that he has "living water" to give, not ordinary water from a cistern. It is clear that the woman wants this water but does not know where to find it. From John's bap- tismal perspective, the discovery of this "living water," this source of life, comes when one keeps company with Jesus. When he says, "The water I shall give will become in him a spring of water welling up to eternal life," Jesus speaks on a spiritual plane. The woman gradually comprehends. The woman displays a sense of urgency as she demands this "living water" from Jesus in order to be thirsty no more. However, faith in Jesus is not a gift imparted all at once; it is a process that takes time as deeper insight is provided.

The woman left her **water** jar
   and went into the **town** and said to the **people**,
     "Come see a **man** who told me **everything** I have **done**.
Could he possibly **be** the **Christ**?"
They went out of the town and **came** to him.
Meanwhile, the disciples urged him, "**Rabbi**, **eat**."
But he said to them,
   "I have **food** to eat of which you do not **know**."
So the disciples said to one another,
   "Could **someone** have brought him something to **eat**?"
Jesus said to them,
   "My **food** is to do the **will** of the one who **sent** me
   and to **finish** his **work**.
Do you not say, 'In **four** months the **harvest** will **be** here'?
I tell you, look **up** and see the fields **ripe** for the **harvest**.
The **reaper** is already **receiving** payment
   and **gathering crops** for eternal **life**,
   so that the **sower** and **reaper** can rejoice **together**.
For **here** the saying is **verified** that 'One **sows** and another **reaps**.'
I sent you to **reap** what you have not **worked** for;
   others have done the **work**,
   and you are **sharing** the fruits of **their** work."

The conclusion returns us to the Samaritan woman; not only does she believe in Jesus, she is able to convert the other Samaritans because of her conviction. The words of the assembled Samaritans are spoken directly to the congregation's own faith.

[Many of the **Samaritans** of that town began to **believe** in him]
   because of the **word** of the woman who **testified**,
     "He told me **everything** I have **done**."
[When the **Samaritans** came to him,
   they invited him to **stay** with them;
   and he stayed there two **days**.
Many more began to **believe** in him because of his **word**,
   and they **said** to the woman,
     "We no longer **believe** because of your **word**;
     for we have **heard** for **ourselves**,
     and we know that this is **truly** the savior of the **world**."]

[Shorter: John 4:5–15, 19b–26, 39a, 40–42 (see brackets)]

When Jesus reveals his knowledge of the woman's marital situation, she takes the opportunity to profess a faith statement of sorts. She first proclaims Jesus to be a prophet and next witnesses to her belief in the coming of the Messiah, who "will tell us everything," a trait that Jesus has just demonstrated. He is indeed the Messiah. Although the woman is not given the chance to affirm her belief in Jesus as Lord, since the disciples interrupt the intimate conversation, it should be evident to us that the woman has indeed been "baptized" in "living water." She has come to faith and is now able to be

an evangelist herself: "Come see a man who told me everything I have done."

The Gospel passage ends with an eschatological tone—a look toward the fulfillment of the kingdom. When Jesus' disciples encourage him to eat, Jesus implies that he is filled with a different kind of food, the satisfaction of gathering people into the kingdom. He sees the world as ripe for the reaping of "crops for eternal life." Just as he has made a disciple out of the woman at the well, Jesus sees that there is much work in sowing the seeds of faith and in reaping a harvest of believers. This is an

ingathering that extends far beyond the land of Jerusalem and includes the most unlikely of outsiders. John leaves no doubt that the "living water" that one finds in Jesus produces new life in abundance in this world and the hope of eternal life in the world to come. S. W.

FOURTH SUNDAY OF LENT

LECTIONARY #33

READING I   Joshua 5:9a, 10–12

A reading from the Book of Joshua

The LORD said to Joshua,
   "**Today** I have **removed** the **reproach** of **Egypt** from you."

While the **Israelites** were encamped at **Gilgal**
      on the plains of **Jericho**,
   they celebrated the **Passover**
   on the **evening** of the **fourteenth** of the **month**.
On the **day** after the **Passover**,
   they **ate** of the **produce** of the **land**
   in the **form** of unleavened **cakes** and parched **grain**.
On that **same day** after the **Passover**,
   on which they **ate** of the **produce** of the **land**,
      the **manna ceased**.
No **longer** was there **manna** for the **Israelites**,
   who that **year** ate of the **yield** of the land of **Canaan**.

RESPONSORIAL PSALM   Psalm 34:2–3, 4–5, 6–7 (9a)

R. Taste and see the goodness of the Lord.

I will bless the LORD at all times;
   his praise shall be ever in my mouth.
Let my soul glory in the LORD;
   the lowly will hear me and be glad.

Glorify the LORD with me,
   let us together extol his name.
I sought the LORD, and he answered me
   and delivered me from all my fears.

Look to him that you may be radiant
   with joy,
   and your faces may not blush with shame.
When the poor one called out, the
   LORD heard,
   and from all his distress he saved him.

Joshua = JOSH-oo-uh *or* JOSH-yoo-uh

A narrative reading about the Israelites coming to the end of the necessity of being fed manna by God.

reproach = rih-PROHCH

Gilgal = GIL-gahl

"On the day" signifies they've come to a new day. Give your proclamation a sense of this change by slowing very slightly down.

"On that same day": draw this repetition out very slightly.

Slight pause between "manna" and "ceased."

Canaan = KAY-n*n

For meditation and context:

There are options for today's readings. Contact your parish staff to learn which readings will be used.

READING I The central theme of the readings for this Fourth Sunday of Lent is an invitation to celebrate the transition to a new state in life or a renewed relationship with God. Therefore, it is fitting that, among Christians of the West, this Sunday was traditionally known as Laetare Sunday, which got its name from the first line of its entrance antiphon, taken from Isaiah 66:10, "Rejoice, O Jerusalem."

The first reading, from the book of Joshua, recalls the story of the arrival of Joshua and the Israelites to the Promised Land. In the preceding chapters, we learned how God's people passed through the Jordan River as the water was held back by the priests who carried the Ark of the Covenant in front of them. We also learned of the rituals that were celebrated at Gilgal and the circumcisions that were performed at Gibeath-haaraloth, because none of those born during the Exodus journey had been circumcised. Circumcision is a sign of the covenant that God made with Abraham and his descendants, so it was fitting that the ritual would be performed before they celebrated their first Passover in the Promised Land.

But notice how the Lord associates circumcision with the removal of the "reproach" (Hebrew *cherpah*, meaning "condition of shame or disgrace") of Egypt, presumably referring to the many times that the Israelites failed to trust in God's protection and benevolence during their desert journey. In essence, with this ritual, God reconsecrates the people of Israel. This is a new time for God's people. The manna that

Corinthians = kohr-IN-thee-uhnz

A didactic reading in which the focus is on reconciliation.

Note parallels between old and new things.

All the variations of "reconcile" provide the focus for this passage. Proclaim directly and clearly.

Slight pause between "trespasses" and "against."

Final repetition of "reconciled."

READING II   2 Corinthians 5:17–21

A reading from the second Letter of Saint Paul to the Corinthians

Brothers and **sisters**:
Whoever is in **Christ** is a new **creation**:
    the **old things** have passed **away**;
    behold, **new things** have **come**.
And all **this** is from **God**,
    who has **reconciled** us to **himself** through **Christ**
    and given us the **ministry** of **reconciliation**,
    namely, **God** was **reconciling** the **world** to **himself** in **Christ**,
    not **counting** their **trespasses against** them
    and **entrusting** to us the **message** of **reconciliation**.
So we are **ambassadors** for **Christ**,
    as if **God** were appealing **through** us.
We **implore** you on behalf of **Christ**,
    be **reconciled** to God.
For **our sake** he made him to be **sin** who did not **know** sin,
    so that we might become the **righteousness** of **God** in **him**.

A narrative reading with a strong didactic message: the parable of the Prodigal Son, as cinematic as a great film.

Immediately, in the context of the Pharisee's complaints, Jesus begins his parable.

GOSPEL   Luke 15:1–3, 11–32

A reading from the holy Gospel according to Luke

Tax collectors and **sinners** were all drawing **near**
        to listen to **Jesus**,
    but the **Pharisees** and **scribes** began to complain, saying,
    "**This man** welcomes **sinners** and **eats** with them."
So to **them** Jesus addressed this **parable**:
"**A man** had two sons, and the **younger son** said to his father,
    '**Father** give me the **share** of your estate that should come
        to **me**.'
So the father **divided** the property **between** them.

they needed to survive in the wilderness had ceased, because now they could eat the Passover from the produce of their own land. The phrase "that year," which appears at the end of today's reading, refers to the fortieth year since the Exodus from Egypt. The number forty is a symbol of transition from one state to another; in this case, from slavery to freedom.

READING II   This reading from Paul's Second Letter to the Corinthians is also focused on reconciliation and recognition of a new status for God's people.

It is part of a section that began at 2:14, which addresses what it means to be an authentic apostle of Christ. The images he employs are striking. He calls himself and those with him the "aroma of Christ" (2 Corinthians 2:15) and suggests that they are ministers of the Spirit (2 Corinthians 3:8), capable of "gazing with unveiled face on the glory of the Lord" and "being transformed into the same image from glory to glory" (2 Corinthians 3:18). Paul is careful to say that this is not a ministry that he and his companions can claim for themselves.

Rather, it is a ministry impelled by the love of Christ (2 Corinthians 5:14).

This lectionary reading begins with the phrase "whoever is in Christ," meaning anyone who belongs to the Christian community, because, for Paul, the Church is the body of Christ. This community, he says, is a new creation (Greek *ktisis*, meaning "a thing created or generated") because of Christ's saving action as God's agent to bring about the reconciliation of humanity to God (see also 1 Corinthians 15:22 and Romans 5:12–21). As a consequence, everyone who is in Christ has died to their old

dissipation = dihs-ih-PAY-shuhn
Slight emphasis on "dissipation."

After a **few days**, the younger son collected **all** his belongings
and set **off** to a distant **country**
where he **squandered** his inheritance on a **life** of **dissipation**.
When he had **freely spent** everything,
a severe **famine** struck that country,
and he found himself in **dire need**.
So he **hired** himself **out** to one of the local **citizens**
who sent him to his **farm** to tend the **swine**.

Emphasis on "swine fed."

And he **longed** to eat his **fill** of the **pods** on which the **swine fed**,
but **nobody** gave him **any**.
Coming to his **senses** he thought,
'**How** many of my **father's** hired **workers**
have **more** than enough **food** to eat,
but **here** am I, **dying** from **hunger**.
I shall get **up** and go to my **father** and I shall **say** to him,

Speech within a speech; make sure it's clear to your assembly.

"**Father**, I have **sinned** against **heaven** and against **you**.
I no longer **deserve** to be called your **son**;
treat me as you would treat one of your hired **workers**." '
So he got **up** and went **back** to his **father**.
While he was still a **long way off**,
his **father** caught **sight** of him, and was **filled** with **compassion**.
He ran to his **son**, **embraced** him and **kissed** him.
His son **said** to him,

Direct repetition of the speech above.

'**Father**, I have **sinned** against **heaven** and against **you**;
I no longer **deserve** to be called your **son**.'
But his **father** ordered his **servants**,
'**Quickly** bring the **finest robe** and put it **on** him;
put a **ring** on his **finger** and **sandals** on his **feet**.

It's appropriate to add a little excitement and tenderness to your proclamation in the words of the father.

Take the fattened **calf** and **slaughter** it.
Then let us **celebrate** with a **feast**,

Note the rhythm: "COME to LIFE aGAIN."

because this **son** of **mine** was **dead**, and has **come** to **life again**;
he was **lost**, and has been **found**.'

Slight pause between "celebration" and "began."

Then the **celebration began**. »

way of life and now is called to imitate Christ's total self-giving love toward humanity. Moreover, Paul sees his ministry as an imitation of Christ's suffering so that others can experience new life in Christ, but again he insists that this reconciliation or restoration to favor comes entirely from God. He and his colleagues are merely ambassadors or emissaries of Christ in the sense that they carry on his mission by "carrying about in the body the dying of Jesus, so that the life of Jesus may also be manifested" in their bodies (2 Corinthians 4:10). As ministers of

reconciliation today, are we willing to do the same?

GOSPEL Today's Gospel reading recounts one of three Lukan parables about God's desire to be reconciled to humanity and the lengths to which God is willing to go to make that happen. The first parable compares God to a shepherd who lost a single sheep, leaves the others to find that one sheep, and, upon finding it, returns home to host a big celebration over his found sheep (Luke 15:4–7). The second

compares God to a woman who cleans her house from top to bottom looking for a lost coin. When she finds it, she throws a big party in celebration of having found the coin, approximately the equivalent of a day laborer's pay.

The third parable, the one that is the subject of today's Gospel, is traditionally known as the Prodigal Son story, but, in light of these other two parables, it should be known as the Prodigal Father story. The word "prodigal" means "spendthrift" or "wastefully extravagant," and that is what

The perspective shifts to the older son. Allow for a slight change to a more sober tone.

Slight pause between "back" and "safe."

The son's tone can express justified exasperation.

Repetition of the rhythm above: "COME to LIFE aGAIN."

Now the **older** son had been **out** in the **field**
   and, on his way **back**, as he neared the **house**,
   he heard the sound of **music** and **dancing**.
He **called** one of the **servants** and asked what this might mean.
The servant **said** to him,
   'Your **brother** has **returned**
   and your **father** has **slaughtered** the **fattened calf**
   because he has him **back safe** and **sound**.'
He became **angry**,
   and when he **refused** to enter the **house**,
   his **father** came out and **pleaded** with him.
He said to his **father** in **reply**,
   '**Look**, all these years I **served** you
   and not **once** did I disobey your **orders**;
   yet you **never** gave me even a young **goat**
      to **feast on** with my **friends**.
But when your **son** returns
   who swallowed up your **property** with **prostitutes**,
   for **him** you **slaughter** the fattened **calf**.'
He **said** to him,
   '**My son**, you are **here** with me **always**;
   everything I **have** is **yours**.
But **now** we must **celebrate** and **rejoice**,
   because your **brother** was **dead** and has **come** to **life again**;
   he was **lost** and has been **found**.' "

the father is. The younger son of this man asks for his inheritance, which, in the honor-shame culture of the first-century Mediterranean world, is tantamount to saying, "You're dead to me!" A self-respecting father of this time would have said to this impertinent young man, "I disown you; get out of my sight!" but this father did what was asked of him. After the son had squandered his inheritance, he came to his senses when he was reduced to a most demeaning job, feeding swine, even as he was starving. He decided that he had no

other recourse but to return to his father's house and ask forgiveness, but already his father was watching and waiting for his return. Any of his neighbors who saw this father running to meet his son would have thought, "How disgusting! This father is running and hugging and kissing this son who wished him dead. Has he no shame?"

And what about the older son? He is angry over his father's actions on behalf of the errant son, so much so that he will not even address him as his brother. When this other son refuses to enter the house, the

father once again makes himself vulnerable to shame by going outside to talk to the outraged son and trying to encourage him to join the party. Unfortunately, Luke leaves us wondering what this older son will do, but his main point is clear. God is like the father who is willing to extravagantly and recklessly spend everything, even his greatest asset, his honor, to reconcile with his children, who treated him so badly. C.C.

FOURTH SUNDAY OF LENT, YEAR A

LECTIONARY #31

Samuel = SAM-yoo-uhl
Jesse = JES-ee
Eliab = ee-LĪ-uhb

A narrative reading with a dramatic conclusion, in which Samuel, chosen by the Lord and endowed with power, is sent among the sons of Jesse to find and anoint a new king. Samuel's power is the ability to recognize this king, whose appearance, when Samuel sees him at last, thrills him. The words themselves convey the drama of this reading compellingly.

Emphasize the parallel: not as man sees does God see.

Samuel cannot see the chosen king among the sons. Subtle emphasis on "one."

TO KEEP IN MIND
On the Third, Fourth and Fifth Sundays of Lent, the readings from Year A are used when the Scrutinies—prayers for purification and strength—are celebrated with the elect, those who will be baptized at the Easter Vigil.

READING I   1 Samuel 16:1b, 6–7, 10–13a

A reading from the first Book of Samuel

The Lord said to **Samuel**:
  "Fill your **horn** with **oil**, and **be** on your **way**.
I am **sending** you to **Jesse** of **Bethlehem**,
  for I have **chosen** my king from among his **sons**."

As Jesse and his sons **came** to the **sacrifice**,
  Samuel looked at **Eliab** and thought,
  "**Surely** the Lord's anointed is **here before** him."
But the Lord said to Samuel:
  "**Do not judge** from his **appearance** or from his **lofty** stature,
  because I have **rejected** him.
Not as **man sees** does **God see**,
  because **man** sees the **appearance**
  but the Lord looks into the **heart**."
In the same way **Jesse** presented seven **sons** before **Samuel**,
  but **Samuel** said to **Jesse**,
  "The Lord has not chosen any **one** of these."
Then Samuel asked Jesse,
  "Are **these** all the **sons** you **have**?"
Jesse replied,
  "There is still the **youngest**, who is **tending** the **sheep**." »

There are options for today's readings. Contact your parish staff to learn which readings will be used.

READING I As so often happens throughout Old Testament, the story of David's anointing by Samuel as King of Israel is a story of divine reversal, whereby God selects the most unlikely candidate as his chosen servant. The key to this reading is the reminder that God gives the job to Samuel after rejecting the most likely candidate, Eliab, the eldest son of Jesse who makes a great appearance due to his "lofty stature." God suggests to Samuel that his requirements for a king do not follow the apparent wisdom of human thinking: "Not as man sees does God see, because man sees the appearance but the Lord looks into the heart." How true this message is! How easily people make mistakes by judging on appearances and failing to probe what lies beneath the surface.

The commissioning of Samuel to seek out, call forward, and anoint a new king for Israel takes place shortly after God rejects the kingship of Saul (1 Samuel 15:35). The reason for God removing Saul as king is very important for the future history of Israel. If Israel was to be guided by a king other than God, then it was expected that this king would approximate divinity. While Saul was indeed a successful leader according to human judgment, he failed to make proper sacrifice to God. Instead of choosing offerings that were the choicest fruits and the best of the herd, Saul settled for a less than desirable sacrifice (1 Samuel 15:9). This represented a misuse of authority on Saul's part; he failed to give God what was his due.

ruddy = RUHD-ee =
having a reddish complexion

Samuel can see the chosen king at last.
Equal emphases on "There," "anoint," "this,"
and "one."

Samuel said to Jesse,
"**Send** for him;
we will not **begin** the sacrificial **banquet** until he **arrives** here."
Jesse **sent** and had the young man **brought** to them.
He was **ruddy**, a youth **handsome** to behold
and making a **splendid** appearance.
The LORD said,
"**There**—anoint **him**, for **this** is the **one**!"
Then **Samuel**, with the **horn** of oil in hand,
anointed **David** in the presence of his **brothers**;
and from that day on, the **spirit** of the LORD **rushed**
upon David.

For meditation and context:

RESPONSORIAL PSALM   Psalm 23:1–3a, 3b–4, 5, 6 (1)

R. The Lord is my shepherd; there is nothing I shall want.

The LORD is my shepherd; I shall not want.
In verdant pastures he gives me repose;
beside restful waters he leads me;
he refreshes my soul.

He guides me in right paths
for his name's sake.
Even though I walk in the dark valley
I fear no evil; for you are at my side
with your rod and your staff
that give me courage.

You spread the table before me
in the sight of my foes;
you anoint my head with oil;
my cup overflows.

Only goodness and kindness follow me
all the days of my life;
and I shall dwell in the house of the LORD
for years to come.

READING II   Ephesians 5:8–14

Ephesians = ee-FEE-zhuhnz

An exhortatory reading in which Paul tries
to convince the Ephesians to live as children
of the light. The concluding exhortation,
after "Therefore," (next page) is the
culmination of this reading.

A reading from the Letter of Saint Paul to the Ephesians

Brothers and sisters:
You were **once darkness**,
but now you are **light** in the **Lord**.
Live as **children** of **light**,
for **light** produces every kind of **goodness**
and **righteousness** and **truth**.

While God chooses to put an end to Saul's line of kingship in Israel, he has no intention of ending the monarchy itself. He turns to the family of Jesse, from which the nation will renew itself. Making such a radical shift in leadership (a new family and the youngest of the family) may appear to be a risky move on God's part. However, once again, in keeping with God's pattern of selecting the lowly in order to overturn the authority of the mighty, the selection of David coincides perfectly with the mysterious ways of God. We need only to ponder the many ways in which David's character

will grow and mature from his roots as a lowly shepherd. Not only will he prove his strength by destroying the mighty Goliath (1 Samuel 17:40–51), but he will provide proper worship for God, especially by delighting him with the many songs we know as psalms (see 1 Samuel 22:1–51). David's strength will be found not only in military might but in his deference to divine authority as displayed in proper worship.

Although David is not officially anointed in a public ceremony until later (2 Samuel 5:1–5), today's reading witnesses to the prophet's anointing of the young David,

upon whom "the spirit of the Lord rushed" and remained for all time. In the Christian process of initiation, anointing with oil is understood to communicate the indwelling of the Holy Spirit. Oil not only serves to heal the body, but it is also used to highlight strength. Such was the purpose for its use in setting apart a king who was to be commissioned with authority as the people's leader. In a Christian initiatory context, oil is used in the sacrament of baptism to indelibly mark the neophyte in the image Christ. In confirmation, oil is used once again to not only visibly manifest a chosen

Try to **learn** what is **pleasing** to the **Lord**.
Take no **part** in the fruitless works of **darkness**;
   rather **expose** them, for it is **shameful** even to **mention**
   the things done by them in **secret**;
   but **everything** exposed by the light becomes **visible**,
   for **everything** that becomes visible is **light**.
Therefore, it says:
   "**Awake**, O sleeper,
   and **arise** from the **dead**,
   and **Christ** will give you **light**."

GOSPEL   John 9:1–41

A reading from the holy Gospel according to John

[As Jesus passed by he saw a man **blind** from **birth**.]
His disciples asked him,
   "**Rabbi**, who **sinned**, this **man** or his **parents**,
   that he was **born blind**?"
Jesus answered,
   "Neither **he** nor his **parents** sinned;
   it is so that the **works** of God might be made **visible**
      through him.
We have to do the **works** of the one who sent me while it is **day**.
Night is coming when **no one** can **work**.
While I am in the **world**, I am the **light** of the **world**."
When he had **said** this, [he **spat** on the ground
   and made **clay** with the **saliva**,
   and **smeared** the clay on his **eyes**, and said to him,
   "**Go wash** in the **Pool** of **Siloam**"—which means **Sent**—.
So he **went** and **washed**, and came back **able** to see.

His neighbors and those who had seen him **earlier**
   as a **beggar** said,
   "Isn't this the one who used to **sit** and **beg**?" »

Take note of the parallels and shifts in these lines: from "everything" to "visible," and then "everything" to "light."

"Awake," "arise," and "light" are the focal points of these final lines. Don't rush through them.

Rabbi = RAB-ī

This is a complex narrative reading with many characters, each with different motivations, as well as several scene changes. In this reading, Jesus upturns traditional rabbinic understanding of blindness as a punishment for immorality. It also relies on a defiant tone to make its point. Keep this in mind as you proclaim.

This line has an anticipatory, prophetic quality, characteristic of John's Gospel.

These details of Jesus' healing powers are interesting; don't rush through them.

Siloam = sih-LOH-uhm

---

status but to suggest through the sense of smell that the Holy Spirit has "rushed upon" the candidate with wisdom and strength. In the sacrament of holy orders, the candidate's hands are anointed with chrism to signal Christ's connection to the hands of the one who will stand at the altar to make an offering on the people's behalf. Thus, oil serves to make visible God's choice of men and women whose election was made not according to appearances but by his having looked into the heart.

READING II A characteristic motif of Paul's writings, as well as of the social world in which Paul lived, is the contrast between honor and shame. To shame a person was to exercise control over that individual, while to honor another was to express one's allegiance. Honor and shame functioned particularly well in the context of the family; parents readily taught their children of the importance of bringing honor to the household and avoiding shame. Thus, Paul will warn the Christian household in Rome: "Let us live honorably as in the daylight: no drunken orgies, no promiscuity or licentiousness, and no wrangling or jealousy" (Romans 13:13).

Here, in his letter to the Ephesians, Paul makes the contrast between living in darkness and living as "children of light." While the former brings shame, the latter is a way of life that has tremendous positive consequences for the honor of the entire Christian community at Ephesus. Paul says that living together as light in the Lord exhibits at least three characteristics: goodness, righteousness, and truth. For the author, these not only continue to bring honor to those baptized into Christ, but

Any expression of "I am" in John's Gospel is freighted with authority.

The (formerly) blind man's tone here is somewhat exasperated.

Once again, the man who had been blind has to explain his story, this time to the Pharisees. His exasperation mounts to defiance when he proclaims Jesus a prophet.

Some said, "It **is**,"
  but others said, "**No**, he just **looks** like him."
He said, "I **am**."]
So they said to him, "How were your eyes opened?"
He replied,
  "The man called **Jesus** made **clay** and anointed my **eyes**
    and told me, 'Go to **Siloam** and **wash**.'
So I **went** there and washed and was able to **see**."
And they said to him, "Where is he?"
He said, "I don't **know**."

[They brought the one who was once blind to the **Pharisees**.
Now Jesus had made **clay** and opened his **eyes** on a **sabbath**.
So then the **Pharisees** also asked him **how** he was able to **see**.
He **said** to them,
  "He put **clay** on my **eyes**, and I **washed**, and now I can **see**."
So some of the Pharisees said,
  "This man is **not** from God,
    because he **does not keep** the **sabbath**."
But others said,
  "How can a sinful man do such **signs**?"
And there was a **division** among them.
So they said to the blind man again,
  "What do you have to **say** about him,
    since he **opened** your **eyes**?"
He said, "He is a **prophet**."]

Now the Jews did not **believe**
  that he had been **blind** and gained his **sight**
    until they **summoned** the parents of the one who had **gained**
      his sight.
They asked them,
  "Is this your **son**, who you say was born **blind**?
How does he now **see**?"
His parents answered and said,
  "We **know** that this is our son and that he was born **blind**.

they also serve to unite the community as one. Where goodness, righteousness, and truth prevail, the community is able to live honorably, without attempting to hide itself from the Lord.

Thus, Paul will continue in his letter to suggest the need to expose the things of darkness to the light. Although the human tendency is to keep hidden those things that may lead to shame, the notion here is that exposure to the light will heal them. The light not only exposes what is caught up in darkness, it has the power to over-

whelm, so that "everything that becomes visible is light."

Finally, Paul equates the darkness to death and challenges those outside the realm of Christ's light to awaken and receive the gift of light. For those in the final weeks of preparing for the waters of Baptism, the call to hear Christ inviting them into the light may be particularly poignant. The celebration of the scrutiny rite today will serve to remind them that the ways that constitute living in darkness are often subtle but no less deserving of the healing that exposure to the light will provide. However, not only

the elect, but all members of the Church will certainly hear in these words from Ephesians the call to ongoing conversion. "Awake, O sleeper, and arise from the dead, and Christ will give you light."

GOSPEL Today's reading from the Gospel of John constitutes the entirety of the ninth chapter, which in the Bible immediately follows the story of the scribes and the Pharisees presenting an adulterous woman to Jesus for his judgment and his use of the occasion as an opportunity to reveal himself to be the "light of the

Because the Pharisees don't believe the man who had been blind, they question his parents. Crucially, they repeat that he is of age and can speak for himself. Their tone is defiant. They believe their son.

We do not **know** how he sees **now**,
  nor do we know who **opened** his eyes.
Ask him, he is of **age**;
  he can **speak** for **himself**."
His parents said this because they were **afraid** of the **Jews**,
  for the **Jews** had already **agreed**
    that if anyone **acknowledged** him as the **Christ**,
  he would be **expelled** from the **synagogue**.
For this **reason** his parents said,
  "He is of **age**; **question** him."

So a second time they **called the man** who had been blind
  and said to him, "**Give God** the praise!
We **know** that this man is a **sinner**."
He replied,
  "If he is a **sinner**, I do not **know**.
One thing I **do know** is that I was **blind** and now I **see**."
So they said to him,
  "What did he **do** to you?
  How did he open your **eyes**?"
He answered them,
  "I told you already and you did not **listen**.
Why do you want to hear it **again**?
Do you **want** to become his **disciples**, **too**?"
They **ridiculed** him and said,
  "**You** are that man's disciple;
  we are disciples of **Moses**!
We **know** that God **spoke** to **Moses**,
  but we do not **know** where this one is **from**."
The man answered and said to them,
  "This is what is so **amazing**,
  that you do not **know** where he is **from**,
    yet he **opened** my **eyes**.
We know that **God** does **not** listen to sinners,
  but if one is **devout** and does his **will**, he listens to **him**. »

Exasperation and defiance.

The Pharisees cannot believe his temerity. This disbelief intensifies to the point where they throw him out because he has the gall to try to teach them. Ridiculous as they are, don't ridicule the Pharisees with your tone of voice.

world" (John 7:12). In this encounter with the man blind since birth, Jesus is able to demonstrate that darkness has no place in the kingdom of God. If the light has entered the world, then blindness stands as a contradiction to the reception of God's grace.

Thus, the story begins with the age-old dilemma: is bodily illness or disease a curse that comes from sin committed either in the present or as something handed down through the generations? Jesus answers this quandary by turning the condition of the man's blindness into a positive trait—it is through his blindness that God is

able to work wonders in him for others to see. While society may want to exclude the blind man from participation in all of its dealings and relationships, Jesus suggests that the man plays a missionary role in the kingdom. He says to the man: "While I am in the world, I am the light of the world." Clearly, the presence of blindness in his midst is simply unacceptable for Jesus. It contradicts the existence of God's kingdom.

Added to this is the recognition that the blind man does not ask to be healed. Instead, Jesus initiates the healing process without a plea coming from either the man

or any other intercessor. Jesus spits on the ground, makes clay with his saliva, and applies the clay to the man's eyes. Step one of the healing process is complete. But Jesus requires something more. He desires that the man demonstrate his own cooperation, which he has the freedom to withhold. Therefore, Jesus sends the man off to wash himself. In other words, the blind man has an important role to play in his healing; he is asked to cooperate with grace.

A powerful transformation takes place in the blind man after he returns with his newfound sight. Up to this point, he has

It is **unheard** of that anyone ever opened the eyes of a person
  born **blind**.
If this man were **not** from God,
  he would **not** be able to do **anything**."
[They **answered** and said to him,
  "You were born **totally** in sin,
  and are **you** trying to teach **us**?"
Then they **threw** him out.

When Jesus heard that they had **thrown him out**,
  he found him and said, "Do you **believe** in the Son of **Man**?"
He answered and said,
  "Who **is** he, sir, that I may believe in **him**?"
Jesus said to him,
  "You have **seen** him,
  and the one **speaking** with you is **he**."
He said,
  "I **do believe**, Lord," and he **worshiped** him.]
Then Jesus said,
  "**I came** into this world for **judgment**,
  so that **those** who do not see might **see**,
  and **those** who do see might become **blind**."

Some of the Pharisees who were with him **heard** this
  and said to him, "**Surely** we are not also blind, **are** we?"
Jesus said to them,
  "**If** you were **blind**, you would have no **sin**;
  but now you are saying, 'We **see**,' so your **sin** remains."

[Shorter: John 9:1, 6–9, 13–17, 34–38 (see brackets)]

Jesus validates the belief of the man who had been blind.

The reading concludes with a crucial inversion: blindness to sight, sight to blindness. The sin tradition indicated in the blind man has been shifted to the Pharisees. When we believe something blindly, are we believing or are we blind?

said nothing, but now, he uses his words to testify to Jesus having "anointed" his eyes and giving him the gift of sight. The man who is perceived at the outset of the story to be blind because of some sin now becomes a disciple and stands as a primary witness to the power in Jesus that frustrates and frightens the religious authorities. Rather than seeing the tremendous good that Jesus is doing in overturning the people's suffering, the scribes and the Pharisees continue to reject the possibility that his is the work of God. "This man is not from God, because he does not keep the Sabbath." Soon, however, the man is able to come to deeper insight: "If this man were not from God, he would not be able to do anything." The questioning leads to exhaustion on the part of the religious establishment, who, after recognizing that the man has been teaching them, throw him out from their midst! The evangelist has painted here a situation that overturns expectations: the man born blind, who comes to see the truth, is able to express faith, while those who consider themselves to be fully knowledgeable of the workings of the law prove themselves to be blind and faithless. When the man who now sees professes his belief in Jesus—"I do believe, Lord"—Jesus is given the opportunity to once again define his mission as the light of the world: "I came into this world for judgment, so that those who do not see might see and those who do see might become blind." S.W.

FIFTH SUNDAY OF LENT

LECTIONARY #36

READING I Isaiah 43:16–21

Isaiah = ī-ZAY-uh

An exhortatory reading filled with vivid imagery and compelling language characterizing the power of God, reading as much like a poem as an exhortation.

A reading from the Book of the Prophet Isaiah

Thus says the LORD,
   who **opens** a way in the **sea**
   and a **path** in the mighty **waters**,
who leads out **chariots** and **horsemen**,
   a powerful **army**,
till they lie **prostrate** together, never to **rise**,
   snuffed **out** and **quenched** like a **wick**.
Remember **not** the events of the **past**,
   the **things** of long ago consider **not**;
see, I am doing something **new**!
   Now it springs **forth**, do you not **perceive** it?
In the **desert** I make a **way**,
   in the **wasteland**, **rivers**.
Wild beasts honor me,
   jackals and **ostriches**,
for I put **water** in the **desert**
   and **rivers** in the **wasteland**
   for my chosen **people** to **drink**,
the **people** whom I **formed** for **myself**,
   that they might **announce** my **praise**.

jackals = JAK-uhls
Slight pause between "Wild beasts" and "honor."

There are options for today's readings. Contact your parish staff to learn which readings will be used.

READING I Our first reading comes from the second major section of the book of Isaiah, which is addressed to the exiles of Judea, who were deported to Babylon in the sixth century BC. It was a very dark time in Israel's history. Jerusalem and the Temple had been destroyed, God's people were forced off the land, and the Davidic king was killed. In the midst of such despair, the prophet becomes God's voice of consolation and hope. Using the imagery of a new Exodus, the prophet tells the people that God will crush the Babylonians and snuff them out, as he put an end to the Egyptian pharaoh's armies when he drowned them in the sea (see Exodus 14:23–31). But this time, the prophet announces, God will do something so wonderful and new that they will forget the first Exodus. He will make a path through the wilderness to aid their journey and provide rivers in the desert so that God's creatures and especially God's chosen ones will have water to drink. This God is worthy of praise because he is their redeemer and because they are precious in God's eyes (see Isaiah 43:1, 4, 14).

For meditation and context:

RESPONSORIAL PSALM   Psalm 126:1–2, 2–3, 4–5, 6 (3)

R. The Lord has done great things for us; we are filled with joy.

When the LORD brought back the captives
    of Zion,
  we were like men dreaming.
Then our mouth was filled with laughter,
  and our tongue with rejoicing.

Then they said among the nations,
  "The LORD has done great things
    for them."
The LORD has done great things for us;
  we are glad indeed.

Restore our fortunes, O LORD,
  like the torrents in the southern desert.
Those that sow in tears
  shall reap rejoicing.

Although they go forth weeping,
  carrying the seed to be sown,
they shall come back rejoicing,
  carrying their sheaves.

Philippians = fih-LIP-ee-uhnz

A didactic reading that also sounds like an exhortatory defense of St. Paul himself. Paul's view here that everything is a loss is a challenging one to make. His argument builds on five parts; let his structure guide your proclamation. It opens with the statement that everything is a loss.

The second part of Paul's argument states why he accepts these losses, noting what he has gained.

Even emphasis on "but that which comes through."

READING II   Philippians 3:8–14

A reading from the Letter of Saint Paul to the Philippians

Brothers and **sisters:**
I consider **everything** as a **loss**
    because of the supreme **good** of knowing Christ **Jesus**
        my **Lord.**
For **his sake** I have **accepted** the **loss** of all **things**
    and I consider them **so much rubbish,**
    that I may gain **Christ** and be **found** in him,
    not having any **righteousness** of my own based on the **law**
    but that which comes through **faith** in **Christ,**
    the **righteousness** from **God,**
    depending on **faith** to know him and the **power**
        of his **resurrection**
    and the **sharing** of his **sufferings** by being **conformed**
        to his **death,**
    if **somehow** I may attain the **resurrection** from the **dead.**

READING II Today's second reading comes from Paul's Letter to the Philippians. The overall theme of this letter is rejoicing in our call to share in the suffering of Christ so that we might share in his resurrection. What a fitting message to ponder as we enter into this fifth week of Lent and prepare for Holy Week! Having introduced a bit of autobiography immediately preceding this section of his letter, Paul writes about how his experience of Christ has utterly transformed him. When

he speaks of "knowing Christ Jesus," he is not talking about catechetical or even theological knowledge. Rather, he is talking about a deep and personal experience of the life of Christ *in him.* Paul employs accounting language to explain how this gain makes everything else look like loss on the spreadsheet of life's accomplishments. Later, he changes his imagery and describes these losses in rather gross language—the Greek word *skybala* means "excrement"—to describe the things that people value in life

compared to his experience of Christ. He knows that his right relationship with God comes not through the Law but through faith in Jesus Christ, which requires knowing and trusting in Christ to the extent that Christ is joined to him in his suffering. Paul ends with a beautiful metaphor of running a race and someday being called up to the stage to receive the victor's crown of sharing in Christ's resurrection.

It is **not** that I have already taken **hold** of it
  or have already attained perfect **maturity**,
  but I **continue** my **pursuit** in **hope** that I may **possess** it,
  since I have **indeed** been taken **possession** of by Christ **Jesus**.
Brothers and **sisters**, I for my **part**
  do not **consider** myself to have taken **possession**.
Just one thing: forgetting what lies **behind**
  but straining **forward** to what lies **ahead**,
  I continue my **pursuit** toward the **goal**,
  the **prize** of God's **upward calling**, in Christ **Jesus**.

GOSPEL   John 8:1–11

A reading from the holy Gospel according to John

Jesus went to the Mount of **Olives**.
But **early** in the **morning** he arrived **again** in the **temple** area,
  and all the **people** started **coming** to him,
  and he sat **down** and **taught** them.
Then the **scribes** and the **Pharisees** brought a **woman**
  who had been **caught** in **adultery**
  and made her **stand** in the **middle**.
They **said** to him,
  "**Teacher**, this **woman** was **caught**
  in the very **act** of committing **adultery**.
Now in the **law**, Moses **commanded** us to **stone** such women.
So what do **you** say?"
They **said** this to **test** him,
  so that they could have some **charge** to bring **against** him.
Jesus bent **down** and began to **write** on the **ground** with
    his **finger**.
But when they continued **asking** him,
  he **straightened** up and **said** to them,
  "Let the one **among** you who is **without sin**
  be the **first** to throw a **stone** at her." »

The third part, in which Paul attributes his perseverance to Christ.

The fourth part, in which he downplays his own role in his perseverance.

The fifth part, his conclusion. Shift your tone to reflect Paul's own uplifting conclusion.

A narrative reading in which Jesus is challenged by the Pharisees. It reads like a short, dramatic scene from a play, in which even Jesus' actions take on a dramatic quality, as when he scribbles on the ground with his finger.

Pharisees = FAYR-uh-seez

Though the Pharisees are here to challenge Jesus, don't overdo your tone here. The question they are asking Jesus is legitimate, after all.

Given that Jesus has been scribbling in the dirt before answering, he appears to have come to his decision after some deliberation. Let your tone reflect this prospect.

GOSPEL The story of the woman caught in adultery is a striking one. It appears to interrupt the section of John's Gospel called the Tabernacles Discourse, and its rhetorical style is very different from the rest of the Gospel. Many biblical scholars who study this text think it was not originally part of this Gospel. Some ancient manuscripts place it at the end of chapter 21 in Luke's Gospel. In any case, it is a beautiful story that shows the full extent of Jesus' kindness toward sinners.

However, if we understand the cultural and religious context of this story, we should also be troubled by some of its features. The story begins with Jesus seated in the temple area, preparing to teach those who had gathered around him. Some scribes and Pharisees bring in a woman caught in adultery and make her stand before Jesus and in the midst of this group of men. To charge her, there had to be at least two male witnesses to the act, so were these witnesses also peeping Toms? Was the woman a willing participant, or was she being raped? The story does not tell us, but the latter is at least as likely as the former. Unless she lived on the margins of society, a marriageable young woman would not be out and about without the protection of family. Also, the story indicates that the only reason for shaming this woman and dragging her before this crowd was to catch Jesus in a legal trap. Will he judge this woman and condemn her according to the rule in Deuteronomy 22:22–24 or not?

Jesus' words are both stern and compassionate.

Again he bent down and **wrote** on the ground.
And in **response**, they went **away one** by **one**,
    beginning with the **elders**.
So he was left **alone** with the **woman before** him.
Then Jesus **straightened** up and **said** to her,
    "**Woman**, where **are** they?
Has **no** one **condemned** you?"
She replied, "**No** one, sir."
Then Jesus said, "Neither do **I condemn** you.
Go, and from now **on** do not **sin** any **more**."

PRAYERFUL READING, OR *LECTIO DIVINA*

1. *Lectio:* Read a Scripture passage aloud slowly. Notice what phrase captures your attention and be attentive to its meaning. Silent pause.

2. *Meditatio:* Read the passage aloud slowly again, reflecting on the passage, allowing God to speak to you through it. Silent pause.

3. *Oratio:* Read it aloud slowly a third time, allowing it to be your prayer or response to God's gift of insight to you. Silent pause.

4. *Contemplatio:* Read it aloud slowly a fourth time, now resting in God's Word.

Since the scribes and Pharisees brought only the woman forward, she would likely be the only one to be punished. But Jesus' judgment forces their nefarious plot to be revealed. Traditionally, witnesses had the right to execute punishment, so when Jesus says, "Let the one among you who is without sin be the first to throw a stone at her," they all slowly depart the scene. After confirming that none of the accusers had condemned her, he added that he did not condemn her, either. We should not take this story to mean that Jesus condones adultery but rather that sins of self-righteousness, duplicity, and violation of human dignity are deserving of much greater punishment. C.C.

FIFTH SUNDAY OF LENT, YEAR A

LECTIONARY #34

READING I   Ezekiel 37:12–14

A reading from the Book of the Prophet Ezekiel

Thus says the Lord GOD:
O my people, I will **open** your **graves**
and have you **rise** from them,
and bring you **back** to the land of **Israel**.
Then you shall **know** that I am the LORD,
when I **open** your graves and have you **rise** from them,
O my people!
I will **put** my spirit **in** you that you may **live**,
and I will **settle** you upon your **land**;
thus you shall **know** that I am the LORD.
I have **promised**, and I will **do** it, says the LORD.

RESPONSORIAL PSALM   Psalm 130:1–2, 3–4, 5–6, 7–8 (7)

R. With the Lord there is mercy and fullness of redemption.

Out of the depths I cry to you, O LORD;
  LORD, hear my voice!
Let your ears be attentive
  to my voice in supplication.

If you, O LORD, mark iniquities,
  LORD, who can stand?
But with you is forgiveness,
  that you may be revered.

I trust in the LORD;
  my soul trusts in his word.
More than sentinels wait for the dawn,
  let Israel wait for the LORD.

For with the LORD is kindness
  and with him is plenteous redemption;
and he will redeem Israel
  from all their iniquities.

Ezekiel = ee-ZEE-kee-uhl

An exhortatory reading in which a small number of promises are repeated and varied a few times to impressive effect. Focus on the phrase "O my people," which includes all the feelings of care and connection that motivate this reading.

This line rephrases the opening lines. Slow down very slightly to signal the repetition.

Emphasize "promised" and "do" to conclude the exhortation.

For meditation and context:

TO KEEP IN MIND
On the Third, Fourth and Fifth Sundays of Lent, the readings from Year A are used when the Scrutinies—prayers for purification and strength—are celebrated with the elect, those who will be baptized at the Easter Vigil.

There are options for today's readings. Contact your parish staff to learn which readings will be used.

READING I   Ezekiel was perhaps born roughly thirty years before the destruction of the Temple in 586 BC and the subsequent exile of the Hebrew people to the land of Babylon. It is during the time of captivity that Ezekiel receives visions and the call to announce the Lord's desire to restore the former glory of Israel.

In the vision found in today's reading, Ezekiel sees the restoration of Israel depicted by the opening of graves. This is truly the language of resurrection: "O my people, I will open your graves and have you rise from them, and bring you back to the land of Israel" (v. 12). Earlier, Ezekiel painted Israel as a desert land filled with dry bones (vv. 1–11). Death has totally overwhelmed the people; there is nothing here that is filled with life. Yet the hope that Ezekiel impresses upon his hearers is that from the dryness of death will come the promise of future life: "I will put my spirit in you that you may live." Just as God breathed his spirit into his human creation at the outset of the world (Genesis 2:7), so here do we see God re-creating humanity by breathing new life into what was dead.

The subtext in Ezekiel's prophecy is that the gift of resurrection and the people's return to the land once theirs will be accomplished by the work of the Lord. Over and over the Lord takes responsibility for saving his people. "I have promised, and I will do it, says the Lord" (v. 14). The Lord will follow through on his promise to restore the bond of the covenant with Israel in which they recognize him as their God. Having been immersed in the polytheistic worldview of

Paul's didactic reading contrasts the flesh and the spirit. In Paul's letters, the spirit is superior to the flesh, which desires, fades, and dies, while the spirit lives. This can make it challenging to read him to an assembly, each member of whom is in the flesh, in a body. However you regard this aspect of Paul's thinking, proclaim this reading as straightforwardly as you can.

READING II   Romans 8:8–11

A reading from the Letter of Saint Paul to the Romans

Brothers and sisters:
Those who are in the **flesh cannot** please **God**.
But you are **not** in the flesh;
    on the **contrary**, you are in the spirit,
    if only the **Spirit** of God dwells in you.
Whoever does not **have** the Spirit of **Christ** does not **belong**
      to him.
But if **Christ** is **in** you,
    although the **body** is dead because of **sin**,
    the **spirit** is alive because of **righteousness**.
If the **Spirit** of the one who raised **Jesus** from the **dead** dwells
     in you,
    the One who raised **Christ** from the dead
    will give **life** to your mortal bodies **also**,
    through his Spirit dwelling in **you**.

The sense of life is decidedly in the spirit, but it can enter the mortal body, too. Emphasize the phrase "give life."

Lazarus = LAZ-uh-ruhs
Bethany = BETH-uh-nee
A long and complex narrative reading energized by the intense emotions of the figures in the story. The outcome of this story is well known. Its mysteries reside in the power over death that Jesus demonstrates, as well as his declarations about himself ("I am the resurrection and the life"). There are also the curious details that texture the imagination, such as the days Lazarus has been dead and the potential stench of his corpse. You can linger on these details in your proclamation.

GOSPEL   John 11:1–45

A reading from the holy Gospel according to John

Now a man was **ill**, **Lazarus** from Bethany,
    the village of **Mary** and her sister **Martha**.
Mary was the one who had **anointed** the Lord with perfumed **oil**
    and **dried** his feet with her **hair**;
    it was her brother **Lazarus** who was **ill**.
So [the sisters (of Lazarus) sent word to Jesus saying,
    "**Master**, the one you love is **ill**."
When Jesus **heard** this he said,
    "This **illness** is not to **end** in death,
    but is for the **glory** of God,
    that the **Son** of God may be glorified **through** it."
Now Jesus loved **Martha** and her **sister** and **Lazarus**.

These are the four main characters in the story.

the Babylonians for several decades, the people's commitment to worshipping God alone must be restored; this is necessary for the reconstruction of Jerusalem and the flourishing of the people.

READING II   Paul devotes the eighth chapter of his correspondence with the Romans to a positive appraisal of the Christian life. He does this by employing the dichotomy of "flesh" (*sarx*), understood as the person enslaved by the powers of sin, and "spirit" (*pneuma*), the person who "is alive because of righteous-

ness" (Romans 8:10). To live "in the flesh" means to live completely for oneself, whereas to live with the Spirit dwelling in you is to live for God.

The entirety of the Christian life is truly focused on the indwelling of the Holy Spirit and the enactment of spiritual gifts. The Holy Spirit is the first fruit of Christ's Resurrection, and therefore, wherever death to self is transcended by life directed to God and others, the Spirit is active and is fully operational.

Those who have been baptized do not wait solely for a future moment of redemp-

tion; rather, salvation is taking place right now for those who have been grafted onto Christ. Phrases such as "you are not in the flesh," "you are in the spirit," and "Christ is in you," make certain that the Christian is seen by God not as being in any lingering sin but rather as being in the fullness of the Spirit. Salvation occurs today. Yet this is not to abandon the attitude of hope for the appearance of some long-awaited future glory. This is the very essence of the last sentence of today's reading: "If the Spirit of the one who raised Jesus from the dead dwells in you, the One who raised Christ from

Rabbi = RAB-ī

Emphasize the relationships between walking and day, walking and night, stumbles and light.

Didymus = DID-uh-muhs = twin

So when he **heard** that he was **ill**,
 he remained for **two days** in the place where he **was**.
Then **after** this he said to his disciples,
 "Let us go **back** to Judea."]
The disciples said to him,
 "**Rabbi**, the Jews were just trying to **stone** you,
 and you want to go **back** there?"
Jesus answered,
 "Are there not **twelve hours** in a day?
If one **walks** during the **day**, he does not **stumble**,
 because he **sees** the **light** of this **world**.
But if one **walks** at **night**, he **stumbles**,
 because the **light** is not in him."
He said this, and then told them,
 "Our friend **Lazarus** is **asleep**,
 but I am going to **awaken** him."
So the disciples said to him,
 "**Master**, if he is **asleep**, he will be **saved**."
But **Jesus** was talking about his **death**,
 while they **thought** that he meant **ordinary sleep**.
So then Jesus said to them clearly,
 "**Lazarus** has **died**.
And I am **glad** for you that I was not **there**,
 that you may **believe**.
Let us **go** to him."
So **Thomas**, called **Didymus**, said to his fellow disciples,
 "Let us **also** go to **die** with him."

[When Jesus **arrived**, he found that **Lazarus**
 had already been in the **tomb** for four days.]
Now Bethany was near **Jerusalem**, only about **two miles** away.
And many of the **Jews** had come to **Martha** and **Mary**
 to **comfort them** about their **brother**.
[When **Martha** heard that **Jesus** was coming,
 she went to **meet** him;
 but **Mary** sat at home. »

---

the dead will give life to your mortal bodies also, through his Spirit dwelling in you."

To summarize this brief excerpt of Paul's theology: Baptism causes one to switch allegiances from sin to God, thereby bringing about the death of life in the flesh in order to live fully in the spiritual realm.

 GOSPEL | The story of the raising of Lazarus takes place immediately after Jesus made several claims to being the Son of God. He retreats to the far side of the Jordan River to escape the religious authorities who wanted to arrest him.

Thus, the story begins with Martha and Mary, Lazarus' sisters, sending word to Jesus that their brother is gravely ill. John the Evangelist plunges us into the cosmic realm whereby the evil forces of this world (represented by those seeking to put Jesus to death) and the power of God's glory are at war with each other. Jesus is very certain that the outcome will testify to the victory of God.

At first, Jesus' reaction to the news that his friend is very ill might surprise us. He makes the decision to stay where he was for two more days. His delay in returning to Bethany allows Lazarus to die and be

buried. If Jesus had returned when Lazarus was merely dying, his return to life may not have had the same effect on the crowds of people who witness Jesus raising Lazarus from the dead. The last line of this reading is therefore critical to the purpose of the passage: "Now many of the Jews who had come to Mary and seen what he had done began to believe in him."

Jesus knows that waiting for Lazarus' death and burial will allow him to perform the miracle that will draw many people over to his side, thereby waging an even greater threat to the religious establishment. In

This exchange, concluding with "everyone who lives and believes in me will never die," expresses the core of this reading. Read it with care, allowing for Jesus' striking expression that he is the resurrection and the life to arise directly, even irrefutably, from this exchange.

Martha said to Jesus,
  "**Lord**, if you had **been** here,
  my **brother** would not have **died**.
But even **now** I know that whatever you ask of **God**,
  God will **give** you."
Jesus said to her,
  "Your **brother** will **rise**."
Martha said to him,
  "I **know** he will rise,
  in the **resurrection** on the last **day**."
Jesus told her,
  "I am the **resurrection** and the **life**;
  whoever **believes** in me, **even if he dies**, will **live**,
  and **everyone** who lives and **believes** in me will **never** die.
Do **you** believe this?"
She said to him, "**Yes**, Lord.
I have **come** to **believe** that you are the **Christ**, the Son of God,
  the one who is **coming** into the world."]

When she had **said** this,
  she went and called her sister Mary **secretly**, saying,
  "The **teacher** is here and is **asking** for you."
As soon as she **heard** this,
  she rose **quickly** and **went** to him.
For Jesus had not yet come into the village,
  but was **still** where Martha had **met** him.
So when the **Jews** who were **with her** in the house **comforting** her
  saw Mary get up **quickly** and go **out**,
  they **followed** her,
  presuming that she was going to the **tomb** to **weep** there.
When Mary came to where Jesus was and saw him,
  she **fell** at his feet and **said** to him,
  "**Lord**, if you had **been** here,
  my **brother** would not have **died**."
When Jesus saw her **weeping** and the **Jews** who had come with
    her **weeping**,

Even emphasis on the words in this line.

Even emphasis here as well.

Mary repeats the same words as her sister, Martha. Repeat them yourself plainly.

addition, the evangelist wants to leave no doubt that Lazarus is dead and that his raising will be far greater than resuscitation, shown by the detail that Lazarus has been dead for four days and that the stone had been rolled over the entrance to the tomb.

There are two important dimensions of Johannine eschatology that are represented in this story. Both are knitted together when Jesus makes the proclamation: "I am the resurrection and the life; whoever believes in me, even if he dies, will live, and everyone who lives and believes in me will never die." For John, the one who believes in Jesus has

already died and is on the journey from death to life, with final resurrection as the confirmation of what has already occurred. Thus, the raising of Lazarus is meant to symbolize the resurrection of Christians. What happens to him will happen to all those who put their faith in Jesus.

The first to express such faith in Jesus is Martha. She makes three faith statements that are meant to be the utterances of every believing Christian, and when taken today, reveal the sense of *anamnesis* in which the past, the present, and the future coincide. First she declares her faith regarding the

past: "Lord, if you had been here, my brother would not have died. But even now I know that whatever you ask of God, God will give you." Next, Martha declares her hope for the future: "I know he will rise, in the resurrection on the last day." Martha professes her faith in the present moment: "Yes, Lord. I have come to believe that you are the Christ, the Son of God, the one who is coming into the world."

John uses the extension of an invitation to Mary to come and see Jesus as the opportunity to have many Jews follow her in order to witness to the miracle about to

perturbed = per-TERBD = agitated and upset

Jesus weeping over Lazarus is a foretaste of his own Passion.

From here to the conclusion of the reading, Jesus is in complete command. He has an audience, to whom he relates his miracle. Take note of the rhythm of the words, "Take away the stone."

Even emphasis on this line with a slight additional emphasis on "believe."

[he became **perturbed** and deeply **troubled**, and said,
"**Where** have you **laid** him?"
They said to him, "Sir, **come** and **see**."
And Jesus wept.
So the Jews said, "See how he **loved** him."
But some of them said,
"Could **not** the one who opened the eyes of the **blind** man
have done **something** so that this man would not have **died**?"

So **Jesus**, perturbed again, **came** to the tomb.
It was a **cave**, and a **stone** lay across it.
Jesus said, "**Take away the stone**."
Martha, the dead man's sister, said to him,
"**Lord**, by now there will be a **stench**;
he has been **dead** for four **days**."
Jesus said to her,
"Did I not tell you that if you **believe**
you will see the **glory** of God?"
So they **took away** the **stone**.
And Jesus raised his eyes and said,
"**Father**, I thank you for **hearing** me.
I know that you **always** hear me;
but because of the **crowd** here I have **said** this,
that they may **believe** that you **sent** me."
And when he had **said** this,
he cried out in a **loud voice**,
"**Lazarus**, come **out**!"
The dead man came **out**,
tied **hand** and **foot** with **burial** bands,
and his **face** was wrapped in a **cloth**.
So Jesus said to them,
"**Untie** him and let him **go**."

Now **many** of the Jews who had come to **Mary**
and seen what he had **done** began to **believe** in him.]

[Shorter: John 11:3–7, 17, 20–27, 33b–45 (see brackets)]

be performed. Upon arriving at the burial site, Mary greets Jesus as her sister had earlier: "Lord, if you had been here, my brother would not have died." However, she fails to make the statement of faith made by her sister: "But even now I know that whatever you ask of God, God will give you." Furthermore, Mary approaches Jesus with a different disposition than Martha had; Mary falls to her knees before the feet of Jesus and, along with the Jews who had accompanied her, was weeping. John tells us that Jesus "became perturbed and deeply troubled."

The Jewish audience perceives Jesus' weeping as a sign of his love for his friend, which would be a purely natural perception; however, they fail to perceive that his tears are for those who have been given so many opportunities yet fail to see that he is the Messiah of God. John tells us that Jesus became "perturbed again" and ordered the stone to be rolled away.

How frustrated Jesus has become with the people's unwillingness to believe. Even Martha now displays some degree of doubt as she declares: "Lord, by now there will be a stench, he has been dead for four days."

After attempting to bolster Martha's fledgling faith, Jesus raises his eyes and prays that this miracle may produce faith: "Father, I thank you for hearing me. I know that you always hear me; but because of the crowd here I have said this, that they may believe that you sent me." With that, Jesus commands Lazarus to "come out!" and gives the instructions to untie him.

While the story acknowledges that "many" came to believe, the reality is that the opposition against Jesus gains strength, "So Jesus no longer went about openly among the Jews." S.W.

PALM SUNDAY OF THE PASSION OF THE LORD

LECTIONARY #37

GOSPEL AT THE PROCESSION   Luke 19:28–40

A reading from the holy Gospel according to Luke

Jesus proceeded on his **journey** up to **Jerusalem**.
As he drew **near** to **Bethphage** and **Bethany**
    at the **place** called the **Mount** of **Olives**,
    he sent **two** of his **disciples**.
He said, "**Go** into the village **opposite** you,
    and as you **enter** it you will find a **colt** tethered
    on which **no one** has ever **sat**.
Untie it and **bring** it here.
And if **anyone** should **ask** you,
    '**Why** are you **untying** it?'
    you will **answer**,
    'The **Master** has **need** of it.'"
So **those** who had been **sent** went **off**
    and found **everything** just as he had **told** them.
And as they were **untying** the **colt**, its **owners** said to them,
    "**Why** are you **untying** this **colt**?"
They **answered**,
    "The **Master** has **need** of it."
So they brought it to **Jesus**,
    threw their **cloaks** over the **colt**,
    and helped **Jesus** to **mount**.

A narrative reading that sets the tone for the liturgy to follow. The tone is preparatory, moving in the direction of consummation.
Bethphage = BETH-fuh-jee
Bethany = BETH-uh-nee

tethered = TETH-*rd

Repeat this phrase "The Master has need of it" in the same tone used the first time it is proclaimed above.

PROCESSION GOSPEL Palm Sunday of the Passion of the Lord is the first day of Holy Week and the day that commemorates Jesus' entry into Jerusalem before his arrest and crucifixion. All four Gospels have a version of this story, and we hear one of these versions as part of the blessing and procession of the palms each year of the three-year lectionary cycle. This reading is typically part of the procession that precedes the celebration of the Eucharist. Our first evidence of this ritual dates back to the fourth century AD in Jerusalem, but in the West, it is not until the eighth century that we have a sacramentary that includes the ritual of the procession with palms.

Luke's version of the story of Jesus' entrance into Jerusalem begins with a mention that Jesus was "going up" to Jerusalem. This mention of Jesus' arrival in Jerusalem is important. For Luke, the journey began ten chapters earlier with a similar statement in which we are told that Jesus "resolutely determined to journey to Jerusalem," and where the narrator tells us that the days leading to Jesus' being "taken up" (i.e., suffering, death, resurrection, and ascension) had come to fulfillment (Luke 9:51). Along the way to Jerusalem, Jesus focused on teaching his disciples about topics such as missionary activity, prayer, and the dangers of riches. He offered many parables and example stories, like the Good Samaritan, the Rich Fool, the Fig Tree, the Mustard Seed and the Yeast, the Wedding Feast and the Great Banquet, the Lost Sheep, the Lost Coin, and the Lost Son. In sum, Jesus had been teaching his disciples about what it would mean to follow him to death.

Now Jesus is about to enter Jerusalem, but he is not a victim here. Luke shows that

As he rode **along**,
 the people were **spreading** their **cloaks** on the **road**;
 and **now** as he was **approaching** the **slope** of the Mount
  of **Olives**,
 the whole **multitude** of his **disciples**
 began to **praise God aloud** with **joy**
 for **all** the mighty **deeds** they had **seen**.
They proclaimed:
 "**Blessed** is the **king** who **comes**
  in the **name** of the **Lord**.
 Peace in **heaven**
  and **glory** in the **highest**."
Some of the **Pharisees** in the **crowd** said to him,
 "**Teacher**, **rebuke** your **disciples**."
He said in **reply**,
 "I **tell** you, if they keep **silent**,
 the **stones** will cry **out**!"

LECTIONARY #38

READING I   Isaiah 50:4–7

A reading from the Book of the Prophet Isaiah

The **Lord GOD** has **given** me
 a **well-trained** tongue,
that I might **know** how to speak to the **weary**
 a **word** that will **rouse** them.
Morning after **morning**
 he opens my **ear** that I may **hear**;
and I have not **rebelled**,
 have not turned **back**.
I gave my back to **those** who **beat** me,
 my **cheeks** to those who **plucked** my beard;
my face I did not **shield**
 from **buffets** and **spitting**. »

Margin notes (left column):

Slight pause between "praise God" and "aloud."

Don't overdo it with the insistence of the Pharisees, or in Jesus' reply. You can raise the pitch of your voice just slightly.

Isaiah = ī-ZAY-uh

A short and powerful exhortatory reading in which Isaiah asserts his trust in God.

Note the poetic rhythm that begins with the phrase "Morning after morning."

TO KEEP IN MIND
The attention you bring to your proclaiming enables you to pray the Word of God with the assembly.

buffets = BUF-its = slaps

Jesus is fully in control of his fate by demonstrating his divine foreknowledge about securing the colt that he wanted for his entrance into Jerusalem. Luke might have borrowed the detail about the colt not yet having been ridden from Mark (see Mark 11:2). What is the significance of introducing this animal into the story? It might have been Luke's way of pointing to a prophecy from the book of Zechariah about God taking on his kingly role and coming to restore Israel: Exult greatly, O daughter Zion! / Shout for joy, O daughter Jerusalem! / Behold: your king is coming to you, / a just savior is he, /

Humble, and riding on a donkey, on a colt, the foal of a donkey (Zechariah 9:9). Or perhaps the owner of this creature was keeping it ritually pure for religious purposes, and now the time was right for it to be enlisted into the service of this holy man. Probably we will never know.

 Where are the palm branches? Luke makes no mention of them in his account of this event. Instead, the people put down their cloaks to cover the path where Jesus was riding. Similarly, the disciples use their cloaks to create a riding blanket for him. Palm branches would have been plentiful in

the area, but cloaks were another matter. Especially for the poor, one's cloak was a precious thing. It was used as a coat to keep out the cold, but it also served as a sleeping bag. Only the most unscrupulous of lenders would take a man's cloak as security for a loan (Exodus 22:26; Deuteronomy 24:13). Does Luke intend us to understand that the crowds accompanying Jesus on this final leg of his journey are willing to give all they have to support him in his mission?

 As Jesus and his disciples made their way into Jerusalem from the Mount of Olives, Luke tells us that the crowds praised

The Lord GOD is my **help**,
   therefore I am not **disgraced**;
I have set my **face** like **flint**,
   knowing that I shall **not** be put to **shame**.

Give "not" and "shame" equal emphasis.
These last lines can be read with conviction.

For meditation and context:

RESPONSORIAL PSALM   Psalm 22:8–9, 17–18, 19–20, 23–24 (2a)

R. My God, my God, why have you abandoned me?

All who see me scoff at me;
   they mock me with parted lips, they wag
      their heads:
"He relied on the LORD; let him deliver him,
   let him rescue him, if he loves him."

Indeed, many dogs surround me,
   a pack of evildoers closes in upon me;
they have pierced my hands and my feet;
   I can count all my bones.

They divide my garments among them,
   and for my vesture they cast lots.
But you, O LORD, be not far from me;
   O my help, hasten to aid me.

I will proclaim your name to my brethren;
   in the midst of the assembly I will
      praise you:
"You who fear the LORD, praise him;
   all you descendants of Jacob, give glory
      to him;
   revere him, all you descendants of Israel!"

Philippians = fih-LIP-ee-uhnz

An exhortation in which Paul seems to quote to the members of the Church at Philippi an early Christian hymn, whose focus is the *kenosis*, or emptying, mentioned in the fourth line of the reading. It's an utterly mysterious presentation of the power of Jesus' Incarnation. When you get to "emptied," give the word extra emphasis.

Give emphasis and rhythm to the words "human," "human," and "humbled."

READING II   Philippians 2:6–11

A reading from the Letter of Saint Paul to the Philippians

Christ **Jesus**, though he was in the **form** of God,
   did not regard **equality** with God
   something to be **grasped**.
Rather, he **emptied** himself,
   taking the form of a **slave**,
   coming in **human** likeness;
   and found **human** in appearance,
   he **humbled** himself,
   becoming **obedient** to the point of **death**,
   even **death** on a **cross**.
Because of this, God **greatly** exalted him
   and **bestowed** on him the name
   which is above **every** name,
   that at the name of **Jesus**

God for the mighty deeds (Greek *dunamis*, meaning "miracle working") that were revealed through Jesus, which should remind us of how Luke describes Jesus' work at the beginning of his ministry. We are told that he came to "bring glad tidings to the poor . . . proclaim liberty to captives and recovery of sight to the blind, to let the oppressed go free" (Luke 4:18). When the crowds proclaimed the words of the pilgrimage Psalm 118:26, "Blessed is the king who comes," they are declaring what kind of king Jesus is: one who is merciful and

who brings peace and well-being to the sick and disenfranchised.

When the Pharisees ask Jesus to silence his disciples, perhaps they are afraid that the Roman occupiers would take the shouting of the crowd as an act of rebellion. Jesus' response is striking. Biblical scholars have suggested that Luke is alluding to the book of the prophet Habakkuk. In a vision directed against rich and powerful tyrants who built their homes and cities on bloodshed and injustice and who try to remove themselves from the consequences of their behavior, God says, "the stone in the wall

shall cry out and the beam in the frame shall answer" about their wickedness (Habakkuk 2:11). So too here. If those who are willing to give all that they have to follow Jesus are silenced, the created world itself will shout out in witness of Jesus' kingship and the justice it will bring. Praise God!

READING I   This reading is taken from the part of the book of Isaiah that was written during the Babylonian Exile, a desperate time for the Jewish people. Jerusalem and the Temple had been destroyed, the elite of Judah had been

every **knee** should **bend**,
of those in **heaven** and on **earth** and **under** the earth,
and every **tongue** confess that
Jesus Christ is Lord,
to the **glory** of God the **Father**.

PASSION   Luke 22:14 — 23:56

The Passion of our Lord Jesus Christ according to Luke

When the **hour** came,
    Jesus took his **place** at **table** with the **apostles**.
He said to them,
    "I have **eagerly** desired to eat this **Passover** with you
        before I **suffer**,
    for, I **tell** you, I **shall not eat** it again
    until there is **fulfillment** in the **kingdom** of **God**."
Then he took a **cup**, gave **thanks**, and **said**,
    "**Take** this and **share** it among **yourselves**;
    for I **tell** you that from **this time** on
    I shall not **drink** of the **fruit** of the **vine**
    until the **kingdom** of God **comes**."
Then he took the **bread**, said the **blessing**,
    broke it, and **gave** it to them, saying,
    "**This** is my **body**, which will be **given** for **you**;
    do this in **memory** of **me**."
And **likewise** the **cup** after they had **eaten**, saying,
    "**This cup** is the new **covenant** in my **blood**,
    which will be **shed** for **you**.

"And yet **behold**, the **hand** of the one who is to **betray** me
    is **with** me on the **table**;
    for the **Son** of **Man** indeed **goes** as it has been **determined**;
    but **woe** to that **man** by **whom** he is **betrayed**."
And they began to **debate** among **themselves**
    who among them would **do** such a **deed**. »

An intensely powerful narrative reading of the story at the core of our faith. This is also the longest reading that most congregants experience during the annual cycle. It is as dramatic as a novel, told with vivid shifts and striking language. Although the reading is dramatic, its drama is inherent in the language and the pacing of the story. You may have an instinct to intensify the drama by "acting out" some of the voices and scenes. Better to avoid that by allowing the language to dictate the drama. You need mainly to stay focused.

It is commonplace for lectors to be involved in the proclamation of this Gospel. Whether passages in the Gospel are divided up among a group of readers, including the priest, the deacon, and some lectors, or with a narrator and then readers for each of the speakers, avoid theatricality in favor of proclaiming boldly, clearly, and slowly.

"When the hour came" are the words that initiate your assembly into the mystery of this proclamation.

Jesus begins with words of fulfillment.

And the familiar words of the consecration, first of the cup, and then of the bread. Imagine in proclaiming these words that this is the first time they are being uttered.

Jesus foretells his betrayal; don't overdo it—proclaim the words as they stand.

deported to Babylon, and their king had been killed. Many would have concluded that God had completely abandoned them. In response, the prophet delivers words of divine consolation to the exiles and, occasionally, even oracles of hope, such as we have in today's reading.

In the verses immediately preceding this reading, God is addressing the exiles in a series of rhetorical questions indicating that they have not been abandoned. The prophet reminds them that God did not write a bill of divorce against their mother, Jerusalem, nor did he sell them to his credi-

tors. God continues, "Why was no one there when I came? Why did no one answer when I called?" (Isaiah 50:2). In other words, the people's feeling of abandonment was less about God's faithfulness and more about their own weak faith.

Then the one who describes himself as God's disciple speaks. He explains that God gave him a "well-trained tongue," or learned speech, to know how to awaken the weary exiles from their stupor and that he accepts God's call willingly. But, as was the case with many of the prophets, the disciple's words are not heeded. Rather, he

is rejected, beaten, and subjected to shameful abuse. Not to be deterred, he hardens his determination to obey God's will, because he knows that he cannot be put to shame when God is his help. Although this was not Isaiah's intention, early Christians took this beautiful poetic oracle to refer to Jesus. Can you see why?

READING II Today's second reading is often described as the "Christ hymn." There is good evidence that Paul did not write this hymn or poem himself; it is likely that it was already in use

Here begins an important scene depicting
the humanity and foolishness of the disciples,
especially Peter.
Jesus' words here are complex, even a little
hard to follow in response to the argument
as to which among the disciples is the
greatest. Proclaim them clearly at an
even pace.
benefactors = BEN-eh-fak-tehrs

This speech sets up Peter's denial. Imagine
saying these words to a trusted friend.

Don't overdramatize Peter's response. In his
heart, he knows he is capable of this denial.

Then an **argument** broke out **among** them
  about **which** of them should be **regarded** as the **greatest**.
He said to them,
  "The **kings** of the **Gentiles** lord it **over** them
  and **those** in **authority** over them are **addressed** as
    '**Benefactors**';
  but among **you** it shall **not** be **so**.
Rather, let the **greatest** among you be as the **youngest**,
  and the **leader** as the **servant**.
For **who** is **greater**:
  the one **seated** at table or the one who **serves**?
Is it **not** the one **seated** at **table**?
I am among you as the **one** who **serves**.
It is **you** who have stood **by** me in my **trials**;
  and I confer a **kingdom** on you,
  just as my **Father** has **conferred** one on **me**,
  that you may **eat** and **drink** at my **table** in my **kingdom**;
  and you will **sit** on **thrones**
  judging the **twelve tribes** of Israel.

"**Simon, Simon**, behold **Satan** has demanded
  to sift **all of you** like **wheat**,
  but I have **prayed** that your own faith may not **fail**;
  and **once** you have turned **back**,
  you must **strengthen** your **brothers**."
He said to him,
  "**Lord**, I am **prepared** to go to **prison** and to **die** with you."
But he replied,
  "I **tell** you, Peter, before the **cock crows** this **day**,
  you will **deny three times** that you **know** me."

He said to them,
  "When I **sent** you **forth** without a **money bag** or a **sack**
    or **sandals**,
  were you in **need** of **anything**?"
"No, **nothing**," they replied.

among early Christian communities and that Paul adapted it for his purposes. He includes it in his letter to the Philippians to encourage fellow believers to rejoice in suffering as Christ suffered for them. Although biblical scholars disagree on how to interpret certain aspects of the hymn, we can affirm that it follows the general pattern of humiliation-exaltation Christologies that are found in the works of other early Christian writers.

Because Jesus was willing to become like a slave and even give himself over to death (humiliation), God exalted him and made him Lord over all creation (exaltation).

To better understand the message that Paul wanted to convey with this "Christ hymn," we need to look at the verses that precede and follow it. He wants his beloved community at Philippi to have the same mind or attitude among themselves as

Christ had for them. Thus, he tells them, "Do nothing out of selfishness or out of vainglory; rather, humbly regard others as more important than yourselves" (Philippians 2:3). After sharing the poem, he reminds the community to continue in obedience, allowing God to work in them for God's good pleasure (Philippians 2:13). His words then turn deeply personal as he anticipates his own end: "But, even if I am poured out as a liba-

He said to them,
"But now **one** who has a **money bag** should **take** it,
and **likewise** a **sack**,
and one who does **not** have a **sword**
should sell his **cloak** and **buy** one.
For I **tell** you that this **Scripture** must be **fulfilled** in me,
namely, *He was* **counted** *among the* **wicked**;
and indeed what is written about **me** is coming to **fulfillment**."
Then they said,
"**Lord, look**, there are **two swords** here."
But he replied, "It is **enough**!"

Then going **out**, he **went**, as was his **custom**, to the Mount
of **Olives**,
and the disciples **followed** him.
When he **arrived** at the place he **said** to them,
"**Pray** that you may not undergo the **test**."
After **withdrawing** about a **stone's throw** from them and **kneeling**,
he **prayed**, saying, "**Father**, if you are **willing**,
take this cup **away** from me;
still, not **my** will but **yours** be done."
And to **strengthen** him an **angel** from heaven **appeared** to him.
He was in **such** agony and he prayed so **fervently**
that his **sweat** became like drops of **blood**
falling on the **ground**.
When he **rose** from prayer and **returned** to his disciples,
he found them **sleeping** from **grief**.
He **said** to them, "**Why** are you **sleeping**?
Get **up** and **pray** that you may **not** undergo the **test**."

While he was still **speaking**, a crowd approached
and in **front** was one of the **Twelve**, a man named **Judas**.
He went up to **Jesus** to **kiss** him.
Jesus said to him,
"**Judas**, are you **betraying** the Son of **Man** with a **kiss**?" »

Luke's telling of the passion is laden with symbolic figures and language. The "two swords" are an example of this.

This prayer of Jesus in agony in the garden is as vivid as it is solemn. Slow your pace to allow these words to sink in.

Avoid a tone that's too angry here.

Ask this question in a plain and neutral tone.

tion upon the sacrificial service of your faith, I rejoice and share my joy with all of you. In the same way you also should rejoice and share your joy with me" (Philippians 2:17–18). This is the way of the Christian who truly has the mind of Christ. Let us pray for one another this week, especially, that we have the courage to set our face "like flint" in obedience to God's will as we follow Jesus

to the cross so that we might one day enjoy his resurrection.

GOSPEL On this Palm Sunday of the Lord's Passion, we are honored to experience the reading of Luke's entire passion narrative. The lectionary presents us with a long form that begins with the story of the Passover meal that

Jesus shares with his disciples. The short form begins with the story of Jesus being brought before Pontius Pilate for trial and sentencing.

The Gospel accounts of Jesus' passion (arrest, trial, and crucifixion) are so compelling that, if we allow them to enter into our hearts and minds, we can find ourselves transported to that place and to the sights

His disciples **realized** what was about to **happen**, and they asked,
    "**Lord**, shall we **strike** with a **sword**?"
And one of them struck the high priest's **servant**
    and cut **off** his right **ear**.
But Jesus said in reply,
    "**Stop**, no **more** of this!"
Then he **touched** the servant's **ear** and **healed** him.
And Jesus **said** to the chief **priests** and temple **guards**
    and **elders** who had **come** for him,
    "Have you come **out** as against a **robber**, with **swords** and **clubs**?
Day after **day** I was **with** you in the **temple** area,
    and you did not **seize** me;
    but **this** is your **hour**, the **time** for the power of **darkness**."

After **arresting** him they led him **away**
    and **took** him into the **house** of the high **priest**;
    Peter was following at a **distance**.
They lit a **fire** in the middle of the **courtyard** and sat around it,
    and **Peter** sat **down** with them.
When a maid saw him **seated** in the light,
    she looked intently at him and **said**,
    "**This** man **too** was **with** him."
But he **denied** it saying,
    "**Woman**, I do **not know** him."
A short while later someone else **saw** him and **said**,
    "You **too** are **one** of them";
    but Peter answered, "My **friend**, I am **not**."
About an hour **later**, still **another** insisted,
    "**Assuredly**, this man **too** was **with** him,
    for he **also** is a **Galilean**."
But Peter said,
    "My **friend**, I **do not know** what you are **talking** about."
Just as he was saying this, the cock **crowed**,
    and the Lord **turned** and looked at **Peter**;
    and Peter **remembered** the word of the Lord,
    how he had **said** to him,

Jesus is angry and exasperated here.

Note the rhythm of this line: "but THIS is your HOUR, the TIME for the power of DARKness."

Here begins the drama involving Peter's denial.

The emphasis here is on "not," as is so in each of the subsequent expressions of denial.

Galilean = gal-ih-LEE-uhn

and sounds surrounding the story, even to the point of sharing in the emotions of the characters of the story as they observe this horrific execution unfold before their eyes. However, in hope, we can also anticipate the resurrection story that we will soon celebrate on Easter.

Because of the length of the passion narratives, it is possible to become overwhelmed by all the details that tend to blur together or pass us by entirely. When we focus on the distinctive elements of a particular Gospel passion narrative, however, we can discern the Gospel writer's theology of Jesus and the cross, thus opening

our eyes to a greater appreciation of its meaning. Let us focus on what makes Luke's passion narrative unique.

In the scene leading up to the last supper, the narrator of Luke's Gospel tells us that the religious leaders were seeking a way to put Jesus to death and that Satan entered into Judas to conspire with them to

Prophesy = PROF-uh-sī

Sanhedrin = san-HEE-druhn.

No need to play up the mocking tone in the words of the Sanhedrin.

Jesus' reply has a blasphemous implication in the words "I am." Pause slightly after "am."

Pilate= PĪ-luht

Pilate's repeated emphasis is that Jesus is not guilty. You can likewise emphasize "not," "no," and "guilty" in the following several verses.

"Before the **cock crows** today, you will **deny** me
　　three times."
He went **out** and began to weep **bitterly**.
The **men** who held **Jesus** in **custody** were **ridiculing** and
　　beating him.
They **blindfolded** him and **questioned** him, saying,
　"**Prophesy!** Who is it that **struck** you?"
And they **reviled** him in saying many other **things against** him.

When **day** came the **council** of **elders** of the people met,
　　both **chief priests** and **scribes**,
　　and they **brought** him before their **Sanhedrin**.
They said, "If you are the **Christ, tell** us,"
　　but he **replied** to them, "If I **tell** you, you will not **believe**,
　　and if I **question**, you will not **respond**.
But from **this time on** the **Son** of **Man** will be **seated**
　　at the **right hand** of the **power** of **God**."
They all asked, "**Are you then** the **Son** of **God**?"
He **replied** to them, "You **say** that I **am**."
Then they said, "What further **need** have we for **testimony**?
We have **heard** it from his own **mouth**."

[Then the whole **assembly** of them **arose** and brought him
　　before **Pilate**.
They brought **charges against** him, saying,
　"We **found** this man **misleading** our people;
　he **opposes** the payment of **taxes** to Caesar
　and **maintains** that he is the **Christ**, a **king**."
Pilate **asked** him, "Are **you** the **king** of the **Jews**?"
He said to him in **reply**, "You **say** so."
Pilate then addressed the **chief priests** and the **crowds**,
　"I **find** this man **not guilty**."
But they were **adamant** and **said**,
　"He is **inciting** the people with his **teaching**
　　throughout all **Judea**,
　from **Galilee** where he **began** even to **here**." »

betray Jesus for a sum of money (Luke 22:2–4). Although Luke was not opposed to Christians having wealth, throughout his Gospel he writes about the dangers of wealth.

After the meal, the Lukan Jesus singles out Peter and tells him that Satan demanded to "sift" all of them like wheat, but that Jesus was praying for him that his faith would not fail and that once he had denied Jesus he would be able to turn back and strengthen his fellow disciples. In between, Jesus talks to his disciples about how he will not eat again of the Passover "until there is fulfillment in the kingdom of God." Later, when Jesus is arrested, he rebukes the scribes and temple guards, saying, "This is your hour, the time for the power of darkness." Luke wants us to understand that we are about to enter into a cosmic, eschatological battle with Satan. But it is a battle that God will surely win in the resurrection of his Son. Luke is the only one to contextualize these scenes in this way.

The interlude with Herod underscores a complicity between Herod and Pilate, and so by extension between the Jewish and Roman leadership. Nevertheless, proclaim this interlude in a neutral tone.

On **hearing** this Pilate asked if the **man** was a **Galilean**;
and upon **learning** that he was under **Herod's** jurisdiction,
he sent him to **Herod**, who was in **Jerusalem** at that time.
Herod was very **glad** to see **Jesus**;
he had been wanting to **see** him for a long **time**,
for he had **heard** about him
and had been **hoping** to see him **perform** some **sign**.
He questioned him at **length**,
but he gave him no **answer**.
The chief **priests** and **scribes**, meanwhile,
stood by **accusing** him **harshly**.
Herod and his **soldiers** treated him **contemptuously**
and **mocked** him,
and after **clothing** him in resplendent **garb**,
he sent him **back** to **Pilate**.
Herod and **Pilate** became **friends** that very **day**,
even though they had been **enemies** formerly.
Pilate then **summoned** the chief **priests**, the **rulers**,
and the **people**
and **said** to them, "You **brought** this man to me
and **accused** him of **inciting** the **people** to **revolt**.
I have **conducted** my **investigation** in your **presence**
and have **not** found this man **guilty**
of the **charges** you have brought **against** him,
nor did **Herod**, for he sent him **back** to us.
So **no capital crime** has been **committed** by him.
Therefore I shall have him **flogged** and then **release** him."

Once again, the emphasis is that Jesus is *not guilty*.

But all **together** they shouted **out**,
"**Away** with this **man**!
Release **Barabbas** to us."
—Now **Barabbas** had been **imprisoned** for a **rebellion**
that had taken **place** in the **city** and for **murder**.—
Again **Pilate** addressed them, still **wishing** to release **Jesus**,
but they **continued** their **shouting**,
"**Crucify** him! **Crucify** him!"

When the crowd is shouting, you can raise your voice.

Likewise, raise your voice with "Crucify him! Crucify him!"

Notice also how the Lukan Jesus expresses compassion toward other characters in the story, even moments before his death. After the Passover meal, he teaches his disciples about servanthood and true greatness and he tells them what lies ahead as they go out to evangelize after his death. In the garden scene on the Mount of Olives, the narrator says that Jesus returned from prayer and found the disciples asleep not because of their cluelessness, as Matthew and Mark suggest, but from great sorrow. Later, on the road to the place of the crucifixion, Jesus stops to minister to the women of Jerusalem who are weeping for him. After being crucified, the Lukan Jesus prays to God, "Father, forgive them; they know not what they do." And we cannot forget the criminal who was crucified next to Jesus and to whom Jesus promises a place in paradise. None of these details are included in the other passion narratives.

Pilate **addressed** them a **third time**,
  "What **evil** has this man **done**?
  I found him **guilty** of **no capital crime**.
Therefore I shall have him **flogged** and then **release** him."
With **loud shouts**, however,
  they **persisted** in calling for his **crucifixion**,
  and their **voices** prevailed.
The **verdict** of **Pilate** was that their **demand** should be **granted**.
So he **released** the man who had been **imprisoned**
  for **rebellion** and **murder**, for whom they **asked**,
  and he handed Jesus **over** to them to **deal with** as they **wished**.

As they **led** him **away**
  they took **hold** of a certain **Simon**, a **Cyrenian**,
  who was coming **in** from the **country**;
  and after laying the **cross** on him,
  they made him **carry** it behind **Jesus**.
A **large crowd** of people followed **Jesus**,
  including many **women** who **mourned** and **lamented** him.
Jesus **turned** to them and **said**,
  "**Daughters** of **Jerusalem**, do not **weep** for me;
  weep **instead** for **yourselves** and for your **children**,
  for **indeed**, the days are **coming** when people will **say**,
  '**Blessed** are the **barren**,
  the **wombs** that never **bore**
  and the **breasts** that never **nursed**.'
At **that time** people will say to the **mountains**,
  '**Fall upon** us!'
  and to the **hills**, '**Cover** us!'
  for if these **things** are **done** when the **wood** is **green**
  what will **happen** when it is **dry**?"
Now **two others**, both **criminals**,
  were led **away** with him to be **executed**. »

Even while being led away to his death, Jesus is ever the revealer, making vivid, even visionary claims about life to come. Your tone should be stern and emphatic.

Finally, Luke's Gospel portrays Jesus as unafraid and resolute about the fate that lies before him. In the garden, before his arrest, he prays only once, "Father, if you are willing, take this cup away from me; still, not my will but yours be done." Matthew and Luke describe a similar prayer, but Jesus prays it three times in these two Gospels, returning to his clueless disciples each time, as if abandoned by them. Further, we are also told that Jesus was "sorrowful even to death" as he went to pray (Matthew 26:38; Mark 14:34). Not so in Luke's Gospel. At the beginning of this journey, Jesus "steadfastly set his face" toward Jerusalem (Luke 9:51), and he will remain steadfast to the end.

During this Holy Week, let us walk with Jesus on this journey, which will lead us toward a transformed life in God's kingdom. C.C.

Pause after "Father." Emphasize "know not."

Slight pause between "criminals" and "hanging."

Here begin the memorable words of St. Dismas, the Repentant Thief. This is an especially moving exchange with Jesus, as clear a sign of his full humanity and his full divinity as found in the Gospels. Don't rush through it.

The celestial event of the eclipse reflects the tragic event of the crucifixion.

When they **came** to the place called the **Skull**,
    they **crucified** him and the **criminals** there,
    one on his **right**, the **other** on his **left**.
Then Jesus said,
    "**Father, forgive** them, they **know not** what they **do**."
They **divided** his **garments** by casting **lots**.
The people stood **by** and **watched**;
    the **rulers**, meanwhile, **sneered** at him and said,
    "He saved **others**, let him save **himself**
    if he is the **chosen** one, the **Christ** of **God**."
Even the **soldiers** jeered at him.
As they **approached** to offer him **wine** they called **out**,
    "If you are **King** of the **Jews**, **save** yourself."
Above him there was an **inscription** that read,
    "**This** is the **King** of the **Jews**."

Now one of the criminals **hanging** there **reviled Jesus**, saying,
    "Are you **not** the **Christ**?
    Save yourself and **us**."
The **other**, however, **rebuking** him, said in **reply**,
    "Have you **no fear** of **God**,
    for you are **subject** to the same **condemnation**?
And **indeed**, we have been **condemned justly**,
    for the **sentence** we **received corresponds** to our **crimes**,
    but **this man** has done **nothing criminal**."
Then he said,
    "**Jesus, remember** me when you **come** into your **kingdom**."
He **replied** to him,
    "**Amen**, I **say** to **you**,
    today you will be **with** me in **Paradise**."

It was **now** about **noon** and **darkness** came
        over the **whole land**
    until **three** in the **afternoon**
    because of an **eclipse** of the **sun**.
Then the **veil** of the **temple** was torn **down** the **middle**.

These are words of exquisite solemnity. Though Jesus cries them out, there's no need for you to shout. Proclaim them in a measured and solemn tone.

Jesus cried out in a loud **voice**,
"**Father**, into your **hands** I commend my **spirit**";
and when he had **said** this he **breathed** his last.

[Here all kneel and pause for a short time.]

The **centurion** who witnessed what had **happened** glorified **God**
and said,
"**This man** was **innocent** beyond **doubt**."
When all the **people** who had gathered for this spectacle **saw**
what had **happened**,
they returned **home** beating their **breasts**;
but all his **acquaintances** stood at a **distance**,
including the **women** who had **followed** him from **Galilee**
and **saw** these **events**.]

The scene of Jesus' burial shifts the tone. Jesus has died; this begins to read as an epilogue, even though in many respects it is a new beginning. There's a practical tone to this passage that you can reflect by proclaiming this matter-of-factly.

Now there was a **virtuous** and **righteous** man
named **Joseph** who,
though he was a **member** of the **council**,
had not **consented** to their plan of **action**.
He came from the Jewish town of **Arimathea**
and was awaiting the **kingdom** of **God**.
He went to **Pilate** and asked for the **body** of **Jesus**.
After he had taken the body **down**,
he wrapped it in a linen **cloth**
and laid him in a **rock-hewn tomb**
in which **no one** had yet been **buried**.
It was the **day** of **preparation**,
and the **sabbath** was about to **begin**.
The **women** who had come from **Galilee** with him
followed **behind**,
and when they had **seen** the tomb
and the **way** in which his body was **laid** in it,
they **returned** and prepared **spices** and perfumed **oils**.
Then they **rested** on the **sabbath** according to the **commandment**.

Allow yourself to slow your pace as you proclaim the sacramental words of this conclusion.

[Shorter: Luke 23:1–49 (see brackets)]

HOLY THURSDAY:
MASS OF THE LORD'S SUPPER

LECTIONARY #39

READING I   Exodus 12:1–8, 11–14

A reading from the Book of Exodus

The LORD said to **Moses** and **Aaron** in the land of **Egypt**,
  "This month shall **stand** at the head of your **calendar**;
  you shall **reckon** it the first month of the **year**.
Tell the **whole** community of **Israel**:
  On the **tenth** of this month every **one** of your families
  must **procure** for itself a lamb, one apiece for each **household**.
If a family is too **small** for a **whole lamb**,
  it shall **join** the nearest household in **procuring** one
  and shall **share** in the **lamb**
  in **proportion** to the number of **persons** who **partake** of it.
The lamb must be a **year-old male** and without **blemish**.
You may **take** it from either the sheep or the **goats**.
You shall **keep it** until the fourteenth day of this **month**,
  and **then**, with the whole assembly of Israel present,
  it shall be **slaughtered** during the evening **twilight**.
They shall take **some** of its blood
  and apply it to the **two doorposts** and the **lintel**
  of **every house** in which they **partake** of the **lamb**.
That **same night** they shall **eat** its roasted **flesh**
  with **unleavened bread** and bitter **herbs**.

Exodus = EK-suh-duhs

A narrative reading that includes detailed instructions from God to Moses and Aaron to convey to the Israelites so that they will be prepared for the events now commemorated as Passover. The instructions have ritual power, anticipating one of the most spectacular narratives in the Old Testament. Read these instructions with some reverence.

These details are part of the appeal of this reading. Don't rush through them.

Emphasis on "slaughtered."

Again, important details.

READING I   The first section of Exodus 12 is called "The Passover Ritual Prescribed" and is followed by a section titled "Promulgation of the Passover." The first is a thorough explanation of the instruction that will govern the annual celebration of Passover for generations to come; the second reiterates some of these instructions that the Lord gave to Moses and Aaron immediately prior to the execution of the tenth plague upon Egypt, the extinction of the firstborn throughout the land.

God had been preparing the Israelites for quite some time to be ready for their lib-

eration from Egypt. Exodus suggests that shortly before God encountered Moses in the Burning Bush, he heard the cry of his people and knew full well their plight (Exodus 2:24). God does not simply rush to their rescue. Instead, the Lord calls Moses, the former prince of Egypt who fled the territory after killing an Egyptian and became a shepherd in the land of Midian, to deliver his people from bondage. Moses, however, would need a great deal of convincing that God's power could be victorious over Pharaoh and his armies. The Hebrew people would as well. Over time, the signs that God

performs in the ten plagues would bind Moses and the Israelites together in their faith that God desires to choose them as his people. Even though Moses failed to understand why God hardened Pharaoh's heart, causing him to prevent the Israelites from leaving Egypt, it later becomes clear to Moses that true freedom to worship God with an unfettered heart takes a great deal of time and effort.

Such a lengthy period of preparation is to be seen in contrast to the events that take place on the night of Passover. Four days after each family has taken an unblemished

girt = gert = belted

This line announces the purpose of this reading; it is followed by the grim details of God's judgment. Give them the emphasis they deserve.

"This is how you are to **eat** it:
    with your loins **girt**, **sandals** on your **feet** and your **staff**
        in hand,
    you shall **eat** like those who are in **flight**.
It is the **Passover** of the LORD.
For on this **same night** I will go through **Egypt**,
    striking down **every firstborn** of the land, both **man** and **beast**,
    and **executing judgment** on all the **gods** of Egypt—I, the LORD!
But the **blood** will mark the **houses** where you **are**.
Seeing the blood, I will **pass over** you;
    thus, when I strike the land of **Egypt**,
    no destructive blow will come **upon** you.

"This **day** shall be a **memorial feast** for **you**,
    which **all** your generations shall **celebrate**
    with **pilgrimage** to the LORD, as a **perpetual** institution."

For meditation and context:

RESPONSORIAL PSALM   Psalm 116:12–13, 15–16bc, 17–18
(see 1 Corinthians 10:16)

R. Our blessing-cup is a communion with the Blood of Christ.

How shall I make a return to the LORD
    for all the good he has done for me?
The cup of salvation I will take up,
    and I will call upon the name of the LORD.

Precious in the eyes of the LORD
    is the death of his faithful ones.
I am your servant, the son of your handmaid;
    you have loosed my bonds.

To you will I offer sacrifice of thanksgiving,
    and I will call upon the name of the LORD.
My vows to the LORD I will pay
    in the presence of all his people.

TO KEEP IN MIND
The responsorial psalm "has great liturgical and pastoral importance, since it fosters meditation on the Word of God," the *General Instruction of the Roman Missal* says. Pray it as you prepare.

---

lamb for itself or together with another household, they are to slaughter the lamb during the "evening twilight" of the Passover, to mark the doorways of their homes with the blood of the lamb, and to eat the meat. The posture during this meal is critical. The Israelites are commanded to eat "like those who are in flight." While the blood on the doorposts will signal to the angel of death that the inhabitants are to be passed over, the Israelites are not to grow complacent. They are to be ready to leave at a moment's notice.

Each spring, the Jewish community celebrates the great feast of the Passover even today. During the Passover Seder, the celebratory meal of the feast, the account of the Israelites' liberation is proclaimed around the family table as a present reality. Just as freedom comes each year to the Jewish people, so Christians see in the Passover the pattern of Christ's own passage from death to life. In the context of the Mass of the Lord's Supper on Holy Thursday, the Exodus story and the prescriptions for celebrating Passover call the Christian commu-

nity to be alert and vigilant for the Lord's invitation into a new liberation and holiness of life.

READING II   Paul's reminder to the Christians at Corinth regarding the Lord's actions and words at the Last Supper are set in the context of his condemnation of the Corinthians' practice when celebrating the Lord's Supper. The more affluent members were failing to wait for the poorer members of the community, who often arrived later because of work, in order

Corinthians = kohr-IN-thee-uhnz

A narrative commemoration of the words at the heart of the Mass. These words of Paul's to the Corinthians echo the words in the reading from Exodus.

Here begin the words of institution, always spoken by a priest, but here, most likely, spoken by a lector. These words can take on a freshness in your proclamation.

In a slow, commemorative rhythm.

READING II   1 Corinthians 11:23–26

A reading from the first Letter of Saint Paul to the Corinthians

Brothers and sisters:
I **received** from the Lord what I also **handed** on to you,
    that the **Lord** Jesus, on the **night** he was handed over,
    took **bread**, and, after he had given **thanks**,
    broke it and said, "**This** is my **body** that is for **you**.
Do this in remembrance of **me**."
In the **same way** also the **cup**, after **supper**, saying,
    "**This cup** is the **new covenant** in my **blood**.
Do this, as **often** as you **drink it**, in **remembrance** of me."
For as **often** as you eat this **bread** and drink the **cup**,
    you **proclaim** the **death** of the **Lord** until he **comes**.

A narrative reading that provides the basis for one of the most powerful of Christian rituals, the washing of feet. Its power resides in the directness of its depiction of the ritual itself but also in the ways the act anticipates Christ's passion.

Iscariot = ih-SKAYR-ee-uht

The details here are important.

GOSPEL   John 13:1–15

A reading from the holy Gospel according to John

Before the feast of **Passover**, Jesus **knew** that his **hour** had **come**
    to **pass** from this **world** to the **Father**.
He **loved** his own in the **world** and he **loved** them to the **end**.
The **devil** had already induced **Judas**, son of **Simon** the **Iscariot**,
    to hand him **over**.
So, during supper,
    fully aware that the **Father** had put **everything** into his **power**
    and that he had **come** from God and was **returning** to God,
    he **rose** from supper and took **off** his outer **garments**.
He took a **towel** and tied it around his **waist**.
Then he **poured water** into a **basin**
    and **began** to wash the disciples' **feet**
    and **dry them** with the **towel** around his **waist**.

to participate together in the sharing of the meal (1 Corinthians 11:17–22). Paul chastises them: "For in eating, each one goes ahead with his own supper, and one goes hungry while another gets drunk" (v. 21).

The "words of institution," the liturgical formula that is spoken over the bread and the wine, are found in this letter as the earliest testimony to what Jesus might actually have said at the Last Supper. Scripture scholars are quite certain that by the time of Paul's writing his letter in the mid-50s, the Church would have known this formula. Liturgical scholars generally

employ the four action words found in this recalling of the Last Supper—*take, bless, break,* and *give*—as the important structural components of the Eucharistic rite. These words themselves serve as a corrective to the inappropriate behavior of the Christians. The food and the drink that they have been given are to be blessed and given for the sake of others. There is to be no suggestion of hoarding in the celebration of the Lord's Supper.

Eating and drinking are important ways of remembering the Lord. It matters to Paul how the Corinthians engage in these

actions: "For as often as you eat this bread and drink the cup, you proclaim the death of the Lord until he comes." Our assemblies would do well to ask themselves how the manner in which we eat and drink at the Lord's Supper testifies to our true faith in his future coming.

GOSPEL   John opens his account of the Last Supper with the theological statement that Jesus knew when "his hour" would come. He is aware and in control: "fully aware that the Father had put everything into his power and that

Peter's inability to understand what Jesus is doing reflects the congregation's. Though Peter is a bit thick, Jesus is gentle but authoritative in his responses.

He **came** to Simon **Peter**, who **said** to him,
  "**Master**, are you going to **wash** my **feet**?"
Jesus answered and said to him,
  "What I am **doing**, you **do not** understand **now**,
  but you will **understand later**."
Peter said to him, "You will **never** wash my **feet**."
Jesus answered him,
  "Unless I **wash** you, you will have no **inheritance** with **me**."
Simon Peter said to him,
  "**Master**, then not only my **feet**, but my **hands** and **head**
    as well."
Jesus said to him,

Emphasis on "feet washed."

  "**Whoever** has bathed has no **need** except to have his
    feet washed, for he is clean all over;
  so you are **clean**, but not **all**."
For he **knew** who would **betray** him;
  for this **reason**, he said, "Not **all** of you are **clean**."

So when he had **washed** their feet
  and put his **garments** back on and **reclined** at table again,
  he said to them, "Do you **realize** what I have **done** for you?

These lines to the end of the reading are firm and mysterious.

You call me '**teacher**' and '**master**,' and rightly so, for **indeed**
    I **am**.
If I, therefore, the **master** and **teacher**, have **washed** your feet,
  you ought to wash one another's feet.
I have **given** you a model to **follow**,
  so that as I have done for **you**, **you** should also **do**."

he had come from God and was returning to God." Even knowing all that he does, Jesus continues to love his disciples to the very end, and he wants to leave them with a clear understanding of what this love means.

John is the only one of the four Gospels not to contain the institution narrative. Instead of leaving his disciples with the commandment to remember him after his death by sharing a cup and breaking bread, Jesus wants them to make him present through the enactment of charity. The selflessness of the Lord's washing his disciples' feet, known by tradition as the *mandatum*

(commandment), is vividly portrayed in the Gospel by the image of Jesus removing his garments, in he *himself* tying a towel around his waist, in the pouring of water, and in the washing and drying of feet. Jesus performs all of these selfless actions without any assistance. Jesus gives his entire self in this expression of service.

The opposite stance, and perhaps the one that most clearly represents the typical human response to other people's acts of kindness, is Peter's simple statement, "You will never wash my feet." So quick are we to respond to people's charity and generos-

ity toward ourselves with the words "No, thank you. I am OK. I do not need your help." We are usually suspicious when others approach us with unsolicited compassion. Yet this is precisely what Jesus is attempting to communicate in this newly established ritual. Wash the feet of others without being asked. "I have given you a model to follow, so that as I have done for you, you should also do." Holy Thursday establishes that the emptying of self for the sake of others is the entry point to contemplating the Paschal Mystery of Christ. S.W.

GOOD FRIDAY: CELEBRATION OF THE LORD'S PASSION

LECTIONARY #40

READING I   Isaiah 52:13—53:12

A reading from the Book of the Prophet Isaiah

> **See**, my servant shall **prosper**,
>> he shall be **raised high** and greatly **exalted**.
> Even as **many** were **amazed** at him—
>> so **marred** was his look beyond **human semblance**
>> and his **appearance** beyond that of the **sons of man**—
> so shall he startle many nations,
>> because of **him kings** shall stand **speechless**;
> for those who have not been **told** shall see,
>> those who have not **heard** shall **ponder** it.
>
> **Who** would **believe** what we have **heard**?
>> To **whom** has the **arm** of the LORD been **revealed**?
> He grew **up** like a sapling **before** him,
>> like a **shoot** from the parched **earth**;
> there was **in him** no stately bearing to make us **look** at him,
>> nor **appearance** that would **attract** us to him.
> He was **spurned** and **avoided** by **people**,
>> a man of **suffering**, accustomed to **infirmity**,
> one of **those** from whom people hide their **faces**,
>> **spurned**, and we held him in no **esteem**.
>
> Yet it was our **infirmities** that he **bore**,
>> our **sufferings** that he **endured**,
> while we **thought** of him as **stricken**,
>> as one **smitten** by God and **afflicted**.

Isaiah = ī-ZAY-uh

An exhortatory reading whose power arises from bold claims and compelling rhythms. Allow these elements to ring out in your proclamation. Isaiah's prophecy speaks directly to the congregation and the mystery into which it is immersed.

Even emphasis on the words in this line.

The questions Isaiah asks set the tone for the lines to follow.

TO KEEP IN MIND
Use the pitch and volume of your voice to gain the attention of the assembly.

Note the rhythms in the lines in this section, many of which place an emphasis on two of the words in the line, "infirmities" and "bore"; "sufferings" and "endured"; and so forth. Let these rhythms carry your proclamation.

READING I   This section from the prophet Isaiah constitutes the fourth and final Suffering Servant song, which accentuates God's fidelity to an unidentified servant, one who is the victim of great torture and pain. Scholars have long debated whether the four servant songs in Isaiah were written as a personification of Israel as God's servant subjected to suffering. However, most agree that this last song is composed with a messianic context. It foretells the coming of God's chosen servant, who will undergo oppression and hardship in announcing God's reign. As the

Christian community contemplates the redemptive value of Christ's suffering on the cross, and thus the redemptive value of suffering endured in the context of self-sacrifice, the Suffering Servant song places before the heart many vivid images of the one who serves God through a willingness to embrace hardship for the sake of others.

The song begins with God claiming the unnamed figure as "my servant." Although he has endured horrific suffering, this servant "shall prosper," will "be raised high," and will be "greatly exalted." Everything about his condition suggests the opposite.

Isaiah states that his appearance is marred "beyond human semblance." We are left to wonder how the servant will "startle many nations" and leave kings standing "speechless." Is it because the servant's physical appearance is so ghastly, or because he will overturn the ways of the world by establishing a kingdom grounded not in power but in service and compassion?

Isaiah accentuates that this person was rejected from the very beginning. People refused to look at him and to face the challenge he posed. Isaiah labels him as "a man

The story of the Suffering Servant is of course anticipatory of the passion in John's Gospel.

But he was **pierced** for our offenses,
    crushed for our sins;
upon him was the **chastisement** that makes us **whole**,
    by his **stripes** we were **healed**.
We had all gone **astray** like **sheep**,
    each following his **own** way;
but the LORD laid upon him
    the **guilt** of us **all**.

The rhythms that prevail in the previous section continue in this one, often with an emphasis on two words in the line. Once again, let these rhythms carry your proclamation.

Though he was **harshly treated**, he **submitted**
    and **opened not** his mouth;
like a **lamb** led to the **slaughter**
    or a **sheep** before the **shearers**,
he was **silent** and opened not his **mouth**.
Oppressed and **condemned**, he was taken **away**,
    and who would have thought any **more** of his **destiny**?
When he was cut **off** from the land of the **living**,
    and **smitten** for the sin of his **people**,
a **grave** was **assigned** him among the **wicked**
    and a **burial** place with **evildoers**,
though he had **done** no **wrong**
    nor **spoken** any **falsehood**.
But the LORD was pleased
    to **crush him** in **infirmity**.

Words like "slaughter," "condemned," "wicked," and "evildoers" are loaded with significance. Recite them clearly and that significance will be evident to the assembly. No need to over-dramatize the words when you proclaim them.

If he **gives** his life as an **offering** for sin,
    he shall **see** his descendants in a **long life**,
    and the **will** of the LORD shall be **accomplished**
        through him.

As the reading concludes, the mood lifts. There is a sense of promise and redemption. Don't, however, overdo it. The hope will come through when you proclaim these words straightforwardly.

Because of his **affliction**
    he shall **see** the light in **fullness** of days;
through his **suffering**, my servant shall **justify many**,
    and their **guilt** he shall **bear**.
Therefore I will give him his **portion** among the **great**,
    and he shall **divide** the spoils with the **mighty**, »

of suffering" throughout his entire life. Suffering simply became a part of his identity.

"Yet it was our infirmities that he bore, our sufferings that he endured." While the people looked at this man and thought that he was being punished by God, Isaiah makes it clear that he was taking the sins of the people upon himself. By not struggling for acceptance and not hiding from those who would mock and deride him, this servant willingly took upon himself all that evildoers would inflict.

Isaiah likens the attitude of this servant to sheep that are led to be shorn or killed. He does not resist and or even protest. He suffers in silence, soon to be forgotten. But no! Fulfilling the opening words of the song, "my servant shall prosper," God promises that if this servant fulfills his mission and suffers for others' sins, he will have accomplished the Lord's will and will see his descendants flourish in the freedom he brought them. God promises to reward this servant with a place among the great—those men and women who have sacrificed themselves for others. How appropriate it is for the Christian assembly to contemplate the Suffering Servant on Good Friday, when we venerate the wood of the cross. We approach the symbol of suffering not with fear, bitterness, or anger but rather with loving gratitude: "by his stripes we were healed."

READING II A priest is one who makes an offering on behalf of others. The term "high priest," which we encounter at the outset of this reading from the Letter to the Hebrews, was used for the chief religious leader in Jerusalem during the Second Temple era (450 BC to AD 70). The introduction of the term "high priest"

because he **surrendered** himself to **death**
and was **counted** among the **wicked**;
and he shall **take away** the sins of **many**,
and win **pardon** for their **offenses**.

For meditation and context:

RESPONSORIAL PSALM   Psalm 31:2, 6, 12–13, 15–16, 17, 25 (Luke 23:46)

R. Father, into your hands I commend my spirit.

In you, O LORD, I take refuge;
  let me never be put to shame.
In your justice rescue me.
Into your hands I commend my spirit;
  you will redeem me, O LORD,
    O faithful God.

For all my foes I am an object of reproach,
  a laughingstock to my neighbors, and a
    dread to my friends;
  they who see me abroad flee from me.
I am forgotten like the unremembered dead;
  I am like a dish that is broken.

But my trust is in you, O LORD;
  I say, "You are my God.
In your hands is my destiny; rescue me
  from the clutches of my enemies and
    my persecutors."

Let your face shine upon your servant;
  save me in your kindness.
Take courage and be stouthearted,
  all you who hope in the LORD.

READING II   Hebrews 4:14–16; 5:7–9

A reading from the Letter to the Hebrews

Brothers and sisters:
Since we have a **great high priest** who has passed **through**
    the heavens,
  Jesus, the Son of **God**,
  let us **hold fast** to our **confession**.
For we do not have a **high priest**
  who is unable to **sympathize** with our **weaknesses**,
  but one who has similarly been tested in **every** way,
  yet **without** sin.
So let us **confidently** approach the **throne** of **grace**
  to receive **mercy** and to find **grace** for timely **help**.

An exhortatory reading that prepares the assembly to understand the sacrifice of Jesus portrayed in the passion to follow. The theology suggested in this reading is as mysterious as it is natural. Christ is our model, our exemplar. As a man, he felt things just as we feel them. And yet his suffering, as God, is inconceivable. Though framed in a negative construction ("We do not have . . ."), this statement expresses the crucial sympathy Christ has for us and that we should have for him. Proclaim this sentence with care.

after the Babylonian Exile brought with it an exaggerated sense of ritual and political power. The high priest essentially ruled as king and was certainly venerated as such in the Temple precincts.

Against this backdrop of a powerful political figure, the author of the Letter to the Hebrews designates Jesus as "a great high priest who has passed through the heavens." The high priests known to the people would not have exhibited compassion or empathy; they were too absorbed with their own status to be concerned about others. But Jesus, the Son of God, is

not an ordinary high priest, "unable to sympathize with our weaknesses." Jesus knows thoroughly the sufferings of the people because he has been tested by the sufferings of humanity. Jesus is in communion with the suffering of this world.

This is precisely why we may "confidently approach the throne of grace" and from that throne receive the gifts of God's mercy and grace. The letter suggests that the offering of this high priest is all that Jesus encountered in humanity. Human illness and disease, war and violence, tragedy and loss are all offered as sacrifice

because of this man's willingness to become one with the weaknesses of humanity. The image of the Suffering Servant encountered in the first reading should come into view here in the midst of having heard Hebrews as well. This is a high priest who denounced pride and power so that he could be "pierced for our offenses, crushed for our sins" (Isaiah 53:5).

The end of this portion of the letter underscores the humanity of Jesus. "In the days when Christ was in the flesh," he experienced complete union with humanity. He did not observe the messiness of

To intensify the sympathy, "In the days when Christ was in the flesh. . ."

Even stresses on "source," "salvation," and "obey."

Kidron = KID-ruhn
The passion narrative in John's Gospel depicts Jesus foreknowing all that will happen to him, giving him an appearance of calm in a storm. John's passion, like those in the synoptic Gospels, is full of drama, with scenes as vivid as those in any novel or film, but whose focus, Jesus, is defined by quiet intensity. Let that guide your recitation and let the drama inherent in the narrative express itself through you.
Don't overdo these expressions of "I AM."

It is not uncommon, because of the length of this reading, for it to be shared among a group of lectors as well as a deacon and priest. While there are several characters in this narrative, including different speakers, avoid the tendency to do voices or to add drama by raising your voice unnecessarily. Let this narrative speak for itself through you.

Even stresses on "let these men go."

In the **days** when Christ was in the **flesh**,
he offered **prayers** and **supplications** with loud **cries**
and **tears**
to the **one** who was able to **save** him from **death**,
and he was **heard** because of his **reverence**.
Son though he was, he learned **obedience** from what he **suffered**;
and when he was made **perfect**,
he became the **source** of eternal **salvation** for all who
obey him.

GOSPEL   John 18:1—19:42

The Passion of our Lord Jesus Christ according to John

Jesus went out with his **disciples** across the Kidron **valley**
to where there was a **garden**,
into which he and his disciples **entered**.
Judas his betrayer also **knew** the place,
because Jesus had often **met** there with his **disciples**.
So **Judas** got a band of **soldiers** and guards
from the **chief priests** and the **Pharisees**
and **went** there with **lanterns**, **torches**, and **weapons**.
Jesus, knowing **everything** that was going to **happen** to him,
went out and said to them, "**Whom** are you **looking** for?"
They answered him, "**Jesus** the **Nazorean**."
He said to them, "**I AM**."
Judas his betrayer was also **with** them.
When he said to them, "**I AM**,"
they turned **away** and fell to the **ground**.
So he again **asked** them,
"**Whom** are you looking for?"
They said, "**Jesus** the **Nazorean**."
Jesus **answered**,
"I **told** you that **I AM**.
So if you are **looking** for me, **let these men go**." »

human life from afar; instead, he mingled with it. Like all humans, Jesus prayed to God "with loud cries and tears." He recognized the agony that was inflicted upon him—he felt it to the very depths of his being—and he asked God to defend him in his suffering. What Jesus did not do was to shirk any aspect of his suffering. He sought to learn from it, and thus, God recognized both his "reverence" and his complete "obedience." On this day, Good Friday, Christians are challenged to make these attitudes of Christ's their own. The perfection of Jesus, his willingness to sacrifice himself utterly and com-

pletely, is indeed our salvation. But it must be the pattern for a way of life that is practiced every day.

GOSPEL The four Gospels contain similar stories of the passion of Jesus Christ but with very different nuances. In the passion narrative from the Gospel of John, what is important is that Jesus is portrayed as a divine figure who is completely aware of how and why the events unfold as they do. John's Jesus knows what is demanded of him for the Law to be fulfilled, and he has foreknowledge of

the outcome itself. For this reason, throughout the passion narrative, Jesus displays compassion and forgiveness toward his disciples, who are seen making great acts of betrayal in the end.

One of the details of John's passion is that it is separated from the Last Supper. Rather than moving directly from the table to the garden where Jesus wishes to pray, John interjects several chapters devoted to Jesus' "farewell discourses" directed to his disciples. From these discourses come many well-known sayings, such as "I am the way and the truth and the life" (14:6), "I am

Even stresses on "struck the high priest's slave."

Malchus = MAL-kuhs

Annas = AN-uhs
Caiaphas = KĪ-uh fuhs
John's Gospel tends to heap scorn upon the Jews, which has contributed to an ugly tendency toward anti-Semitism in Christianity. Mindfulness of this history can empower your proclamation.

The story of Peter's denial provides a sympathetic note in an often harsh narrative. Peter's weakness is the assembly's; his denials ("I am not") speak directly to our spiritual struggles.

Even emphasis on the words in this line.

This was to fulfill what he had said,
  "I have not lost any of those you gave me."
Then Simon Peter, who had a sword, drew it,
  struck the high priest's slave, and cut off his right ear.
The slave's name was Malchus.
Jesus said to Peter,
  "Put your sword into its scabbard.
Shall I not drink the cup that the Father gave me?"

So the band of soldiers, the tribune, and the Jewish guards
    seized Jesus,
  bound him, and brought him to Annas first.
He was the father-in-law of Caiaphas,
  who was high priest that year.
It was Caiaphas who had counseled the Jews
  that it was better that one man should die rather than
    the people.

Simon Peter and another disciple followed Jesus.
Now the other disciple was known to the high priest,
  and he entered the courtyard of the high priest with Jesus.
But Peter stood at the gate outside.
So the other disciple, the acquaintance of the high priest,
  went out and spoke to the gatekeeper and brought Peter in.
Then the maid who was the gatekeeper said to Peter,
  "You are not one of this man's disciples, are you?"
He said, "I am not."
Now the slaves and the guards were standing around
    a charcoal fire
  that they had made, because it was cold,
  and were warming themselves.
Peter was also standing there keeping warm.

The high priest questioned Jesus
  about his disciples and about his doctrine.
Jesus answered him,
  "I have spoken publicly to the world.

the vine, you are the branches" (15:5), and "No one has greater love than this, to lay down one's life for one's friends" (15:13). In these farewell words, Jesus speaks clearly of the need for his disciples to maintain faith in him in a hostile world. This is the intent for John's Gospel as a whole: the maintenance of faith in Jesus even though his return seems to be delayed. Only after John tells of Jesus commissioning his disciples in the arduous task of remaining in him does John tell of the passion, beginning with Jesus' arrest. The disciples have been prepared for what is to come.

As Jesus enters the garden with his disciples, we learn that Judas, who "also knew the place," has arrived ahead of them. Instead of suggesting that Judas hands Jesus over to hostile authorities, John portrays Judas as the organizer of a sort of posse, complete with "lanterns, torches, and weapons." There is no kiss given by Judas to Jesus to signal that he is the one to be arrested; instead Jesus steps forward to make himself more visible and accessible. John tells us that Jesus begins the dialogue with the mob precisely because he knows what was going to hap-

pen to him. In the synoptic Gospels, Jesus is described as suffering great agony as he spends time in prayer, but here in John, there is no display of emotion, only his calm reply to the crowd's question: he is the one they are looking for.

When Jesus identifies himself as "I AM"—the name by which God instructs Moses to reveal the divine nature to the Israelites and Pharaoh in the Book of Exodus (3:14)—the crowd accompanying Judas turns away from him and falls to the ground. From this display of humility, it is clear that deep down they recognize the

I have **always taught** in a **synagogue**
or in the **temple** area where all the **Jews** gather,
and in **secret** I have said **nothing**. Why **ask** me?
Ask **those** who **heard me** what I said to **them**.
They **know** what I **said**."
When he had **said** this,
one of the temple guards standing there struck Jesus and said,
"Is **this** the way you **answer** the high **priest**?"
Jesus **answered** him,
"If I have spoken **wrongly**, **testify** to the wrong;
but if I have spoken **rightly**, why do you strike **me**?"
Then **Annas** sent him bound to **Caiaphas** the high **priest**.

Now **Simon Peter** was standing there keeping **warm**.
And they **said** to him,
"You are not one of his **disciples**, **are you**?"
He **denied** it and said,
"I am **not**."
One of the **slaves** of the high **priest**,
a **relative** of the one whose **ear Peter** had cut **off**, said,
"Didn't I **see** you in the **garden** with him?"
Again Peter **denied** it.
And **immediately** the cock **crowed**.

Then they **brought Jesus** from Caiaphas to the **praetorium**.
It was **morning**.
And they themselves did not enter the praetorium,
in order **not** to be **defiled** so that they could **eat** the **Passover**.
So **Pilate** came out to them and said,
"**What charge** do you bring **against** this **man**?"
They **answered** and **said** to him,
"If he were **not** a criminal,
we would **not** have handed him **over** to you."
At this, Pilate said to them,
"**Take him yourselves**, and **judge** him according
to your **law**." »

Even emphasis on the words in this line.

Jesus' response suggests the core of his resolve to face the suffering to come.

Again, a return to the story of Peter. Don't overly dramatize the denial. Peter's shame will come through clearly when you proclaim this passage deliberately and clearly.

praetorium = prih-TOHR-ee-uhm
Here begins a long passage of exceptional vividness and power. It contrasts the conversation between Pilate and Jesus in the praetorium with the more aggressive exchanges between Pilate and the crowd. It is told from Pilate's point of view, which allows us to sympathize with Pilate. It's a truly remarkable passage whose drama need not be exaggerated. Pace your reading to allow its potent drama to come through on its own.

Pilate is dismissive here, but don't exaggerate his dismissiveness.

---

divine presence in their midst. Even as Jesus repeats the question "Whom are you looking for?" his persecutors respond with the same response: "Jesus of Nazareth." Jesus again applies the divine name to himself, and the crowd continues to act in a passive way, almost as if they are in a trance. The first to act with aggression is Simon Peter, who draws his sword and cuts off the ear of the high priest's slave. Jesus reprimands Peter and proceeds to offer a teaching on the necessity of his impending death: "Shall I not drink the cup that the Father gave me?" Such a statement is much

different from the request Jesus makes in prayer in Luke's Gospel, read this past Sunday: "Take this cup away from me" (Luke 22:42).

Without further questioning or altercation, the soldiers and Jewish guards bind Jesus and escort him to Annas, the father-in-law of the high priest. Unlike the synoptic Gospels, in which Peter is said to have been present when Jesus arrived, John states that Peter and another disciple followed Jesus. While the unnamed disciple is allowed entrance into the courtyard of the high priest, Peter remains at the gate. This

gate clearly marks a separation between those in proximity to Jesus and those distant from him. Just as Peter is about to be brought inside, closer to Jesus, he begins his denial of the Lord. The gatekeeper allows Jesus entrance, and Peter moves to a fire to keep himself warm. He continues to remain at a physical distance from Jesus.

Meanwhile Annas begins his interrogation of Jesus, first inquiring about his disciples and then about his doctrine. Jesus' reply may seem caustic as he tells Annas to find out about these things from those who heard him teaching. His reply carries the

The Jews answered him,
  "We do **not** have the right to execute **anyone**,"
  in **order** that the word of **Jesus** might be **fulfilled**
  that he said **indicating** the kind of **death** he would **die**.
So Pilate went back into the **praetorium**
  and **summoned Jesus** and **said** to him,
  "**Are you** the **King** of the **Jews?**"
Jesus answered,
  "Do you **say this** on your **own**
  or have others **told** you **about** me?"
Pilate answered,
  "I am not a Jew, am I?
Your own **nation** and the chief **priests** handed you **over** to me.
What have you done?"
Jesus answered,
  "My kingdom does not belong to this **world**.
If my kingdom **did** belong to this world,
  my **attendants** would be **fighting**
  to **keep** me from being handed **over** to the **Jews**.
But as it **is**, my **kingdom** is not **here**."
So Pilate said to him,
  "Then you **are** a king?"
Jesus answered,
  "You **say** I am a king.
For **this** I was born and for **this** I came into the world,
  to **testify** to the **truth**.
Everyone who **belongs** to the truth **listens** to my **voice**."
Pilate said to him, "What is **truth?**"

When he had **said** this,
  he **again** went out to the Jews and **said** to them,
  "I find no **guilt** in him.
But you have a **custom** that I release one **prisoner** to you
    at **Passover**.
Do you want me to **release** to you the **King** of the **Jews?**"

The crucial question. Again, don't exaggerate it. Pilate, a government official, is asking an earnest question.

Even emphasis on the words in this question.

Jesus' answer is completely mysterious but supercharged with confidence. Read these words clearly and plainly.

Again, mysterious and confident.

Almost even emphasis on the words in this line, with extra added to "guilt."

---

tone of a prophet. One of the guards strikes Jesus and reproves him for his bold speech. Jesus' reaction, like his demeanor in the garden, is calm; he simply suggests that he is merely speaking words of truth: the people he taught ought to be able to answer all their questions about Jesus' orthodoxy. John then turns our attention back to Peter, who should have been one of those capable of testifying to Jesus' right teaching. Such is not the case. Rather, Peter denies him two more times before the cock crowed, as Jesus had predicted.

Although John tells us that Annas had Jesus bound and sent to Caiaphas, we are not told anything regarding the interchange between Caiaphas and Jesus. We next encounter Jesus at the Roman praetorium, the seat of Roman authority in occupied Jerusalem. Because entering the praetorium would mean automatic defilement for the Jews, it was necessary that Pilate come to the entrance to meet them. When Pilate, the leading Roman official, asks the crowd outside regarding the charges against Jesus, they are suddenly vague in their response, suggesting that the act of handing him over

to a Roman official ought to make the severity of the charge clear enough. Thus, Pilate must return inside to question Jesus. Pilate discovers that Jesus will not be much help in providing an answer to the simple question "What have you done?"

Jesus chooses not to address this question; instead, he returns to one posed moments earlier by Pilate: "Are you the King of the Jews?" Jesus does not deny being a king, but he defines the nature of his kingdom as one not belonging to this world. Nevertheless, Jesus does not directly utter the words "I am a king," which would have

Barabbas = buh-RAB-uhs
Avoid the tendency to shout this line.

"Scourged" is a wicked word. Read it slowly, one elongated syllable.

No need to shout this line. It's all too clear what is happening.

Even stresses on the words in this line.

Pilate is at a loss, but he's also a dutiful Roman bureaucrat.

Lower your voice here. Don't exclaim.

Don't shout.

This question has a note of astonishment.

They cried out again,
    "Not **this** one but **Barabbas**!"
Now **Barabbas** was a **revolutionary**.

Then **Pilate** took Jesus and had him **scourged**.
And the **soldiers** wove a **crown** out of **thorns**
    and **placed** it on his **head**,
    and **clothed him** in a purple **cloak**,
    and they **came** to him and said,
    "**Hail**, **King** of the **Jews**!"
And they **struck** him **repeatedly**.
Once more Pilate went out and said to them,
    "**Look**, I am **bringing** him out to you,
    so that you may **know** that I find no **guilt** in him."
So **Jesus** came out,
    wearing the **crown** of **thorns** and the **purple cloak**.
And he **said** to them, "**Behold**, the **man**!"
When the **chief priests** and the **guards** saw him they cried **out**,
    "**Crucify** him, **crucify** him!"
Pilate **said** to them,
    "**Take** him **yourselves** and crucify him.
I **find** no **guilt** in him."
The Jews answered,
    "We have a **law**, and according to that **law** he ought to **die**,
    because he **made** himself the Son of **God**."
Now when Pilate **heard** this statement,
    he became even more **afraid**,
    and went **back** into the **praetorium** and said to Jesus,
    "**Where** are you **from**?"
Jesus did not **answer** him.
So Pilate **said** to him,
    "Do you not **speak** to me?
Do you not **know** that I have **power** to **release** you
    and I have **power** to **crucify** you?"
Jesus **answered** him,
    "You would have **no power** over **me**
    if it had not been **given** to you from **above**. ≫

been a sufficient threat against Rome to put him to death as an insurrectionist. He continues by suggesting that the title "king" comes from the lips of Pilate. In contrast to the political understanding of being a king, Jesus tells Pilate that he was born into this world to testify to the truth. So, tying the logic of Jesus together, this means that Jesus' kingdom is based on truth, where "everyone who belongs to the truth listens to my voice." Pilate's question, "What is truth?" suggests that he has neither listened to Jesus' voice nor does he belong to his kingdom.

Undoubtedly, Pilate wishes to bring this controversy to a resolution, but it could be that he has begun to listen to what Jesus is communicating about himself. Pilate once again moves outside and tells the crowd that he finds "no guilt in him." He gives the people the opportunity to release Jesus, but the people call instead for the release of Barabbas.

If Pilate wants to prevent an uprising among the people, he has no choice but to bow to their request to put Jesus to death. The Roman soldiers scourge Jesus, dress him in the clothes of a king, place a crown

of thorns on his head, and mock him with the words "Hail, King of the Jews!" Pilate goes outside the praetorium once more and presents a bruised and beaten Jesus to the crowd: "Behold, the man!" Undoubtedly, Pilate is underscoring the weakness of Jesus, as if to say, "Does he look like he could pose any threat?" After Pilate tells the mob that he finds Jesus to be innocent, they remind him that their law demands death for the one who claims to be the Son of God. John tells us that Pilate became even more afraid and retreated back into the praetorium to confront Jesus once again.

Jesus' answer to Pilate's question once again is mysterious and confident.

For this **reason** the one who handed me over to you
    has the greater **sin**."
Consequently, Pilate tried to **release** him; but the Jews cried out,
    "If you **release** him, you are not a **Friend** of **Caesar**.
Everyone who makes himself a **king** opposes **Caesar**."

When Pilate **heard these words** he brought Jesus **out**
    and **seated** him on the judge's **bench**
    in the **place** called Stone **Pavement**, in Hebrew, **Gabbatha**.

Gabbatha = GAB-uh-thuh

It was **preparation** day for **Passover**, and it was about **noon**.
And he **said** to the Jews,
    "**Behold**, your **king**!"

Don't shout.

They cried out,
    "**Take him away, take him away! Crucify** him!"
Pilate **said** to them,
    "Shall I **crucify** your **king**?"
The chief priests answered,

This line of the chief priests is dismissive; don't overdo the dismissiveness.

    "We have no **king** but **Caesar**."
Then he handed him **over** to them to be **crucified**.

So they took **Jesus**, and, carrying the **cross** himself,
    he went out to what is called the **Place** of the **Skull**,
    in Hebrew, **Golgotha**.

Golgotha = GAWL-guh-thuh

In two short lines the act of Jesus' crucifixion, to which this whole passion has been building, is expressed. Read these lines plainly and slowly.

There they **crucified** him, and **with** him two **others**,
    one on either **side**, with **Jesus** in the **middle**.
Pilate also had an **inscription** written and put on the **cross**.
It read,
    "**Jesus** the **Nazorean**, the **King** of the **Jews**."
Now **many** of the Jews **read** this inscription,
    because the **place** where Jesus was crucified was near the **city**;
    and it was **written** in **Hebrew**, **Latin**, and **Greek**.
So the **chief priests** of the Jews said to **Pilate**,
    "Do not write 'The **King** of the **Jews**,'
    but that he said, 'I **am** the King of the **Jews**.'"
Pilate answered,
    "What I have **written**, I have **written**."

Pilate's are his final, ominous words in this passion. Pause slightly after proclaiming them.

Now the confrontation between Pilate and Jesus grows more contentious, primarily because of Pilate's fear of an uprising, but also because Jesus answers his question with silence. Nevertheless, Pilate still does not discover a real reason for putting Jesus to death. John tells us that Pilate wanted to release Jesus, but the crowd would not have it. They persuade Pilate that he would be seen as disloyal to Caesar if he allowed this supposed king to live. Consequently, Pilate brings Jesus out of the praetorium once more, takes his seat at the judge's bench, and introduces Jesus to the people with the words "Behold, your king!" Pilate is surely mocking the Jews by declaring the weak and battered Jesus their king. They demand that he be taken away and crucified. John tells us that the time is about noon, the time when the lambs were beginning to be slaughtered in the Temple. That the beginning of Jesus' final journey to death coincides with the killing of the Passover lambs is important for John.

The carrying of the cross between the praetorium and Golgotha is omitted in John. We are simply told that Jesus "went out to" the place of his crucifixion, where he is crucified between "two others." John does not identify these two as criminals or engage them in dialogue with Jesus. Instead, John wants the reader to focus on the identity of Jesus alone, as seen in Pilate's ordering the inscription "Jesus the Nazorean, the King of the Jews" to be placed above his head. Meanwhile, the soldiers are busy dividing Jesus, clothes and gambling for his tunic. The seamlessness of his tunic allows for John to demonstrate how Scripture is being fulfilled.

As Jesus hangs upon the cross, John turns our attention to Jesus' mother and

When the **soldiers** had crucified **Jesus**,
>   they took his **clothes** and divided them into **four shares**,
>   a **share** for each **soldier**.
They also took his **tunic**, but the tunic was **seamless**,
>   **woven** in one piece from the **top down**.
So they said to one **another**,
>   "Let's not **tear** it, but cast **lots** for it to see whose it will **be**,"
>   in order that the passage of Scripture might be fulfilled
>   that says:
>   *They **divided** my garments among them,*
>   *and for my **vesture** they cast **lots**.*
This is what the soldiers **did**.
Standing by the cross of **Jesus** were his **mother**
>   and his mother's **sister**, **Mary** the wife of **Clopas**,
>   and Mary of **Magdala**.
When Jesus saw his **mother** and the disciple there whom
>   he **loved**
>   he said to his **mother**, "**Woman**, **behold**, your **son**."
Then he said to the **disciple**,
>   "**Behold**, your **mother**."
And from **that hour** the **disciple** took her into his **home**.

After **this**, aware that everything was now **finished**,
>   in order that the **Scripture** might be **fulfilled**,
>   Jesus said, "**I thirst**."
There was a **vessel** filled with **common wine**.
So they put a **sponge** soaked in wine on a sprig of **hyssop**
>   and put it up to his **mouth**.
When **Jesus** had taken the wine, he said,
>   "**It is finished**."
And **bowing** his head, he **handed** over the **spirit**.

[Here all kneel and pause for a short time.]

Now since it was **preparation** day,
>   in **order** that the bodies might not remain
>   on the **cross** on the **sabbath**, »

Be sure to read the names of these women clearly.

Almost even stresses on the words in this line.

"I thirst," concentrates the agony of the crucifixion. Say it simply and clearly.

hyssop = HIS-uhp

These words, "It is finished," culminate the drama of the passion. Give each word even stress, pausing ever so slightly between them, almost: "It. Is. Finished."

The details in the passage that concludes John's passion are of interest because they speak to the awful economy of torture and execution (on the part of the Roman soldiers)

---

the other disciples who remain with him at the foot of the cross. John is unique in including Jesus' mother and the "beloved disciple." Jesus speaks to his mother using language reminiscent of the wedding at Cana, when he addressed her as "Woman." The scene of Jesus presenting his mother to the beloved disciple and presenting the beloved disciple to his mother has long been interpreted as Jesus instituting the new familial relationship that is to take place in the Church. Great care for this relationship is suggested with the words, "And from that hour the disciple took her into his home."

All Jesus must yet do is fulfill the words of Psalm 69:4: "I am weary with crying out; my throat is parched." Thus, Jesus says the simple words "I thirst" joined with the words "It is finished." John's Jesus is not only aware of how events will unfold, he is in complete control. He determines when all has been fulfilled and when his mission is finished.

Pilate orders the soldiers to break the legs of those who had been crucified to hasten their deaths before the beginning of the Sabbath. Breaking the last bit of support for the upper body would cause

instant suffocation. However, the guards discover that Jesus is already dead. Because his death takes place simultaneous to the killing of the lambs in the Temple, John wishes us to see that Jesus' legs must be unbroken for him to be likened to an unblemished lamb. Another important symbol for John here is the blood and water that flow from Jesus' side. Both blood and water are primary symbols of the Exodus story, as the Israelites marked their doorposts with the blood of the lamb before they were set free to cross through the waters of the Red Sea. The cross stands as

as well as the requirements of the burial of a corpse according to Jewish custom. It's effective to read these words with scrutiny and openness.

John is speaking directly to his audience in these words; through you, directly to the assembly.

Arimathea = ayr-ih-muh-THEE-uh

Nicodemus = nik-uh-DEE-muhs

Don't hurry over these details.

myrrh = mer

aloes = AL-ohz

Read this concluding phrase, "for the tomb was close by," slowly.

for the **sabbath** day of that **week** was a **solemn** one,
the **Jews** asked Pilate that their **legs** be broken
and that they be taken **down**.
So the **soldiers** came and broke the **legs** of the first
and then of the other one who was **crucified** with **Jesus**.
But when they came to **Jesus** and saw that he was already **dead**,
they did **not** break his **legs**,
but one **soldier** thrust his **lance** into his **side**,
and immediately blood and **water** flowed **out**.
An **eyewitness** has testified, and his **testimony** is true;
he **knows** that he is speaking the **truth**,
so that **you also** may come to **believe**.
For this **happened** so that the **Scripture** passage might
be **fulfilled**:
*Not a **bone** of it will be **broken**.*
And again another passage says:
*They will look **upon him** whom they have **pierced**.*

After **this**, Joseph of **Arimathea**,
secretly a disciple of **Jesus** for **fear** of the **Jews**,
asked **Pilate** if he could **remove** the body of **Jesus**.
And Pilate **permitted** it.
So he came and took his **body**.
Nicodemus, the one who had **first come** to him at **night**,
also came bringing a mixture of **myrrh** and **aloes**
weighing about one **hundred** pounds.
They took the body of **Jesus**
and bound it with **burial cloths** along with the **spices**,
according to the **Jewish burial custom**.
Now in the **place** where he had been **crucified** there was
a **garden**,
and in the **garden** a new **tomb**, in which **no one** had yet
been **buried**.
So they laid **Jesus** there because of the Jewish **preparation** day;
for the **tomb** was close **by**.

a sign of Paschal liberation in the Gospel of John.

The final element of the passion in John is the abundance of ritual connected with the burial of Jesus. We are told that Joseph of Arimathea is assisted by Nicodemus, "the one who had first come to him at night." Nicodemus first appeared in the third chapter of John and recognized Jesus as "a teacher who has come from God," and he is the first disciple whom Jesus instructs on the kingdom of God. Clearly, John wants

us to see that, unlike the disciples that accompanied Jesus along the way, Nicodemus has come out of the shadows as a figure of light who takes great care in attending to Jesus' body. John tells us that the spices Nicodemus brings with him to anoint Jesus' body weigh almost one hundred pounds. Joseph and Nicodemus proceed to bind Jesus' body in burial clothes, placing it in a new tomb in the garden. Even in the midst of death, there is the reverent care for life. S.W.

HOLY SATURDAY: EASTER VIGIL

LECTIONARY #41

READING I   Genesis 1:1—2:2

Genesis = JEN-uh-sihs

A narrative reading of one of the most familiar passages in all of Scripture. Because the language in this reading is so grand, you maybe tempted to dramatize your proclamation. No need. The language is so finely wrought that if you read at a measured pace, its glories will come through.

The word "and" appears repeatedly in this reading. It's one of the main sources of its power. It functions almost like a verb. Let the word do the work for you as you proclaim.

Pause ever so slightly after "first day." You will repeat this slight pause five more times.

Pause slightly after "second day."

A reading from the Book of Genesis

[In the **beginning**, when God created the **heavens** and the **earth**,]
    the **earth** was a formless **wasteland**, and **darkness** covered
        the **abyss**,
    while a **mighty wind** swept **over** the **waters**.

Then God said,
    "Let there be **light**," and there was **light**.
God saw how **good** the light was.
God then **separated** the **light** from the **darkness**.
God called the light "**day**," and the darkness he called "**night**."
Thus **evening** came, and **morning** followed—the **first** day.

Then God said,
    "Let there be a **dome** in the **middle** of the **waters**,
    to separate one **body** of water from the **other**."
And so it **happened**:
    God **made** the dome,
    and it separated the water **above** the dome from the water
        below it.
God called the dome "the **sky**."
Evening came, and **morning** followed—the **second** day.

Then God said,
    "Let the **water** under the **sky** be gathered into a **single basin**,
    so that the **dry land** may appear." »

There are options for today's readings. Contact your parish staff to learn which readings will be used.

READING I   The seven Old Testament readings that precede the two New Testament readings in the Liturgy of the Word for the Easter Vigil constitute the broad brushstrokes of salvation history. After the creation of the world, in which God calls everything good, sin enters the world and calls for redemption. The readings we hear this night recall the many voices and events leading Israel, and the entire created world, back to the fullness of relationship with God. At the Vigil, we hear these stories as the context for participating in the baptism of new Christians, renewing our own baptismal promises, and celebrating the Eucharist. This whole event is an act of *anamnesis*, a way of remembering in which these tales of salvation do not simply remain historical fact, but constitute the community's living present. They call us to ponder how God continues to be active in the world, saving all things and drawing creation to himself.

The very first words of the Old Testament, Genesis 1:1—2:2, present the primordial creation story, in which everything that exists was brought into being in the course of six days, with the seventh day of the week designated as a day for God to rest from all his labors. Although science convinces us that the world came into being through something like the Big Bang theory, which suggests that the expansion of the cosmos began 13.8 billion years ago through the chaotic combination of dense gases and high temperatures, this ancient story is still to be taken seriously. It reveals

And so it **happened**:
  the **water** under the **sky** was gathered into its **basin**,
  and the **dry land** appeared.
God called the dry land "the **earth**,"
  and the basin of the water he called "the **sea**."
God saw how **good** it was.
Then God said,
  "Let the **earth** bring **forth** vegetation:
  every **kind** of plant that bears **seed**
  and every **kind** of fruit tree on **earth**
  that bears **fruit** with its seed **in** it."
And so it **happened**:
  the **earth** brought forth every **kind** of plant that bears **seed**
  and every **kind** of fruit tree on **earth**
  that bears **fruit** with its **seed** in it.
God saw how **good** it was.
Evening came, and **morning** followed—the **third** day.

Then God said:
  "Let there be **lights** in the **dome** of the **sky**,
  to separate **day** from **night**.
Let them mark the **fixed times**, the **days** and the **years**,
  and serve as **luminaries** in the **dome** of the **sky**,
  to shed **light** upon the **earth**."
And so it **happened**:
  God **made** the two great **lights**,
  the **greater** one to govern the **day**,
  and the **lesser** one to govern the **night**;
  and he made the **stars**.
God set them in the **dome** of the **sky**,
  to shed light upon the **earth**,
  to govern the **day** and the **night**,
  and to separate the **light** from the **darkness**.
God saw how **good** it was.
Evening came, and **morning** followed—the **fourth** day.

the love of God, who meticulously cares for each detail of that which comes forth from the utterance of his Word. From this foundational account of creation, we can say that all things are meant to exist in perfect harmony; chaos is not a piece of how the world's puzzle fits together. All that is works together.

Genesis opens with a description of what was before God showed his desire to create: Genesis describes this as a "formless wasteland," filled with darkness. This is meant to be viewed as chaotic—there is simply no point to it. Then God speaks, and from his voice comes light, which changes everything. Light serves to balance darkness. The two are not seen as waging some sort of cosmic war against each other; rather, they complement each other and serve as the foundation of time. Light is called the time of "day," and darkness is called the time of "night."

Over the course of days, God creates a highly coordinated and patterned material world. On the second day, God distinguishes the waters by the dome of the sky. This separation makes way for God's work on the third day, when he creates the earth and the vegetation upon it. This moment in the creation story suggests that God takes great care for the endurance of life, as all the plants and trees are to bear seed to regenerate life. After focusing his attention upon the earth, God centers the work of the fourth day on the skies and creates the sun and the moon—"the greater one to govern the day, and the lesser one to govern the night"—and the stars. Once again, Genesis depicts God creating distinction and separation as a means of governing all things in harmony.

TO KEEP IN MIND

Smile when you share good news. Nonverbal cues like a smile help the assembly understand the reading.

Pause slightly after "fifth day."

Keep an even pace through this line.

This passage repeats the word "kinds" four times. These "kinds" anticipate the image of "humankind" shortly to come.

Don't treat the appearance of humankind at this point as a break, as something separate; rather, treat it as part of a continuum. The tone and pitch of your proclamation does not need to change here.

Then God said,
"Let the **water teem** with an abundance of **living creatures**,
and on the **earth** let birds fly **beneath** the dome of the sky."
And so it **happened**:
God created the great **sea monsters**
and all kinds of **swimming creatures** with which the
water **teems**,
and all kinds of **winged birds**.
God saw how **good** it was, and God **blessed** them, saying,
"Be **fertile**, **multiply**, and **fill** the water of the **seas**;
and let the **birds** multiply on the **earth**."
Evening came, and **morning** followed—the **fifth** day.

Then God said,
"Let the **earth** bring **forth** all kinds of **living creatures**:
cattle, **creeping things**, and wild **animals** of all **kinds**."
And so it **happened**:
God made **all kinds** of wild **animals**, all **kinds** of **cattle**,
and all **kinds** of **creeping things** of the earth.
God saw how **good** it was.

Then [God said:
"Let us make **man** in our image, **after** our **likeness**.
Let them have **dominion** over the **fish** of the **sea**,
the **birds** of the **air**, and the **cattle**,
and over **all** the wild **animals**
and **all** the creatures that **crawl** on the **ground**."
God created **man** in his **image**;
in the **image** of **God** he created **him**;
male and **female** he created **them**.
God **blessed** them, saying:
"Be **fertile** and **multiply**;
fill the earth and **subdue** it.
Have **dominion** over the **fish** of the **sea**, the **birds** of the **air**,
and **all** the living things that move on the earth." ❯❯

On the fifth day, God continues his focus on the sky, but he also looks at the waters and brings forth "living creatures" to inhabit the seas. The sixth day's work turns to providing inhabitants for the dry land. It is significant that God commands, "Let the earth bring forth all kinds of living creatures." The earth itself has a role to play in providing for the life that is to dwell upon its surface. Then comes the crown of creation, God's final mark of care for creation: humanity. The human creature is distinguished from the other aspects of creation in two primary ways. First, male

and female are created in the divine image. Rather than thinking of this as a similarity in physical form, it is better to understand that the divine image is able to understand the significance of generative love. To multiply is meant to be a means of expressing divine love. Second, God creates human beings to "have dominion" over all the living creatures of the world. Instead of conceiving of "dominion" as a form of rule, we better understand it in terms of stewardship. In all that they do, men and women are to care for God's good creation.

Finally, on the seventh day, God rests. Jewish Law will come to understand the Sabbath rest as a command for all of creation. Genesis suggests that God did not create the world to have its various components labor against one another in order to survive. Darwin's theory of the survival of the fittest, while a recognizable characteristic of the cosmos, really has no place in this primeval story of creation. Here, God takes a rest from the labor of creating, and all creation is called to do the same in order to restore the original intention of God's creation—all things existing together in

God also said:
"**See**, I give you every **seed-bearing** plant all over the **earth**
and every **tree** that has seed-bearing **fruit** on it
      to be your **food**;
and to all the **animals** of the land, all the **birds** of the air,
and all the **living creatures** that crawl on the **ground**,
I give all the green plants for **food**."
And so it **happened**.
God looked at **everything** he had made, and he found it
      very good.]
Evening came, and **morning** followed—the **sixth** day.

Thus the **heavens** and the **earth** and all their **array**
      were **completed**.
Since on the **seventh** day God was **finished**
      with the **work** he had been **doing**,
      he **rested** on the seventh day from **all** the work he
      had **undertaken**.

[Shorter: Genesis 1:1, 26–31a (see brackets)]

Pause slightly after "sixth day."

For these concluding lines of this reading, which describe the sabbath, you can allow your proclamation to relax a little without overdoing it.

For meditation and context:

RESPONSORIAL PSALM   Psalm 104:1–2, 5–6, 10, 12, 13–14, 24, 35 (30)

R. Lord, send out your Spirit, and renew the face of the earth.

Bless the LORD, O my soul!
    O LORD, my God, you are great indeed!
You are clothed with majesty and glory,
    robed in light as with a cloak.

You fixed the earth upon its foundation,
    not to be moved forever;
with the ocean, as with a garment,
    you covered it;
    above the mountains the waters stood.

You send forth springs into the watercourses
    that wind among the mountains.
Beside them the birds of heaven dwell;
    from among the branches they send forth
    their song.

You water the mountains from your palace;
    the earth is replete with the fruit
    of your works.
You raise grass for the cattle,
    and vegetation for man's use,
producing bread from the earth.

How manifold are your works, O LORD!
    In wisdom you have wrought them all—
the earth is full of your creatures.
    Bless the LORD, O my soul!

Or:

---

perfect harmony. This is the ultimate hope of our salvation.

 READING II Moving on from creation, Genesis continues to unfold with the introduction of sin into the world and the subsequent return of chaos. Quickly we see how jealousy between brothers leads to death (Cain and Abel), how the corruption of humanity can move God to destroy it (Noah and the flood), and how the desire to be like God produces confusion among the peoples of the earth (Tower of Babel). These stories are read at

different times in the liturgical cycle. They demonstrate how far humanity moves itself away from God's original designs and exploits creation for its own success.

Finally, we are introduced to Abraham in Genesis 12. He will be called by God to be the father of a great nation, with descendants as numerous as the stars of heaven and the sands on the shore of the sea. What God intended to accomplish with the goodness of the original creation, he hopes to restore in the people established through Abraham's lineage.

Although Abraham's story of departing from his homeland to take possession of the land God would bestow upon him would include many hardships, there is no harsher test for him than the story we read this night, the binding of Isaac. It is important to remember that when Abraham receives God's covenant assuring him that he would be the father of a great nation, he was already an old man and his wife, Sarah, was well beyond childbearing years. The two of them wrestled long and hard with the question of how they would ever have offspring. Taking matters into their own

For meditation and context:

RESPONSORIAL PSALM   Psalm 33:4–5, 6–7, 12–13, 20 and 22 (5b)

R. The earth is full of the goodness of the Lord.

Upright is the word of the LORD,
   and all his works are trustworthy.
He loves justice and right;
   of the kindness of the LORD the earth
   is full.

By the word of the LORD the heavens
   were made;
   by the breath of his mouth all their host.
He gathers the waters of the sea as in a flask;
   in cellars he confines the deep.

Blessed the nation whose God is the LORD,
   the people he has chosen for his own
   inheritance.
From heaven the LORD looks down;
   he sees all mankind.

Our soul waits for the LORD,
   who is our help and our shield.
May your kindness, O LORD, be upon us
   who have put our hope in you.

Genesis = JEN-uh-sihs
Moriah = moh-RĪ-uh
A narrative reading of another very familiar story from Scripture. The reading is mythic: its elements, including its conclusion, are known, but that does not diminish its power. A passage such as this is already so dramatic, your task is to proclaim as clearly as you can. Even though there are several exclamations in this passage, you will not need to raise your voice any more than you normally do when proclaiming.

Case in point: the first acclamation. There is an aura of otherworldly silence around Abraham's name. No need to shout.

The great literary critic Erich Auerbach describes this passage as "fraught with background," a delicious phrase. He means that while the action is spare, the scene itself is filling with tension. When you proclaim "On the third day," you are skipping over two full days of traveling.

READING II   Genesis 22:1–18

A reading from the Book of Genesis

[God put **Abraham** to the **test**.
He called to him, "**Abraham**!"
"**Here** I am," he replied.
Then God said:
   "Take your son **Isaac**, your **only** one, whom you **love**,
   and go to the land of **Moriah**.
There you shall offer him up as a **holocaust**
   on a **height** that I will point **out** to you."]
Early the next morning Abraham saddled his **donkey**,
   took with him his son **Isaac** and two of his **servants** as well,
   and with the **wood** that he had cut for the **holocaust**,
   set **out** for the place of which **God** had told him.

On the third day **Abraham** got sight of the place from **afar**.
Then he **said** to his servants:
   "**Both** of you stay here with the **donkey**,
   while the **boy** and I go on over **yonder**.
We will **worship** and then come **back** to you." ≫

hands, Abraham sleeps with Sarah's maidservant, Hagar, who bears a child named Ishmael. God is greatly displeased with their lack of faith and declares to Hagar that her descendants will be too numerous to be counted (Genesis 16:10). Even though God will return to Abraham, restore the covenant with him, and make it possible for Sarah to give birth to Isaac, the great nation descending from his name will forever be at odds with the great nation descending from Hagar and her son, Ishmael. (Note that Muslims believe themselves to be descendants of Ishmael.)

All of this is background to understanding the weighty significance of Abraham's being willing to sacrifice Isaac. At stake here is not only the death of a precious child, but the potential end to the future of the nation as a whole. The future of Abraham's great nation relies upon the flourishing of his son Isaac. The story begins with God's call, "Abraham," and he replies with the conventional words of a servant: "Here I am." God instructs Abraham to take his son Isaac up the mountain, where Abraham is to offer him as a holocaust. In its original sense, a holocaust is a specific type of offering, one

that is to be burned. Thus, not only is Abraham to kill his son, but the sacrifice will obliterate Isaac entirely from the world.

While we might wonder what kind of thoughts were running through Abraham's head as he made the journey up the mountain, we are given no insight into Abraham's interior disposition. We see only his obedience put into action. Certainly the three days of travel that it took to reach the site for the sacrifice had to increase Abraham's horror and dread of what he believed he would be called to do.

Thereupon Abraham took the **wood** for the **holocaust**
    and laid it on his son Isaac's **shoulders**,
    while he himself carried the **fire** and the **knife**.
As the two walked on together, Isaac **spoke** to his
        father Abraham:
    "**Father**!" Isaac said.
"Yes, son," he replied.
Isaac continued, "**Here** are the **fire** and the **wood**,
    but **where** is the **sheep** for the **holocaust**?"
"Son," Abraham answered,
    "God **himself** will provide the **sheep** for the **holocaust**."
Then the two **continued** going forward.

[When they **came** to the place of which **God** had told him,
    Abraham built an **altar** there and arranged the **wood** on it.]
Next he tied up his son **Isaac**,
    and put him on **top** of the **wood** on the **altar**.
[Then he **reached out** and took the **knife** to **slaughter** his son.
But the LORD's messenger **called** to him from **heaven**,
    "**Abraham**, **Abraham**!"
"**Here** I am," he answered.
"Do **not** lay your **hand** on the **boy**," said the messenger.
"Do **not** do the **least thing** to him.
I know **now** how devoted you are to **God**,
    since you did not **withhold** from me your **own beloved** son."
As Abraham looked about,
    he spied a **ram** caught by its **horns** in the **thicket**.
So he **went** and took the **ram**
    and offered it up as a **holocaust** in place of his **son**.]
Abraham named the site **Yahweh-yireh**;
    hence people now say, "On the **mountain** the LORD will **see**."

[Again the LORD's **messenger** called to Abraham from **heaven**
        and said:
    "I **swear** by myself, **declares** the LORD,
    that **because** you acted as you **did**

Second exclamation: Don't shout.

"Continued": This word is "fraught with background."

Take note of the details. Abraham is preparing an altar for sacrifice.

Third exclamation: Don't shout.

Yahweh-yireh = YAH-way-YEER-ay

Though an angel of God is relaying these words, it's God himself who speaks here. Set off the phrase "declares the Lord" in such a way to make it clear that God is speaking.

When Abraham finally detects the place that would be suitable for the sacrifice, he and Isaac depart from the two servants that accompanied them and proceed alone to the site, with Isaac carrying the wood for the fire on his shoulders. In a metaphorical sense, it is the future of all of Israel that is laid upon his shoulders. When Isaac asks his father about the missing sheep for the holocaust, Abraham makes a great profession of faith: "God himself will provide the sheep for the holocaust." This statement will have lasting significance for salvation history; only God can provide the

means for a sacrifice that is truly worthy of his reception. Christians will understand that Jesus must be given by God to be a sacrifice for all of creation.

The gruesomeness of the event builds as Abraham prepares the altar for sacrifice, ties up his beloved son, and places him upon the wood on the altar. Then comes the call of God once again: "Abraham! Abraham!" His reply changes not at all: "Here I am." With this loving exchange between God and Abraham, the test is over. God has no doubt that Abraham is filled with faith, willing even to sacrifice his beloved son. Abraham

expresses his gratitude to God by making the sacrifice of a ram placed there, no doubt, by God himself. Seeing the beauty of Abraham's faith, God blesses him and restores the covenant with him: "I will bless you abundantly and make your descendants as countless as the stars of the sky and the sands of the seashore."

READING III   The third reading for the Easter Vigil continues the story of salvation history with the account of Moses leading the Israelites out of Egypt by passing through the sea. This story, which

in not **withholding** from me your beloved **son**,
I will **bless you** abundantly
and make your **descendants** as **countless**
as the **stars** of the **sky** and the **sands** of the **seashore**;
your **descendants** shall take **possession**
of the **gates** of their **enemies**,
and in your **descendants** all the **nations** of the earth shall
    find **blessing**—
all **this** because you **obeyed** my command."]

[Shorter: Genesis 22:1–2, 9a, 10–13, 15–18 (see brackets)]

For meditation and context:

RESPONSORIAL PSALM   Psalm 16:5, 8, 9–10, 11 (1)

R. You are my inheritance, O Lord.

O LORD, my allotted portion and my cup,
    you it is who hold fast my lot.
I set the LORD ever before me;
    with him at my right hand I shall
        not be disturbed.

Therefore my heart is glad and my
    soul rejoices,
    my body, too, abides in confidence;

because you will not abandon my soul to the
    netherworld,
    nor will you suffer your faithful one to
        undergo corruption.

You will show me the path to life,
    fullness of joys in your presence,
    the delights at your right hand forever.

READING III   Exodus 14:15—15:1

A reading from the Book of Exodus

The LORD said to Moses, "**Why** are you crying **out** to me?
Tell the **Israelites** to go **forward**.
And you, lift up your **staff** and, with **hand** outstretched
    over the **sea**,
    split the sea in **two**,
    that the **Israelites** may pass through it on **dry land**.
But I will make the **Egyptians** so **obstinate**
    that they will go in **after** them. »

Exodus = EK-suh-duhs

Another very familiar story, this reading is full of action, with occasional instruction by God himself. But mostly action. Its drama will come through your proclamation if you allow the details of the action to be voiced. Let the words of the reading speak for themselves.

Here, God instructs Moses on how to perform a miraculous act. He's a little impatient, but he's also providing the details of a carefully considered plan.

is told in the context of the annual Passover Seder in the Jewish community, has great importance for Christians; the natural element of water becomes a primary symbol in the story of salvation. Remember that water is created by God in the Book of Genesis to provide life for the creatures of the sea. In the Book of Exodus, the water is not only a symbol of new life for the Israelites as they pass through to safety on dry land, but is also a symbol of death, as the Egyptians are completely destroyed as the waters flow in upon them. The Christian "Passover," the celebration of Christ's res-

urrection, is the celebration of God's infinite love that is capable of producing new life at the hour of death.

This passage opens with Moses and Aaron having just led the Israelites south of the land of Goshen in Egypt only to be given the instructions to circle around to the north again to set up camp at the shore of the sea (Exodus 14:1–4). Seeing the Israelites wandering with no direct escape route, Pharaoh recognizes his mistake in letting them go, and once again, his heart is hardened so that he orders his armies to chase after the Israelites. This will provide

God with the opportunity to defeat the powers (meaning gods) of Egypt once and for all. By defeating the Egyptians in the neutral territory of the Red Sea, the whole world will be able to see God's great power. Thus, the exodus of the Hebrews is seen as an opportunity to lead those beyond the Israelite community to faith in God.

At the outset of the reading, Moses echoes to God the cry of the Israelites, who see the Egyptians pursuing them and wonder if remaining as slaves in Egypt may have been better than being led out to their death. God promises that he will make the

Then I will **receive glory** through **Pharaoh** and all his **army**,
    his **chariots** and **charioteers**.
The **Egyptians** shall know that I am the LORD,
    when I receive **glory** through **Pharaoh**
    and his **chariots** and **charioteers**."

The passage that follows includes many vivid details.

The **angel** of God, who had been leading Israel's **camp**,
    now **moved** and went around **behind** them.
The column of cloud **also**, leaving the front,
    took up its place **behind** them,
    so that it came **between** the camp of the **Egyptians**
    and that of **Israel**.
But the cloud now became **dark**, and thus the night **passed**
    without the rival camps coming any **closer together** all
        night long.
Then **Moses** stretched out his **hand** over the **sea**,
    and the LORD swept the **sea**
    with a **strong east wind** throughout the night
    and so **turned** it into **dry** land.
When the **water** was thus **divided**,
    the Israelites **marched** into the **midst** of the sea on dry **land**,
    with the **water** like a **wall** to their **right** and to their **left**.

Again, vivid details. Give your voice to them.

The **Egyptians** followed in **pursuit**;
    all Pharaoh's **horses** and **chariots** and **charioteers** went
        after them
    right into the **midst** of the **sea**.
In the **night watch** just before **dawn**
    the LORD cast through the **column** of the fiery **cloud**
    upon the Egyptian force a **glance** that **threw** it into a **panic**;
    and he so **clogged** their chariot wheels
    that they could hardly **drive**.
With that the **Egyptians** sounded the **retreat** before **Israel**,
    because the LORD was fighting for them against the **Egyptians**.

> **TO KEEP IN MIND**
> Be careful not to swallow your words.
> Articulate carefully, especially at the
> end of lines.

Egyptians incapable of recognizing that moving into the waters will result in their being swallowed up to death. God makes it clear that the death of these Egyptians will bring him glory.

The work of the angel of God is particularly important. Throughout their journey from Egypt, the angel had taken a position in front of the Israelites, leading them along the way. At the Red Sea, the angel moves around behind the Israelites to come in between the Israelites and the Egyptians. This move represents a marking out of

sacred space. The angel changes positions, and as a result, the power of the sacred moves forward with the Israelites and is removed from the grasp of the Egyptians. This event becomes a turning point of the passage. At the sea, the Israelites say a final goodbye to the life they knew and are invited to take possession of a new reality. This is their movement into an unknown territory; they will have to come to understand the authority of God in an experiential way.

The Lord parts the sea through the intercession of Moses as he stretched his staff out over the waters. After the Israelites had marched through on dry land, and after the waters receded back upon the Egyptians, the Israelites feared and believed in the Lord and in his servant Moses. This stands as a statement of their being a newly constructed people. Having passed through the waters, the Israelites are now committing themselves to the new way of life that God has in store for them. The song that the Israelites sing with joy,

God speaks, once again instructing Moses on how to perform another miraculous act, one that parallels the earlier act.

Then the LORD told Moses, "**Stretch** out your hand over the **sea**,
  that the **water** may flow **back** upon the **Egyptians**,
  upon their **chariots** and their **charioteers**."
So Moses stretched **out** his hand over the **sea**,
  and at dawn the **sea** flowed **back** to its normal **depth**.
The Egyptians were fleeing head **on** toward the **sea**,
  when the LORD **hurled** them into its **midst**.
As the **water** flowed back,
  it covered the **chariots** and the **charioteers** of Pharaoh's
    whole army
  which had followed the **Israelites** into the **sea**.
Not a single **one** of them **escaped**.
But the **Israelites** had marched on **dry land**
  through the **midst** of the **sea**,
  with the **water** like a **wall** to their right and to their **left**.
Thus the LORD saved **Israel** on that day
  from the **power** of the **Egyptians**.
When Israel saw the **Egyptians** lying dead on the **seashore**
  and beheld the great **power** that the LORD
  had **shown** against the **Egyptians**,
  they **feared** the LORD and **believed** in him and in his
    servant **Moses**.

Then **Moses** and the Israelites sang this song to the LORD:
  I will sing to the LORD, for he is **gloriously** triumphant;
  horse and **chariot** he has **cast** into the **sea**.

Don't overly dramatize the doom that comes to Pharaoh and his army. Let the grim details speak for themselves.

"Power": Its manifestation defines this reading.

The reading concludes with the words of a song. The song is triumphant, but its contents are a little grim. The entire song is sung as the responsorial psalm.

"I will sing to the Lord, for he is gloriously triumphant; horse and chariot he has cast into the sea," is the verbal recognition that the Israelites want to be God's people. Although we know that the story of Exodus proceeds with many failures on the part of the people to remain faithful to God, here at the Red Sea we have the establishment of a new nation. What the Israelites must yet discover is that freedom from slavery in Egypt is not simply liberation from oppression; true freedom is found in loving and serving God.

READING IV | The next stop in our hearing of salvation history comes from the time of the Babylonian Exile, which can be dated to 586 BC, and the destruction of Solomon's Temple in the city of Jerusalem. After the northern tribes of Israel fell to the Assyrians earlier in the previous century, the stronger tribes of the southern kingdom (Judah) fell into the hands of the Babylonians, who forced the people from their land and deported them as slaves to Babylon. Just as happened during their captivity in Egypt, many of the

Hebrews during the Babylonian captivity found it easy to assimilate into the surrounding culture and were able to take advantage of the situation. Many found their new life to be much more rewarding than they had experienced in Jerusalem. And for those Hebrews born in Babylon, this was the only life they knew.

Thus, the reading from Isaiah, which was almost certainly constructed in the final days of the Babylonian captivity, is part of a sweeping call to the exiles to return home to their land. Because the

For meditation and context:

RESPONSORIAL PSALM Exodus 15:1–2, 3–4, 5–6, 17–18 (1b)

R. Let us sing to the Lord; he has covered himself in glory.

I will sing to the LORD, for he is
    gloriously triumphant;
    horse and chariot he has cast into the sea.
My strength and my courage is the LORD,
  and he has been my savior.
He is my God, I praise him;
  the God of my father, I extol him.

The LORD is a warrior,
  LORD is his name!
Pharaoh's chariots and army he hurled
  into the sea;
  the elite of his officers were submerged
    in the Red Sea.

The flood waters covered them,
  they sank into the depths like a stone.
Your right hand, O LORD, magnificent
  in power,
  your right hand, O LORD, has shattered
    the enemy.

You brought in the people you redeemed
  and planted them on the mountain of
    your inheritance—
the place where you made your seat, O LORD,
  the sanctuary, LORD, which your
    hands established.
The LORD shall reign forever and ever.

READING IV Isaiah 54:5–14

Isaiah = ī-ZAY-uh

An exhortatory reading in which the prophet speaks on behalf of God to the people, seeking to intensify the intimacy between them.

The core of the reading is this simile comparing the people ("you") to a forsaken wife whom God, as the husband, wants back. The conflict described and the strife implied in this passage should be familiar to many in the assembly. Don't get too dramatic with your proclamation, but don't shy away from its implications.

A reading from the Book of the Prophet Isaiah

The **One** who has become your **husband** is your **Maker**;
  his **name** is the LORD of hosts;
your **redeemer** is the **Holy One** of Israel,
  called **God** of all the **earth**.
The LORD calls you **back**,
  like a **wife** forsaken and **grieved** in spirit,
  a wife **married** in youth and then **cast off**,
  says your God.
For a **brief moment** I **abandoned** you,
  but with **great tenderness** I will take you **back**.
In an **outburst** of wrath, for a **moment**
  I hid my **face** from you;
but with enduring **love** I take **pity** on you,
  says the LORD, your **redeemer**.
This is for me like the **days** of Noah,
  when I **swore** that the waters of Noah
  should **never again** deluge the **earth**;

people have long been surrounded by the gods of the Babylonians, it is necessary to remind the people just who their God is. Isaiah reminds the people that God is their "husband," their "Maker," "your redeemer," the "God of all the earth." Isaiah wants to restore the people's faith in God's fidelity. Like a wife who has been abandoned yet wants nothing more than for her husband to return, so does God yearn for his people's restoration.

    Isaiah continues to describe God's invitation to Israel to come home with pow-

erful relational language in which God admits to having allowed Israel to fall from his grace. Thus, speaking in the Lord's name, Isaiah writes, "For a brief moment I abandoned you, but with great tenderness I will take you back." God recognizes that his wrath may have gotten the better of him, likening the exile to Noah and the flood. He promised then that he would never again destroy creation. Certainly, the exiles believed that the destruction of their Temple and all of Jerusalem signaled that God, in his wrath, was once again punishing

them for some grave sin. But God does not wish them to see their situation in this light anymore: "so I have sworn not to be angry with you, or to rebuke you."

    The final portion of this reading dwells not on the afflictions of the past but on hope for the future. The Lord promises his people the gift of his mercy and the assurance that his love will never abandon them again. The Lord will provide the strength for the founding of a restored nation. He will lay the stones of the foundation and will provide for the building of its walls. Perhaps

so I have **sworn** not to be **angry** with you,
  or to **rebuke** you.
Though the **mountains** leave their **place**
  and the **hills** be shaken,
my **love** shall never **leave** you
  nor my **covenant** of peace be **shaken**,
  says the LORD, who has **mercy** on you.
O **afflicted** one, storm-battered and **unconsoled**,
  I lay your **pavements** in **carnelians**,
  and your **foundations** in **sapphires**;
I will make your **battlements** of **rubies**,
  your **gates** of **carbuncles**,
  and all your **walls** of precious **stones**.
All your **children** shall be **taught** by the LORD,
  and **great** shall be the **peace** of your **children**.
In **justice** shall you be **established**,
  far from the **fear** of **oppression**,
  where **destruction** cannot come **near** you.

God promises peace, despite previously turbulent times.

Many jewels. The names of jewels are appealing to say and hear.
carnelians = kahr-NEEL-yuhnz = red semiprecious stones
carbuncles = KAHR-bung-k*lz = bright red gems

The peace God promises is like the jewels: enduring, precious, and consoling.

For meditation and context:

RESPONSORIAL PSALM Psalm 30:2, 4, 5–6, 11–12, 13 (2a)

R. I will praise you, Lord, for you have rescued me.

I will extol you, O LORD, for you drew me clear
and did not let my enemies rejoice over me.
O LORD, you brought me up from the netherworld;
you preserved me from among those going down into the pit.

Sing praise to the LORD, you his faithful ones,
and give thanks to his holy name.
For his anger lasts but a moment; a lifetime, his good will.
At nightfall, weeping enters in, but with the dawn, rejoicing.

Hear, O LORD, and have pity on me; O LORD, be my helper.
You changed my mourning into dancing; O LORD, my God, forever will I give you thanks.

the greatest gift of all, the Lord promises that the children of the new Israel will be taught by the Lord himself, so great is the personal relationship he wishes to establish with them, "and great shall be the peace of your children." The words and the tone of Isaiah's prophecy make the invitation to return one that would be foolish to ignore; no matter what fortune has been discovered in Babylon, nothing can match the promises the Lord makes to the people in his desire to make them his own possession once again.

READING V Each year at the Easter Vigil we hear Isaiah calling the thirsty and the poor to "come to the water!" We hear these words knowing that in a matter of moments the Church will immerse men and women into the life-giving waters of baptism. These are waters that do not discriminate and do not distinguish male from female, rich from poor, young from old. These waters equalize and make all people members of Christ. Whether one comes to baptism a millionaire or a pauper, one comes out of the water a disciple of Christ. Thus, the waters of baptism are ulti-

mately about God's justice, which does not condemn but instead desires right relationship. In God's kingdom, where right relationship prevails, all will delight in rich foods and will come to know what truly satisfies.

Following upon the prophecy from tonight's previous reading, also from Isaiah, this prophecy continues the message of great hope. Whereas the previous reading made the invitation to return to Jerusalem hard to refuse, these words of Isaiah embrace a wider audience. The people's return to the land will serve as a witness to all the nations of God's great abundance.

Isaiah = ī-ZAY-uh
An exhortatory reading in which God through the voice of the prophet Isaiah promises forgiveness. The message of this reading is direct and should be relatable to many in your assembly.

"You who have no money": Even in affluent parishes, there are people who have felt this pinch. God is speaking directly to these people.

READING V   Isaiah 55:1–11

A reading from the Book of the Prophet Isaiah

Thus says the LORD:
   All **you** who are **thirsty**,
      come to the **water**!
You who have no **money**,
      come, receive **grain** and **eat**;
come, without **paying** and without **cost**,
      drink **wine** and **milk**!
Why spend your **money** for what is not **bread**,
      your **wages** for what fails to **satisfy**?
Heed me, and you shall **eat** well,
      you shall **delight** in rich **fare**.
Come to me **heedfully**,
      listen, that you may have **life**.
I will **renew** with you the everlasting **covenant**,
      the **benefits** assured to **David**.
As I made him a **witness** to the **peoples**,
      a **leader** and commander of **nations**,
so shall you **summon** a nation you knew **not**,
      and **nations** that knew you not shall **run** to you,
because of the LORD, your **God**,
      the **Holy One** of Israel, who has **glorified** you.

Seek the LORD while he may be **found**,
      call him while he is **near**.
Let the **scoundrel** forsake his **way**,
      and the **wicked man** his **thoughts**;
let him **turn** to the LORD for **mercy**;
      to our **God**, who is generous in **forgiving**.
For my **thoughts** are not **your** thoughts,
      nor are your ways **my** ways, says the LORD.
As **high** as the heavens are above the **earth**,
      so **high** are my **ways** above your **ways**
      and my **thoughts** above your **thoughts**.

"Seek the Lord while he may be found": This command speaks to the hope inherent in this reading. We hope it's true, that God may be found, especially when we call him.

Forgiveness. This is the heart of this reading.

The nations of the world will stand in awe of all that God has done, and Israel will act as missionaries to attract people to God, who says to those still in exile, "So shall you summon a nation you knew not; and nations that knew you not shall run to you." Not only is the return of the people about the establishment of peace in their homeland, it is meant to serve as the means by which the whole world will come to be at peace. The invitation to come to the water goes out to all the inhabitants of the earth.

Toward the middle of the passage is another invitation to the whole world: "Seek the Lord while he may be found, call him while he is near." The prophet's words continue to elaborate on the theme of developing a relationship with the One who is always faithful. All one has to do is to abandon former ways, turn to the Lord, and accept his gift of mercy. The cost of such a relationship is not based on wealth or material possessions; all it requires is the desire to forsake the past and to try to discern the Lord's ways.

Those who are about to be immersed in the waters of baptism as well as the whole Church, which is about to renew its baptismal promises, hear the words of Isaiah as a call to ongoing conversion. Isaiah suggests that the word of God nurtures the earth, making it "fertile and fruitful." The word of God is meant to be productive. There is nothing unsatisfying about the word of God that is freely given in abundance. All that is necessary is for hearts to attempt to seek such generosity. We look at the men and women who hunger

For **just** as from the **heavens**
    the rain and snow come **down**
and do not **return** there
    till they have **watered** the earth,
    making it **fertile** and **fruitful**,
giving **seed** to the one who **sows**
    and **bread** to the one who **eats**,
so shall my word be
    that goes **forth** from my **mouth**;
my word shall not **return** to me **void**,
    but shall do my **will**,
    achieving the **end** for which I **sent** it.

Even stresses on the words in this line.

For meditation and context:

RESPONSORIAL PSALM   Isaiah 12:2–3, 4, 5–6 (3)

R. You will draw water joyfully from the springs of salvation.

God indeed is my savior;
    I am confident and unafraid.
My strength and my courage is the LORD,
    and he has been my savior.
With joy you will draw water
    at the fountain of salvation.

Give thanks to the LORD, acclaim his name;
    among the nations make known his deeds,
    proclaim how exalted is his name.

Sing praise to the LORD for his glorious
    achievement;
    let this be known throughout all
    the earth.
Shout with exultation, O city of Zion,
    for great in your midst
    is the Holy One of Israel!

READING VI   Baruch 3:9–15, 32—4:4

A reading from the Book of the Prophet Baruch

Hear, O Israel, the **commandments** of life:
    listen, and know **prudence**!
How **is** it, Israel,
    that you are in the **land** of your **foes**,
    grown **old** in a foreign **land**,
defiled with the **dead**,
    accounted with those **destined** for the **netherworld**? »

Baruch = buh-ROOK

An exhortation on wisdom, personified in this reading in her ancient feminine principle. A powerful reminder.

The reading makes use of rhetorical questions. Use these questions—this first one stretches over several lines—to organize the pace of your proclamation.

for baptism this night, and we see evidence of such conversion, seeking the Lord "while he is near."

 The sixth reading is a rather obscure poem/hymn from Baruch in praise of Wisdom. The poem opens with the acknowledgment that the Babylonian exile still lingers in the minds and hearts of the Hebrew people, but its main focus is an invitation to embrace the Law as a lasting treasure and the source of life. Placing this reading into the overall context of salvation history, we know that people too often forsake the commands of the Law because they are distracted by the concerns of this world. Baruch reminds us that attuning one's heart to Wisdom, which he says is "the book of the precepts of God, the law that endures forever," will never disappoint.

Baruch establishes the authority of Wisdom in the middle stanza of this poem. Here he suggests that just as God created every aspect of the world to reflect the glory of God, so too has God "probed [Wisdom] by his knowledge." Similarly, just as every part of creation responds to the voice of God with the words "Here we are!" so is the Wisdom of God contained in the law meant to help all creation respond to God with joy. God "has traced out the whole way of understanding, and has given her to Jacob, his servant, to Israel, his beloved Son." If human beings are to be good stewards over all the things of the world, then they must cherish the gift that is the Law.

You have **forsaken** the fountain of **wisdom**!
  Had you **walked** in the way of **God**,
  you would have **dwelt** in enduring **peace**.
Learn where prudence is,
  where **strength**, where **understanding**;
that you may know **also**
  where are length of **days**, and **life**,
  where **light** of the eyes, and **peace**.
Who has found the place of **wisdom**,
  who has entered into her **treasuries**?

The One who knows all things **knows** her;
  he has **probed** her by his **knowledge**—
the One who established the **earth** for all time,
  and **filled** it with four-footed **beasts**;
he who **dismisses** the light, and it **departs**,
  calls it, and it obeys him **trembling**;
before whom the **stars** at their posts
  shine and **rejoice**;
when he **calls** them, they **answer**, "**Here** we are!"
  shining with joy for their **Maker**.
Such is our **God**;
  no **other** is to be **compared** to him:
he has **traced out** the whole way of understanding,
  and has **given** her to Jacob, his **servant**,
  to **Israel**, his beloved **son**.

Since then she has **appeared** on **earth**,
  and **moved** among people.
She is the **book** of the precepts of **God**,
  the **law** that endures **forever**;
all who **cling** to her will **live**,
  but those will **die** who **forsake** her.
Turn, O Jacob, and **receive** her:
  walk by her light toward **splendor**.

Take note of the questions here.

"Her" refers to Wisdom, *Hokhmah* in Hebrew, *Sophia* in Greek, always personified in feminine form in the ancient imagination.

Wisdom's divinity—the part she plays in God's creative imagination—is implied in this closing passage.

Baruch ends the poem by suggesting that Wisdom has been with creation from the foundation of the world. To all those who know of her, a choice is to be made: "All who cling to her will live, but those will die who forsake her." The people God has chosen as his own is richly blessed with the knowledge of the Law. This is their prized possession, the treasure they should cherish above all things. The challenge is for us today as it was for Israel of old: "Give not your glory to another." Follow the commandments of God as the source of unfailing light, and the way of darkness will never prevail.

READING VII Previous readings this night from the prophet Isaiah and from Baruch concern the crushing blow dealt to Israel by the Babylonian Exile; the prophet Ezekiel also writes from this perspective. In this seventh reading, he attributes the exile to the misdeeds committed by the people, especially idol worship. Rather than seeing the people of Israel as the victims of the Babylonian conquest, Ezekiel holds them responsible for defiling the land and bringing ruin to the nation. Furthermore, says Ezekiel, it is not the Babylonians who expel the people from the Land. Rather, the Lord himself scattered the people to captivity, "dispersing them over foreign lands."

Give not your **glory** to another,
    your **privileges** to an alien **race**.
Blessed are **we**, O Israel;
    for what **pleases** God is **known** to us!

For meditation and context:

RESPONSORIAL PSALM Psalm 19:8, 9, 10, 11 (John 6:68c)

R. Lord, you have the words of everlasting life.

The law of the LORD is perfect,
    refreshing the soul;
the decree of the LORD is trustworthy,
    giving wisdom to the simple.

The precepts of the LORD are right,
    rejoicing the heart;
the command of the LORD is clear,
    enlightening the eye.

The fear of the LORD is pure,
    enduring forever;
the ordinances of the LORD are true,
    all of them just.

They are more precious than gold,
    than a heap of purest gold;
sweeter also than syrup
    or honey from the comb.

Ezekiel = ee-ZEE-kee-uhl
A challenging exhortatory reading. Challenging because the tone of this passage is largely wrathful and accusatory. The language in this reading is so charged, the wrath will come through. It consists almost entirely of the words of God spoken to Ezekiel.

Here the tone is clear: the words *fury*, *defiled*, and *profane* set that tone.

READING VII Ezekiel 36:16–17a, 18–28

A reading from the Book of the Prophet Ezekiel

The **word** of the LORD **came** to me, saying:
    Son of man, when the **house** of Israel lived in their **land**,
    they **defiled** it by their **conduct** and **deeds**.
Therefore I poured **out** my fury **upon** them
    because of the **blood** that they poured **out** on the **ground**,
    and because they **defiled** it with idols.
I **scattered** them among the **nations**,
    dispersing them over foreign **lands**;
    according to their **conduct** and **deeds** I **judged** them.
But when they **came** among the nations wherever they **came**,
    they served to **profane** my holy **name**,
    because it was **said** of them:
        "**These** are the **people** of the **LORD**,
    yet they had to **leave** their land." »

In the covenantal relationship between God and the Chosen People, the land that God gave them is the bond between them. For the people to act in a way that detracts from the sacredness of the land is a true act of idolatry; it exhibits a forgetfulness of God. However, the Lord recognizes that the dispersal of his people also profanes his name. When people from other nations see that the Chosen People have been forced from their land, they mock and ridicule the relationship God has with those he has cho-

sen. They doubt God's power and authority, and they question his generosity. What kind of God would abandon his people and disperse them?

There is only one way to restore the honor of God's holy name: restore the people to the land. The Lord makes it clear: his desire to return Israel back to their home is not out of concern for them, but rather "for the sake of my holy name" among the nations. What the prophecy of Ezekiel suggests here is that the restoration of Israel

serves God's desire to draw the entire world to himself. No longer will he simply show concern for his people; now God will see to it that all nations seek to rid themselves of idolatry and strive to speak his holy name.

God will perform a sign for all to see so that his name be profaned no more. This sign will be the gathering together again of all the people dispersed from their land. God tells the people that he will "sprinkle clean water" upon them, cleansing them

God is so worked up, he begins quoting himself!

So I have **relented** because of my holy **name**
which the **house** of Israel **profaned**
among the **nations** where they **came**.
Therefore say to the house of Israel: **Thus** says the Lord GOD:
Not for **your sakes** do I act, house of Israel,
but for the **sake** of my holy **name**,
which you **profaned** among the **nations** to which you **came**.
I will **prove** the holiness of my great **name**, profaned among
the **nations**,
in whose **midst** you have **profaned** it.
Thus the **nations** shall know that **I** am the LORD,
says the Lord GOD,
when in their sight I prove my **holiness** through **you**.

Note the shift into the future tense. The tone doesn't change significantly, but from here to the conclusion of the reading, God is speaking about the future.

For I will take you **away** from among the **nations**,
gather you from **all** the foreign lands,
and bring you **back** to your own land.

God wants to cleanse the future of its impurities.

I will **sprinkle** clean water upon you
to **cleanse** you from all your **impurities**,
and from **all** your idols I will **cleanse** you.

And give people a new heart.

I will give you a new **heart** and place a new spirit **within** you,
taking from your bodies your **stony hearts**
and **giving** you **natural** hearts.
I will put my **spirit** within you and make you **live** by my statutes,
careful to observe my **decrees**.
You shall **live** in the land I **gave** your fathers;
you shall be my **people**, and I will be your **God**.

God's hope: this is his covenant.

from their past sins. In this symbolic act of purification, the Lord makes a new creation, a new nation, with a "new heart" and a "new spirit"—God's very own. This is so that the people will abide by God's commandments and decrees. Thus, the sign of salvation for the world in this prophecy of Ezekiel is found in the words of the very last sentence: "You shall live in the land I gave your fathers; you shall be my people, and I will be your God." When all the world sees the relationship between God and his

people flourishing, they too will profess his holy name.

EPISTLE   It is important to take note of a liturgical shift that takes place in the Liturgy of the Word at the Easter Vigil after the final reading from the Old Testament: the candles at the altar are lit, the bells sound, and the assembly sings the Gloria. In our hearing of the various readings from the Old Testament, we have been invited to contemplate the mystery of

salvation history. Ours is a God who is intimately involved with the goodness of his creation, who leads people out of bondage into freedom, and who asks only that we love him in return for his many expressions of care and kindness. Our telling of salvation history now approaches the pinnacle in our preparation for hearing from the New Testament. We Christians believe that salvation history comes to a definitive resolution through the Incarnation of Jesus, his life and ministry on earth, and the ultimate

For meditation and context:

RESPONSORIAL PSALM   Psalm 42:3, 5; 43:3, 4 (42:2)

R. Like a deer that longs for running streams, my soul longs for you, my God.

Athirst is my soul for God, the living God.
  When shall I go and behold the face
    of God?

I went with the throng
  and led them in procession to the house
    of God,
amid loud cries of joy and thanksgiving,
  with the multitude keeping festival.

Send forth your light and your fidelity;
  they shall lead me on
and bring me to your holy mountain,
  to your dwelling-place.

Then will I go in to the altar of God,
  the God of my gladness and joy;
then will I give you thanks upon the harp,
  O God, my God!

Or:

For meditation and context:

RESPONSORIAL PSALM   Isaiah 12:2–3, 4bcd, 5–6 (3)

R. You will draw water joyfully from the springs of salvation.

God indeed is my savior;
  I am confident and unafraid.
My strength and my courage is the LORD,
  and he has been my savior.
With joy you will draw water
  at the fountain of salvation.

Give thanks to the LORD, acclaim his name;
  among the nations make known his deeds,
  proclaim how exalted is his name.

Sing praise to the LORD for his glorious
    achievement;
  let this be known throughout all
    the earth.
Shout with exultation, O city of Zion,
  for great in your midst
  is the Holy One of Israel!

Or:

For meditation and context:

RESPONSORIAL PSALM   Psalm 51:12–13, 14–15, 18–19 (12a)

R. Create a clean heart in me, O God.

A clean heart create for me, O God,
  and a steadfast spirit renew within me.
Cast me not out from your presence,
  and your Holy Spirit take not from me.

Give me back the joy of your salvation,
  and a willing spirit sustain in me.
I will teach transgressors your ways,
  and sinners shall return to you.

For you are not pleased with sacrifices;
  should I offer a holocaust, you would
    not accept it.
My sacrifice, O God, is a contrite spirit;
  a heart contrite and humbled, O God,
    you will not spurn.

---

gift of his Paschal Mystery (his suffering, death, and resurrection). Our joy is not to be contained, because we are not simply waiting for some future savior. Our savior has already appeared and is among us still; he will not abandon us until the day when all things will be gathered together as one in God's great love. We live in a new age.

Paul's address to the Christians at Rome could very well be used as a piece of final catechesis for the elect as they prepare to be immersed in the waters of baptism. The question that opens Paul's

address could be asked directly to them: "Are you unaware that we who were baptized into Christ Jesus were baptized into his death?" How good it is not only for the elect, but for the entire Church as well, to be reminded that baptism entails a fundamental death—and not a death that occurs only once, but again and again as a Christian learns self-sacrifice over a lifetime.

To add to the notion of baptism as death, Paul employs the image of being buried with Christ. Not only does one have to die to self when immersed in the waters

of baptism, the person must also be ready to bury the past. It is precisely in burial that God can perform the mighty task of raising to new life.

Paul continues his address by linking death to self with the abandonment of sin. For Paul, membership in Christ necessitates ridding oneself of attractions and allurements that might distract from living fully the new life of Christ. When Paul writes, "We know that our old self was crucified with him, so that our sinful body might be done away with, that we might no longer be in

A didactic reading focused on Baptism. Because the Easter Vigil often includes the Baptism of the elect, you should imagine you are speaking directly to those about to be baptized.

Paul begins by making a connection between Baptism, life and death, and resurrection. These are the terms that define this passage from his letter to the Romans.

To die with Christ is also to live with him, to be resurrected with him. Baptism is rebirth.

Paul reemphasizes this point about resurrection in these concluding words.

For meditation and context:

EPISTLE   Romans 6:3–11

A reading from the Letter of Saint Paul to the Romans

Brothers and **sisters**:
Are you **unaware** that **we** who were **baptized** into Christ **Jesus**
    were **baptized** into his **death**?
We were **indeed** buried with him through **baptism** into **death**,
    so that, **just** as Christ was **raised** from the dead
    by the **glory** of the Father,
    we **too** might live in **newness** of life.

For if we have **grown** into union with him through a **death**
        like his,
    we shall also be **united** with him in the **resurrection**.
We know that our **old self** was **crucified** with him,
    so that our sinful **body** might be done **away** with,
    that we might no longer be in **slavery** to **sin**.
For a **dead** person has been **absolved** from sin.
If, then, we have **died** with Christ,
    we **believe** that we shall also **live** with him.
We know that **Christ**, **raised** from the **dead**, **dies** no more;
    death no longer has **power** over him.
As to his **death**, he **died** to **sin once** and for **all**;
    as to his **life**, he lives for **God**.
Consequently, **you too** must think of yourselves as being **dead**
        to sin
    and **living** for God in Christ **Jesus**.

RESPONSORIAL PSALM   Psalm 118:1–2, 16–17, 22–23

R. Alleluia, alleluia, alleluia.

Give thanks to the LORD, for he is good,
    for his mercy endures forever.
Let the house of Israel say,
    "His mercy endures forever."

The right hand of the LORD has
        struck with power;
    the right hand of the LORD is exalted.

I shall not die, but live,
    and declare the works of the LORD.

The stone which the builders rejected
    has become the cornerstone.
By the LORD has this been done;
    it is wonderful in our eyes.

slavery to sin," we might very well hear in the background the prophecy of Ezekiel, who told the people that the Lord would place in them a "new heart" and his very own spirit. The bottom line for Paul is that baptism entails becoming a new creation in Christ—"living for God in Christ Jesus"—which means that nothing in life can be the same as it was before baptism.

 GOSPEL   The Gospel of Luke is book-ended by divine announcements made to holy women. At the outset

of Luke's Gospel, the angel Gabriel appears to the Virgin Mary and announces to her that she has won God's favor and will bear a child who is to be named Jesus, a message she quickly shares with her cousin Elizabeth. These two women set the stage for the wonders that will be performed by God's gift of grace.

At the end of the story, after Jesus suffers and dies on the cross and is buried, a group of women, at first unnamed, come to his tomb to anoint his body. There they encounter two angels in the form of men,

who announce to them a message of great hope. Just as Mary and Elizabeth were filled with a holy fear in the presence of divine power, so these women at Jesus' tomb are said to be "terrified and bowed their faces to the ground." The message delivered by the angels is meant to calm their fear and to instill in them the courage to carry the message to Jesus' disciples.

It is not by accident that the Evangelist Luke chooses women to be the bearers of a world-changing message. Other great female messengers in the Gospel of Luke

GOSPEL   Luke 24:1–12

A reading from the holy Gospel according to Luke

At **daybreak** on the **first day** of the **week**
    the **women** who had come from **Galilee** with **Jesus**
    took the **spices** they had **prepared**
    and went to the **tomb**.
They found the **stone** rolled **away** from the **tomb**;
    but when they **entered**,
    they did not find the **body** of the Lord **Jesus**.
While they were **puzzling** over this, **behold**,
    two men in **dazzling garments appeared** to them.
They were **terrified** and bowed their **faces** to the ground.
They **said** to them,
    "**Why** do you seek the **living one** among the **dead**?
He is not **here**, but he has been **raised**
Remember what he **said** to you while he was **still** in **Galilee**,
    that the **Son** of **Man** must be handed **over** to sinners
    and be **crucified**, and **rise** on the **third day**."
And they **remembered** his words.
Then they **returned** from the **tomb**
    and **announced** all these **things** to the **eleven**
    and to **all** the **others**.
The **women** were Mary **Magdalene**, **Joanna**,
        and **Mary** the mother of **James**;
    the **others** who accompanied them also **told** this
        to the **apostles**,
    but their **story** seemed like **nonsense**
    and they did not **believe** them.
But **Peter** got up and ran to the **tomb**,
    bent **down**, and saw the burial cloths **alone**;
    then he went home **amazed** at what had **happened**.

A narrative reading of great power and solemnity. The emphasis in Luke's depiction of the empty tomb is on the women there to attend to the body of Jesus. Their puzzlement is that of women expected to tend to this task but who suddenly cannot because the tomb is empty. Allow the details of the reading, the spices and the dazzling garments of the two men (presumably angels), to guide your proclamation.

The two messengers speak directly here to the women, reminding them of what Jesus has prophesied.

Magdalene =
MAG-duh-luhn or MAG-duh-leen
Luke names the women specifically here. Let their names ring out.

Finally, Peter believes the women and goes to take a look for himself. Treat Peter's amazement as a confirmation of the words of the women.

include Anna the prophetess, who foretold the greatness of Jesus' ministry (Luke 2:36–38); the sinful woman who anointed Jesus' feet (Luke 7:36–50); and Martha and Mary (Luke 10:38–42). Women play a special role in Luke's theology; they seem to have a better understanding of the divine will than men. The same paradigm can be found in the Book of Exodus, in which all of the leading female characters—the midwives, Moses' mother, Pharaoh's daughter, Miriam, and Zipporah—exhibit a holy fear and discern God's will quickly and without resistance.

The women who come to honor the Lord by anointing his dead body become the first eyewitnesses to Jesus' resurrection. It is only after they have received the angels' announcement and have returned to share their remarkable finding with the eleven that Luke provides their identity: Mary Magdalene, Joanna, and Mary the mother of James. Despite the great joy exhibited by these women, the apostles did not believe their story, as it "seemed like nonsense." Unlike the women who quickly come to belief, these men are stubborn and slow in their willingness to believe. Nevertheless, Peter runs to the tomb, peers into its emptiness, and goes home amazed. Luke describes nothing extraordinary about Peter's discovery. Indeed, it will take several resurrection appearances to convince these men that the living one is not to be found among the dead, but rather has been raised (Luke 24:5). S.W.

EASTER SUNDAY

LECTIONARY #42

READING I   Acts of the Apostles 10:34a, 37–43

A didactic reading in the form of a narrative. Peter is telling an assembled crowd the story of Jesus' life and the important lessons learned from his instructions.
Judea = joo-DEE-uh

A reading from the Acts of the Apostles

Peter **proceeded** to speak and said:
  "You **know** what has **happened** all over **Judea**,
  beginning in **Galilee** after the **baptism**
  that **John** preached,
  how **God** anointed **Jesus** of **Nazareth**
  with the Holy **Spirit** and **power**.

Here is the first point: Jesus went about doing good.

He went **about** doing **good**
  and healing all those **oppressed** by the **devil**,
  for **God** was **with** him.
We are **witnesses** of all that he **did**
  both in the country of the **Jews** and in **Jerusalem**.

Here is the second point: He was crucified.

They put him to **death** by hanging him on a **tree**.

Here is the third point: He was resurrected. Mostly even stresses on the words in this line.

This man God raised on the third day and **granted** that he
      be **visible**,
  not to all the people, but to **us**,
  the **witnesses** chosen by **God** in advance,
  who **ate** and drank with him after he **rose** from the dead.

Here is the fourth point: He commissioned Peter and the other disciples to preach.

He **commissioned** us to preach to the **people**
  and **testify** that he is the one **appointed** by God
  as **judge** of the living and the **dead**.

And finally, the fifth point: If you believe in Jesus, your sins will be forgiven. This point speaks directly to the assembly.

To him all the **prophets** bear **witness**,
  that everyone who **believes** in him
  will receive **forgiveness** of sins through his **name**."

There are options for today's readings. Contact your parish staff to learn which readings will be used.

READING I Peter's speech concerning "what has happened all over Judea" most certainly stems from catechetical preaching in the early Church and has been accommodated by Luke to fit Peter's address in the house of Cornelius. This house represents a Gentile audience, therefore Peter attempts to be all-encompassing in summarizing the events surrounding the life and ministry of Jesus. Peter's speech is crafted to be evangelizing; his words suggest that it would be foolish not to give oneself over to a life of discipleship.

This discourse underscores the credibility of the apostles: "We are witness of all that he did both in the country of the Jews and in Jerusalem." This is particularly important for the effectiveness of Peter's speech. Because they witnessed the ministry of the Lord, his death on the cross, and numerous encounters with his resurrected body, these witnesses make present the deeds of the Lord. Peter suggests that Jesus com-missioned his followers to preach, to witness, to judge, and to herald the "forgiveness of sins through his name." There is no denying the great responsibility handed on to those who have been called to testify to the Lord's resurrection.

Another form of witness that Peter provides in this address is his highlighting the actions of eating and drinking with Jesus after his resurrection. The theme of sharing a meal is seen throughout Luke's Gospel and occurs in Acts as a means of demonstrating the particular people that God has carved out in calling forth wit-

For meditation and context:

RESPONSORIAL PSALM   Psalm 118:1–2, 16–17, 22–23 (24)

R. This is the day the Lord has made; let us rejoice and be glad.
or R. Alleluia.

Give thanks to the LORD, for he is good,
  for his mercy endures forever.
Let the house of Israel say,
  "His mercy endures forever."

"The right hand of the LORD has struck
  with power;
  the right hand of the LORD is exalted.

I shall not die, but live,
  and declare the works of the LORD."

The stone which the builders rejected
  has become the cornerstone.
By the LORD has this been done;
  it is wonderful in our eyes.

Colossians = kuh-LOSH-uhnz

An exhortatory reading, compressed in its length but powerful in its message.

The focal word in this reading is "above."

The syntax here is strange. Be sure to practice.

READING II   Colossians 3:1–4

A reading from the Letter of Saint Paul to the Colossians

Brothers and **sisters**:
If then you were raised with **Christ**, seek what is **above**,
  where **Christ** is seated at the **right hand** of God.
Think of what is **above**, not of what is on **earth**.
For you have **died**, and your life is hidden with **Christ** in God.
When Christ your life **appears**,
  then **you too** will appear with him in **glory**.

Or:

Corinthians = kohr-IN-thee-uhnz

An exhortatory reading, compressed in its length but powerful in its message.

Yeast is Paul's metaphor for Christ's sacrifice. Just as there would be no feast without bread, so there is no spiritual life without leaven.

READING II   1 Corinthians 5:6b–8

A reading from the first Letter of Saint Paul to the Corinthians

Brothers and **sisters**:
Do you not **know** that a little **yeast** leavens all the **dough**?
Clear **out** the old **yeast**,
  so that you may become a fresh **batch** of **dough**,
  inasmuch as you are **unleavened**.
For our **paschal lamb**, Christ, has been **sacrificed**.
Therefore, let us **celebrate** the feast,
  not with the **old yeast**, the yeast of **malice** and **wickedness**,
  but with the **unleavened bread** of **sincerity** and **truth**.

---

nesses. This was granted "not to all the people, but to us." Luke substantiates his catechesis on the mystery of the Lord with the authority of Peter and the apostles.

As Peter concludes his preaching, he leaves those assembled in Cornelius' household with an unspoken choice that they must make: to believe in this man raised up by God on the third day or not. In some ways, Peter makes the choice a simple one. Since the prophets have foretold his coming for many ages, and because belief brings with it the forgiveness of sins, it would be foolish not to believe.

READING II **Colossians.** In these four sentences from his letter to the Colossians, Paul insists that the truth of being raised with Christ demands striving for things that are above. The things of this world are no longer to hold the attention of those refashioned into Christ. Instead, those who are grafted onto Christ are to see life from the perspective of being "seated at the right hand of God."

Nevertheless, Paul hints at the reality that living a life focused on "what is above" is no easy task; it will not be possible to make sense of a life "hidden with Christ"

until the glory of his return. Those baptized into Christ must ask themselves how their lives manifest the presence of Christ. Although we do not hear of them in this reading, Paul provides a list of vices that the baptized must avoid at all cost (Colossians 3:5–8). By leading a life that is so contrary to the ways of the world, Christians reveal the Lord's glory in a gradual way.

What is most fundamental in this reading is the present effect of baptism. Death and resurrection have actually taken place for those baptized into Christ. If these actions have already taken place, then baptism

For meditation and context:

A narrative reading relating a scene of enduring power.

Magdala = MAG-duh-luh

SEQUENCE   Victimae paschali laudes

Christians, to the Paschal Victim
   Offer your thankful praises!
A Lamb the sheep redeems;
   Christ, who only is sinless,
   Reconciles sinners to the Father.
Death and life have contended in that
   combat stupendous:
   The Prince of life, who died, reigns
   immortal.
Speak, Mary, declaring
   What you saw, wayfaring.

"The tomb of Christ, who is living,
   The glory of Jesus' resurrection;
Bright angels attesting,
   The shroud and napkin resting.
Yes, Christ my hope is arisen;
   To Galilee he goes before you."
Christ indeed from death is risen, our new
   life obtaining.
   Have mercy, victor King, ever reigning!
   Amen. Alleluia.

GOSPEL   John 20:1–9

A reading from the holy Gospel according to John

On the **first day** of the week,
   Mary of **Magdala** came to the tomb **early** in the morning,
   while it was still **dark**,
   and saw the **stone removed** from the **tomb**.
So she ran and went to Simon **Peter**
   and to the other **disciple** whom Jesus **loved**, and told them,
   "They have **taken** the Lord from the **tomb**,
   and we don't **know** where they **put** him."
So **Peter** and the other **disciple** went out and came to the **tomb**.
They both **ran**, but the other **disciple** ran faster than **Peter**
   and **arrived** at the tomb **first**;
   he bent **down** and saw the **burial cloths** there, but did **not**
      go in.
When Simon **Peter** arrived **after** him,
   he went into the **tomb** and saw the **burial cloths** there,
   and the **cloth** that had covered his **head**,
   not **with** the burial cloths but rolled **up** in a separate **place**.
Then the **other** disciple also went **in**,
   the one who had arrived at the tomb **first**,
   and he **saw** and **believed**.
For they did not yet **understand** the Scripture
   that he had to **rise** from the **dead**.

The detail of the burial cloths is important. When Peter recognizes that the head cloth has been folded up, he understands that the body of Jesus was not stolen (since thieves wouldn't take the time to fold up the linens).

Seeing is believing: belief dawns on them here. Believing and understanding are two separate things. Understanding can take more time than belief.

simply squeezes out behavior that is at odds with life in Christ. Salvation is not something to be waited for in the end; it is something to be lived out every day.

1 Corinthians. Paul's exhortation concerning the need to "clear out the old yeast so that you may become fresh batch of dough" takes place in the context of his condemnation of the Corinthians for apparent sexual immorality, which begins a few verses earlier. Paul makes no attempt to withhold his contempt: "I have been told as an undoubted fact that one of you is living with his father's wife" (1 Corinthians 5:1).

Not only is this act shameful for the individual accused, but the entire community is judged culpable by Paul. This community of Christians has been noted for being prideful when they have reason to fear the Lord's judgement for actions so contrary to the Body of Christ.

This sinful "old yeast" has the potential for them to "rise" in a way that nurtures immorality. Nevertheless, Paul's instructions are clear: to become a new batch of dough that rises to become Christ's body, you must get rid of the old yeast.

Just as the Jews keep the annual celebration of Passover, which commemorates their freedom from slavery in Egypt, so Christians celebrate the passage from sin to freedom in the sacrifice of the Lord. Similarly, just as the Jewish community marks the enduring nature of their liberation by eating unleavened bread, made without yeast, for seven days after the Passover, so too do Christians mark their freedom in Christ with the unleavened bread of sincerity and truth. The purification of life that comes with baptism is to be lived out by

AFTERNOON GOSPEL Luke 24:13–35

A reading from the holy Gospel according to Luke

That very day, the first **day** of the week,
    two of Jesus' **disciples** were going
    to a **village** seven miles from Jerusalem called **Emmaus**,
    and they were **conversing** about all the things
        that had occurred.
And it **happened** that while they were **conversing** and debating,
    Jesus **himself** drew **near** and walked **with** them,
    but their **eyes** were prevented from **recognizing** him.
He asked them,
    "What are you **discussing** as you walk **along**?"
They **stopped**, looking downcast.
One of them, named **Cleopas**, said to him in **reply**,
    "Are you the **only visitor** to Jerusalem
    who does not **know** of the things
    that have taken **place there** in these days?"
And he **replied** to them, "What **sort** of things?"
They said to him,
    "The **things** that happened to **Jesus** the Nazarene,
    who was a **prophet** mighty in **deed** and **word**
    before **God** and all the **people**,
    how our **chief priests** and rulers both **handed** him **over**
    to a **sentence** of **death** and **crucified** him.
But we were **hoping** that he would be the **one** to redeem Israel;
    and **besides** all this,
    it is now the **third day** since this took **place**.
Some women from our group, however, have **astounded** us:
    they were at the tomb **early** in the morning
    and did not find his **body**;
    they came **back** and reported
    that they had **indeed seen** a vision of **angels**
    who **announced** that he was **alive**. »

A narrative reading with great drama built into it. The focus of the reading is recognition, specifically the time it takes Jesus' two disciples to recognize that he has been raised from the dead. The build-up of the narrative intensifies the excitement and joy of their recognition.

This phrase introduces the motif of recognition that guides the passage. Recognition is connected initially to seeing.

It's interesting that only one of these two disciples are named.

Note that "they" are speaking, both of them, even though it's one unified speech. The purpose of this description of Jesus' deeds and words is to build toward recognition.

Note "a vision of angels." Recognition and seeing are still urgently connected.

keeping the post-Passover spirit alive by their moral conduct.

GOSPEL | John is the only evangelist to report Mary Magdalene as the sole visitor to the tomb of Jesus, "early in the morning." John's simplification of Mary's first visit—she neither encounters an angel nor is she invited to peer into the empty tomb—downplays Mary as a primary witness to the Lord's resurrection. Instead, John places the emphasis on Peter "and the other disciple."

There is great urgency in the way Peter and his companion run to the tomb. The unnamed disciple runs faster than Peter and is the first to see the burial cloths. Nevertheless, he refrains from entering the tomb. This honor belongs to Simon Peter alone. He is to be seen as the first of the apostles to witness to the resurrection of the Lord. Peter enters by himself and sees the burial cloths. Only after this does the other disciple enter. John reports that "he saw and believed." John intended this unnamed disciples to symbolize the believing Christian. Therefore, while Peter is the

first to "see," it is every faithful and loving Christian who is called to "believe." Because this is the "beloved disciple," the one who stood by the cross of Christ, we are to see the connection between faith and love.

AFTERNOON GOSPEL | Surely there must have been tears shed and cries of anger uttered by the two disciples on that dusty road. Amid their grief and anxiety, the resurrected Lord appears to them and inquires about the nature of their conversation. They proclaim Jesus as a mighty prophet, witness to the

After spending time with Jesus (whom they still don't recognize), these disciples have a desire for further fellowship with him. They are beginning to sense something different than seeing something.

In the breaking of the bread—the ritual that repeats the Passover when they last were in Jesus' company—there is recognition. Ritual reveals presence.

Confirmation of their recognition, repeated in the phrase "the breaking of bread," the message of this reading.

Then some of those with us went to the **tomb**
    and found things **just as** the women had **described**,
    but him they did not **see**."
And he said to them, "**Oh**, how **foolish** you are!
How slow of heart to believe **all** that the prophets **spoke**!
Was it not **necessary** that the Christ should **suffer** these things
    and **enter** into his **glory**?"
Then beginning with **Moses** and all the **prophets**,
    he **interpreted** to them what referred to him
    in all the **Scriptures**.
As they **approached** the village to which they were **going**,
    he gave the **impression** that he was going on **farther**.
But they **urged** him, "**Stay** with us,
    for it is **nearly evening** and the day is almost **over**."
So he went in to **stay** with them.
And it happened that, while he was **with** them at table,
    he took bread, said the **blessing**,
    broke it, and **gave** it to them.
With **that** their eyes were **opened** and they **recognized** him,
    but he **vanished** from their **sight**.
Then they **said** to each other,
    "Were not our **hearts** burning **within** us
    while he **spoke** to us on the **way** and opened the **Scriptures**
        to us?"
So they set out at once and **returned** to Jerusalem
    where they found **gathered together**
    the eleven and those with them who were **saying**,
    "The **Lord** has truly been **raised** and has **appeared** to Simon!"
Then the two recounted
    what had taken **place** on the **way**
    and how he was made **known** to them in the **breaking** of **bread**.

charges lodged at Jesus and his subsequent death, reveal their hope that he was the Messiah, and attest that Jesus has been discovered to be alive. These are the developing strains of the faith that would be professed by the early Church.

Telling the story is precisely what the risen Lord seeks to do when he takes over and interprets the Scriptures for them. Although we are given no indication that the preaching opens their eyes, we can detect that it is indeed opening their hearts. They

invite the stranger to remain with them for the evening and to share a meal with them. Three things happen simultaneously: "their eyes were opened and they recognized him but he vanished from their sight. "If fear and a sense of failure filled their hearts when they left the city, joy and zeal fill them as they return to tell the other disciples of their good news. Upon their reunion with the other disciples, we see a grand collision of stories of the Lord's appearances, all of which must have produced a sense of over-

whelming peace. It is the testimony to the growth of Easter faith, as Luke leaves us with the words "Then they told what had happened on the road, and how he had been made known to them in the breaking of the bread." S.W.

SECOND SUNDAY OF EASTER

LECTIONARY #45

READING I   Acts 5:12–16

A straightforward, narrative reading describing the powers of the apostles in the early days of their ministry. Proclaim this passage with the even intonation of a seasoned storyteller.
portico = POHR-tih-koh

A reading from the Acts of the Apostles

Many **signs** and **wonders** were **done** among the **people**
    at the **hands** of the **apostles**.
They were **all together** in **Solomon's portico**.
None of the others **dared** to join them, but the **people**
      esteemed them.
Yet **more** than ever, **believers** in the Lord,
    great numbers of men and women, were **added** to them.
Thus they even **carried** the **sick out** into the **streets**
    and **laid** them on **cots** and **mats**
    so that when **Peter** came **by**,
    at least his **shadow** might fall on **one** or **another** of them.
A large number of **people** from the **towns**
    in the **vicinity** of Jerusalem also **gathered**,
    bringing the **sick** and those **disturbed** by unclean **spirits**,
    and they were **all cured**.

Slight pause between "sick" and "out."

Slow your pace to add emphasis to "all cured" at the end of this reading.

READING I The opening chapters of the Acts of the Apostles describe an infant Church that is very much concerned with the generous outpouring of gifts and talents to be shared with the Christian community. Today's reading immediately follows a story of greed: Ananias and Sapphira were a married couple who schemed to withhold more money than they needed from the sale of property. Their avarice led to both of them dying suddenly at Peter's feet.

Today's reading is one of life. Not only do we witness the grand multiplication of believers in the fold of the Church, but we also see Peter's gift of curing the sick and tormented.

Although we do not hear the story of the fraud of Ananias and Sapphira in the liturgy today, it is helpful to read the success of the growth and faith of the early Church in tandem with their story. We are tempted to imagine the early Church as a perfect utopia, with everyone sharing all things in common and the needs of the poor satisfied without any difficulty. We should be careful not to romanticize the fledgling community. The explosion of faith and the ability of the apostles to work wonders in the Lord's name most likely came with growing pains, disappointments, and stress. Yes, we should see the early Church in a positive light and take to heart the charitable attitude engendered there, but we must also recognize that the work of achieving unity in Christ was and is possible only with perseverance and trials.

READING II The Book of Revelation, written as an oracle given to John, looks to the eschatological future of the Christian Church. Scripture scholars

For meditation and context:

RESPONSORIAL PSALM   Psalm 118:2–4, 13–15, 22–24 (1)

R. Give thanks to the Lord for he is good, his love is everlasting.
or R. Alleluia.

Let the house of Israel say,
  "His mercy endures forever."
Let the house of Aaron say,
  "His mercy endures forever."
Let those who fear the LORD say,
  "His mercy endures forever."

I was hard pressed and was falling,
  but the LORD helped me.
My strength and my courage is the LORD,
  and he has been my savior.
The joyful shout of victory
  in the tents of the just.

The stone which the builders rejected
  has become the cornerstone.
By the LORD has this been done;
  it is wonderful in our eyes.
This is the day the LORD has made;
  let us be glad and rejoice in it.

READING II   Revelation 1:9–11a, 12–13, 17–19

A reading from the Book of Revelation

I, **John**, your **brother**, who **share** with you
  the **distress**, the **kingdom**, and the **endurance** we have
    in **Jesus**,
  found myself on the **island** called **Patmos**
  because I **proclaimed** God's word and gave **testimony** to Jesus.
I was **caught up** in **spirit** on the **Lord's day**
  and heard behind me a **voice** as **loud** as a **trumpet**, which said,
  "**Write** on a **scroll** what you see."
Then I turned to see whose **voice** it was that **spoke** to me,
  and when I **turned**, I saw **seven gold lampstands**
  and in the **midst** of the **lampstands** one like a **son** of man,
  wearing an **ankle-length robe**, with a **gold sash**
    around his **chest**.

When I caught **sight** of him, I fell **down** at his feet
  as though **dead**.
He **touched** me with his right hand and said, "**Do not** be **afraid**.
I am the **first** and the **last**, the one who **lives**.

A visionary narrative reading from Revelation that initiates six weeks in which the second reading comes from Revelation. The language from Revelation is as vivid as it is mysterious. It requires of its proclaimer confident, steady intonation which will more than adequately convey a sense of its value to your assembly.

This statement, "Write on a scroll what you see," expresses the entirety of the Christian visionary imperative. Emphasis on "write," "scroll," and "see."

Slightly heavier emphasis on "first" and "last."

approximate that it was written in about AD 95. This date is well past the apostolic period and is approaching the time when the Church began to develop marks of institutional authority and worship. The overall purpose of this book is to help maintain belief in the Second Coming of the Lord, which would usher in the Kingdom of God and when all the dead would be raised to eternal life. John acknowledges that he has shared the "distress, the kingdom, and the endurance" of remaining faithful to Jesus, despite the fact that the Lord has yet to come again.

John shares a beautiful vision of what that day will look like. He sees seven gold lampstands, symbols of the seven Churches of Asia Minor and thus the totality of the Christian Church. In the midst of them John sees "one like a son of man" wearing a robe stretching down to his ankles and a sash of gold around his chest, denoting both a priest and a king. John's reaction foretells the posture of the entire Church when Jesus returns in glory: he prostrates himself at the Lord's feet. Not only to John, but to the whole distressed Church, this figure declares, "Do not be afraid" and names himself "the first

and the last, the one who lives." As the one who was dead and now lives forever, he holds the keys to death and the world beyond it; it is he who will judge. He commands John: "Write down, therefore, what you have seen, and what is happening, and what will happen afterwards." The final words present the vision as an *anamnesis,* a form of remembering the past as present in order to live into the future as the speaker in the vision commands.

Once I was **dead**, but **now** I am **alive forever** and **ever**.
I hold the **keys** to **death** and the **netherworld**.
Write **down**, therefore, what you have **seen**,
and what is **happening**, and what will happen **afterwards**."

GOSPEL John 20:19–31

A reading from the holy Gospel according to John

On the **evening** of that first day of the **week**,
when the **doors** were locked, where the **disciples** were,
for **fear** of the **Jews**,
Jesus came and stood in their **midst**
and said to them, "**Peace** be with you."
When he had **said** this, he **showed** them his hands and his **side**.
The disciples **rejoiced** when they saw the **Lord**.
Jesus said to them again, "**Peace** be with you.
As the **Father** has sent me, so I send **you**."
And when he had **said** this, he **breathed** on them and **said**
to them,
"**Receive** the Holy Spirit.
Whose sins you **forgive** are **forgiven** them,
and whose **sins** you **retain** are **retained**."

Thomas, called **Didymus**, one of the **Twelve**,
was not **with** them when Jesus **came**.
So the other disciples said to him, "We have **seen** the Lord."
But he said to them,
"Unless I see the **mark** of the nails in his **hands**
and put my **finger** into the nailmarks
and put my **hand** into his side, I will **not** believe."

Now a **week later** his disciples were **again** inside
and **Thomas** was with them. **»**

Repetition of the visionary imperative, extending from the present into the future.

A narrative reading of a passage containing a great deal of inherent and relatable mystery. Thomas not only stands for the person who needs to see in order to believe; he is also a stand-in for the reluctant believer or for anyone struggling with belief, giving his recognition of Jesus and his expression of faith even greater resonance.

Jesus announces his presence with the word "peace" in this passage. The word is focal.

Repetition of "peace."

Didymus = DID-uh-muhs

Thomas' expressions of doubt in this passage should be treated with care.

GOSPEL | It is important to situate this passage from John according to the liturgical calendar. Since the year 2000, the Second Sunday of Easter has been designated Divine Mercy Sunday. While the background of the feast centers on a devotion stemming from the apparitions given to St. Faustina Kowalska, the Church is invited to contemplate the risen Lord as the ambassador of mercy. His Easter appearance to the apostles as they huddle in fear behind locked doors is a most suitable Scripture story by which to consider the resurrected Jesus as the perfect revelation of divine mercy.

An important detail to be considered in this passage is that the risen Lord appears to his closest friend on the evening of that first day of the week. This is the eighth day, the Day of the Lord, is to be considered beyond time. The eighth day is understood as the day when the Lord will appear again in glory and usher in the fullness of God's kingdom. Thus, the day of this resurrection appearance is meant to signal that it is a moment that stands outside of the ordinary.

Another significant aspect of the encounter is that the disciples neither ask for Jesus to come, nor does he need to break down doors in order to approach his friends. Instead, he simply came and stood among them. The connection to divine mercy is clear. Mercy is always before us, and it is most often we who put up barriers preventing us from seeing it. This is precisely what Thomas does. Rather than believing in the testimony of his companions, Thomas closes himself off to mercy; he will not believe.

Another repetition of "peace."

Jesus' words to Thomas are spoken with gentleness.

Thomas' recognition is joyful—its expression conveys the joy. No need to overemphasize it.

The conclusion of this Gospel reading speaks directly to the assembly, using the second person pronoun. Even though the word isn't rhythmically emphasized, it is thematically focal.

Jesus came, although the doors were **locked**,
    and stood in their **midst** and said, "**Peace** be with you."
Then he said to Thomas, "Put your finger **here** and see my **hands**,
    and bring your **hand** and put it into my **side**,
    and do not be **unbelieving**, but **believe**."
Thomas answered and said to him, "My **Lord** and my **God**!"
Jesus said to him, "Have you come to **believe**
    because you have **seen** me?
Blessed are those who **have not seen** and have **believed**."

Now Jesus did many other signs in the presence of his **disciples**
    that are not **written** in this **book**.
But these are **written** that you may come to **believe**
    that **Jesus** is the **Christ**, the Son of **God**,
    and that **through this belief** you may have **life** in his name.

PRAYERFUL READING, OR *LECTIO DIVINA*

1. *Lectio:* Read a Scripture passage aloud slowly. Notice what phrase captures your attention and be attentive to its meaning. Silent pause.

2. *Meditatio:* Read the passage aloud slowly again, reflecting on the passage, allowing God to speak to you through it. Silent pause.

3. *Oratio:* Read it aloud slowly a third time, allowing it to be your prayer or response to God's gift of insight to you. Silent pause.

4. *Contemplatio:* Read it aloud slowly a fourth time, now resting in God's Word.

The risen Lord had already breathed the Holy Spirit on the other apostles and charged them with the ability to forgive and retain sins, but this occurred in Thomas' absence. The unleashing of the Holy Spirit would surely have strengthened Thomas' faith as his friends recalled all that they had experienced. And this is precisely what happens. A week later, Jesus again appears to the apostles, and this time Thomas is with them. Once again, Jesus greets them: "Peace be with you." Undoubtedly, Thomas has had a chance to experience the peace that was upon the other apostles through-out the past week. Now he has no need to place his hands into the Lord's side or his fingers into the nail holes in his hands. Through the peace bestowed upon the apostles, he has been able to grow in his faith and is able to make one of the strongest biblical statements of faith ever: "My Lord and my God!" Thomas did not come to believe because he saw the risen Jesus but because he witnessed the transformative power of the Holy Spirit and the gift of mercy. S.W.

THIRD SUNDAY OF EASTER

LECTIONARY #48

READING I   Acts 5:27–32, 40b–41

A reading from the Acts of the Apostles

When the **captain** and the **court officers** had brought
    the **apostles** in
  and made them **stand** before the **Sanhedrin**,
  the high priest **questioned** them,
    "We gave you **strict orders**, did we **not**,
  to stop **teaching** in that **name**?
Yet you have **filled** Jerusalem with your **teaching**
  and want to bring this man's **blood upon** us."
But **Peter** and the **apostles** said in **reply**,
  "We must obey **God** rather than **men**.
The **God** of our **ancestors** raised **Jesus**,
  though you had him **killed** by **hanging** him on a **tree**.
God **exalted** him at his **right hand** as **leader** and **savior**
  to grant **Israel** repentance and **forgiveness** of sins.
We are **witnesses** of these things,
  as is the **Holy Spirit** whom **God** has given to **those** who
    obey him."

The **Sanhedrin** ordered the **apostles**
  to stop **speaking** in the name of **Jesus**, and **dismissed** them.
So they left the **presence** of the **Sanhedrin**,
  rejoicing that they had been found **worthy**
  to **suffer dishonor** for the **sake** of the **name**.

A narrative reading that consists of an accusation by the Sanhedrin about the apostles' activity, followed by Peter's response. It's an inherently dramatic reading because of this; the final sentences express relief.

Sanhedrin = san-HEE-druhn

Slight pause between "blood" and "us."

TO KEEP IN MIND
Pay attention to the pace of your reading. Varying the pace gives listeners clues to the meaning of the text. The most common error for proclaimers new to the ministry is speaking too fast.

Even emphasis on "So they left."

READING I The story of the nascent Church spreading through the Mediterranean region is really the story of the apostles' display of courageous faith. For instance, the Gospel would not have arrived in Antioch if it were not for the conviction of Paul and Barnabas. Likewise, Peter is seen in today's reading as remaining steadfast in faith despite the suffering that is to be inflicted upon him by the Sanhedrin.

Even stronger than the apostles' faith and their resolve to undergo persecution for the sake of the Lord's name is the overall power and authority of God's Word.

When the high priest berates Peter and his companions for teaching in Jesus' name, Peter responds simply that obedience to God is more important than following a human mandate. Those who are witnesses of Jesus' execution and exaltation, those who have been granted the power of the Holy Spirit, must teach in Jesus' name.

What we are to see in this debate is that Peter and those with him are not speaking by their own authority; it is by the power of God that they are able to testify to God's amazing desire to forgive those who are willing to embrace repentance.

Furthermore, we see in this encounter the beginning of a sense of revelry in martyrdom; the apostles leave the Sanhedrin rejoicing because they were "worthy to suffer dishonor for the sake of the name."

READING II In this apocalyptic vision, John sees and hears things never before encountered: the voices of angels, elders gathered around the throne, and "every creature in heaven and on earth and under the earth and in the sea" singing praise to the One on the throne. And four living creatures shouting, "Amen!" This is

For meditation and context:

RESPONSORIAL PSALM   Psalm 30:2, 4, 5–6, 11–12, 13 (2a)

R. I will praise you, Lord, for you have rescued me.
or R. Alleluia.

I will extol you, O LORD, for you drew me clear
    and did not let my enemies rejoice over me.
O LORD, you brought me up from the netherworld;
    you preserved me from among those going down into the pit.

Sing praise to the LORD, you his faithful ones,
    and give thanks to his holy name.
For his anger lasts but a moment;
    a lifetime, his good will.
At nightfall, weeping enters in,
    but with the dawn, rejoicing.

Hear, O LORD, and have pity on me;
    O LORD, be my helper.
You changed my mourning into dancing;
    O LORD, my God, forever will I give you thanks.

Revelation = rehv-uh-LAY-shuhn

A narrative reading of a visionary scene. While verbs of sight (to see, to look) are the primary verbs, verbs of hearing (to listen, to hear) are nearly as important. This passage includes more hearing than it does seeing, making it well suited to proclamation.

READING II   Revelation 5:11–14

A reading from the Book of Revelation

I, John, looked and heard the voices of many **angels**
    who **surrounded** the **throne**
    and the **living creatures** and the **elders**.
They were **countless** in number, and they cried **out**
      in a loud **voice**:
      "**Worthy** is the **Lamb** that was **slain**
        to receive **power** and **riches**, **wisdom** and **strength**,
        honor and **glory** and **blessing**."
Then I heard **every creature** in **heaven** and on **earth**
    and **under** the earth and in the sea,
    everything in the **universe**, cry **out**:
      "To the **one** who sits on the **throne** and to the **Lamb**
        be **blessing** and **honor**, **glory** and **might**,
        forever and **ever**."
The **four living creatures** answered, "**Amen**,"
    and the **elders** fell down and **worshiped**.

Emphasis on "out."

Ritual expressions such as "forever and ever" are easy to overdo in the recitation of a passage such as this. Treat the words directly, simply.

---

the heavenly liturgy, the work of every creature attuned to the praise of God. The beauty of this multitude of God's creation focused upon the divine throne is beyond compare.

    In the two stanzas of the song sung around the throne, "honor and glory and blessing" are given first to the "Lamb that was slain," the risen Lord who sits at the Father's right hand and, subsequently, to both the Lamb of God and the Father who sits upon the throne. This reveals that the Church is called to bow down in utter self-

lessness before the power of God who alone is worthy to receive the fullness of worship.

| GOSPEL | Chapter 21 of John's Gospel is considered to be an |

appendix to the original manuscript. It represents the third and final time that Jesus appeared to his disciples after his resurrection.

    What makes this story so compelling is imagining the underlying mood of Peter and the other disciples as they continue to grieve the loss of their friend and try to make sense of what life will look like going

forward. It is Peter who first announces to his friends, "I am going fishing." We who are reading the story might well say to ourselves, "Well, of course you are, Peter! What took you so long? After all, you once were a great fisherman." It should make perfect sense to us that in this moment of crisis and transition, Peter would want to return to his former profession.

    The other disciples make no hesitation in following Peter into the boat, "but that night they caught nothing." Perhaps we are to see in their inability to make a catch that their former skills at fishing have been

A multilayered narrative reading of the disciples encountering Jesus after the resurrection. Effectively, the reading is split in half. In the first half, the disciples who are fishing slowly recognize Jesus who is already among them. In the second half, Jesus seemingly forgives Peter for having denied knowing him three times. Both narratives are unusually powerful, requiring very little embellishment.

Tiberias = tĭ-BEER-ee-uhs
Didymus = DID-uh-muhs
Nathanael = nuh-THAN-ay-uhl
Galilee = GAL-ih-lee
Zebedee = ZEB-uh-dee

Not realizing it's Jesus is a motif of post-resurrection stories.

First recognition that it's Jesus.

Even emphasis on "one hundred fifty-three large fish."

GOSPEL John 21:1–19

A reading from the holy Gospel according to John

[At that time, **Jesus revealed** himself **again** to his **disciples**
    at the **Sea** of **Tiberias**.
He revealed himself in **this** way.
Together were **Simon Peter**, **Thomas** called **Didymus**,
    Nathanael from **Cana** in **Galilee**,
    Zebedee's sons, and **two others** of his **disciples**.
Simon Peter said to them, "I am going **fishing**."
They said to him, "We **also** will **come** with you."
So they went out and got into the **boat**,
    but **that night** they caught **nothing**.
When it was **already dawn**, Jesus was **standing** on the **shore**;
    but the **disciples** did not **realize** that it was **Jesus**.
Jesus said to them, "**Children**, have you caught **anything** to **eat**?"
They answered him, "**No**."
So he said to them, "**Cast** the net **over** the right side of the **boat**
    and you will **find something**."
So they **cast** it, and were **not able** to pull it **in**
    because of the **number** of fish.
So the **disciple** whom Jesus **loved** said to **Peter**, "It is the **Lord**."
When Simon Peter **heard** that it was the **Lord**,
    he tucked in his **garment**, for he was lightly **clad**,
    and **jumped** into the sea.
The other **disciples** came in the **boat**,
    for they were not **far** from **shore**, only about a hundred **yards**,
    dragging the **net** with the **fish**.
When they climbed **out** on **shore**,
    they saw a charcoal **fire** with **fish** on it and **bread**.
Jesus said to them, "**Bring** some of the **fish** you just **caught**."
So Simon Peter went **over** and dragged the net **ashore**
    full of **one hundred fifty-three large fish**.
Even though there were so **many**, the net was not **torn**. »

replaced by a new skill: hearing and following the voice of the Lord. In the morning, after returning to shore with their empty nets, they hear the command of the unrecognizable risen Jesus to cast the net on the right side of the boat. Their obedience yields to a catch so big that they are unable to haul it ashore.

Who is the first to make sense of the mysterious catch? It is the beloved disciple of the Lord, the one to whom Jesus commended the care of his mother as the two stood below at the cross. He announces to Peter, "It is the Lord." Simon Peter hears

this prophetic voice and responds with an overwhelming display of awe, reverence, and joy. Scholars suggest that Peter jumping into the sea is a form of self-baptism by which he symbolizes a newly found commitment to the risen Lord.

What follows this baptismal allusion is a scene that is very Eucharistic in nature. Jesus commands the disciples to bring ashore some of the newly caught fish. John is oddly precise about the number: 153 large fish. Some believe that the number corresponds to the 153,000 men that were needed to construct the Temple in Jerusalem.

The meal continues with the risen Jesus uttering the invitation for the disciples to join him, as he "took" bread and "gave" it to them, and "in like manner the fish." Clearly, the discovery of Jesus' true identity is linked to Eucharistic hospitality, by which he is able to nurture and sustain the faith of those who follow him.

Just as the contemporary celebration of the Eucharist leads to a commissioning of those who have been fed, so too does this breakfast on the seashore end in a grand commissioning. As Jesus elicits from Peter three statements of faith, he also

Widespread recognition of Jesus.

Jesus **said** to them, "**Come**, have **breakfast**."
And none of the disciples dared to ask him, "Who **are** you?"
  because they **realized** it was the **Lord**.
Jesus came **over** and took the **bread** and **gave** it to them,
  and in like **manner** the fish.
This was now the **third time** Jesus was **revealed** to his disciples
  after being **raised** from the **dead**.]

It shifts here to the forgiveness narrative.

Among the words for love in the New Testament are *agape* and *philo*. *Agape* signifies a higher love; *philo* signifies familiar love and the love among friends. When Jesus asks Peter whether he loves him, he uses a form of *agape,* but Peter answers using a form of *philo*. Since English only has one word for love, it's a challenge to convey this nuance. When Jesus asks, keep your intonation neutral, while when Peter asks, make your intonation more pleading. (Presumably, Peter feels slightly insulted that Jesus would even ask.)
The second time, Jesus uses *agape* and Peter replies with *philo*.
This third time, however, Jesus uses *philo* in his question, coming down to Peter's level. Peter's response perhaps indicates that he has understood that Jesus is condescending to him (in a good way). He is a little exasperated and relieved.

When they had **finished breakfast, Jesus** said to Simon **Peter**,
  "**Simon**, son of **John**, do you **love me** more than **these**?"
Simon Peter answered him, "**Yes**, Lord, you **know** that
    I **love** you."
Jesus said to him, "**Feed** my **lambs**."
He then **said** to Simon **Peter** a **second** time,
  "**Simon**, son of **John**, do you **love** me?"
Simon Peter answered him, "**Yes**, Lord, you **know**
    that I **love** you."
Jesus said to him, "**Tend** my **sheep**."
Jesus said to him the **third** time,
  "**Simon**, son of **John**, do you **love** me?"
Peter was **distressed** that Jesus had said to him a **third** time,
  "Do you **love** me?" and he **said** to him,
  "**Lord**, you know **everything**; you **know** that I **love** you."
Jesus said to him, "**Feed** my sheep.
Amen, amen, I **say** to you, when you were **younger**,
  you used to **dress** yourself and go where you **wanted**;
  but when you grow **old**, you will stretch out your **hands**,
  and someone **else** will **dress** you
  and **lead** you where you do not want to **go**."
He **said** this signifying by what **kind** of death he would
    glorify **God**.
And when he had **said** this, he said to him, "**Follow me**."

Emphasize "Follow me."

[Shorter: John 21:1–14 (see brackets)]

commands Peter and the other disciples to go out into the world to care for his flock. First, he tells Peter, "Feed my lambs." Then he instructs him, "Tend my sheep." Finally, a third time, Jesus makes an allusion to the kind of death Peter will die in offering his service to the Lord. In suffering persecution and resentment, Peter "will stretch out [his]hands" and will be led to where he does not want to go. This is meant to parallel the Lord's own passion, during which Peter denied having any sort of relationship with Jesus. At the end this intimate post-resurrection appearance, the Lord utters the same words he used to summon Peter and the other fishermen away from their nets and boats at the beginning of his earthly mission: "Follow me." S.W.

FOURTH SUNDAY OF EASTER

LECTIONARY #51

READING I   Acts 13:14, 43–52

An exultant narrative reading that details the successes of the apostles' efforts to spread the word of God.
Barnabas = BAHR-nuh-buhs
Perga = PER-guh
Antioch = AN-tee-ahk
Pisidia = pih-SID-ee-uh
Synagogue = SIN-uh-gog

Slight pause between "whole city" and "gathered."

Slight pause between "violent abuse" and "contradicted."

A reading from the Acts of the Apostles

Paul and **Barnabas** continued on from **Perga**
    and reached **Antioch** in **Pisidia**.
On the **sabbath** they entered the **synagogue** and took their **seats**.
Many **Jews** and **worshipers** who were **converts** to **Judaism**
    followed **Paul** and **Barnabas**, who **spoke** to them
    and **urged** them to remain **faithful** to the grace of **God**.

On the following **sabbath** almost the **whole city gathered**
    to hear the **word** of the **Lord**.
When the **Jews** saw the **crowds**, they were **filled** with **jealousy**
    and with **violent abuse contradicted** what Paul said.
Both **Paul** and **Barnabas** spoke out **boldly** and said,
    "It was **necessary** that the **word** of God be **spoken** to you **first**,
    but since you **reject** it
    and **condemn yourselves** as **unworthy** of eternal **life**,
    we now **turn** to the **Gentiles**.
For so the **Lord** has **commanded** us,
    *I have made you a **light** to the **Gentiles**,*
    *that you may be an **instrument** of **salvation***
    *to the **ends** of the **earth**."* »

READING I   Today's reading from the Acts of the Apostles finds Paul and Barnabas in the synagogue in this Gentile region of Antioch. They take their seats, showing us that they are connected to their Jewish roots. Acts suggests that at first these missionaries were welcomed by "many Jews and worshippers."

The reading suggests that their work to reveal the risen Lord to the people of the city was highly effective; on the following Sabbath, "almost the whole city" came together to hear the preaching of Paul and Barnabas. Nevertheless, the response of the leading Jews is one of jealousy, as they witness the success of the missionaries' preaching. Paul's response to their fear is to announce that the work of preaching the Word of God would be focused from that point upon the Gentiles rather than the Jews. Paul proclaims that he and Barnabas have been commissioned by the Lord to be "a light to the Gentiles"—reminiscent of Simeon's words in Luke's Gospel when the infant Jesus was presented in the Temple—and "an instrument of salvation" for all the world.

At the declaration that they have been made the worthy recipients of the Lord's care, the Gentiles in Antioch were "delighted" and came to belief in the Gospel. The Jews, however, distanced themselves more from the way of Jesus. For those who are willing to listen and come to faith, the gift of great joy and ongoing spread of the Word is granted, but for those who choose to reject the teaching of the apostles, fear and jealousy will prevent them from accepting the gift of salvation. We are meant to see in this reading the power of God's Word to triumph

This sentence characterizes the successes of the apostles. Emphasis on "all" and "believe."

The **Gentiles** were **delighted** when they **heard** this
    and **glorified** the word of the **Lord**.
All who were **destined** for eternal **life** came to **believe**,
    and the **word** of the **Lord** continued to **spread**
    through the **whole region**.
The **Jews**, however, incited the **women** of **prominence**
      who were **worshipers**
    and the **leading men** of the **city**,
      stirred up a persecution against **Paul** and **Barnabas**,
    and **expelled** them from their **territory**.

Iconium = ī-KOH-nee-uhm

Emphasis on "joy" and the "Holy Spirit."

So they **shook** the **dust** from their **feet** in **protest against** them,
    and went to **Iconium**.
The **disciples** were filled with **joy** and the Holy **Spirit**.

For meditation and context:

RESPONSORIAL PSALM   Psalm 100:1–2, 3, 5 (3c)

R. We are his people, the sheep of his flock.
or R. Alleluia.

Sing joyfully to the LORD, all you lands;
   serve the LORD with gladness;
   come before him with joyful song.

Know that the LORD is God;
   he made us, his we are;
   his people, the flock he tends.

The LORD is good:
   his kindness endures forever,
   and his faithfulness, to all generations.

Revelation = rehv-uh-LAY-shuhn

A visionary narrative reading from Revelation consisting primarily of the symbolically loaded speech of a celestial elder.

The Lamb is a predominant, mysterious figure in Revelation, obviously Christ, endowed with otherworldly power.

READING II   Revelation 7:9, 14b–17

A reading from the Book of Revelation

I, John, had a **vision** of a great **multitude**,
    which **no one** could **count**,
    from every **nation**, **race**, **people**, and **tongue**.
They stood before the **throne** and before the **Lamb**,
    wearing **white robes** and holding **palm branches**
      in their **hands**.

---

over disbelief, as the disciples were "filled with joy and the Holy Spirit."

READING II The Book of Revelation is often used to engender fear in those who contemplate the world's end. However, the vision given to John is one of anticipated beauty. John sees the throne of God surrounded by a "great multitude," incapable of being counted. This multitude is far from homogenous, for it is constituted by people of "every nation, race, people, and tongue." While the members of this great multitude may have come from a variety of origins, they are joined together in Christ. While Revelation does not mention his name, Christ's identity is indicated in the multitudes' wearing of white robes and carrying of palm branches. These are participants in the Lord who have purified themselves and who share in the kingship of the cross.

John not only sees a vision, but he also hears the voice of one of the elders, who clarifies the scene and explains that they have "washed their robes" which leaves them "white in the blood of the Lamb." A few things might strike the reader about the symbolism here. First, washing in blood should turn something red, but in this case, the "blood of the Lamb" produces the color associated with purity. Second, the participation and faith of each individual member of the throng is accounted for, as each person is responsible for washing his or her own garment. Furthermore, alluding to Psalm 23, the elder suggests that those who surround the throne will be so focused on worship that they will neither hunger nor thirst and will be shepherded "to springs of life-giving water."

Here, the unnamed elder begins to speak. The vision's authority comes from what is seen and what is heard.

The strangeness of robes turning white in the blood of the Lamb can be noted simply by reading this passage a little slowly.

The Lamb and his connection to "life-giving water," which you should emphasize.

Then one of the **elders said** to me,
    "**These** are the ones who have **survived** the time
        of **great distress**;
they have **washed** their **robes**
and made them **white** in the **blood** of the **Lamb**.

    "For this **reason** they stand before God's **throne**
        and **worship** him **day** and **night** in his **temple**.
    The one who **sits** on the throne will **shelter** them.
    They will not **hunger** or **thirst** anymore,
        nor will the **sun** or any heat **strike** them.
    For the **Lamb** who is in the **center** of the **throne**
        will **shepherd** them
        and **lead** them to springs of **life-giving water**,
        and **God** will wipe away **every tear** from their **eyes**."

GOSPEL   John 10:27–30

A short, potent didactic reading that reads almost like a logical proof or a story problem.

Parallel emphasis between "know" and "follow."

This speech of Jesus serves to make the connection between Jesus and the protection he provides and God, who has granted Jesus his protective powers, and Jesus himself. Even emphasis on "Father," "I", and "one."

A reading from the holy Gospel according to John

Jesus said:
"My **sheep** hear my **voice**;
    I **know** them, and they **follow** me.
I give them **eternal life**, and they shall **never perish**.
No one can take them **out** of my **hand**.
My **Father**, who has **given** them to me, is **greater** than all,
    and **no one** can take them **out** of the Father's **hand**.
The **Father** and **I** are **one**."

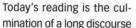

GOSPEL   Today's reading is the culmination of a long discourse in the Gospel of John in which Jesus calls himself the Good Shepherd. The shepherd serves as a beautiful image of kindness and compassion. At the same time, shepherds must also be strong and courageous in protecting their flocks.

In these few lines from John's Gospel, the focus is on the relationship between the shepherd and the sheep. First, the sheep are able to hear the shepherd's voice. John says nothing about the quality or strength of this particular voice, only

that it allows the flock to follow the shepherd. Moreover, the relationship between the shepherd and the sheep is one of trust: "I know them, and they follow me." The point here is that leadership of the flock is not provided from the outside but from inside the fold; Jesus has an intimate knowledge of those he came to save.

Finally, and perhaps most importantly, the relationship between the shepherd and the sheep is based upon the gift of eternal life, where "they shall never perish." Jesus has handed his followers over to the Father, and no power is capable of removing them

from his care. Even though we might envision the Good Shepherd as a tender caretaker, the reality is that his grasp over his own is mighty. As easy as it might be to wander from the voice of the shepherd, it is far more difficult to be taken out of his grasp. S.W.

FIFTH SUNDAY OF EASTER

LECTIONARY #54

READING I   Acts 14:21–27

A reading from the Acts of the Apostles

After **Paul** and **Barnabas** had **proclaimed** the good **news**
    to that **city**
    and made a **considerable** number of **disciples,**
      they **returned** to **Lystra** and to **Iconium** and to **Antioch.**
They **strengthened** the spirits of the **disciples**
    and **exhorted** them to **persevere** in the **faith,** saying,
    "It is **necessary** for us to **undergo** many **hardships**
    to enter the **kingdom** of **God.**"
They appointed **elders** for them in each **church** and,
    with **prayer** and **fasting,** commended them to the **Lord**
    in whom they had **put** their **faith.**
Then they **traveled** through **Pisidia** and reached **Pamphylia.**
After proclaiming the **word** at **Perga** they went **down** to **Attalia.**
From **there** they sailed to **Antioch,**
    where they had been **commended** to the **grace** of **God**
    for the **work** they had now **accomplished.**
And when they **arrived,** they **called** the church **together**
    and **reported** what **God** had **done** with them
    and how he had **opened** the door of **faith** to the **Gentiles.**

A narrative reading that recounts the movements of Sts. Paul and Barnabas as they worked to spread the word of God. Its general tone is appreciative of the hardships the apostles endured and the success they achieved.

Lystra = LIS-truh
Iconium = Ī-KOH-nee-uhm
Antioch = AN-tee-ahk

This reading is filled with place names, each of which signifies a place where these apostles found some success in sharing the good news.

Pisidia = pih-SID-ee-uh
Pamphylia = pam-FIL-ee-uh
Perga = PER-guh
Attalia = at-uh-LĪ-uh

Your tone here should be purposeful.

READING I   Chapter 14 of Acts opens with the success of the Paul and Barnabas' preaching inciting persecution by Jewish officials aiming to prevent the evangelization of the Gentiles. The chapter also relates the story of Paul curing a crippled man, which leads to the crowd mistaking them to be gods sent to destroy them. While today's reading may open at verse 21 with the mere mention that "Paul and Barnabas had proclaimed the good news to that city," it is important to understand that such preaching took place in the midst of high drama.

Even with intermittent opposition waged by Jewish authorities, Paul and Barnabas were able to secure many followers for Christ. Throughout their travels, they recognize that discipleship will come with its share of hardships. Not only do the two apostles work to fortify the faith of new disciples in the infant Churches spreading throughout the Mediterranean region, but they also are responsible for appointing leaders within the various Christian communities. It is likely that already by this time (AD 46–49) these elders would have

been installed by a ritual laying on of hands and prayer.

After passing through several more cities, where they undoubtedly took time to proclaim the good news, Paul and Barnabas eventually return to Antioch, where they had begun their journey. Acts makes clear that the two had accomplished all that they had been appointed to do. Nevertheless, when they summon the Christian community of Antioch together to tell them all that they had done, Paul and Barnabas attribute all the credit to the grace of God; he was

For meditation and context:

RESPONSORIAL PSALM   Psalm 145:8–9, 10–11, 12–13 (see 1)

R. I will praise your name for ever, my king and my God.
or
R. Alleluia.

The LORD is gracious and merciful,
   slow to anger and of great kindness.
The LORD is good to all
   and compassionate toward all his works.

Let all your works give you thanks, O LORD,
   and let your faithful ones bless you.
Let them discourse of the glory of
   your kingdom
   and speak of your might.

Let them make known your might to the
   children of Adam,
   and the glorious splendor of your kingdom.
Your kingdom is a kingdom for all ages,
   and your dominion endures through
   all generations.

A visionary narrative reading that includes an exhortation spoken by a loud voice in new Jerusalem. Because the reading seethes with images, you will serve it best by reading it clearly and firmly in a measured tone.

Slight pause between "bride" and "adorned."

TO KEEP IN MIND
Be careful not to swallow your words. Articulate carefully, especially at the end of lines.

This statement is one of the boldest, most striking and original claims in all of the New Testament; it resides at the mystical core of our Christian faith. Emphasize "Behold" and give even stresses to "all things new."

READING II   Revelation 21:1–5a

A reading from the Book of Revelation

Then **I, John**, saw a **new heaven** and a **new earth**.
The **former heaven** and the **former earth** had **passed away**,
   and the **sea** was no **more**.
I also saw the **holy city**, a **new Jerusalem**,
   coming **down** out of **heaven** from **God**,
   prepared as a **bride adorned** for her **husband**.
I heard a **loud voice** from the **throne** saying,
   "**Behold**, God's **dwelling** is with the human **race**.
He will **dwell** with them and they will be his **people**
   and **God himself** will a**lways be** with them as their **God**.
He will wipe **every tear** from their **eyes**,
   and there shall be **no more death** or **mourning**,
      wailing or **pain**,
   for the **old order** has passed **away**."

The One who sat on the throne said,
   "**Behold**, I make **all things new**."

---

the one who "had opened the door of faith to the Gentiles."

READING II The vision of a "new heaven and a new earth" constitutes the final scene of the Book of Revelation, and John intends these words to inaugurate a new beginning. Revelation is written to a Christian community in the throes of a violent persecution, and its people have grown weary in their hope for the Lord's return. Their primary concern is undoubtedly how much longer they must endure this world as they know it. John's

response is the command to see what he has seen: "Behold, I make all things new."

Yet, where are the people to look? The answer to this question is precisely the Church. The Lord has established the Church as "the holy city, a new Jerusalem." It is the Church that is "prepared as a bride adorned for her husband." Because the Church exists on earth, the "former heaven and the former earth" are no more. All things have been made new in the creation of Christ's Church. Yet the lived reality feels nothing like a new creation. Thus, the voice from heaven cries out with words of assur-

ance. The Lord promises to be with his people. He will dry the tears from their eyes, destroy death, and take away their "mourning," "wailing," and "pain." These signs of despair have no place in a Church guided by hope.

GOSPEL This Gospel passage precedes and introduces Jesus' final discourse with his disciples (John 14—17). This brief introduction focuses on two main points: first, Jesus announces his departure ("I will be with you only a little while longer") and, second,

GOSPEL   John 13:31–33a, 34–35

A reading from the holy Gospel according to John

When **Judas** had left them, Jesus said,
    "**Now** is the Son of Man **glorified**, and **God** is glorified in **him**.
If **God** is glorified in **him**,
    God will also **glorify** him in **himself**,
    and God will **glorify** him at **once**.
My **children**, I will be **with you** only a little while **longer**.
I give you a **new commandment: love one another**.
As **I** have loved **you**, so **you also** should **love** one another.
This is how **all will know** that **you** are my **disciples**,
    if you have **love** for one **another**."

An exhortatory reading which contains the core commandment of Jesus' teachings. Crucially, Jesus doesn't utter it until Judas has left.

To follow the track of Jesus' use of "glorify," note the parallels: "glorify" him in "himself" / "glorify" him "at once."

Proclaim this commandment slowly: "love one another."

Likewise, proclaim this conclusion slowly.

Jesus speaks of providing his disciples with a "new commandment." In presenting these two themes to his closest followers, Jesus expresses great affection for his hearers, addressing them as "my children."

First, Jesus foretells of his departure as a time of glorification. In fact, he uses a form of the word "glorify," either referring to himself or his Father, five times in this short passage. Jesus' gift of utter obedience gives glory to the Father, and in turn, the Father glorifies him. John's Jesus also states that God will "glorify him at once." This temporal reference is most likely the author's way of reassuring his community, which has long been awaiting the Lord's return. Words of glory are meant to keep alive hope in his future coming.

Second, this reading introduces the giving of a "new commandment." Jesus will make the discussion of this commandment the centerpiece of his final discourse in chapter 15. The Hebrew covenant had made love of God and love of neighbor a primary mandate of the Law, so one must ask what is new about Jesus' command to love. The answer lies in the difference between a love based upon law and a love based upon a heartfelt relationship. Jesus will instruct his disciples very soon in this final discourse that "no one has greater love than this, to lay down one's life for one's friends" (John 15:13), and he will put this love into action as he hangs upon the Cross. S.W.

SIXTH SUNDAY OF EASTER

LECTIONARY #57

A narrative reading whose focus is on some of the mundane elements of the work the apostles were engaged in, including traveling about to deliver letters to people in the early Church. It has the quality of a chronicle.

circumcised = SER-kuhm-sīzd
Mosaic = moh-ZAY-ihk

Barnabas = BAHR-nuh-buhs

"Apostles" and "elders" signal a focal point of the reading. Give slight additional emphasis to these words and the names of the apostles that follow.
Antioch = AN-tee-ahk

A recitation from the letter the apostles delivered to Antioch. Straightforward delivery.
Syria = SEER-ee-uh
Cilicia = suh-LISH-ee-uh

READING I   Acts 15:1–2, 22–29

A reading from the Acts of the Apostles

Some who had come down from **Judea** were instructing
the **brothers**,
"**Unless** you are **circumcised** according to the **Mosaic** practice,
you **cannot** be **saved**."
Because there arose **no little dissension** and **debate**
by **Paul** and **Barnabas with** them,
it was **decided** that **Paul, Barnabas**, and **some** of the others
should go up to **Jerusalem** to the **apostles** and **elders**
about this **question**.

The **apostles** and **elders**, in **agreement** with the whole **church**,
decided to choose **representatives**
and to **send** them to **Antioch** with **Paul** and **Barnabas**.
The ones **chosen** were **Judas**, who was called **Barsabbas**,
and **Silas**, **leaders** among the **brothers**.
This is the letter **delivered** by them:

"The **apostles** and the **elders**, your **brothers**,
to the brothers in **Antioch**, **Syria**, and **Cilicia**
of **Gentile** origin: **greetings**.
Since we have **heard** that some of our **number**
who went **out** without any **mandate** from us
have **upset** you with their **teachings**
and **disturbed** your peace of **mind**, »

READING I   Today's reading from the Acts of the Apostles is a sort of bookend account of a major controversy in Jerusalem concerning how Gentiles should be accepted into the faith. First, we have visitors from Judea arriving in Antioch, who demand that converts need to be circumcised. Then, the reading jumps to the written response prepared in Jerusalem and delivered to the Church in Antioch announcing that Gentiles would be exempt from circumcision. What is missing in today's reading is the debate that took place in between. Peter and James offer

brief, but eloquent testimony that God does not wish to place distinctions among his people. Thus, the decision is made not to make things unnecessarily difficult for those who were turning from paganism to belief in Christ.

While Paul covers the discussion in his letter to the Galatians (2:1–10), Luke's reporting of the story is much more peaceful. The debate at Jerusalem produces three resolutions. First, those Jewish Christians who had stirred up the Gentiles lacked authority in their teaching. For this reason, the Jerusalem Church now sends

Judas (Barsabbas) and Silas as credible witnesses to the truth. Second, those who turn from paganism to Christ are to be considered exempt from the Mosaic Law and the tradition of circumcision. Finally, Gentile Christians are to abstain from several customs held by some outside the faith, namely, eating meat that was sacrificed to idols, eating meat with blood in it, eating meat of strangled animals (instead of meat from ritual slaughter), and marriages with close family members.

There is a genuine sense of collaboration in this Scripture passage, as the apostles

we have with **one accord** decided to **choose** representatives
and to **send** them to you along with our beloved **Barnabas**
    and **Paul**,
who have **dedicated** their **lives** to the **name**
    of our **Lord Jesus Christ**.
So we are sending **Judas** and **Silas**
    who will also convey this **same message** by **word** of **mouth**:
'It is the **decision** of the Holy Spirit and of **us**
    not to **place** on you any **burden** beyond these **necessities**,
    namely, to abstain from **meat** sacrificed to **idols**,
    from **blood**, from **meats** of strangled **animals**,
    and from **unlawful marriage**.
If you keep **free** of these,
    you will be **doing** what is **right. Farewell**.'"

The letter includes a quoted message, which is the heart of the teaching. Proclaim at a slightly slower pace.

For meditation and context:

RESPONSORIAL PSALM   Psalm 67:2–3, 5, 6, 8 (4)

R. O God, let all the nations praise you!
or R. Alleluia.

May God have pity on us and bless us;
    may he let his face shine upon us.
So may your way be known upon earth;
    among all nations, your salvation.

May the nations be glad and exult
    because you rule the peoples in equity;
    the nations on the earth you guide.

May the peoples praise you, O God;
    may all the peoples praise you!
May God bless us,
    and may all the ends of the earth fear him!

READING II   Revelation 21:10–14, 22–23

A reading from the Book of Revelation

The **angel** took me in **spirit** to a **great, high mountain**
    and **showed** me the **holy city Jerusalem**
    coming **down** out of **heaven** from **God**.
It **gleamed** with the **splendor** of God.

A visionary narrative reading, describing what John saw when taken up in the spirit to the heavenly city of Jerusalem. Great wonders, celestial and worldly, are recounted. No need to overdo it. Allow the drama inherent in the reading to do the work for you.

"in agreement with the whole church" calmly select representatives to quiet the turmoil instigated by the Jewish Christians at Antioch. In their wise debate, the apostles restore the credibility of Paul and Barnabas, "who have dedicated their lives to the name of our Lord Jesus Christ." Furthermore, the letter sent from Jerusalem acknowledges the work of the Holy Spirit in guiding the deliberation. As the early Church spread rapidly throughout the Mediterranean region, one of the central concerns was the unity of faith. The dispute concerning the requirement of circumcision

provides the Church with the opportunity to enter into the work of discernment and clearly define what is necessary for Christian unity.

READING II When reading excerpts from the Book of Revelation, it is always important to place its apocalyptic nature within the context of the late first century. Revelation is believed to have been composed around the year 96, which corresponds to the end of the reign of Domitian (AD 89–96), a Roman emperor who intensely persecuted Christians and Jews alike. Thus,

the end-times description of the heavenly city (the new Jerusalem) that comes "down out of heaven from God" would surely have instilled hope in the hearts of believers who witnessed the Church being destroyed one martyr at a time.

Biblical symbolism plays a major role in this vision given to John. First, John is led to a "great, high mountain." As seen in Exodus, Ezekiel, and the Gospels as well, the setting of a mountain is well suited to divine revelation. Second, the city symbolizes completeness or fullness, as its twelve doors, each designated for one of the

Its **radiance** was like that of a precious **stone**,
   like **jasper**, clear as **crystal**.
It had a **massive**, **high wall**,
   with **twelve gates** where **twelve angels** were **stationed**
   and on which **names** were **inscribed**,
   the **names** of the **twelve tribes** of the **Israelites**.
There were **three gates** facing **east**,
   three **north**, three **south**, and three **west**.
The **wall** of the city had **twelve courses** of stones
      as its **foundation**,
   on which were inscribed the **twelve names**
   of the **twelve apostles** of the **Lamb**.

I saw **no temple** in the **city**
   for its **temple** is the **Lord God almighty** and the **Lamb**.
The **city** had **no need** of **sun** or **moon** to **shine** on it,
   for the **glory** of **God** gave it **light**,
   and its **lamp** was the **Lamb**.

Twelve is the celestial number repeated most frequently in this reading. Give it slight emphasis.

John seeing "no temple" would be like seeing a house without walls or a river without banks. That the temple is almighty God, and the Lamb is total revelation.

GOSPEL   John 14:23–29

A reading from the holy Gospel according to John

Jesus said to his **disciples**:
   "Whoever **loves me** will **keep** my **word**,
   and my **Father** will **love him**,
   and we will **come** to him and make our **dwelling** with him.
Whoever does **not** love me does **not** keep my **words**;
   yet the **word** you **hear** is not **mine**
   but that of the **Father** who **sent** me. **»**

An exhortatory reading of puzzling complexity in which Jesus elaborates on his relationship to the Father.

Equal emphasis on "love" and "him."

---

twelve tribes of Israel, welcome people from every corner of the earth, from the north and the south, the east and the west. Furthermore, the foundation stones, also twelve in number, are named after the twelve apostles. This city is fortified through and through, and it gleams with the Glory of God!

The centerpiece of the historical Jerusalem was the Temple, which by the time of Revelation's writing, had been leveled by the Romans. However, the heavenly city that John beholds needs no temple. Its temple is the "Lord God almighty and the Lamb." In this city God's glory is its light

and the Lamb is the lamp. Although the author is not concerned here with Trinitarian theology, it might be possible to equate the light with the Spirit that is generated in the relationship between the Father and the Son. Regardless, this vision is designed to bring great hope to a Church struggling for its earthly survival.

GOSPEL   This passage from the Gospel of John, which constitutes a portion of Jesus' farewell discourse, reads as a series of sayings. Jesus intends to inform his disciples with easy-to-

recall phrases: "Whoever loves me will keep my word," "Peace I leave with you, my peace I give to you," "Do not let your hearts be troubled." But the overall umbrella of Jesus' teaching is the command to allow God to dwell with them by imitating the pattern of divine love: "Whoever loves me will keep my word, and my Father will love him, and we will come to him and make our dwelling with him." As Jesus prepares to take leave of his disciples, he wishes to make it abundantly clear that he is not abandoning them, but rather, he will lead them home.

Advocate = AD-vuh-k*t

Light emphasis on "teach you"; heavier emphasis on "everything."

The point: the "Father" is "greater" than "I" am. Emphasize all three words equally.

"I have **told** you this while I am **with** you.
The **Advocate**, the Holy **Spirit**,
    whom the **Father** will **send** in my **name**,
    will **teach you everything**
    and **remind** you of **all** that I **told** you.
Peace I **leave** with you; my **peace** I **give** to you.
Not as the world **gives** do I **give** it to you.
Do not let your **hearts** be **troubled** or **afraid**.
You **heard** me **tell** you,
    'I am going **away** and I will come **back** to you.'
If you **loved** me,
    you would **rejoice** that I am **going** to the **Father**;
    for the **Father** is **greater** than **I**.
And **now** I have told you this before it **happens**,
    so that when it **happens** you may **believe**."

In order to provide for such guidance here on earth, Jesus instructs them that the Advocate, who will be sent by God, will teach his followers all that they need to know. Furthermore, this Spirit will be responsible for perpetuating the mission of Jesus by reminding the disciples of all that Jesus had taught them. Moreover, Jesus will leave the gift of peace with his disciples. This is not any ordinary kind of peace, but one that comes from the other side of the grave. Jesus will not impart this peace until after he has suffered, died, and been raised to new life. This is a peace that cannot be destroyed by hatred or death; it is a peace that lives for eternity. Because the disciples will be given the gift of the Lord's peace, they should be able to rejoice that the Lord is going to return to the Father. Jesus posits himself as inferior to the Father precisely because his is the role of obedience—as he gives up his life for others, and ultimately as an act of perfect love for the Father, the Father has only the fullness of his love to return without fail. S.W.

THE ASCENSION OF THE LORD

LECTIONARY #58

READING I   Acts 1:1–11

A reading from the Acts of the Apostles

In the **first** book, Theophilus,
    I dealt with **all** that Jesus **did** and **taught**
    until the **day** he was taken **up**,
    after giving **instructions** through the Holy **Spirit**
    to the **apostles** whom he had **chosen**.
He presented himself **alive** to them
    by many **proofs** after he had **suffered**,
    appearing to them during forty **days**
    and **speaking** about the **kingdom** of God.
While **meeting** with them,
    he **enjoined** them not to **depart** from **Jerusalem**,
    but to **wait** for "the **promise** of the **Father**
    about which you have **heard** me **speak**;
    for John baptized with **water**,
    but in a few days you will be **baptized** with the Holy **Spirit**."

When they had gathered **together** they asked him,
    "**Lord**, are you at this time going to **restore**
        the **kingdom** to Israel?"
He answered them, "It is not for you to know the **times**
        or **seasons**
    that the **Father** has established by his own **authority**.
But you will **receive** power when the Holy **Spirit**
        comes **upon** you, »

Theophilus = thee-AWF-uh-luhs
A narrative reading that recounts the ascension of Jesus, along with some of last words. The reading is dramatic and visionary. You will only need to proclaim it with care for its power to come through.

"The day he was taken up": the ascension. The vertical direction is important.

This question allows Jesus to provide the disciples specific details of their task as well as advice before he departs.

There are options for today's readings. Contact your parish staff to learn which readings will be used.

READING I Luke begins the Acts of the Apostles with a systematic presentation of God's plan, which culminates with the exaltation of Jesus. Specifically, Luke is concerned with describing the forty-day period of preparation that begins with the Lord's resurrection day and progresses to the ascension. The number forty is symbolic for preparedness: Noah's forty days in the ark, Moses' forty days on Mount Sinai, Elijah's forty days of wandering in the desert, and Jesus' own forty days of preparation for ministry in the desert. Thus, even though the liturgical season of Easter is nearing completion, the celebration of the Lord's ascension on the fortieth day points us in the direction of preparedness for the future.

How has the Church as a whole been preparing? What is the goal of this preparation? Luke answers the first question by testifying that the Lord "presented himself alive to [the apostles] by many proofs after he had suffered." During his post-resurrection appearances, Christ commanded the apostles to remain in Jerusalem. The Lord wished for those closest to him to remain together in order to strengthen one another before he would finally depart from their sight. Regarding the goal of these forty days of preparation, Luke also provides the answer: The apostles will "receive power" from the coming of the Holy Spirit to witness to "the ends of the earth." This resurrected Jesus reveals this only after they reveal their misunderstanding of the nature of the kingdom that is to come.

Emphasize "witnesses." Witnessing is
essential to discipleship.
Judea = joo-DEE-uh
Samaria = suh-MAYR-ee-uh

and you will be my **witnesses** in Jerusalem,
throughout **Judea** and **Samaria**,
and to the **ends** of the **earth**."
When he had **said** this, as they were looking **on**,
he was lifted **up**, and a **cloud** took him from their **sight**.
While they were looking **intently** at the sky as he was **going**,
suddenly two men **dressed** in white **garments**
stood **beside** them.
They said, "Men of **Galilee**,
why are you **standing** there looking at the **sky**?
This Jesus who has been taken **up** from you into **heaven**
will **return** in the same way as you have seen him
going into **heaven**."

The reading concludes with a vision of two
angelic beings. Give their speech that
follows emphasis by slowing your pace
ever so slightly.

For meditation and context:

RESPONSORIAL PSALM   Psalm 47:2–3, 6–7, 8–9 (6)

R. God mounts his throne to shouts of joy: a blare of trumpets for the Lord.
or R. Alleluia.

All you peoples, clap your hands,
  shout to God with cries of gladness
For the LORD, the Most High, the awesome,
  is the great king over all the earth.

God mounts his throne amid shouts of joy;
  the LORD, amid trumpet blasts.

Sing praise to God, sing praise;
  sing praise to our king, sing praise.

For king of all the earth is God;
  sing hymns of praise.
God reigns over the nations,
  God sits upon his holy throne.

Ephesians = ee-FEE-zhuhnz

READING II   Ephesians 1:17–23

A reading from the Letter of Saint Paul to the Ephesians

An exhortatory reading, filled with
high-hearted blessings.
The first blessing comes from God to the
people of Ephesus.

Brothers and **sisters**:
May the **God** of our Lord Jesus **Christ**, the Father of **glory**,
  give you a Spirit of **wisdom** and **revelation**
  resulting in **knowledge** of him.
May the **eyes** of your hearts be **enlightened**,
  that you may **know** what is the **hope** that belongs to his **call**,
what are the **riches** of glory
  in his **inheritance** among the holy **ones**,

The second blessing comes from Paul to
the people of Ephesus, including knowledge,
hope, and the riches of glory. Give each
aspect of this blessing its due by emphasizing
it slightly.

READING II **Ephesians.** This reading is a prayer for the heart's enlightenment and for the maturing of the virtue of hope. Such a prayer is able to be uttered precisely because of the pattern of Christ. It is through attachment to Christ alone (that is, baptism) that such a rich and glorious inheritance comes and can be understood. Phrases such as "the surpassing greatness of his power" and "the exercise of his great might" nearly stretch the limits of language in trying to express the unimaginable power God has revealed in Christ. For this we need a spirit of wisdom

and revelation. With the evidence provided in this passage, it would be foolish not to desire being a beneficiary of this prayer.

As if God's greatness in raising up Jesus from the dead is not enough to enlighten the hearts of believers and unbelievers alike, Ephesians points to the position of power that God has given to the glorified Christ: dominion and authority over all that exists, even the things of heaven. The Father has "put all things beneath his feet" and has provided for Christ's continued relationship with the temporal Church; Christ is forever to be the head of his body,

the Church. Even though the Church experiences persecution and unrest, it shares in the "fullness" of Christ's universal rule, which is possible only because of the Father's great love of Christ.

Hebrews. Today's reading from Hebrews alludes to the feast of Atonement, the annual occasion when the high priest enters the holy of holies and sprinkles blood as a means of rededication to and reunion with God. The high priest offered sacrifice for the remission of his own sins and for the sins of the Israelite nation.

and what is the surpassing **greatness** of his **power**
for **us** who **believe**,
in **accord** with the exercise of his **great might**:
which he **worked** in **Christ**,
raising him from the **dead**
and **seating** him at his right **hand** in the **heavens**,
far above every **principality**, **authority**, **power**, and **dominion**,
and every **name** that is **named**
not only in this **age** but also in the one to **come**.
And he put **all things** beneath his **feet**
and gave him as **head** over all things to the church,
which is his **body**,
the **fullness** of the one who fills **all things** in every **way**.

Or:

READING II   Hebrews 9:24–28; 10:19–23

A reading from the Letter to the Hebrews

Christ did not **enter** into a sanctuary made by **hands**,
a **copy** of the **true** one, but **heaven** itself,
that he might now **appear** before **God** on our **behalf**.
Not that he might **offer** himself **repeatedly**,
as the **high priest** enters each **year** into the **sanctuary**
with **blood** that is not his **own**;
if that were **so**, he would have had to **suffer repeatedly**
from the **foundation** of the **world**.
But **now** once for **all** he has **appeared** at the end of the **ages**
to take away **sin** by his **sacrifice**.
Just as it is **appointed** that men and **women** die **once**,
and after **this** the **judgment**,
so also **Christ**, offered **once** to take away the **sins** of **many**,
will **appear** a second time, not to take away **sin**
but to bring **salvation** to those who eagerly **await** him. **»**

These are the traditional names of some of the angelic powers.

Paul concludes by invoking the power of Jesus himself.

A didactic reading about the Christian attitude toward Christ's sacrifice told with great eloquence. A complex reading but one very pleasing to proclaim.

TO KEEP IN MIND
Use the pitch and volume of your voice to gain the attention of the assembly.

Note the "just as / so also" construction. This allows for rhetorical tension to be built up and then released.

The atonement in Christ's blood, however, is permanent. His sacrifice made on the altar of the cross makes the repetition of offerings by humans unnecessary. Christ, the perfect priest, enters into the heavenly presence of God and intercedes on our behalf. Perhaps Christ does not need to use words to make intercession, but rather, his presence before the Father suffices to make all our needs known. The love exchanged between the Father and the Son unites our humanity with divine love and atones for our sins. Christ has offered himself "once to take away the sins of many."

The human temptation is to be led into thinking that this sacrifice does not really happen once and for all, and that we must do something on our own to bring about salvation (this is the heresy called Pelagianism). This passage from Hebrews intends to restore our confidence in the permanence of all that Christ accomplishes. The second half of the reading suggests that, because of Christ's offering, we too will enter into the heavenly sanctuary. While we cannot add anything to perfect the sacrifice of Christ, we are to foster a "sincere heart" and hold fast "to our confession that gives us hope,"

made at our baptism. Where Christ, is we hope one day to follow.

GOSPEL The account of Jesus providing a final instruction that is linked to the event of his ascension serves as the conclusion to Luke's Gospel. In the first part of this passage, Jesus provides his disciples with a way of interpreting Scripture that is based on his suffering, death, and resurrection. Jesus' statement that everything that he has suffered and overcome has already been written means that his mission is to be understood as

"Therefore" signals that the important points of the argument are about to be stated.

Therefore, brothers and **sisters**, since **through** the blood of **Jesus**
  we have **confidence** of **entrance** into the **sanctuary**
  by the **new** and **living way** he opened for us through the veil,
  that is, his **flesh**,
  and since we have "a **great priest** over the **house** of **God**,"
  let us **approach** with a sincere **heart** and in absolute **trust**,
  with our **hearts** sprinkled **clean** from an evil **conscience**
  and our **bodies** washed in pure **water**.

Slightly uplifted tone for this conclusion.

Let us hold **unwaveringly** to our **confession** that gives us **hope**,
  for he who made the **promise** is **trustworthy**.

GOSPEL   Luke 24:46–53

A narrative reading of the verses that conclude the Gospel of Luke, which ends on an uplifting high note.

A reading from the holy Gospel according to Luke

Jesus said to his **disciples**:
"**Thus** it is written that the **Christ** would **suffer**
  and **rise** from the **dead** on the **third day**
  and that **repentance**, for the forgiveness of **sins**,
  would be **preached** in his **name**
  to all the **nations**, beginning from **Jerusalem**.
You are **witnesses** of these things.

These are Jesus' last words in Luke. They have the quality of great conviction and inspiration.

And **behold** I am sending the **promise** of my **Father upon** you;
  but **stay** in the **city**
  until you are **clothed** with power from on **high**."

Then he led them **out** as far as **Bethany**,
  raised his **hands**, and **blessed** them.
As he **blessed** them he **parted** from them
  and was **taken up** to **heaven**.

"Taken up to heaven": These four words depict the ascension.

They did him **homage**
  and then **returned** to **Jerusalem** with great **joy**,
  and they were **continually** in the temple praising **God**.

Joy is the feeling of this last verse in Luke.

---

preordained by the Father. Further, Jesus teaches that the proclamation of his name must be tied to the bestowal of forgiveness. Finally, while the disciples are called to be witnesses to all that Jesus has lived and taught, it is the outpouring of the Holy Spirit that will provide the power for all that is to come. With these instructions the Lord's voice falls silent, and he says nothing more in Luke's Gospel.

However, what he does not say in words, the quiet drama of the ascension makes clear what attachment to Jesus and his way will bring. Luke tells us in Acts 1:3 that the ascension takes place on the fortieth day after the Lord's resurrection. The number forty conveys the symbolic meaning of preparation in Scripture; the resurrected Lord needed the full forty-day period to bolster the faith of his disciples. Here, at the end of Luke's Gospel, the drama of the ascension itself is rather low-key: Jesus bestows a blessing upon his followers and then is "taken up to heaven." After worshipping the Lord, the apostles returned to Jerusalem and were seen "continually in the temple praising God." As the Gospel concludes, we are left to imagine that the disciples are strong in their faith as they await the coming of the Spirit. With this passage, Luke has opened the way for a Christological interpretation of all Scriptures already written, and he has paved the way for the apostles to follow the guidance of the Spirit and provide for the foundation of the Church. S.W.

SEVENTH SUNDAY OF EASTER

LECTIONARY #61

READING I   Acts 7:55–60

A reading from the Acts of the Apostles

Stephen, **filled** with the Holy **Spirit**,
   looked up **intently** to **heaven** and saw the **glory** of **God**
   and **Jesus standing** at the right hand of **God**,
   and Stephen said, "**Behold**, I see the **heavens opened**
   and the Son of **Man standing** at the right hand of **God**."
But they cried **out** in a loud **voice**,
   covered their **ears**, and **rushed** upon him **together**.
They threw him **out** of the **city**, and began to **stone** him.
The **witnesses** laid down their **cloaks**
   at the **feet** of a young man named **Saul**.
As they were **stoning Stephen**, he called **out**,
   "Lord **Jesus**, receive my **spirit**."
Then he **fell** to his **knees** and cried **out** in a loud **voice**,
   "**Lord**, do not **hold** this sin **against** them";
   and when he **said** this, he fell **asleep**.

A narrative reading of the martyrdom of St. Stephen. Tones of conviction and forgiveness prevail.

After St. Stephen speaks, the scene turns violent. Don't overplay the violence; instead, relate the violence clearly and directly.

The reading concludes on a note of forgiveness, striking in contrast to the violence. Once again, don't over play it. The contrast will come through naturally.

For meditation and context:

RESPONSORIAL PSALM   Psalm 97:1–2, 6–7, 9 (1a, 9a)

R. The Lord is king, the most high over all the earth.
or R. Alleluia.

The LORD is king; let the earth rejoice;
   let the many islands be glad.
Justice and judgment are the foundation of
   his throne.

The heavens proclaim his justice,
   and all peoples see his glory.
All gods are prostrate before him.

You, O LORD, are the Most High over
   all the earth,
   exalted far above all gods.

READING I The young Stephen, who witnesses to the resurrected and exalted Jesus "standing at the right hand of God," rightfully claims the honor of being the Church's first martyr. In this scene from Acts, Stephen is "filled with the Holy Spirit" and endures horrendous suffering in the name of Christ. Just as Jesus surrendered his spirit to the Father and begged forgiveness for his persecutors, Stephen cries out in similar words, offering his spirit to the Lord and praying for those responsible for his death.

As the Church moves from Ascension through the period that leads to Pentecost, the emphasis is on the restoration of creation which, having suffered from sin, is guided in the Spirit to become a new creation. Not only is such restoration highlighted in the death Stephen endures, complete with his vision of the heavens opening up for him, but it is also foreshadowed in Luke's mention of the witnesses laying their cloaks before the feet of Saul, as the crowds once did for Jesus entering Jerusalem. Saul, who will lead a persecution against the followers of Jesus (Acts 8:3),

will eventually himself become a new creation and work tirelessly for the spread of the faith. The death of the Church's first martyr could have brought the Church to a swift end; instead, that death is intimately connected to the raising up of a sinner who will assume the role of an apostle.

READING II The speaker in today's passage from the Book of Revelation is the resurrected Christ, who announces that his return is imminent. The word "behold" at the outset of his proclamation relates a sense of urgency regarding

A visionary exhortatory reading, the sixth and final in a sequence of readings from Revelation that stretch back to the Second Sunday of Easter, preparing us for the feast of Pentecost the following Sunday. Jesus is speaking in this reading, the final words he utters in the New Testament.

recompense = REK-uhm-pens
Alpha = AL-fuh
Omega = oh-MAY-guh

These words are repeated from the first chapter of Revelation, one of the most striking things uttered in all of the New Testament. Essentially, Jesus is saying "I am the alphabet." Parallel emphases: "Alpha/Omega"; "first/last"; "beginning/end."

Even stresses on "bright morning star."

"Yes, I am coming soon" are Jesus' last words in the New Testament. They are followed immediately by an exclamation in the words by John of Patmos himself, whose words stand in for our own.

READING II   Revelation 22:12–14, 16–17, 20

A reading from the Book of Revelation

I, John, heard a voice **saying** to me:
    "**Behold**, I am coming **soon**.
I bring with me the **recompense** I will give to **each**
        according to his **deeds**.
I am the **Alpha** and the **Omega**, the **first** and the **last**,
        the **beginning** and the **end**."

Blessed are they who wash their **robes**
        so as to have the **right** to the tree of **life**
        and enter the **city** through its **gates**.
"**I, Jesus**, sent my **angel** to give you this **testimony**
        for the **churches**.
I am the **root** and **offspring** of **David**,
        the **bright morning star**."

The **Spirit** and the **bride** say, "**Come**."
Let the hearer say, "**Come**."
Let the one who **thirsts** come forward,
        and the one who **wants** it receive the **gift** of life-giving **water**.

The one who gives this **testimony** says, "**Yes**, I am coming **soon**."
Amen! Come, Lord **Jesus**!

---

his return. This is a revelation for all to hear and ponder. Christ reveals all that will occur when he returns. He will serve as judge, bestowing a "recompense" for each according to the deeds performed in his absence. He encompasses everything and all time; he is the "Alpha and the Omega" (the two ends of the Greek alphabet), the beginning and the end and everything in between.

This vision also has baptismal significance. Those "who wash their robes" are blessed with the inheritance of eternal life, of which he is the beginning and the end. He is the "bright morning star," a promise

of light, the dawn of hope for a Church that has longed for his return and has suffered persecution in the meantime.

The final portion of this vision turns to the appropriate response of the earthly Church, guided by the Spirit: *Maranatha*, "Come, Lord Jesus." The same the cry is on our lips during Advent as we look forward with great hope to the Lord's triumphal return. Like the Samaritan woman in John 4, we thirst for "life-giving water"; like her, we are invited to drink.

As the seal to this revelation given to John, the Lord announces: "Yes, I am com-

ing soon." These final words of the New Testament echo down the ages as a promise of light and hope, not of doom.

GOSPEL   Today's portion of the Gospel of John constitutes a small part of what is called the priestly prayer of Jesus. The Lord at the Last Supper prays as a priest, lifting up to the Father his present disciples and future disciples, asking that they "might be one." This intimate prayer that Jesus addresses to his Father displays his hope that the divine worldview of perfect unity might be realized among his

GOSPEL   John 17:20–26

A reading from the holy Gospel according to John

Lifting up his eyes to **heaven**, Jesus **prayed**, saying:
"**Holy Father**, I pray not **only** for **them**,
     but also for **those** who will **believe** in me through their **word**,
     so that they may **all** be **one**,
     as **you**, Father, are in **me** and I in **you**,
     that they also may be in **us**,
     that the **world** may believe that you **sent** me.
And I have **given** them the glory you **gave** me,
     so that they may be **one**, as we are **one**,
     I in **them** and **you** in me,
     that they may be **brought** to perfection as **one**,
     that the world may **know** that you sent **me**,
     and that you loved **them** even as you loved **me**.
Father, they are your **gift** to me.
I **wish** that where I **am** they also may be with **me**,
     that they may **see** my glory that you **gave** me,
     because you **loved** me before the **foundation** of the **world**.
Righteous Father, the world also does not **know** you,
     but **I** know you, and they **know** that you **sent** me.
I made **known** to them your **name** and I will make it **known**,
     that the **love** with which you **loved** me
     may **be** in **them** and **I** in **them**."

A complex exhortatory reading in which Jesus pleads to the Father while positioning himself as the intermediary between God and the people he is praying for. Parallels, from the Father to Jesus, from Jesus to the people, define this reading.

The reading involves four direct addresses to God, each time named "Father." Use these to drive your reading forward through its complexities.

The second address to God, which leads to the "me/you" parallel.

The third address to God.

The fourth address to God, as "Righteous Father." Emphasize the repetitions of "know" and "known" through to the end of the reading.

---

followers on earth. This intercession is not only for the benefit of the disciples, but also for the sake of the whole world, "that the world may know that you sent me."

Jesus states that he has given his followers a share in the glory that was bestowed upon him by his Father. This glory is nothing less than perfect unity with God. Thus, perfect unity with them is the perfection of our humanity. It is the hope of the Church that eternal life will consist of participation in divine oneness.

In the final verses of his priestly prayer, knowing that he will soon be betrayed, Jesus asks that the love he shares with the Father may be in those he will soon leave behind. The disciples know this love because they know that the Father sent Jesus into the world. Thus, with the possession of both knowledge and love, the disciples are sure to grow in unity and faith. S.W.

PENTECOST SUNDAY:
VIGIL

LECTIONARY #62

READING I   Genesis 11:1–9

A reading from the Book of Genesis

The whole **world** spoke the same **language**, using the same **words**.
While the **people** were migrating in the east,
   they came upon a **valley** in the land of **Shinar** and settled there.
They said to one another,
   "**Come**, let us mold **bricks** and harden them with **fire**."
They used **bricks** for stone, and **bitumen** for mortar.
Then they said, "**Come**, let us **build** ourselves a **city**
   and a **tower** with its **top** in the **sky**,
   and so make a **name** for ourselves;
   otherwise we shall be **scattered** all over the **earth**."

The LORD came down to see the **city** and the **tower**
   that the **people** had built.
Then the LORD said: "If **now**, while they are one **people**,
   all **speaking** the same **language**,
   they have **started** to do this,
   nothing will later stop them from doing **whatever** they
      presume to do.
Let us then go **down** there and **confuse** their language,
   so that **one** will not **understand** what another **says**."
Thus the LORD **scattered** them from **there** all over the **earth**,
   and they **stopped** building the city.

Genesis = JEN-uh-sihs

A narrative reading of a story absorbed in mysterious power. As much a parable as it is a demonstration of the incomprehensible mind of God, it can seem almost like science fiction. It's probably best to treat it that way in terms of proclaiming it: Read what's in the text, straightforwardly and clearly.

Shinar = SHĬ-nahr

bitumen = bih-TYOO-m*n

The two repetitions of "Come" stand for the aspirations—or arrogance—of the people. Give a little edge to the word when you speak it.

TO KEEP IN MIND
The words in bold are suggestions for ways to express the meaning of the reading. Consider using them as you practice the reading, then choose to stress them or to find your own way of proclaiming.

God's use of "let us" repeats the use of the builders of the tower. Here, God's intention is unhelpful, destructive even. "Confuse" is the loaded word.

There are options for today's readings. Contact your parish staff to learn which readings will be used.

READING I   The story of Babel is part of the Genesis account of sin and its rootedness in the world. After the fall of humanity in the Garden of Eden, men and women continued to disobey God in a variety of ways; the chief act of disobedience was to aspire to the greatness of God.

Although the descendants of Noah were meant to be dispersed throughout the world (Genesis 10), they chose instead to settle all together in the land of Shinar and build there a city with a tower that would demonstrate their unified force.

This halt in the people's migration eastward ended their nomadic way of life, which would be replaced by a form of urban living. We might question whether God intended humanity to cluster together in cities rather than embrace life lived as a

journey. In any case, the people's pursuit of building a tower into the skies that will make a name for themselves was an attempt to rival pagan temples, and thus was itself a form of idolatry.

Needless to say, the Lord is not happy with the arrogance of the people, who wish to plot their own destiny upon the earth. Thus, in a conversation with his heavenly helpers, the Lord determines that an appropriate punishment would be the confusion of their speech, thereby making human

Babel = BAB-*l

Note the repetition of "confuse" in "confused." The word suggests something of the power of God.

That is why it was called **Babel**,
    because **there** the Lord **confused** the speech of **all** the world.
It was from **that** place that he **scattered** them all over the **earth**.

For meditation and context:

RESPONSORIAL PSALM   Psalm 33:10–11, 12–13, 14–15

R. Blessed the people the Lord has chosen to be his own.

The Lord brings to nought the plans
   of nations;
  he foils the designs of peoples.
But the plan of the Lord stands forever;
  the design of his heart, through
   all generations.

Blessed the nation whose God is the Lord,
   the people he has chosen for his own
   inheritance.
From heaven the Lord looks down;
  he sees all mankind.

From his fixed throne he beholds
  all who dwell on the earth,
He who fashioned the heart of each,
  he who knows all their works.

Exodus = EK-suh-duhs

A narrative reading of the sealing of the covenant between God and humankind, attended by powerful natural phenomena. The scene of this reading is especially vivid.

READING II   Exodus 19:3–8a, 16–20b

A reading from the Book of Exodus

Moses went up the **mountain** to God.
Then the Lord **called** to him and said,
   "**Thus** shall you **say** to the house of **Jacob**;
   tell the **Israelites**:
   You have **seen** for yourselves how I **treated** the Egyptians
   and how I **bore** you up on **eagle wings**
   and **brought** you here to **myself**.
Therefore, if you **hearken** to my voice and **keep** my covenant,
   you shall be my **special** possession,
   dearer to me than **all** other people,
   though **all** the earth is **mine**.
You shall be to me a **kingdom** of priests, a **holy** nation.
That is what you must **tell** the Israelites."
So **Moses** went and summoned the **elders** of the people. »

"Therefore" initiates the terms of the covenant. Say it with authority.

---

communication a means for division rather than unity. The Hebrew word "to confuse" is in fact the word *babel*. As a result, when God scatters the people across the earth, as was his initial plan after the flood, human beings will forever struggle to understand one another. Their pride has been dashed by a God who does not tolerate attempts to supplant the divine will.

READING II | Near the beginning of the Book of Exodus, after Moses has become a young man, flees Egypt because he has killed an Egyptian guard, marries the daughter of the priest of Midian, and settles into his new role as a shepherd, he encounters the voice of God in a burning bush. Whatever this meeting may have looked like, it was a divine appearance to one person. At the point that this reading occurs, Moses has liberated more than 600,000 Hebrews from

slavery in Egypt, and he returns to the mountain on which he first encountered God. What we have in this second divine revelation, however, is no small burning bush. It is a great theophany, complete with thunder and lightning, the blast of the shofar, and the entire mountain "wrapped in smoke."

When Moses first encountered God in the burning bush and debated with him regarding the command to lead God's people out of Egypt, he asked God what kind of

When he set **before** them
 all that the LORD had **ordered** him to tell them,
 the people all answered together,
 "**Everything** the LORD has **said**, we will **do**."

On the **morning** of the third **day**
 there were **peals** of thunder and lightning,
 and a heavy **cloud** over the mountain,
 and a very loud trumpet blast,
 so that all the **people** in the camp **trembled**.
But **Moses** led the people out of the camp to meet **God**,
 and they **stationed** themselves at the foot of the **mountain**.
Mount **Sinai** was all wrapped in **smoke**,
 for the LORD came down **upon** it in **fire**.
The smoke **rose** from it as though from a **furnace**,
 and the whole **mountain** trembled **violently**.
The trumpet blast grew **louder** and **louder**, while Moses
  was speaking,
 and God **answering** him with **thunder**.

When the LORD came **down** to the top of Mount **Sinai**,
 he summoned **Moses** to the top of the **mountain**.

"Everything the Lord has said, we will do":
With these words, the covenant is sealed.
Emphasis on "do."
Natural forces express themselves vividly
in response.

Even stresses on the words in this line.

The vision of smoke and fire signals the
power of God. These words paint a potent
picture. No need, however, to raise your
voice. Keep it steady.

For meditation and context:

RESPONSORIAL PSALM   Daniel 3:52, 53, 54, 55, 56

R. Glory and praise for ever!

"Blessed are you, O Lord, the God of
 our fathers,
 praiseworthy and exalted above
 all forever;
And blessed is your holy and glorious name,
 praiseworthy and exalted above all for
 all ages."

"Blessed are you in the temple of
 your holy glory,
 praiseworthy and glorious above
 all forever."

"Blessed are you on the throne of
 your Kingdom,
 praiseworthy and exalted above
 all forever."

"Blessed are you who look into the depths
 from your throne upon the cherubim,
 praiseworthy and exalted above
 all forever."
"Blessed are you in the firmament of heaven,
 praiseworthy and glorious forever."

Or:

---

authority a poor shepherd from Midian would have to command Pharaoh to release the Hebrews. God tells him that the sign that will reveal Moses' credibility is when the people return to this very spot and worship God on the mountain (Exodus 3:11–12). Therefore, the theophany on Mount Sinai is not only a display of divine power, but it is also a way of welcoming God's people home, having "brought [them] to myself," as God tells Moses. This homecoming, fearful as it might have been, was

to be the beginning of the formation of a covenantal relationship. This people, called by God to be "a kingdom of priests, a holy nation," would offer daily sacrifice, and God would continue to display his might as he guided Israel home to the Promised Land.

READING III   The Prophet Ezekiel is believed to have been born in the year 622 BC and lived through the duration of the Babylonian Exile. It is likely that Ezekiel was already a prophet when

Jerusalem was occupied by the Babylonians prior to the destruction of the temple in 586 BC and the exile of the Jews. However, it is during the time of exile in Babylon that his prophesies take on an apocalyptic nature, with visions of the resurrection of Israel.

Today's reading from Ezekiel is the well-known vision of the dry bones scattered on a desolate plain. As Ezekiel beholds the countless number of lifeless bones, he is led by God to walk among them, and he notes how dry they were. Such dryness

For meditation and context:

RESPONSORIAL PSALM   Psalm 19:8, 9, 10, 11

R. Lord, you have the words of everlasting life.

The law of the LORD is perfect,
   refreshing the soul;
The decree of the LORD is trustworthy,
   giving wisdom to the simple.

The precepts of the LORD are right,
   rejoicing the heart;
The command of the LORD is clear,
   enlightening the eye.

The fear of the LORD is pure,
   enduring forever;
The ordinances of the LORD are true,
   all of them just.

They are more precious than gold,
   than a heap of purest gold;
Sweeter also than syrup
   or honey from the comb.

READING III   Ezekiel 37:1–14

A reading from the Book of the Prophet Ezekiel

The **hand** of the LORD came **upon** me,
   and he led me **out** in the **spirit** of the LORD
   and set me in the **center** of the **plain**,
   which was now **filled** with **bones**.
He made me **walk** among the **bones** in every **direction**
   so that I saw how **many** they were on the **surface** of the plain.
How **dry** they were!
He asked me:
   Son of **man**, can these **bones** come to **life**?
I answered, "Lord GOD, **you alone** know that."
Then he said to me:
   Prophesy over these **bones**, and **say** to them:
   Dry bones, **hear** the **word** of the LORD!
Thus **says** the Lord GOD to these **bones**:
   See! I will bring spirit into you, that you may come to **life**.
I will put **sinews** upon you, make flesh grow **over** you,
   cover you with **skin**, and put spirit **in** you
   so that you may come to **life** and know that I am the LORD.

Ezekiel = ee-ZEE-kee-uhl

A narrative reading with visionary passages of exquisite strangeness and power. God speaks to and through Ezekiel throughout this reading. Because the punctuation isn't entirely clear, it's useful to have markers for when God is speaking and when Ezekiel is speaking for himself.

The vision, which is frightening, begins here with the valley of dry bones. The life of this vision relies on these dry bones coming to life.

God begins to speak here.

This reading makes use of the verb "prophesy" as well as its past tense, "prophesied." Pronunciation is important. Prophesy = PROPH-eh-sigh (not PROPH-eh-see); prophesied = PROPH-eh-side (not PROPH-eh-seed). Be sure to practice! sinews = sin-yooz

Emphasis on "know."

symbolizes the hopelessness of the remnant of the People of Israel, who labor and mourn in a foreign land. God leading Ezekiel to walk among the bones helps him internalize the destruction.

The Lord then uses Ezekiel to speak words of prophecy over the bones so that God can place his life-giving spirit in them. With the gift of life will come the regrowth of the body, complete with "sinews" and "flesh." Obeying the Lord, Ezekiel prophesies, and the bones knit themselves back

together into human bodies, completely regenerated with the covering of skin. Then, the voice of God commands Ezekiel to prophesy to the spirit, thereby directing the spirit to breathe life into these still-lifeless bodies. With this command, the bodies come to life and form a great army.

This vision ends with God revealing to Ezekiel that what he has witnessed is the house of Israel. At first, this is a people without hope, a nation that is completely dried up. But the word of the Lord has the

power to change that. God instructs Ezekiel to tell the people that he will raise them to new life and restore them to the land of Israel. The grave will not be the abode of the dead, but instead, it will contain the promise of new life. God's spirit will live in the people and give them life in abundance. Thus God says, "I have promised, and I will do it." Who can doubt such a prophecy?

Ezekiel himself is speaking here.

God begins to speak again here.

Ezekiel himself is speaking again here.

From here to the end of the reading, God is speaking, even as he quotes the house of Israel.

TO KEEP IN MIND
Make eye contact with the assembly. This helps keep the assembly engaged with the reading.

I, **Ezekiel**, **prophesied** as I had been **told**,
  and even as I was **prophesying** I heard a noise;
  it was a **rattling** as the bones came together, **bone**
    joining **bone**.
I saw the **sinews** and the **flesh** come **upon** them,
  and the skin **cover** them, but there was no spirit in them.
Then the LORD said to me:
  Prophesy to the **spirit**, **prophesy**, son of man,
  and **say** to the spirit: **Thus** says the Lord GOD:
  From the **four winds come**, O spirit,
  and **breathe** into these **slain** that they may **come** to life.
I **prophesied** as he told me, and the spirit came **into** them;
  they came **alive** and stood **upright**, a vast **army**.
Then he said to me:
  Son of **man**, these **bones** are the **whole house** of Israel.
They have been **saying**,
  "Our **bones** are dried up,
  our **hope** is lost, and we are cut **off**."
Therefore, **prophesy** and say to them: **Thus** says the Lord GOD:
  O my **people**, I will open your **graves**
  and have you **rise** from them,
  and bring you **back** to the land of **Israel**.
Then you shall **know** that I am the LORD,
  when I open your **graves** and have you **rise** from them,
  O my **people**!
I will put my **spirit** in you that you may **live**,
  and I will **settle** you upon your **land**;
  thus you shall **know** that I am the LORD.
I have **promised**, and I will **do** it, says the LORD.

READING IV | This brief passage from the book of Joel presents a scene that is both constructive and destructive. First, the Lord God reveals to Joel that he will pour out his spirit "upon all flesh." Many people will be given the ability to prophesy and to receive dreams regarding the future. Even the servants will be beneficiaries of God's spirit. Thus, this pouring out of the spirit serves as a leveling agent by God. No longer will just a few be able to discern the will of God, but now God makes it possible for "all flesh" to behold his coming. This constitutes the constructive portion of the text.

As the more destructive aspect of this prophetic vision unfolds, God promises to work wonders in the heavens and on earth. Natural signs of destruction, such as blood, fire, and smoke, will be visible for all to see. The sun will become dark, while the moon will be turned to blood. This "day of the Lord" will be "great and terrible."

If this were the end of the story, there would be no hope. But God assures Joel that a remnant will survive this great destruction, and God will call them forth. Apocalyptic writings such as the prophecy of Joel were not meant to instill fear in the people but to call for *metanoia*, a true change of heart and a transformation of lifestyles. Undoubtedly, the hope here is that the people will embrace the spirit and seek to discern the will of God.

For meditation and context:

RESPONSORIAL PSALM   Psalm 107:2–3, 4–5, 6–7, 8–9

R. Give thanks to the Lord; his love is everlasting.
or
R. Alleluia.

Let the redeemed of the Lord say,
  those whom he has redeemed from the
    hand of the foe
And gathered from the lands,
  from the east and the west, from the north
    and the south.

They went astray in the desert wilderness;
  the way to an inhabited city they did
    not find.
Hungry and thirsty,
  their life was wasting away within them.

They cried to the Lord in their distress;
  from their straits he rescued them.
And he led them by a direct way
  to reach an inhabited city.

Let them give thanks to the Lord for
  his mercy
  and his wondrous deeds to the children
    of men,
Because he satisfied the longing soul
  and filled the hungry soul with
    good things.

READING IV   Joel 3:1–5

An exhortatory reading, with a prophetic vision of a cataclysmic event. Scripture often shifts into this visionary mode, which can be exciting to proclaim because the language is so vivid.
prophesy = PROF-uh-sī

A reading from the Book of the Prophet Joel

> **Thus** says the Lord:
> I will **pour out** my spirit upon all **flesh**.
> Your **sons** and **daughters** shall **prophesy**,
>   your old men shall dream **dreams**,
>   your young men shall see **visions**;
> even upon the **servants** and the **handmaids**,
>   in those days, I will pour out my **spirit**.
> And I will work **wonders** in the **heavens** and on the **earth**,
>   **blood**, **fire**, and columns of **smoke**;
> the **sun** will be turned to **darkness**,
>   and the **moon** to **blood**,
> at the **coming** of the day of the Lord,
>   the **great** and terrible **day**.
> Then **everyone** shall be **rescued**
>   who **calls** on the name of the Lord; »

"The great and terrible day": with these words, Joel concludes his vision.

The vision is immediately followed by the promise of rescue from God, which continues to the end of the reading.

EPISTLE   In the chapters immediately prior to the one our reading is taken from, Paul discusses the death that takes place for those who are baptized into Christ and their death to the Hebrew Law. In this reading, Paul turns to the topic of spiritual birth. He uses the image of a woman in labor to portray the experience of yearning and crying out for the "redemption of our bodies," and thus ultimate union with God. All of creation, in fact, groans for a spiritual rebirth in God.

Paul continues to associate the birthing image with the theme of hope. A pregnancy is an extended period of waiting in hopeful expectation. The baby grows unseen by human eyes, and yet the presence of life is very much detectable, especially to the mother herself. Paul suggests that this is the hope of Christians who wait "with endurance" for salvation. Hope is not

hope if the future is known. Hope in what is not seen is the very hallmark of the Christian vocation.

An enduring sense of hopefulness is made possible because of the Spirit's presence in the world. The Spirit knows the truth of our final salvation, and thus, the Spirit is able to intercede "with inexpressible groanings," a yearning that far exceeds any that we are capable of uttering by ourselves. This is precisely the "weakness" of

Don't overdo your reading, but you can shift to a slightly more optimistic tone.

for on Mount **Zion** there shall be a **remnant**,
 as the LORD has said,
and in **Jerusalem** survivors
 whom the LORD shall **call**.

For meditation and context:

RESPONSORIAL PSALM   Psalm 104:1–2, 24 and 35, 27–28, 29–30 (see 30)

R. Lord, send out your Spirit, and renew the face of the earth.
or
R. Alleluia.

Bless the LORD, O my soul!
 O LORD, my God, you are great indeed!
You are clothed with majesty and glory,
 robed in light as with a cloak.

How manifold are your works, O LORD!
 In wisdom you have wrought them all—
the earth is full of your creatures;
 bless the LORD, O my soul! Alleluia.

Creatures all look to you
 to give them food in due time.
When you give it to them, they gather it;
 when you open your hand, they are filled
 with good things.

If you take away their breath, they perish
 and return to their dust.
When you send forth your spirit,
 they are created,
 and you renew the face of the earth.

EPISTLE   Romans 8:22–27

A reading from the Letter of Saint Paul to the Romans

An exhortatory reading that contains a potent and not easily digested message: that life is challenging—Paul compares it to childbirth —and its pain does not abate, even as we hope for its end. Nevertheless, we hope.

The first line after the greeting contains the core of Paul's message. Emphasize "know," "groaning," and "now."

Brothers and **sisters**:
We **know** that all creation is **groaning** in labor pains even
 until **now**;
 and not only **that**, but we **ourselves**,
 who have the **firstfruits** of the **Spirit**,
 we also groan within **ourselves**
 as we wait for **adoption**, the **redemption** of our **bodies**.
For in **hope** we were **saved**.
Now hope that **sees** is not **hope**.
For who **hopes** for what one **sees**?
But if we **hope** for what we do not **see**,
 we wait with **endurance**.

Slight extra emphasis on "endurance."

---

which Paul speaks, namely, the inability to know the will of God in relationship to the salvation of the world. Christian hope is bolstered by the gift of the Spirit, who knows the will of God and is able to move human hearts toward union with God's will.

GOSPEL   The seventh chapter of John's Gospel opens with Jesus' disciples trying to convince him to leave Galilee and journey to Jerusalem, where his followers there might see the righteous works that he had been accomplishing (John 7:2–4). Although Jesus tells them that it is not yet his time to make such a revelation, he sends them on their way to the Holy City for the celebration of the Feast of Tabernacles, quietly making his way alone. It is important to the story that Jesus wants to keep a low profile as he moves amid the crowds in Jerusalem.

One of the distinctive rituals of the Feast of Tabernacles is performed by a priest who draws a bucket of water from the Siloam pool and pours it out before the people, reminding them that God provides life-giving water for his people. This ritual was also enacted as an accompaniment to prayers for rain, much needed for the fields

"In the same way": Paul intends to compare our life to the work of the Holy Spirit, who comes to our aid. In the Spirit lies our hope.

In the **same way**, the Spirit too comes to the **aid** of our **weakness**;
for we do not **know** how to pray as we **ought**,
but the Spirit himself **intercedes** with inexpressible **groanings**.
And the one who searches **hearts**
knows what is the **intention** of the Spirit,
because he **intercedes** for the **holy** ones
according to God's **will**.

GOSPEL   John 7:37–39

A reading from the holy Gospel according to John

A brief narrative reading with an extraordinary exhortation embedded in it.

On the **last** and greatest **day** of the **feast**,
Jesus stood up and **exclaimed**,
"Let anyone who **thirsts** come to me and **drink**.
As Scripture says:

"Rivers of living water" is an especially evocative phrase, especially as a sign of belief.

*Rivers of living water will **flow** from within him who
believes in me."*

He said this in reference to the **Spirit**
that **those** who came to **believe** in him were to **receive**.

The reading concludes with an anticipatory claim about Jesus' eventual glorification.

There was, of course, no **Spirit** yet,
because **Jesus** had not yet been **glorified**.

in the off-season. Far from keeping his identity hidden, Jesus suddenly stands up and proclaims himself to be life-giving water for anyone who thirsts. According to John, this is the means by which Jesus refers to the outpouring of the Spirit that will be given to his followers after his resurrection. Thus, the Spirit's work is directly related to the quote Jesus uses from Scripture: "Rivers of living water will flow from within him" (possibly a reference to

Proverbs 4:23). Belief in Jesus provides for the abundant flowing of this life-giving river.
S.W.

PENTECOST SUNDAY: DAY

A narrative reading that directly inverts the Tower of Babel passage from Genesis. (See the first reading for the Pentecost Vigil.) This kind of inverted symmetry is one of the enduring pleasures of reading Scripture. Babel doesn't need to be mentioned in order for your assembly to sense its presence.

Air and fire are the two elements associated with the Holy Spirit. Here, it's air in the form of wind.

And here in the form of tongues of fire.

And here, the Holy Spirit becomes language.

Read all of these names with care. Be sure to practice their pronunciation:
Parthians = PAHR-thee-uhnz
Medes = meedz
Elamites = EE-luh-mīts
Mesopotamia = mes-uh-poh-TAY-mee-uh
Judea = joo-DEE-uh
Cappadocia = cap-uh-DOH-shee-uh

> **TO KEEP IN MIND**
> Pause to break up separate thoughts, set apart significant statements, or indicate major shifts. Never pause in the middle of a thought. Your primary guide for pauses is punctuation.

LECTIONARY #63

READING I   Acts 2:1–11

A reading from the Acts of the Apostles

When the **time** for Pentecost was **fulfilled**,
     they were all in one place **together**.
And suddenly there came from the **sky**
     a **noise** like a strong driving **wind**,
     and it filled the entire **house** in which they **were**.
Then there appeared to them **tongues** as of fire,
     which **parted** and came to **rest** on each **one** of them.
And they were all **filled** with the Holy **Spirit**
     and began to **speak** in different **tongues**,
     as the Spirit **enabled** them to **proclaim**.

Now there were devout **Jews** from every **nation** under **heaven**
     staying in **Jerusalem**.
At this **sound**, they gathered in a large **crowd**,
     but they were **confused**
     because each one heard them **speaking** in his own **language**.
They were **astounded**, and in amazement they **asked**,
     "Are not all these **people** who are speaking **Galileans**?
Then how does each of us **hear** them in his native **language**?
We are **Parthians**, **Medes**, and **Elamites**,
     inhabitants of **Mesopotamia**, **Judea** and **Cappadocia**,

READING I — This account of the Holy Spirit's descent at Pentecost is often heralded for its drama, complete with tongues of fire and the cacophony of diverse languages. While it is dramatic, it is the theological value of the story that deserves our attention. First, the descent of the Holy Spirit occurs during the Jewish festival of *Shavuot*. This originally was one of three pilgrimage festivals to Jerusalem; it later came to commemorate the giving of the Law on Mount Sinai. The

Shavuot festival probably had taken on the second meaning by the time of Luke's writing. Therefore, it is likely that the Spirit's descent is intended to enact the giving of the New Law.

The second theological point to consider is the meaning of the tongues of fire. The tongue is a symbol of speech or language. Because the Spirit descends upon each person individually, we are meant to see the validation of a diversity of languages. What takes place at Pentecost is

the overturning of the punishment at Babel (Genesis 11:1–9), where the unity of speech was brought to confusion, causing the people to separate into many tribes. The Spirit unites what has been previously divided.

Finally, this leads to the third theological principle, universalism. From the upper room, where they had previously huddled in fear, the Holy Spirit moves them to the outside world. They are to reach out to all. Because there were many foreigners gathered in Jerusalem for the celebration of the

Pontus = PON-tuhs
Phrygia = FRIJ-ee-uh
Pamphylia = Pam-FIL-ee-uh
Libya = LIB-ee-uh
Cyrene = sī-REE-nee
Cretans = KREE-tuhnz

Pontus and **Asia**, **Phrygia** and **Pamphylia**,
Egypt and the districts of **Libya** near **Cyrene**,
as well as **travelers** from **Rome**,
both **Jews** and converts to **Judaism**, **Cretans** and **Arabs**,
yet we **hear them** speaking in our own **tongues**
of the **mighty acts** of **God**."

For meditation and context:

RESPONSORIAL PSALM   Psalm 104:1, 24, 29–30, 31, 34 (30)

R. Lord, send out your Spirit, and renew the face of the earth.
or R. Alleluia.

Bless the Lord, O my soul!
　O Lord, my God, you are great indeed!
How manifold are your works, O Lord!
　The earth is full of your creatures.

If you take away their breath, they perish
　and return to their dust.
When you send forth your spirit,
　they are created,
　and you renew the face of the earth.

May the glory of the Lord endure forever;
　may the Lord be glad in his works!
Pleasing to him be my theme;
　I will be glad in the Lord.

Corinthians = kohr-IN-thee-uhnz

READING II   1 Corinthians 12:3b–7, 12–13

A didactic reading with claims of enduring force.

A reading from the first Letter of Saint Paul to the Corinthians

Brothers and **sisters**:
No one can say, "**Jesus** is Lord," **except** by the Holy Spirit.

The invocation of the Holy Spirit is meant to echo the same in the first reading at Pentecost. Here the Holy Spirit is understood in terms of spiritual gifts.

There are different **kinds** of spiritual gifts but the same **Spirit**;
　there are different **forms** of service but the same **Lord**;
　there are different **workings** but the same **God**
　who produces **all** of them in **everyone**.
To each individual the **manifestation** of the Spirit
　is given for some **benefit**.

Even stress on these three words: "so also Christ."

As a **body** is one though it has many **parts**,
　and all the **parts** of the body, though **many**, are one **body**,
　so also Christ. ❯❯

feast, Luke is demonstrating that the infant Church has the mission to take the Good News beyond the confines of Jerusalem.

READING II | **1 Corinthians.** Just before this passage from the First Letter to the Corinthians, Paul reprimanded the community for the way they celebrate the Lord's Supper. According to Paul's assessment, a meal meant to fortify unity has become a sign of division. The wealthy arrive early and eat and drink their fill, while the poor, who must labor, arrive late and have little to eat or drink.

　Here in chapter 12, Paul continues to challenge the Christian believers at Corinth to see their participation in the Church as the work of maintaining unity in Christ. First, he articulates the foundation of Christian faith, the gift of the Spirit in which all are baptized. Without the Spirit, profession that "Jesus is Lord" is simply impossible. Paul believes that the bestowal of a multitude of gifts by the Spirit is for the

fruitfulness of the Church. Members have different gifts, which are neither for the purpose of competing with each other nor for the ability to make claims of superiority. Rather, the different gifts are to be used for the good of the whole.

　Paul employs the body as an analogy for such unity and the use of many gifts. The body is one because the parts work together, not because any one part outshines the others. Further, Paul makes the great theological claim that baptism makes

The vision of radical equality that Paul stresses in these lines is something the Church continues to aspire to.

For in one **Spirit** we were all **baptized** into one **body**,
   whether **Jews** or **Greeks**, **slaves** or free **persons**,
   and we were all **given** to drink of one **Spirit**.

Or:

___

READING II   Romans 8:8–17

A reading from the Letter of Saint Paul to the Romans

A complex, exhortatory reading from St. Paul, who is making an argument that builds from phrase to phrase. Follow Paul's cues to guide your proclamation: words such as *consequently* and *for.*
Slight pause between *flesh* and *cannot.*

Slight pause between *God* and *dwells.*

Brothers and **sisters**:
Those who are in the **flesh cannot** please **God**.
But you are **not** in the **flesh**;
   on the **contrary**, you are in the **spirit**,
   if **only** the Spirit of **God dwells** in you.
Whoever does not have the Spirit of **Christ** does **not** belong
      to **him**.
But if Christ is **in** you,
   although the **body** is dead because of **sin**,
   the **spirit** is alive because of **righteousness**.
If the **Spirit** of the one who raised **Jesus** from the dead **dwells**
      in you,
   the **one** who raised **Christ** from the **dead**
   will give **life** to your mortal **bodies** also,
   through his **Spirit** that **dwells** in **you**.
Consequently, brothers and sisters,
   we are not **debtors** to the **flesh**,
   to live **according** to the **flesh**.

Here Paul arrives at one of the first points of his argument, stated in inverted parallel. *If you* live *according to the flesh, (*then*) you will* die. *If you die to the flesh, (*then*) in the Spirit you will* live.

For if you **live** according to the **flesh**, you will **die**,
   but if by the **Spirit** you put to **death** the **deeds** of the **body**,
   you will **live**.

For **those** who are **led** by the **Spirit** of **God** are **sons** of God.
For you did not **receive** a spirit of **slavery** to fall back into **fear**,
   but you **received** a spirit of **adoption**,
   through whom we cry, "**Abba, Father**!"

all members equal in Christ. All forms of outward distinction simply fall away in the waters of baptism.

Romans. In our day and age, it is common to have a holistic understanding of the body and the soul. When Paul wrote, however, this was not the case. As the Christian message moved beyond Palestine into the Mediterranean world, it encountered a philosophy that very much separated the flesh from the spirit. Those who operated according to the needs of the flesh were thought

to be crude, while those who dwelled in the world of things spiritual were considered lofty and sophisticated.

Paul's agenda is not to which side is the more cultured way of living; his interest is in how one approaches God. If one is focused on the things of the earth, then one is focused on the self and not on God: "Those who are in the flesh cannot please God." Paul even goes so far as to say that being grounded in the flesh brings only death to life: "the body is dead because of

sin" and "if you live according to the flesh, you will die."

Baptism changes all of this. According to Paul, anyone who lives in Christ lives according to the Spirit. Life lived according to the Spirit is life lived in relationship to God. Paul states clearly at the end of this passage: "you received a spirit of adoption, through whom we cry, 'Abba, Father!'" Being in Christ brings us into relationship with God as his sons and daughters. Ours is an inheritance of divine life. But this is not

The **Spirit** himself bears **witness** with our **spirit**
    that we are **children** of **God**,
    and if **children**, then **heirs**,
    heirs of God and joint **heirs** with **Christ**,
    if **only** we suffer **with** him
    so that we may **also** be **glorified** with him.

For meditation and context:

SEQUENCE   Veni, Sancte Spiritus

Come, Holy Spirit, come!
And from your celestial home
    Shed a ray of light divine!
Come, Father of the poor!
Come, source of all our store!
    Come, within our bosoms shine.
You, of comforters the best;
You, the soul's most welcome guest;
    Sweet refreshment here below;
In our labor, rest most sweet;
Grateful coolness in the heat;
    Solace in the midst of woe.
O most blessed Light divine,
Shine within these hearts of yours,
    And our inmost being fill!

Where you are not, we have naught,
Nothing good in deed or thought,
    Nothing free from taint of ill.
Heal our wounds, our strength renew;
On our dryness pour your dew;
    Wash the stains of guilt away:
Bend the stubborn heart and will;
Melt the frozen, warm the chill;
    Guide the steps that go astray.
On the faithful, who adore
And confess you, evermore
    In your sevenfold gift descend;
Give them virtue's sure reward;
Give them your salvation, Lord;
    Give them joys that never end. Amen.
    Alleluia.

Emphasize the connection between suffering with Christ and being glorified with him.

TO KEEP IN MIND
Sequences originated as extensions of the sung Alleluia before the proclamation of the Gospel, although they precede the Alleluia now. The Pentecost Sequence, also called the Golden Sequence, is an ancient liturgical hymn praising the Holy Spirit. It is the source of the hymn "Come, Holy Ghost."

A narrative reading that depicts the transmission of the Holy Spirit through Jesus himself to his disciples.

Jesus enters the scene with the word "Peace."

GOSPEL   John 20:19–23

A reading from the holy Gospel according to John

On the **evening** of that first day of the **week**,
    when the **doors** were locked, where the **disciples** were,
    for **fear** of the Jews,
    Jesus came and **stood** in their midst
    and **said** to them, "**Peace** be with you."
When he had **said** this, he **showed** them his hands and his side.
The disciples **rejoiced** when they saw the Lord.
Jesus said to them again, "**Peace** be with you.
As the **Father** has sent me, so I send **you**." »

---

without ethical responsibility. Paul demands that living according to the Spirit means putting "to death the deeds of the body" (verse 13).

 John 20. Today, the fiftieth day of Easter and the Solemnity of Pentecost, brings Easter Time to a close. The Church has been invited to renew its faith during these fifty days of Easter so that it might be prepared to accept the Lord's peace as an invitation to work with the Spirit for the world's transformation.

For John, the giving of the Spirit is one and the same with Jesus' resurrection and glorification. John focuses our attention on two matters of theological importance here: the type of peace that Jesus gives to his followers and the missionary work of forgiving sins that will be guided by the Spirit. First, the peace that Jesus utters before and after he shows the disciples his hands and his side is the gift of peace that comes from the other side of the grave. God has successfully restored oneness between himself and his creation; the

divide that sin creates between God and his beloved creation no longer exists. Second, just as God breathed life into Adam, Jesus breathes on his followers, giving them new life in the Holy Spirit. Peace and new life are given to conquer the apostles' fear, ushering them into service.

John 14. Chapter 14 of John's Gospel (along with the tail end of chapter 13) opens Jesus' lengthy farewell discourse to his disciples at the conclusion of the Last Supper. John's depiction of this important event centers on Jesus' command to wash

Breath is the most ancient sign of life in Scripture. Here, Jesus' powers are transmitted directly through his breath.

Note the parallel construction: forgive/forgiven; retain/retained.

And when he had **said** this, he **breathed** on them
>   and **said** to them,
> "**Receive** the Holy Spirit.
Whose **sins** you **forgive** are **forgiven** them,
>   and whose **sins** you **retain** are **retained**."

Or:

GOSPEL   John 14:15–16, 23b–26

An exhortatory reading in which Jesus introduces the notion of the Holy Spirit as Advocate, while also tracking the complex relationship between Jesus and the Father.

A reading from the holy Gospel according to John

Added emphasis on *Advocate*.

Jesus said to his **disciples**:
> "If you **love** me, you will keep my **commandments**.
And I will **ask** the **Father**,
>   and he will **give** you another **Advocate** to **be** with you **always**.

From this point, Jesus elaborates on his relationship with the Father as a way of setting up the meaning of the Advocate. The tone of this passage is preparatory.

"Whoever **loves** me will keep my **word**,
>   and my **Father** will love **him**,
>   and we will **come** to him and make our dwelling **with** him.
Those who do not **love** me do not **keep** my **words**;
>   yet the **word** you **hear** is not **mine**
>   but that of the **Father** who **sent** me.

"I have **told** you this while I am **with** you.

Once again, emphasis on *Advocate* as well as *Holy Spirit*.

The **Advocate**, the Holy **Spirit** whom the **Father**
>   will **send** in my **name**,
>   will teach you **everything**
>   and **remind** you of **all** that I **told** you."

feet and on a set of instructions meant to preserve the unity of his disciples. There are no commands to celebrate a ritual meal in memory of Jesus in John's Gospel because the content of the farewell discourse is what John believes disciples must remember in order to preserve their unity.

The primary theme of the entire discourse is that love for Jesus is expressed by keeping his commandments, and his commandments may be summarized by the command to "love one another, as I have loved you" (John 13:34). It all seems so very simple, and yet the betrayal of Judas, witnessed shortly before Jesus speaks, suggests that it is not. For this reason, Jesus promises that he will provide an "Advocate" who will be with them "always," teaching them anew and reminding them of what he had taught them. The Holy Spirit preserves the word in the hearts of all believers, so that divine life will dwell within them. S.W.

THE MOST HOLY TRINITY

LECTIONARY #166

READING I   Proverbs 8:22–31

An exhortatory reading of great poetic power, filled with rich images and expressions. The speaker of the exhortation, identified as "the wisdom of God," describes cosmic intimacy with the creation, which is the source of the power in this passage.

The rhetorical effect of this reading is achieved through the repetitions of the words *when* and *before*. Use these words to locate your proclamation.

TO KEEP IN MIND
Pay attention to the pace of your reading. Varying the pace gives listeners clues to the meaning of the text. The most common error for proclaimers new to the ministry is speaking too fast.

Note the shift that happens with the word *then*, a sense of accomplishment and conclusion. Stress the word *craftsman*.

A reading from the Book of Proverbs

Thus says the **wisdom** of **God**:
    "The Lord **possessed** me, the **beginning** of his **ways**,
      the **forerunner** of his **prodigies** of **long ago**;
    from of **old** I was poured **forth**,
      at the **first**, before the **earth**.
    When there were no **depths** I was brought **forth**,
      when there were no **fountains** or **springs** of **water**;
    before the **mountains** were **settled** into **place**,
      before the **hills**, I was brought **forth**;
    while as **yet** the **earth** and **fields** were not **made**,
      nor the first **clods** of the **world**.

    "When the **Lord** established the **heavens** I was **there**,
      when he **marked out** the **vault** over the **face** of the **deep**;
    when he made **firm** the skies **above**,
      when he fixed **fast** the foundations of the **earth**;
    when he **set** for the **sea** its **limit**,
      so that the **waters** should not **transgress** his **command**;
    then was **I beside** him as his **craftsman**,
      and I was his **delight** day by day,
    playing before him all the **while**,
      playing on the **surface** of his **earth**;
      and I found **delight** in the human **race**."

READING I The word "possessed" (from the Hebrew verb *qanah*) is used to describe the relationship between God and Lady Wisdom in the first line from this passage from Proverbs. She is portrayed as God's coworker in the design and construction of creation. She was there with God before anything came into being; she is faithful and true. The "pouring forth" of wisdom suggests God's abundant love in creation.

These lines rehearse the Hebrew understanding of the mystery of creation: the establishing of the heavens, the marking out of a vault over the deep, the placement of the skies. In all of these wondrous acts of bringing harmony out of chaos, Lady Wisdom is beside the Lord "as his craftsman" and his "delight." Proverbs suggests that wisdom "plays" upon the face of the earth to "delight" God. Above all, wisdom delights in humanity. Without calling humanity the stewards of creation, this presentation of the world's beginning associates wisdom with the human person, and thus the responsibility for humanity to act wisely in the care for all that is.

READING II This short passage from Paul's Letter to the Romans presents the author's understanding of justification through faith in the Triune God: Father, Son, and Holy Spirit. This comes as the conclusion to Paul's defense of justification on the basis of faith and not by works (Romans 3:21—4:25). Paul suggests that such reconciliation has been initiated by God for the purpose of allowing humanity to participate in divine life.

In deciphering Paul's theology of justification by faith, it is perhaps best to begin at the end of today's passage and work our

For meditation and context:

RESPONSORIAL PSALM   Psalm 8:4–5, 6–7, 8–9 (2a)

R. O Lord, our God, how wonderful your name in all the earth!

When I behold your heavens, the work of
    your fingers,
  the moon and the stars which you set
    in place—
what is man that you should be mindful
    of him,
  or the son of man that you should care
    for him?

You have made him little less than
    the angels,
  and crowned him with glory and honor.
You have given him rule over the works of
    your hands,
  putting all things under his feet.

All sheep and oxen,
  yes, and the beasts of the field,
the birds of the air, the fishes of the sea,
  and whatever swims the paths of the seas.

READING II   Romans 5:1–5

A reading from the Letter of Saint Paul to the Romans

Brothers and **sisters:**
Therefore, since we have been **justified** by **faith**,
    we have **peace** with **God** through our **Lord** Jesus **Christ**,
    through whom we have gained **access** by faith
    to this **grace** in which we **stand**,
    and we **boast** in hope of the **glory** of **God**.
Not only **that**, but we even **boast** of our **afflictions**,
    knowing that **affliction** produces **endurance**,
    and **endurance**, proven **character**,
    and proven **character**, **hope**,
    and **hope** does not **disappoint**,
    because the **love** of **God** has been **poured** out into our **hearts**
    through the Holy **Spirit** that has been **given** to us.

An exhortatory reading from St. Paul that includes a theological conviction—the justification by faith—that has had far-reaching consequences in Christian history. *Therefore* sticks out like a sore thumb. It's a strange way to begin a reading, signaling that we are already at the conclusion of an argument, one that your assembly likely won't have familiarity with at the moment you are proclaiming. You need simply proceed from here; Paul will fill in the blanks.

Paul concludes his argument by introducing one virtue and then transforming it into another. Allow yourself to go from virtue to virtue as though crossing a stream from one stable rock to another.

way backwards. First, Paul states in verse 5 that it is the Holy Spirit who pours upon us the *love* of God. The gift of love, in turn, creates in us a *hope* that "does not disappoint." This hope is maintained in the dual attitudes of *peace* and *faith*. This chain of divine providence allows those who have gained access by faith in Jesus Christ to stand firm in sufferings and affliction and even to be able to "boast" of one's trials. However, the very essence of Paul's theology is that such boasting is not a puffing up of one's own strength and merit, but rather

a testimony to reliance upon the grace that comes from God.

The thrust of this passage is really the centerpiece of hope. Hope means to be solidly rooted in the love of God and thus to be people of faith and peace. The very opposite of faith and peace is a lifestyle that is filled with anxiety and pessimism regarding the future, especially when it comes to trust in one's worthiness of the gift of God's love. Undoubtedly, the sin against the Holy Spirit, mentioned in all three synoptic Gospels, is the failure to believe in the

enduring gift of love that God pours into our hearts through the work of the Holy Spirit.

GOSPEL   Our passage from John's Gospel returns to Jesus' final discourse with his disciples at the Last Supper. This festive meal, which would quickly lead to Jesus, arrest, was surely marked by an underlying sense of fear on the part of the disciples. Repeatedly in this final instruction, Jesus speaks of his leave-taking. This surely troubled the hearts of those who had abandoned their families

GOSPEL   John 16:12–15

A reading from the holy Gospel according to John

Jesus said to his **disciples**:
   "I have **much more** to **tell** you, but you **cannot** bear it **now**.
But when he **comes**, the Spirit of **truth**,
   he will **guide** you to **all truth**.
He will not **speak** on his **own**,
   but he will **speak** what he **hears**,
   and will **declare** to you the **things** that are **coming**.
He will **glorify** me,
   because he will **take** from what is **mine** and **declare** it to **you**.
Everything that the **Father** has is **mine**;
   for **this reason** I told you that he will **take** from what is **mine**
   and **declare** it to **you**."

An exhortatory reading with a mysterious conclusion auguring future events.

This reading is emphatically in the future tense. Jesus is looking ahead.

Declare it to you is a mysterious phrase. The sense of *declare* is almost a synonym for *show*. It's being used here to signify an alignment: God will take what is Jesus' and then align it to you, therefore revealing it to you. The phrase is repeated at the end of the reading to give it emphasis.

and their means of making a living in order to follow Jesus. The question "Now what?" must have haunted them all. Jesus sensed this question, and yet he is cautious not to answer it in too much detail: "I have much more to tell you, but you cannot bear it now."

Jesus tells them that it will be the role of the Spirit to guide them to "all truth." How will such guidance take place? The disciples' minds and hearts will be opened as the Spirit gives glory to Christ. It is the primary role of the Spirit to reveal Christ, who in turn is the fullness of truth because

he mediates the Father to the world. John's Jesus uses the word "declare" three times here in talking about the revelation of truth, making this truth an oral reality. However, unlike the disciples, who remain in a fog regarding the Lord's imminent death, we know that truth is much more than words spoken; it is love enacted. Jesus' suffering, his death upon the cross, and his resurrection to new life by the Father provide the real evidence of the truth. It will be the work of the Spirit to enlighten the minds of believers to the truth that the cross is a

sign of true power rather than dismal failure. The Spirit will continue to declare such truth to the Church for all ages to come.
S.W.

THE MOST HOLY BODY
AND BLOOD OF CHRIST

LECTIONARY #169

READING I Genesis 14:18–20

A narrative reading rehearsing a moment of blessing.

A reading from the Book of Genesis

In those days, **Melchizedek**, king of **Salem**,
   brought out **bread** and **wine**,
   and being a **priest** of **God** Most **High**,
he blessed **Abram** with these words:
"**Blessed** be **Abram** by **God** Most **High**,
   the **creator** of **heaven** and **earth**;
   and **blessed** be **God** Most **High**,
   who delivered your **foes** into your **hand**."
Then **Abram** gave him a **tenth** of **everything**.

Intone the blessing with authority.

The blessing is followed by a description of recompense.

For meditation and context:

RESPONSORIAL PSALM Psalm 110:1, 2, 3, 4 (4b)

R. You are a priest for ever, in the line of Melchizedek.

The LORD said to my Lord: "Sit at my
   right hand
till I make your enemies your footstool."

The scepter of your power the LORD will
   stretch forth from Zion:
"Rule in the midst of your enemies."

"Yours is princely power in the day of your
   birth, in holy splendor;
before the daystar, like the dew, I have
   begotten you."

The LORD has sworn, and he will not repent:
"You are a priest forever, according to the
   order of Melchizedek."

READING I The brief mention of Melchizedek, king of Salem and a priest of God Most High, takes place at the conclusion of Abram's successful military campaign against forces who inhabited the land that God promised Abram would become his own. Melchizedek is among those kings who have gathered to praise and honor Abram for his victory. Unlike the other kings, who surely brought substantial material gifts to Abram, Melchizedek brings bread and wine and a prayer of blessing. His priestly identity is thereby underscored. Melchizedek makes it clear that Abram fought with the power of God Most High on his side, for he reminds Abram that it was God "who delivered your foes into your hands."

The gifts of bread and wine that Melchizedek brings to this joyful occasion are offered in thanksgiving to God Most High. Although the gift may seem relatively insignificant, it has great ritual meaning, as it is meant to communicate the power of the blessing from which Abram will benefit. In response to this sacrificial offering, Abram tithes ten percent of all that is in his possession. Thus, this story hints at the covenantal relationship that gradually unfolds between God and Abram.

READING II Paul's correspondence with the Corinthians contains the earliest formula for what is known as the "words of institution" that are part of our Eucharistic Prayers. Although this letter was likely composed in the mid-50s AD, it is clear that the words Jesus spoke at the Last Supper were already well known in the Church and had become a ritual phrase. Paul wishes to reestablish the authority of these words. Far from being his own inven-

READING II   1 Corinthians 11:23–26

A didactic reading in which St. Paul instructs the people of Corinth about how properly to remember Jesus.

A reading from the first Letter of Saint Paul to the Corinthians

Brothers and **sisters**:
I **received** from the Lord what I also handed **on** to **you**,
    that the **Lord Jesus**, on the **night** he was handed **over**,
    took **bread**, and, after he had given **thanks**,
    broke it and said, "**This** is my **body** that is for **you**.
Do this in **remembrance** of me."
In the **same** way also the **cup**, after **supper**, saying,
    "This **cup** is the new **covenant** in my **blood**.
Do this, as **often** as you **drink** it, in **remembrance** of me."
For as **often** as you eat this **bread** and drink the **cup**,
    you proclaim the **death** of the **Lord** until he **comes**.

The words of institution. Very ritually familiar. Here, proclaim them as instructions.

The conclusion of this passage also has a liturgical echo. Proclaim it here as a conclusion.

GOSPEL   Luke 9:11b–17

A narrative reading depicting one of Jesus' best-known miracles, the multiplication of the loaves and fishes. Consider as an orientation to this familiar story: Jesus has been preaching all day to many people (over five thousand of them). When he speaks, he is likely exhausted.

A reading from the holy Gospel according to Luke

Jesus spoke to the **crowds** about the **kingdom** of **God**,
    and he **healed** those who needed to be **cured**.
As the **day** was drawing to a **close**,
    the Twelve approached him and said,
    "**Dismiss** the crowd
    so that they can **go** to the surrounding **villages** and **farms**
    and find **lodging** and **provisions**;
    for we are in a **deserted place** here."
He said to them, "**Give** them some food **yourselves**."
They replied, "**Five loaves** and **two fish** are **all** we **have**,
    unless **we ourselves** go and buy **food** for all these **people**."
Now the **men there** numbered about **five thousand**. »

Jesus' tone is exasperated.

---

tion, these words were ones he "received" and therefore "handed on" to the Corinthian community. What is most important for Paul is that the actions of both eating and drinking are done "in remembrance" of Jesus. The eating and drinking of the Eucharist are intended to make a bold statement: they allow members of the community to "proclaim the death of the Lord until he comes." How they are enacted matters.

What follows today's reading is the connection of the actions of eating and drinking with the division that exists in the gathering of the Christians in Corinth

(11:28–32). The problem is that less well-off members of the community must work at the time the wealthier members begin the celebration of the Lord's Supper. The Corinthians fail to honor the oneness of Christ's Body in the unity of its members; therefore, they eat and drink their own "condemnation" (v. 30). Thus, when the words of the Lord are pronounced over the bread and the cup, the unity of the community must be kept in mind. To forget it, as the Corinthians have, is to betray the community's worship "in remembrance" of Jesus.

GOSPEL | The multiplication of the loaves and the fish, a miracle found in all three of the synoptic Gospels, is intended, especially in Luke's Gospel, to be catechesis on the Eucharist and on ministry in general. This story occurs between the commissioning of the Twelve, in which they are to take nothing for their journey, and the profession of Peter's faith, as he proclaims Jesus to be "the Messiah of God." The miraculous feeding of the five thousand therefore serves as the link between the work of proclaiming the Kingdom of God and the heralding of

Now, Jesus is taking charge of the situation.

Then he **said** to his **disciples**,
　"Have them **sit down** in groups of about **fifty**."
They **did** so and made them **all** sit **down**.
Then taking the **five loaves** and the **two fish**,
　and looking up to **heaven**,
　　he said the **blessing** over them, **broke** them,
　　and **gave** them to the **disciples** to set before the **crowd**.
They **all ate** and were **satisfied**.
And when the **leftover fragments** were picked up,
　they filled **twelve wicker baskets**.

Emphatic final rhythm: *twelve wicker baskets*.

PRAYERFUL READING, OR *LECTIO DIVINA*

1. *Lectio:* Read a Scripture passage aloud slowly. Notice what phrase captures your attention and be attentive to its meaning. Silent pause.

2. *Meditatio:* Read the passage aloud slowly again, reflecting on the passage, allowing God to speak to you through it. Silent pause.

3. *Oratio:* Read it aloud slowly a third time, allowing it to be your prayer or response to God's gift of insight to you. Silent pause.

4. *Contemplatio:* Read it aloud slowly a fourth time, now resting in God's Word.

Jesus as savior. The feeding seals the work of ministry with compassion and points to the grace from which it comes.

The miracle in today's Gospel is closely connected to other Eucharist-themed stories in Luke, such as the Last Supper and the account of the two disciples on the road to Emmaus. Meals are an important setting for the demonstration of restoration in Luke's Gospel. This is shown in Jesus asking the crowd to be seated in groups, as if they were celebrating a festive fellowship meal. Moreover, the significance of this particular meal is indicated in the formula that Jesus uses in "taking," "blessing," "breaking," and "giving" the bread to the crowd. Luke clearly intends to present a teaching on the Eucharist: through the gathering of the Church, Jesus feeds those who are attended by the ministry of his followers. The story concludes by noting that Jesus provided for the people in such abundance that all ate with plenty left over. Just as Jesus sent out the Twelve in mission earlier in chapter 9, so the twelve baskets must testify to the extravagant success of the apostles' ministry. S.W.

THIRTEENTH SUNDAY IN ORDINARY TIME

LECTIONARY #99

READING I   1 Kings 19:16b, 19–21

A reading from the first Book of Kings

The LORD said to Elijah:
   "You shall anoint Elisha, son of Shaphat of Abel-meholah,
   as prophet to succeed you."

Elijah set out and came upon Elisha, son of Shaphat,
   as he was plowing with twelve yoke of oxen;
   he was following the twelfth.
Elijah went over to him and threw his cloak over him.
Elisha left the oxen, ran after Elijah, and said,
   "Please, let me kiss my father and mother goodbye,
   and I will follow you."
Elijah answered, "Go back!
Have I done anything to you?"
Elisha left him and, taking the yoke of oxen, slaughtered them;
   he used the plowing equipment for fuel to boil their flesh,
   and gave it to his people to eat.
Then Elisha left and followed Elijah as his attendant.

Elijah = ee-LĪ-juh
Elisha = ee-LI-shuh
Shaphat = SHAY-fat
Abel-meholah = AY-b*l muh-HOH-lah

A narrative reading that recounts the mysterious process of prophetic initiation and succession. The events recorded are remarkable, but the tone of the reading is matter-of-fact.

Elijah initiates Elisha by throwing his cloak over him. Slight emphasis on "cloak."

The most mysterious detail in the reading: slaughtering and then boiling all of the oxen. With this act, Elisha is ready to follow Elijah.

TO KEEP IN MIND
 If you are assigned to proclaim the first reading, read the Gospel for that week as well. They are connected in thematic ways.

READING I Scripture rarely provides any clues to God's method for choosing prophets, those who are given the mission to draw the people back to God and to challenge them to live according to God's justice. This is certainly true in the case of Elijah preparing to transfer the work of prophecy to a younger man. God commands Elijah to anoint Elisha as his successor. Elisha is an unknown figure who is discovered out in a field following a herd of twelve oxen. Elijah throws his cloak over Elisha's shoulders as sign that he is handing over the mantle of prophecy to the younger man, who is quite taken off-guard.

   Nevertheless, it does not take Elisha long to discern the meaning of Elijah's actions. As with all "calling" narratives, Elisha appears not quite ready to take on the new role to which he has been appointed. He runs after Elijah and asks for permission to take proper leave of his family. Elijah's reply seems dismissive; he says nothing to clarify the intention of his bestowal of the cloak. Elisha demonstrates his willingness to leave his old life behind, slaughtering the oxen and even using the plow as fuel to create a feast for his people. Elisha demonstrates himself to be completely faithful to God. Having destroyed the means by which he formerly earned his livelihood, he is now utterly free to begin an apprenticeship with Elijah.

READING II Within the Christian community at Galatia, a powerful faction existed that demanded adherence to the Jewish law, especially the requirement of circumcision. For Paul, however, the law is nothing less than the "yoke

For meditation and context:

RESPONSORIAL PSALM   Psalm 16:1–2, 5, 7–8, 9–10, 11 (see 5a)

R. You are my inheritance, O Lord.

Keep me, O God, for in you I take refuge;
    I say to the LORD, "My Lord are you."
O Lord, my allotted portion and my cup,
    you it is who hold fast my lot.

I bless the LORD who counsels me;
    even in the night my heart exhorts me.
I set the LORD ever before me;
    with him at my right hand I shall not
        be disturbed.

Therefore my heart is glad and my
        soul rejoices,
    my body, too, abides in confidence
because you will not abandon my soul to
        the netherworld,
    nor will you suffer your faithful one to
        undergo corruption.

You will show me the path to life,
    fullness of joys in your presence,
    the delights at your right hand forever.

Galatians = guh-LAY-shuhnz

A didactic reading in which St. Paul provides a sense of the meaning of spiritual freedom.

Slight pause between "freedom" and "Christ."

READING II   Galatians 5:1, 13–18

A reading from the Letter of Saint Paul to the Galatians

Brothers and **sisters**:
For **freedom Christ** set us **free**;
    so **stand firm** and do **not** submit **again** to the yoke of **slavery**.

For you were **called** for **freedom**, brothers and sisters.
But do not **use** this freedom
    as an **opportunity** for the **flesh**;
    rather, **serve** one another through **love**.
For the **whole law** is **fulfilled** in one **statement**,
    namely, *You shall **love** your **neighbor** as **yourself**.*
But if you go on **biting** and **devouring** one another,
    beware that you are not **consumed** by one another.

This core teaching of Scripture simply cannot be overemphasized. The admonition that follows puts it clearly into perspective.

I say, then: **live** by the **Spirit**
    and you will **certainly** not **gratify** the **desire** of the **flesh**.
For the **flesh** has **desires** against the **Spirit**,
    and the **Spirit** against the **flesh**;
    these are **opposed** to each **other**,
    so that you may not **do** what you **want**.
But if you are **guided** by the Spirit, you are **not** under the **law**.

Emphasis on "not."

---

of slavery," from which all who adhere to Christ are free. To promote any form of legalism is to forsake the freedom which is found in Christ. The two simply cannot coexist.

As is quite common in Pauline letters, the author sets up the dichotomy between the "Spirit" and the "flesh." The letter makes it clear that Christian freedom is freedom to love, not freedom to live according to worldly desires. A listing of such desires appears in the verses just after today's reading: "fornication, gross indecency and sexual irresponsibility, idolatry and sorcery; feuds and wrangling, jealousy, bad temper and quarrels; disagreements, factions, envy; drunkenness, orgies, and similar things." Self-indulgence of this sort prevents one from following the dictate to love, and therefore, all of these behaviors move a person in the direction of former slavery.

Elsewhere, Paul has made it very clear that the one who dies to the flesh is the one who has given the self over to Christ in baptism (Romans 6:2). Nevertheless, despite the sin-destroying power of baptism, the psychological order allows for the effects of sin to continue to be felt. The things of the flesh do not cease to be at war with the Spirit. For this reason, the command is issued for Christians to "live by the Spirit." The letter suggests that there is no middle ground between the flesh and the Spirit; rather, one must be totally guided by the Spirit in order to reject the law, resist the attractions of the world, and remain secure in the freedom of Christ.

GOSPEL   Luke 9:51–62

A reading from the holy Gospel according to Luke

When the **days** for Jesus' being taken **up** were **fulfilled**,
    he resolutely **determined** to journey to **Jerusalem**,
    and he sent **messengers ahead** of him.
On the **way** they entered a Samaritan **village**
    to **prepare** for his **reception** there,
    but they would not **welcome** him
    because the **destination** of his **journey** was **Jerusalem**.
When the disciples **James** and **John** saw this they asked,
    "**Lord**, do you want us to call down **fire** from heaven
    to **consume** them?"
Jesus **turned** and **rebuked** them, and they **journeyed**
    to another **village**.

As they were **proceeding** on their **journey** someone said to him,
    "I will **follow** you wherever you **go**."
Jesus answered him,
    "**Foxes** have **dens** and **birds** of the sky have **nests**,
    but the **Son** of **Man** has **nowhere** to rest his **head**."

And to another he said, "**Follow** me."
But he replied, "**Lord**, let me go **first** and bury my **father**."
But he answered him, "Let the **dead** bury their **dead**.
But **you**, **go** and **proclaim** the kingdom of **God**."
And another said, "**I** will follow you, Lord,
    but **first** let me say **farewell** to my family at **home**."
To **him** Jesus said, "**No one** who sets a **hand** to the **plow**
    and **looks** to what was left **behind** is **fit** for the kingdom
    of **God**."

A narrative reading. Jesus is beginning to make demands of his followers that they are finding hard to meet.
rebuked = rih-BYOOKD

Slight pause between "messengers" and "ahead."
Samaritan = suh-MAYR-uh-tuhn

"Rebuked" suggests a tone of frustration, even anger.

Jesus' aphorism is a strange way to respond to the devotion of this potential follower.

Another strange aphorism. This feeds into the overall atmosphere of this reading.

Jesus' tone is unusual; his demands of his followers are high.

GOSPEL Today's Gospel reading opens with a new section in Luke, whereby Jesus suggests that his ministry in Galilee is complete and that he is now prepared to make a final journey to Jerusalem. This journey to Jerusalem occupies a primary place in the overall structure of Luke's Gospel, spanning from the end of chapter 9 until Jesus' ascension in chapter 24. Luke's use of the words "when the days for Jesus' being taken up were fulfilled," reveals the theological import of this journey; Jesus' determination to depart for Jerusalem is seen as salvific.

How is salvation to be received? Luke answers this question at the outset of the journey. When a Samaritan village refuses to welcome him, Jesus' disciples' harsh response is to wish destruction upon the village, which Jesus rebukes. Rather quickly, though, he discovers the weakness of those who would profess to follow him. Disciples must be capable of leaving possessions, responsibilities, and cherished relationships in order to be fully committed to the reign of God. Salvation is to be received with complete devotion to God's reign. S.W.

FOURTEENTH SUNDAY IN ORDINARY TIME

LECTIONARY #102

READING I   Isaiah 66:10–14c

Isaiah = ī-ZAY-uh
An exhortatory reading depicting a river of prosperity, rich with vivid metaphors and poetic invocations.

A reading from the Book of the Prophet Isaiah

Thus says the LORD:
Rejoice with Jerusalem and be glad **because** of her,
  all you who **love** her;
exult, exult with her,
  all you who were **mourning** over her!
Oh, that you may suck **fully**
  of the **milk** of her **comfort**,
that you may **nurse** with **delight**
  at her **abundant breasts**!
  For **thus** says the LORD:
Lo, I will spread **prosperity** over Jerusalem like a **river**,
  and the **wealth** of the **nations** like an overflowing **torrent**.
As **nurslings**, you shall be **carried** in her **arms**,
  and **fondled** in her **lap**;
as a **mother** comforts her **child**,
  so will I **comfort** you;
  in **Jerusalem** you shall find your **comfort**.

When you **see** this, your heart shall **rejoice**
  and your **bodies** flourish like the **grass**;
the LORD's **power** shall be known to his **servants**.

The main metaphor: An infant nursing at the mother's breasts. In this case, Jerusalem is the mother.

nurslings = NERS-lihngz = babies still nursing

Note the parallels to emphasize: "see/rejoice"; "bodies/grass"; and "power/servants."

READING I   The passage we hear today from the Prophet Isaiah is found in the very last chapter of the book and is attributed to *Trito-Isaiah,* author of chapters 56 to 66, who wrote after Israel's return home from the Babylonian exile. These words of prophecy, which proclaim an end to the nation's suffering and a new beginning that promises to be fruitful, contain some of the most beautiful and creative images of God found in all of Scripture.

Although the people return to Jerusalem and see firsthand the complete destruction of the city and the Temple, the Lord demands that they rejoice. How can this be, since all that the people witness is a wasteland? The answer lies in the new birth for the nation that the prophet heralds. The city, like God, is portrayed as a mother who has given birth, her "abundant breasts" are prepared to feed, and her "fondling" of the newborn will provide comfort. Jerusalem may look empty and devoid of life now, but soon the Lord will see to the regeneration of the city. Isaiah employs an image from nature, comparing the success of the new nation to a raging river: "Lo, I will spread prosperity over Jerusalem like a river, and the wealth of the nations like an overflowing torrent." What is suggested here is the speed by which the Lord will accomplish his work of reconstruction, which will occur without hesitation. Thus, the image of Jerusalem as mother and the work of the Lord compared to an "overflowing torrent" portray both tenderness and strength.

Not only will the physical city be transformed, but the people themselves will be a new creation upon their return to Jerusalem. The passage ends with the prophet announcing that when the people

For meditation and context:

RESPONSORIAL PSALM Psalm 66:1–3, 4–5, 6–7, 16, 20 (1)

R. Let all the earth cry out to God with joy.

Shout joyfully to God, all the earth,
  sing praise to the glory of his name;
  proclaim his glorious praise.
Say to God, "How tremendous are
  your deeds!"

"Let all on earth worship and sing praise
  to you,
  sing praise to your name!"
Come and see the works of God,
  his tremendous deeds among the
  children of Adam.

He changed the sea into dry land;
  through the river they passed on foot;
  therefore let us rejoice in him.
He rules by his might forever.

Hear now, all you who fear God,
  while I declare what he has done for me.
Blessed be God who refused me not
  my prayer or his kindness!

Galatians = guh-LAY-shuhnz

A didactic reading from the conclusion of St. Paul's letter to the Galatians. Thus, the valedictory note at the conclusion of the reading. He's wrapping things up.

Note the parallels to emphasize: "world/me" and "I/world."

Circumcision = sehr-kuhm-SIH-zhuhn

Uncircumcision = uhn-sehr-kuhm-SIH-zhuhn

"Uncircumcision": strange word!

READING II Galatians 6:14–18

A reading from the Letter of Saint Paul to the Galatians

Brothers and **sisters**:
May I never **boast** except in the **cross** of our Lord Jesus **Christ**,
  through which the **world** has been **crucified** to **me**,
  and **I** to the **world**.
For neither does **circumcision** mean **anything**,
    nor does **uncircumcision**,
  but **only** a new **creation**.
Peace and **mercy** be to all who **follow** this rule
  and to the **Israel** of God.

From now on, let **no one** make **troubles** for me;
  for I bear the **marks** of **Jesus** on my **body**.

The **grace** of our Lord Jesus **Christ** be with your **spirit**,
  brothers and sisters. Amen.

TO KEEP IN MIND

If you are assigned to proclaim the first reading, read the Gospel for that week as well. They are connected in thematic ways.

---

come to behold the Lord's power, their hearts will "rejoice" and their bodies will "flourish" like the growing grass. For those who return to the land once destroyed, there is nothing to fear: God will provide motherly care and a guiding plan. After years of suffering and abandonment, the people can look to the future with great hope.

 READING II Throughout his letter to the Galatians, Paul reveals a struggle with a group of Judaizers, who taught that the Hebrew law regarding circumcision continued to be in force for all

Christians. The mark of circumcision is meant to be a source of identification that separates a people from others. The Judaizers believes this mark to be particularly important to distinguish faithful believers apart from the pagan world. The mark itself was something that allowed for boasting because it spoke of giving the body over to a new allegiance. However, for Paul, the only mark that matters is the cross of Christ and all that giving oneself over to it demands.

Paul speaks of the world being crucified to him and he to the world. Paul knows

well that the world was created by God as good; he also knows that the world contains many allurements that could take control of the senses. Baptism into Christ means that the world's power to seduce no longer holds sway over Christians, who are a "new creation." Such a new creation cannot come about by the marking of the flesh in circumcision but only with the inner and total transformation into Christ. That is the "rule" to be followed in the Church.

As Paul brings his correspondence with the Galatians to an end, he utters a prayer that his suffering, brought on by

GOSPEL   Luke 10:1–12, 17–20

A narrative reading about the empowering of Jesus' followers.

A reading from the holy Gospel according to Luke

[At that time the Lord appointed **seventy-two others**
    whom he sent **ahead** of him in **pairs**
    to every **town** and **place** he intended to **visit**.
He said to them,

Initially, "harvest" is a focal word for this reading.

    "The **harvest** is abundant but the **laborers** are few;
    so **ask** the master of the **harvest**
    to send out **laborers** for his **harvest**.
Go on your way;
    behold, I am sending you like **lambs** among **wolves**.

Note the details.

Carry no **money bag**, no **sack**, no **sandals**;
    and greet **no one** along the **way**.
Into whatever house you enter, first say,
    '**Peace** to this **household**.'
If a **peaceful person lives** there,
    your **peace** will rest on **him**;
    but if **not**, it will return to **you**.
Stay in the same house and **eat** and **drink** what is **offered** to you,
    for the **laborer** deserves his **payment**.

Even stresses on "Do not move about."

Do not move about from one **house** to **another**.
Whatever **town** you enter and they **welcome** you,
    eat what is set **before** you,
    cure the sick in it and **say** to them,
    'The **kingdom** of God is at **hand** for you.']
Whatever **town** you enter and they do **not** receive you,
    go **out** into the streets and say,
    'The **dust** of your town that **clings** to our feet,
    even **that** we shake off **against** you.'

Proclaim this line slowly.

Yet know this: the **kingdom** of God is at **hand**.

---

such opponents as the Judaizers, may cease and that his word may be heard as authentic, since he bears the marks of Jesus on his body. Paul sees himself as having been branded in the Lord and therefore should be known to be willing to endure great hardships on the Lord's behalf. Such is possible because of the grace that comes through the Lord Jesus Christ.

 GOSPEL   In Luke's account of the commissioning of the disciples, Jesus sends seventy-two followers

ahead of him to the places he plans to visit. This number parallels Moses' appointment of seventy-two elders (seventy plus Eldad and Medad, who were chosen to remain in the camp) for the task of helping with administration and keeping order among the people (Numbers 11:24–30).

As the seventy-two are sent out, it is clear that Luke is more interested in the characteristics that make the work of the mission possible rather than what the mission itself looks like. In other words, Jesus tells the disciples that "the harvest is

abundant," but he does not instruct them how to gather the harvest. Instead, Jesus provides details on how they should be disciples: they are to journey without various provisions that will guarantee their comfort and security along the way. Their witness is the mission that they are sent to accomplish.

Jesus makes it clear that what is at stake is the readiness of the people to hear the Good News of the kingdom. Some people will welcome the disciples with great interest, and some towns will not provide

Sodom = SOD-uhm

I **tell** you,
  it will be more **tolerable** for **Sodom** on that **day**
    than for that **town**."

The seventy-two returned rejoicing, and said,
  "**Lord**, even the **demons** are subject to us because
    of your **name**."

This is an especially striking and poetic image.

Jesus said, "I have observed **Satan** fall like **lightning**
  from the **sky**.
Behold, I have given you the power to '**tread** upon **serpents**'
  and **scorpions**
  and upon the **full force** of the **enemy**
    and **nothing** will harm you.
Nevertheless, do not rejoice because
    the **spirits** are **subject** to **you**,

Emphasis on "written."

  but **rejoice** because your names are **written** in heaven."

[Shorter: Luke 10:1–9 (see brackets)]

any welcome at all. Indeed, some will be ready for conversion, while others will resist. Urgency is more important than persistence for the seventy-two; it is better for them to "shake off" resistance than to try to overcome a lack of reception.

After completing their mission, the disciples return to Jesus "rejoicing." Undoubtedly, they feel a sense of great accomplishment, which Jesus affirms by suggesting that he has witnessed the fall of Satan's power due to their labor. Nevertheless, Jesus provides a final word of caution for them: they are not to revel in the power they have as his disciples; rather, they are to rejoice because they have secured a place in heaven. The seventy-two have gathered together a grand harvest, but there is one to come that will be far greater! S.W.

FIFTEENTH SUNDAY IN ORDINARY TIME

LECTIONARY #105

READING I   Deuteronomy 30:10–14

A reading from the Book of Deuteronomy

Moses said to the **people**:
"If **only** you would heed the **voice** of the Lord, your **God**,
 and **keep** his **commandments** and **statutes**
 that are **written** in this **book** of the **law**,
 when you **return** to the Lord, your God,
 with all your **heart** and all your **soul**.

"For **this command** that I enjoin on you **today**
 is not too **mysterious** and **remote** for you.
It is not **up** in the **sky**, that you should **say**,
 '**Who** will go **up** in the **sky** to **get** it for us
 and **tell** us of it, that we may **carry** it **out**?'
Nor is it across the **sea**, that you should say,
 '**Who** will cross the **sea** to **get** it for us
 and **tell** us of it, that we may **carry** it **out**?'
No, it is something very **near** to you,
 already in your mouths and in your **hearts**;
 you have **only** to carry it **out**."

Deuteronomy = doo-ter-AH-nuh-mee
or dyoo-ter-AH-nuh-mee

A narrative reading in which Moses expresses his frustration that the people are not following the commandments and statutes of God.

Moses expresses his frustration. You can allow a little impatience to enter into your proclamation.

In a series of negative statements—beginning "no" or "nor"—Moses clarifies that the people "should" be able to follow these commandments. But obviously, they are not.

TO KEEP IN MIND
Use the pitch and volume of your voice to gain the attention of the assembly.

READING I God established his covenant with Israel to be a mutual expression of fidelity and love. When God brought the Israelites out of Egypt, led them through the wilderness to Mount Sinai, and there both gave and subsequently renewed a covenant with the people, he left no doubt as to what needed to be attended to in their mutual relationship. God would journey with his people and bring them into the land flowing with milk and honey. The people, for their part, would simply have to demonstrate a daily willingness to sacrifice to God and to trust in him completely. This test would prove difficult for the Israelites.

In today's reading from Deuteronomy, Moses, at the age of one hundred and twenty, assembles the people to renew the covenant. Afterwards, he would pass the leadership of the people to Joshua, who would have the responsibility of guiding them into the Promised Land. The Israelites' forty years of wandering through the desert has come to an end; now is the time for them to confirm their identity as God's Chosen People.

This identity is found primarily in the act of listening to the voice of God. Moses instructs the Israelites at the outset of their journey to "listen closely to the voice of the Lord, your God" (Exodus 15:26). The essential Jewish prayer, the *Shema* ("hear," in Hebrew) begins, "Hear, O Israel: The Lord is our God, the Lord alone" (Deuteronomy 6:4). Moses suggests to the people that they ought not make this hearing overly difficult; the Law is not found way up in the sky or far off on the sea. It is, rather, on the lips and in the hearts of those to whom it has been given. For this very reason, it is

For meditation and context:

RESPONSORIAL PSALM Psalm 69:14, 17, 30–31, 33–34, 36, 37 (see 33)

R. Turn to the Lord in your need, and you will live.

I pray to you, O Lord,
　for the time of your favor, O God!
In your great kindness answer me
　with your constant help.
Answer me, O Lord, for bounteous is
　　your kindness:
　in your great mercy turn toward me.

I am afflicted and in pain;
　let your saving help, O God, protect me.
I will praise the name of God in song,
　and I will glorify him with thanksgiving.

"See, you lowly ones, and be glad;
　you who seek God, may your hearts revive!
For the Lord hears the poor,
　and his own who are in bonds he
　　spurns not."

For God will save Zion
　and rebuild the cities of Judah.
The descendants of his servants shall
　　inherit it,
　and those who love his name shall
　　inhabit it.

Or:

For meditation and context:

RESPONSORIAL PSALM Psalm 19:8, 9, 10, 11 (9a)

R. Your words, Lord, are Spirit and life.

The law of the Lord is perfect,
　refreshing the soul;
the decree of the Lord is trustworthy,
　giving wisdom to the simple.

The precepts of the Lord are right,
　rejoicing the heart;
the command of the Lord is clear,
　enlightening the eye.

The fear of the Lord is pure,
　enduring forever;
the ordinances of the Lord are true,
　all of them just.

They are more precious than gold,
　than a heap of purest gold;
sweeter also than syrup
　or honey from the comb.

Colossians = kuh-LOSH-uhnz

A didactic reading in which St. Paul depicts the possibilities of a cosmic Christ.

The reading is shaped by two rhetorical devices. First, Paul uses the phrase "For in him" to depict cosmic, enduring features of Christ. He uses it twice, as a frame. Between them, he repeats "He is" to attribute cosmic aspects to Christ.

These are traditional names of angelic powers. Let mystery and reverence seep into your proclamation.

READING II   Colossians 1:15–20

A reading from the Letter of Saint Paul to the Colossians

Christ Jesus is the **image** of the invisible **God**,
　the **firstborn** of all **creation**.
For in **him** were created **all things** in **heaven** and on **earth**,
　the **visible** and the **invisible**,
　whether **thrones** or **dominions** or **principalities** or **powers**;
　all things were created **through** him and **for** him. »

crucial for subsequent generations to be taught the fullness of the Law and therefore maintain God's truth within the heart of the nation. In this way, it will be impossible for Israel to abandon the covenant completely.

READING II This excerpt from Paul's letter to the Colossians likely originated as a liturgical hymn of praise and exultation, most appropriate for baptismal celebrations. In it, Christ is heralded as both the center of the cosmos and the head of the Church. The hymn pro-

claims that without Christ nothing has direction, nothing has purpose. Those who have given themselves to Christ in baptism are themselves the holy ones set free from Satan's power.

　The structure of this passage is of particular interest. It begins by extolling Christ's role as "the firstborn of all creation." All things were created "in him." There is no particle of creation that did not involve the participation of God's Son. Moreover, creation itself exists "for him"—Christ gives both value and meaning to all things. One could even think here of the

Paschal imprint on creation itself. Just as Christ died to self and rose again for the sake of others, so does creation often bear the need to die in order to produce new life.

　The second portion of the hymn praises Christ as "the firstborn from the dead." He stands at the head of the Church and thus provides order and shape to the body. Portraying the Church as the body of Christ, in which the unity and equality of all of the members is of paramount importance, is a favored image for Paul (see 1 Corinthians 6:15, Romans 12:4). The mission of Christ's work in the Church points to a return to his

dominions = doh-MIN-yuhns
principalities = prihn-suh-PAL-uh-teez

preeminent = pree-EHM-ih-nuhnt
And here, with "For in him," Paul concludes his argument.

He is **before** all things,
   and in him all things **hold together**.
He is the **head** of the body, the **church**.
He is the **beginning**, the firstborn from the **dead**,
   that in **all things** he himself might be **preeminent**.
For **in** him all the **fullness** was pleased to **dwell**,
   and **through** him to reconcile all things **for** him,
   making **peace** by the **blood** of his **cross**
   through **him**, whether those on **earth** or those in **heaven**.

GOSPEL   Luke 10:25–37

A very energetic narrative reading that depicts a conversation between Jesus and a scholar rich in drama and with all of the qualities of a rabbinic dialogue.

A reading from the holy Gospel according to Luke

There was a **scholar** of the **law** who stood up
   to test Jesus and said,
  "**Teacher**, what must I do to **inherit eternal life**?"
Jesus said to him, "What is **written** in the **law**?
How do you **read** it?"
He said in reply,
  *"You shall **love** the Lord, your God,*
  *with all your **heart**,*
  *with all your **being**,*
  *with all your **strength**,*
  *and with all your **mind**,*
  *and your **neighbor** as **yourself**."*
He replied to him, "You have answered **correctly**;
  do **this** and you will **live**."

The Great Commandment: The irreducible core of all Christian faith.

But because he wished to **justify** himself, he said to Jesus,
  "And **who** is my **neighbor**?"
Jesus replied,
  "A **man** fell victim to **robbers**
  as he went **down** from **Jerusalem** to **Jericho**.
They **stripped** and **beat** him and went off **leaving** him **half-dead**.

When the scholar asks his question, he is goading Jesus to explain the teaching of the love of neighbor.

preeminence in creation: he is responsible for the reconciliation of all things to himself. This task has been accomplished by his blood shed upon the cross. A new order now exists: creation is not simply imprinted with the image of the divine, it has been redeemed by Christ's blood. There is a new fullness in the universe made possible only by the demonstration of Christ's great sacrifice of love.

GOSPEL   In the verses immediately prior to today's Gospel passage, the seventy-two have been appointed for mission and have returned exhilarated from all their work. Upon returning, they learn from Jesus how fortunate they are to know all that they do about the coming of the kingdom. He tells them in private, "Happy the eyes that see what you see" (Luke 10:23). Then, without any mention of a change in setting, a scholar of the law "stood up to test" Jesus. The combination

of the gesture of standing up along with the intention of testing Jesus sets the tone of a courtroom. Jesus has just instructed the disciples regarding all of the good news that has been handed on to them. Surely, this man's testing will be in vain.

The scholar's first question is simple and direct, especially for anyone steeped in Jewish law: What is required for eternal life? Instead of answering, Jesus turns the question on him, clearly taking the upper hand in the argument. After the scholar

Levite = LEE-vĭt

Samaritan = suh-MAYR-uh-tuhn

The tone of the parable shifts more hopefully at "But a Samaritan."

The scholar's final statement summarizes the lesson.

A **priest** happened to be going down that **road**,
  but when he **saw** him, he passed **by** on the opposite **side**.
Likewise a Levite came to the **place**,
  and when he **saw** him, he passed **by** on the opposite **side**.
But a **Samaritan** traveler who came upon him
  was **moved** with **compassion** at the **sight**.
He approached the **victim**,
  poured **oil** and **wine** over his **wounds** and **bandaged** them.
Then he lifted him **up** on his own **animal**,
  took him to an **inn**, and **cared** for him.
The **next day** he took out **two silver coins**
  and gave them to the **innkeeper** with the **instruction**,
  'Take **care** of him.
If you spend **more** than what I have **given** you,
  I shall **repay** you on my way **back**.'
Which of these **three**, in your opinion,
  was **neighbor** to the robbers' **victim**?"
He answered, "The one who treated him with **mercy**."
Jesus said to him, "**Go** and do **likewise**."

provides the correct answer from the Mosaic law, Jesus politely affirms his answer. However, in typical lawyerly fashion, the man presses him again, posing a more complex question to Jesus: How does one define "neighbor"? This time Jesus answers with the parable of the Good Samaritan. Three characters, a priest, a Levite, and a Samaritan, separately come upon a robbery victim beaten up on the side of the road. The first two men (who are very much like the man who knows the law) ignore the

man and pass him by, but the outsider to the Jewish law picks the man up, treats him with compassion, and cares for his needs.

The parable ends with Jesus offering the final question of the debate. When the questioner is asked to identify the neighbor of the man lying in the road, we hope that perhaps he identifies his own arrogance in the priest and the Levite in the parable. He names as neighbor the one who treated the man with mercy. Perhaps the scholar of the law realizes that he has failed to be

neighbor to Jesus in his desire to test him. Regardless, Jesus acts with mercy as well, as he simply sends the man away with the command: "Go and do likewise." S.W.

SIXTEENTH SUNDAY
IN ORDINARY TIME

Genesis = JEN-uh-sihs

terebinth = TAYR-uh-binth

Mamre = MAM-ree *or* MAHM-ray

A narrative reading of great dramatic power and important symbolic resonance. Your proclamation of the story will unfurl as you attend to its details.

Emphasis on "three men." Christian interpretations of these men suggest them to prefigure the persons of the Trinity.

TO KEEP IN MIND

The words in bold are suggestions for ways to express the meaning of the reading. Consider using them as you practice the reading, then choose to stress them or to find your own way of proclaiming.

As Abraham hastens, you too can pick up the pace of your proclamation.

curds = kerds

LECTIONARY #108

READING I   Genesis 18:1–10a

A reading from the Book of Genesis

The **LORD** appeared to **Abraham** by the **terebinth** of **Mamre**,
as he **sat** in the entrance of his **tent**,
while the **day** was growing **hot**.
Looking up, Abraham saw **three men** standing nearby.
When he **saw** them, he ran from the **entrance** of the tent
to **greet** them;
and **bowing** to the ground, he said:
"**Sir**, if I may ask you this **favor**,
please do not go on past your **servant**.
Let some **water** be brought, that you may **bathe** your feet,
and then **rest** yourselves under the **tree**.
Now that you have come this **close** to your servant,
let me **bring** you a little **food**, that you may **refresh** yourselves;
and **afterward** you may go on your **way**."
The men replied, "Very **well, do** as you have **said**."

Abraham **hastened** into the tent and told Sarah,
"**Quick**, three measures of fine **flour**! **Knead** it
and make **rolls**."
He ran to the **herd**, picked out a **tender**, **choice steer**,
and gave it to a **servant**, who quickly **prepared** it.
Then **Abraham** got some **curds** and **milk**,
as well as the **steer** that had been **prepared**,
and set these before the **three men**;
and he **waited** on them under the **tree** while they **ate**.

READING I   In the biblical world, it is a sacred duty to welcome strangers who simply show up in one's life, like the visitors in this reading. Though the narrator tells readers that it is the Lord who appears to Abraham, this is not immediately apparent to Abraham. He looks up and sees three men standing nearby. It is only as their visit unfolds—Abraham sees that the three know Sarah's name and are aware of her silent laughter at their announcement that she will bear a son (omitted from this reading)—that he realizes that the three men are the Lord and two heavenly attendants.

When the strangers arrive, one-hundred-year-old Abraham is sitting at the hottest time of the day in the coolest place he can find, the opening of his tent, where sunshine meets shade and the air temperature suddenly changes and stirs up a slight breeze. He abandons his comfortable spot to welcome people about whom he knows nothing. He runs to greet them and bows to the ground, addressing them as *"Adonai"* or "lord," which like "sir" is a common title of respect. His eagerness, bowing, and respectful address are typical of social interaction in the biblical world. Abraham then asks the strangers to do him the favor of not passing him by, but allowing him to bring "a little water" and "a little food" so they can refresh themselves.

After the visitors accept his invitation, old Abraham hurries to ninety-year-old Sarah and tells her to take a huge amount of their finest flour and make rolls. Then he runs and chooses one of his choicest animals and tells his servant to prepare it

At their question, slow your pace—here is where the drama intensifies.

They asked Abraham, "**Where** is your wife **Sarah**?"
He replied, "**There** in the **tent**."
One of them said, "I will **surely** return to you
     about **this time** next year,
  and **Sarah** will **then** have a **son**."

Note the rhythm of this last line.

For meditation and context:

RESPONSORIAL PSALM   Psalm 15:2–3, 3–4, 5 (1a)

R. He who does justice will live in the presence of the Lord.

One who walks blamelessly and does justice;
  who thinks the truth in his heart
  and slanders not with his tongue.

Who harms not his fellow man,
  nor takes up a reproach against
    his neighbor;
by whom the reprobate is despised,
  while he honors those who fear the Lord.

Who lends not his money at usury
  and accepts no bribe against the innocent.
One who does these things
  shall never be disturbed.

Colossians = kuh-LOSH-uhnz

A didactic reading in which St. Paul extols the virtues of following Christ.

"Now" initiates Paul's argument with a set of observations that follow.

READING II   Colossians 1:24–28

A reading from the Letter of Saint Paul to the Colossians

Brothers and **sisters**:
Now I rejoice in my **sufferings** for your **sake**,
  and in my **flesh** I am filling up
  what is **lacking** in the afflictions of **Christ**
  on **behalf** of his body, which is the **church**,
  of which I am a **minister**
  in **accordance** with God's **stewardship** given to **me**
  to bring to **completion** for you the word of **God**,
  the **mystery hidden** from **ages** and from generations **past**.
But **now** it has been **manifested** to his **holy** ones,
  to whom **God chose** to make known the **riches** of the **glory**
  of this **mystery** among the **Gentiles**;
  it is **Christ** in you, the **hope** for glory. »

Slight pause between "mystery" and "hidden."

"But now" shifts to the second half of Paul's argument, redirecting his observations from himself to God's "holy ones."

quickly. In the end, Abraham sets much more than a little food before his visitors and then stands and waits on them while they eat. In the verses immediately following this reading, one of the visitors announces that Abraham and Sarah will soon have the son for whom they longed.

 Paul, who calls himself a "minister" (Greek *diakonos*) of the Gospel, rejoices in his sufferings because they flow from and provide evidence of his commitment to the stewardship that God gave him. His statement that

he "is filling up what is lacking in the afflictions of Christ" seems to convey that Christ's sufferings were not enough to effect universal salvation. Elsewhere, however, Paul makes it clear that Christ's suffering on the cross and his resurrection removed all sin and effected the forgiveness of all (see, for example, Colossians 2:13–14).

In the context of this passage, Christ's affliction seems to refer to the sufferings of the Body of Christ, the Church. Paul's share in these sufferings brings to completion the word of God, that is, they play a role in the

extension of God's promises to and plans for Israel to the Gentiles. Indeed, Paul's afflictions for the sake of the Gospel become the vehicle that spreads it. They reveal the mystery that "was hidden from ages and from generations past." The revelation of this mystery continues to unfold in the sufferings of the "holy ones," Christ's followers in every era. Paul's commission is to communicate this reality with "all wisdom" so that the baptized grow into more perfect images of Christ.

admonishing = ad-MON-ish-ing

Slight pause between "everyone" and "perfect."

It is **he** whom we **proclaim**,
   admonishing **everyone** and teaching **everyone**
      with all **wisdom**,
   that we may present **everyone perfect** in **Christ**.

GOSPEL   Luke 10:38–42

A reading from the holy Gospel according to Luke

A narrative reading relating a well-known teaching. All the weight in this reading is carried in the names "Martha" and "Mary."

Slight pause between "Martha" and "welcomed.'

Use a compassionate tone here.

Likewise, use a compassionate tone when saying "Mary."

Jesus entered a **village**
   where a woman whose name was **Martha welcomed** him.
She had a **sister** named **Mary**
   who **sat** beside the Lord at his **feet** listening to him **speak**.
Martha, burdened with much serving, came to him and said,
   "**Lord**, do you not **care**
   that my **sister** has left me by **myself** to do the **serving**?
Tell her to **help** me."
The Lord said to her in reply,
   "**Martha, Martha**, you are **anxious** and **worried**
      about **many** things.
There is **need** of only **one** thing.
Mary has chosen the **better part**
   and it will **not** be taken from **her**."

GOSPEL As Jesus enters a village, Martha invites him to her home and busies herself with providing a lavish welcome. Apparently oblivious to Martha's bustle and to the demands of hospitality, her sister, Mary, sits at Jesus' feet "listening to him speak."

Luke describes Martha as "burdened with much serving" (*diakonia*). The Greek behind "burdened," *perispaomai*, can also denote "being dragged or pulled along," in this context, by societal expectations. Martha's dutiful concern, however, seems to be lost on Jesus. He does not prattle on about the delightful cuisine that she sets before him because he did not come to the sisters' home to chat about food and wine. He came to enlighten them about the relationship that God wants to have with them.

Jesus even seems rude. Ignoring the gracious Martha's urging that he tell Mary to help her, he instead tells Martha that she is anxious and worried about many things and is not doing the most important one— listening to him. Jesus' response might well jar Martha and us to evaluate how well we listen to him. Do we welcome him and his views and live differently? Or are we anxious and busy complying with the world's expectations? S.W.

SEVENTEENTH SUNDAY IN ORDINARY TIME

LECTIONARY #111

READING I   Genesis 18:20–32

A reading from the Book of Genesis

In those days, the LORD said:
  "The **outcry** against **Sodom** and **Gomorrah** is so **great**,
  and their **sin** so grave,
  that I must go **down** and see whether or not their **actions**
  fully correspond to the cry **against** them that **comes** to me.
I **mean** to find **out**."

While Abraham's **visitors** walked on farther toward **Sodom**,
  the LORD remained **standing** before **Abraham**.
Then **Abraham** drew nearer and said:
  "Will you **sweep away** the innocent with the **guilty**?
Suppose there were **fifty innocent people** in the city;
  would you **wipe out** the place, rather than **spare** it
  for the sake of the **fifty innocent people** within it?
Far **be** it from you to **do** such a thing,
  to make the **innocent die** with the **guilty**
  so that the **innocent** and the **guilty** would be treated **alike**!
Should not the **judge** of all the world act with **justice**?"
The LORD replied,
  "If I find **fifty innocent people** in the city of Sodom,
  I will spare the **whole place** for their **sake**."
Abraham spoke up again:
  "**See** how I am presuming to **speak** to my Lord,
  though I am but **dust** and **ashes**! »

Genesis = JEN-uh-sihs
A narrative reading whose power lies in the cumulative argument it relates. Its tone combines cunning and mercy, starting with the former and shifting into the latter.
Sodom = SOD-uhm

Establish the tone of the reading with the Lord's words. He is concerned but also curious.

Abraham's initial tone is one of familiarity but also playful engagement.

Here, Abraham's tone is one of playful assuagement.

With each additional test, Abraham is trying to awaken the Lord's mercy. Allow your tone to become ever slightly more earnest with each additional question.

READING I | Though both testaments of the Bible remember Abraham's exemplary faith, this passage focuses on his justice. In the verses preceding our reading, the Lord considers whether to discuss the fate of Sodom and Gomorrah with Abraham. He had grown close to the Lord, trusting him enough that at the Lord's command he left all that provided him with security—his family and tribe, the familiar and or like-minded people with whom he associated—and followed the Lord to a foreign place. Over time, the Lord comes to reckon Abraham a just man (Genesis 15:6)

and trusts that he will persuade his descendants to do the right thing in every situation. For these reasons, the Lord decides to discuss the problem of the two cities with him.

Their dialogue centers on the complaint that the innocent often suffer what seems to be divine punishment of the guilty, but with a twist. Namely, Abraham wants to know how many just people must be found among the wicked for the Lord to save the whole group. His question echoes Jeremiah 5:1, where the Lord commands the prophet: "Roam the streets of Jerusalem . . .

to find even one who acts justly and seeks honesty, and I will pardon (Jerusalem)!" Jeremiah didn't find one. Apparently, neither did the Lord find the ten just people that Abraham bargained for to save Sodom and Gomorrah.

READING II | Paul reminds the Colossians that before they were baptized, they lived like most people. They set personal goals, charted their course through life, and generally followed their contemporaries on the paths worn by the generations before them. Though this

A little more earnest.

A little more earnest.

And now a little more pleading.

At last, with the pleading tone, allow the mercy to come in when you emphasize "Please."

What if there are **five less** than **fifty innocent people**?
Will you destroy the **whole city** because of those **five**?"
He answered, "I **will not** destroy it, if I find **forty-five** there."
But Abraham persisted, saying "What if only **forty** are
found there?"
He replied, "I will **forbear** doing it for the **sake** of the **forty**."
Then Abraham said, "Let **not** my Lord grow **impatient** if I go on.
What if only **thirty** are found there?"
He replied, "I will **forbear** doing it if I can find but **thirty** there."
Still Abraham went on,
"Since I have **thus dared** to speak to my **Lord**,
what if there are no more than **twenty**?"
The LORD answered, "I **will not** destroy it, for the **sake**
of the **twenty**."
But he still persisted:
"**Please**, let not my Lord grow **angry** if I speak up this
last time.
What if there are at least **ten** there?"
He replied, "For the **sake** of those **ten**, I will **not** destroy it."

For meditation and context:

RESPONSORIAL PSALM   Psalm 138:1–2, 2–3, 6–7, 7–8 (3a)

R. Lord, on the day I called for help, you answered me.

I will give thanks to you, O LORD, with all
my heart,
for you have heard the words of my mouth;
in the presence of the angels I will sing
your praise;
I will worship at your holy temple
and give thanks to your name.

Because of your kindness and your truth;
for you have made great above all things
your name and your promise.
When I called you answered me;
you built up strength within me.

The LORD is exalted, yet the lowly he sees,
and the proud he knows from afar.
Though I walk amid distress, you
preserve me;
against the anger of my enemies you raise
your hand.

Your right hand saves me.
The LORD will complete what he has done
for me;
your kindness, O LORD, endures forever;
forsake not the work of your hands.

TO KEEP IN MIND
Make eye contact with the assembly.
This helps keep the assembly engaged
with the reading.

---

seemed to work out well enough for them, Paul declares that before they were baptized the Colossians were, in reality, "dead in transgressions." In other words, before Christ, they sat on a kind of death row. The record of the widespread and irreparable damage that they inflicted on each other and themselves was indisputable and irreversible. Until Christ pardoned everyone. Until Christ obliterated "the bond against us . . . nailing it to the cross," setting us free from the consequences of our sins.

Paul reminds us that in baptism we were both buried with Christ and raised with

him "through faith in the power of God who raised him from the dead." This same divine power is always at work within us, though its effects are often only realized over time. The baptized believe that the risen Lord is changing them from within, working below the level of consciousness and in ways that are not perceptible to the senses.

GOSPEL   One of Jesus' disciples asks him to teach them how to pray. He responds here with Luke's version of the "Our Father." We are so familiar with this prayer that perhaps the impact of its

first word is lost on us. Jesus could have said, "When you pray, say 'God.'" Instead, he tells us to say "Father," an address which draws us into his intimate relationship with God. It is to no distant deity that he prays in the garden before his passion or from the cross. His dying breath does not commend his spirit into the hands of a vague, aloof, supernatural being, but to his Father, from whom he is never separated.

Jesus tells his disciples to pray for five basic things. First, that the Father's "name," or person, be made holy. In Luke's Gospel, disciples contribute to this process by put-

READING II   Colossians 2:12–14

A reading from the Letter of Saint Paul to the Colossians

Brothers and **sisters**:
You were **buried** with him in **baptism**,
  in which you were also **raised** with him
  through **faith** in the **power** of God,
  who **raised** him from the **dead**.
And even when you were dead
  in **transgressions** and the **uncircumcision** of your flesh,
  he **brought** you to life **along** with him,
  having **forgiven** us all our **transgressions**;
  obliterating the bond **against** us, with its **legal** claims,
  which was **opposed** to us,
  he also **removed** it from our **midst**, **nailing** it to the **cross**.

GOSPEL   Luke 11:1–13

A reading from the holy Gospel according to Luke

Jesus was praying in a certain place, and when he had **finished**,
  one of his disciples said to him,
  "**Lord**, teach us to pray just as **John** taught his **disciples**."
He said to them, "When you pray, say:
  Father, **hallowed** be your name,
    your **kingdom come**.
    Give us each **day** our daily **bread**
    and **forgive** us our **sins**
    for we ourselves forgive **everyone** in **debt** to us,
    and do not **subject** us to the **final test**." »

Sidebar notes (left column):

Colossians = kuh-LOSH-uhnz
A didactic reading in which St. Paul uses his considerable rhetorical skills to visualize a metaphor for the forgiveness of sins.

The repetitions of "raised" set the tone for what Paul is trying to teach.

transgressions = trans-GRESH-uhnz
uncircumcision = uhn-sehr-kuhm-SIH-zhuhn
"Uncircumcision": a strange word! It belongs to Paul's spiritual convictions.

Emphasis on "nailing" and "cross."

A powerful narrative reading containing a combination of instruction, parable, and exhortation.

The Lord's Prayer, in context. Imagine you're proclaiming these words to someone hearing them for the first time.

---

ting Jesus' teachings into practice. Their different priorities and lifestyles spread awareness of the Father's interests and concerns.

Second, God's children pray, "your kingdom come." This is the kingdom announced by the prophets from the eighth century before Christ and kept alive by those who believed in the Lord's word. Unlike the sad succession of earthly kingdoms— wherein a few thrive and overindulge themselves while the many lack the basic needs for a decent life—in God's kingdom all people flourish and together share the Lord's bounty.

Third, disciples also petition Jesus' Father, "give us each day our daily bread." In other words, give us what we need to carry on Jesus' work today—not tomorrow or in the coming years. This petition covers all possible personal prayers for daily help.

Fourth, disciples pray: "forgive us our sins *for* we ourselves forgive *everyone* in debt to us." This, the longest of Jesus' petitions, demands that we forgive everyone who insulted or harmed us personally by their words and deeds, or by their failure to help us when they had the means to do so, or by the far-reaching negative conse-

quences of their habits and choices, or by any other way.

Finally, disciples pray, "do not subject us to the final test." In Luke, the Greek for "test" or "temptation," *peirasmos*, denotes Jesus' temptations in the wilderness. And in Jesus' parable of the sower, the seed that falls on rocky ground represents believers who fall away in time of "trial" (or test or temptation). And during Jesus' agony, he twice tells his disciples to pray that they will not be "put to the test."

Jesus' parable teaches, among other things, that God's responses to a disciple's

Immediately, Jesus offers a parable, whose emphasis is on "persistence," proclaimed at the very end of it.

The parallels are repeated for emphasis.

Jesus reinforces the instruction to persist with parallels: "ask/receive"; "seek/find"; and "knock/open."

Jesus concludes with an inverted comparison: If "you" who are "wicked" can nevertheless offer good gifts to your children, imagine what "the Father," who is good, offers of the "Holy Spirit" to those who persistently ask him for something.

And he said to them, "**Suppose** one of you has a **friend**
　　to whom he goes at **midnight** and says,
　　'**Friend**, lend me **three loaves** of **bread**,
　　for a **friend** of mine has arrived at my **house** from a journey
　　and I have **nothing** to offer him,'
　　and he says in reply from within,
　　'Do not **bother** me; the door has already been **locked**
　　and my **children** and **I** are already in **bed**.
I cannot get **up** to give you **anything**.'
I tell you,
　　if he does not get **up** to give the visitor the **loaves**
　　because of their **friendship**,
　　he will get **up** to give him **whatever** he needs
　　because of his **persistence**.

"And I **tell** you, **ask** and you will **receive**;
　　seek and you will **find**;
　　knock and the door will be **opened** to you.
For **everyone** who asks, **receives**;
　　and the one who **seeks**, **finds**;
　　and to the one who **knocks**, the door will be **opened**.
What **father** among you would hand his son a **snake**
　　when he **asks** for a **fish**?
Or hand him a **scorpion** when he **asks** for an **egg**?
If **you** then, who are **wicked**,
　　know how to give good **gifts** to your children,
　　how much **more** will the Father in **heaven**
　　give the **Holy Spirit** to those who **ask** him?"

needs are more suitable and reliable than human responses. Not a single request goes unanswered. Every person who seeks, finds. And to those who knock, the door will be opened. These are not religious fancies, but givens. We often miss them because God does not respond in the way we expect.

That's why the Father gives the Holy Spirit to everyone who asks for it. This Spirit leads and guides disciples from within and helps them perceive how God is active in their life. When they feel that they are not receiving when they ask, or finding when they seek, or when their knock seems to go unheeded, Luke would have them remember that the Spirit who comes upon Mary at the Annunciation; who fills Jesus' fearless forerunner, John the Baptist; who was upon and enabled the just and devout Simeon to recognize Jesus when Joseph and Mary brought him to the temple; who descends upon Jesus at his baptism; and who fills Jesus and leads him is the *same* Spirit who fills and leads the baptized. S.W.

EIGHTEENTH SUNDAY IN ORDINARY TIME

LECTIONARY #114

Ecclesiastes = ih-klee-zee-AS-teez

An exhortatory reading whose straightforward message is repeatedly forgotten despite its irrefutability. Proclaim it with conviction. "Vanity" is clearly the focus.

Qoheleth = koh-HEL-uhth

The message of this reading is condensed in this powerful aphorism. Emphasize its menacing quality.

Rhythm. Land hard on the final "vanity."

READING I Ecclesiastes 1:2; 2:21–23

A reading from the Book of Ecclesiastes

> **Vanity** of **vanities**, says Qoheleth,
>   **vanity** of **vanities**! **All** things are **vanity**!
>
> Here is one who has labored with **wisdom** and **knowledge**
>   and **skill**,
>   and yet to another who has **not** labored over it,
>   he must leave **property**.
> This also is **vanity** and a great **misfortune**.
> For what **profit** comes to man from all the **toil** and **anxiety**
>   of **heart**
>   with which he has **labored** under the **sun**?
> All his days **sorrow** and **grief** are his **occupation**;
>   even at **night** his mind is not at **rest**.
> **This also** is **vanity**.

> **TO KEEP IN MIND**
> If you are assigned to proclaim the first reading, read the Gospel for that week as well. They are connected in thematic ways.

READING I "Ecclesiastes" is the Latin translation of the Hebrew *Qoheleth*, here a proper name which denotes a "speaker in an assembly" or a "teacher." Qoheleth is a sage who writes from personal experience and the observation of people and nature. Today's opening verse sums up his main conclusion about life: "Vanity of vanities says Qoheleth, vanity of vanities. All things are vanity. In Hebrew usage, the phrase "vanity of vanities" conveys superlative or complete vanity, and the doubling of the phrase emphasizes the certainty of this claim.

The meaning of "vanity" (Hebrew *hebel*) in the book of Qoheleth varies depending on its context. Basically, *hebel* denotes "vapor" or "breath." Figuratively, it can indicate something insubstantial and short-lived, or futile, like human efforts that come to nothing. In some contexts, *hebel* connotes something that defies human reasoning, something that is incomprehensible or mysterious, such as effects that seemingly bear no logical relationship to their causes.

In this reading, "*hebel* and great misfortune" describe a situation where a man labors with practical wisdom, knowledge, and skill. But when he dies, he must leave his property to someone who did nothing to help gain it. Qoheleth laments further that work leads to more work and an anxious mind that will not shut down and allow healthy sleep. Sorrow and grief fill the diligent person's life.

Such quandaries lead Qoheleth to conclude that life is a mysterious experience whose meaning and purpose humans cannot ever fully fathom. It's futile to try to do so.

For meditation and context:

RESPONSORIAL PSALM   Psalm 90:3–4, 5–6, 12–13, 14, 17 (95:8)

R. If today you hear his voice, harden not your hearts.

You turn man back to dust,
    saying, "Return, O children of men."
For a thousand years in your sight
    are as yesterday, now that it is past,
    or as a watch of the night.

You make an end of them in their sleep;
    the next morning they are like the
        changing grass,
which at dawn springs up anew,
    but by evening wilts and fades.

Teach us to number our days aright,
    that we may gain wisdom of heart.
Return, O LORD! How long?
    Have pity on your servants!

Fill us at daybreak with your kindness,
    that we may shout for joy and gladness all
        our days.
And may the gracious care of the LORD our
        God be ours;
    prosper the work of our hands for us!
    Prosper the work of our hands!

Colossians = kuh-LOSH-uhnz

A didactic reading that includes some of the most striking claims in all of St. Paul's letters.

Paul orients our gazes heavenward to begin, toward the glory.

Then he shifts our gazes downward, toward earthly passions.

Even emphasis on all of these problematic feelings.
This remains very good advice!

READING II   Colossians 3:1–5, 9–11

A reading from the Letter of Saint Paul to the Colossians

Brothers and **sisters**:
If you were **raised** with Christ, **seek** what is **above**,
    where **Christ** is seated at the **right** hand of **God**.
Think of what is **above**, **not** of what is on **earth**.
For you have **died**,
    and your life is **hidden** with **Christ** in **God**.
When **Christ** your life **appears**,
    then you **too** will appear with him in **glory**.

Put to **death**, then, the **parts** of you that are **earthly**:
    immorality, **impurity**, **passion**, **evil desire**,
    and the **greed** that is **idolatry**.
Stop **lying** to one another,
    since you have taken off the **old self** with its **practices**
    and have put on the **new self**,
    which is being **renewed**, for **knowledge**,
    in the **image** of its **creator**.

| READING II | This reading urges the baptized to seek not "what is of the earth," but rather the things above, where Christ reigns. The Greek for "seek," *phroneo*, also means to "think about," or "be intent on," or "set your mind on." The present tense verb form used here indicates non-stop searching, pondering, and being attentive to one's hidden life with Christ in God.

As Christians grow in Christ, they reject common misbehaviors that society ignores and allows to continue, evils whose ubiquity inures people to the harm going on around them. Today, Paul urges us to "put to death" immorality (Greek *porneia)*, impurity, passion, evil desire, and insatiable avarice. The baptized must also stop lying to one another. They must give up the accepted practices of speaking partial truths and spinning information to accomplish personal goals.

Finally, an unnegotiable Christian belief is that Christ lives in people of every nation and group. Consequently, whatever we say about and do to others, we say about and do to him. The categories of "us" and "them" do not exist in Christ. Neither may Christians label an entire ethnic group as barbarians (terrorists) or as inferiors because, for example, their culture and religion are different or they are less industrialized. In Paul's view, every evil practice hinders one's growth into an image or icon (Greek *eikona*) of the Creator.

| GOSPEL | The Gospel opens with a family quarrel about the division of an inheritance. Jesus uses the occasion to draw attention to the common mistaken notions that a person's life consists in what they possess, and that

This reading concludes with Paul's radicalism in full.
circumcision = sehr-kuhm-SIH-zhuhn
uncircumcision = uhn-sehr-kuhm-SIH-zhuhn
Scythian = SITH-ee-uhn
barbarian = bahr-BAYR-ee-uhn

Here there is not **Greek** and **Jew**,
  circumcision and **uncircumcision**,
  barbarian, **Scythian**, **slave**, **free**;
  but **Christ** is **all** and in **all**.

GOSPEL   Luke 12:13–21

A reading from the holy Gospel according to Luke

A narrative reading in which both a parable and speech from God are embedded, providing a variety of voices.

Someone in the crowd said to **Jesus**,
  "**Teacher**, tell my **brother** to share the **inheritance** with me."
He replied to him,
  "**Friend**, who appointed me as your **judge** and **arbitrator**?"
Then he said to the crowd,
  "Take **care** to guard against all **greed**,
  for though one may be **rich**,
  one's **life** does not consist of **possessions**."

arbitrator = AHR-bih-tray-ter

Jesus' parable expands on his advice to the crowd.

This parable includes speech within speech. There are enough narrative cues to keep straight who is speaking.

The rich man is speaking to himself.

Then he told them a parable.
"There was a **rich** man whose **land** produced a bountiful **harvest**.
He asked himself, 'What shall I **do**,
  for I do not have **space** to store my **harvest**?'
And he said, '**This** is what I shall do:
  I shall **tear down** my **barns** and build **larger ones**.
There I shall store all my **grain** and other goods
  and I shall say to myself, "**Now** as for **you**,
  you have **so many good things** stored up for many **years**,
  rest, **eat**, **drink**, be **merry**!" '
But God said to him,

God interrupts. Land heavy on "You fool."

  'You **fool**, this **night** your **life** will be **demanded** of you;
  and the **things** you have **prepared**, to **whom** will they **belong**?'
Thus will it be for **all** who store up **treasure** for themselves
  but are not **rich** in what **matters** to God."

---

possessions can ensure a good life. Jesus warns the crowd to guard against the constant urge to acquire more stuff because this habit distracts one from acquiring true riches.

In Jesus' view, as in Judaism, all that one has is a gift from God and is earmarked for divine purposes. The rich man does not get this. He does not realize that he is only the steward of a piece of land from which God brought forth a bountiful harvest. In his view, the crop is his alone. And so, he consults himself, not God, about what to do with it. To protect the harvest

and the rest of his belongings—here "many good things"—he decides to build a bigger barn.

The thrice-repeated Greek *psychae* in Luke 12:19–20 highlights how wrong-headed his thinking is. Though in some texts *psychae* can denote "soul," in others, as here, it denotes one's self or one's life. The rich man envisions the security he will feel when he has more storage space: "I shall say to myself (*psychae*), 'Self (*Psychae*), you have so many good things stored up for many years. Rest, eat, drink, and be merry.'" He imagines a future filled with one good

time after another. Then God breaks into his reverie, saying, "You fool, *this night* [not "many years" later] your life [*psychae*] will be demanded of you." The rich man's security evaporates. And what kind of eternal life will his possessions provide for him? E.N.

NINETEENTH SUNDAY IN ORDINARY TIME

An exhortatory reading that in short space accumulates impressive mystery.

> **TO KEEP IN MIND**
> Pause to break up separate thoughts, set apart significant statements, or indicate major shifts. Never pause in the middle of a thought. Your primary guide for pauses is punctuation.

adversaries = AD-vehr-sayr-eez

The mystery of this passage concentrates in the "holy children" offering "sacrifice" in "secret." No need to dispel the mystery. Allow it to spread out from your proclamation.

For meditation and context:

LECTIONARY #117

READING I   Wisdom 18:6–9

A reading from the Book of Wisdom

The **night** of the **passover** was known **beforehand** to
    our **fathers**,
that, with **sure knowledge** of the **oaths** in which they
    put their **faith**,
they might have **courage**.
Your **people** awaited the **salvation** of the **just**
    and the **destruction** of their **foes**.
For when you **punished** our adversaries,
    in this you **glorified** us whom you had **summoned**.
For in **secret** the holy **children** of the good
    were offering **sacrifice**
and **putting** into **effect** with one **accord** the
    divine institution.

RESPONSORIAL PSALM   Psalm 33:1, 12, 18–19, 20–22 (12b)

R. **Blessed the people the Lord has chosen to be his own.**

Exult, you just, in the LORD;
  praise from the upright is fitting.
Blessed the nation whose God is the LORD,
  the people he has chosen for his
    own inheritance.

See, the eyes of the LORD are upon those who
    fear him,
  upon those who hope for his kindness,
to deliver them from death

and preserve them in spite of famine.

Our soul waits for the LORD,
  who is our help and our shield.
May your kindness, O LORD, be upon us
  who have put our hope in you.

READING I   The people of God live by faith. They trust that God, often despite appearances to the contrary, is present and active in their midst. The author of Wisdom writes to a Jewish community in Alexandria, Egypt, at the turn of the BC–AD eras. During this period, the dominant Greek culture and its gods seem more relevant and effective to many Jews than their covenant-based culture and beliefs. The book of Wisdom reminds the Jews living in Alexandria that their God is the one who delivered their ancestors from Egypt.

Today's reading comes from Wisdom 11:2—19:22, a section in which the author draws on Israel's exodus traditions to demonstrate God's power and dependability. Here he cites the last plague that took place on the night of Passover. His point is that this event unfolded just as God had announced it beforehand through Moses.

The final verse describes how "the holy children of the good" await God's salvation. They resolutely worship God by living justly and by following the covenant directives. They reject the worldly wisdom and pastimes of the culture that surrounds

them. The last half of the final verse, omitted in today's reading, gives a motivation for such fidelity, namely "so that your holy ones should share alike the same blessings and dangers." Together, they keep each other's faith alive.

READING II   This passage defines faith as the realization of what is hoped for and the evidence of things that, though unseen, are nevertheless real—like God's dynamic presence in the human realm (Hebrews 11:6). The author cites creation as an example of "evidence of things

Hebrews = HEE-brooz
A didactic reading infused with exhortation and poetic persuasiveness.

The reading is organized by the repetition of "by faith"; use its repetition to structure your proclamation.

sojourned = SOH-jehrnd

READING II Hebrews 11:1–2, 8–19

A reading from the Letter to the Hebrews

[**Brothers** and **sisters:**
Faith is the realization of what is **hoped** for
and **evidence** of things not **seen**.
Because of it the **ancients** were well **attested**.

By **faith** Abraham obeyed when he was called
to go out to a **place**
that he was to **receive** as an **inheritance**;
he went **out**, not knowing where he was to **go**.
By **faith** he sojourned in the **promised land** as
in a **foreign country**,
dwelling in **tents** with **Isaac** and **Jacob**,
heirs of the same **promise**;
for he was looking **forward** to the city with **foundations**,
whose **architect** and **maker** is **God**.
By **faith** he received power to **generate**,
even though he was **past** the normal **age**
—and Sarah **herself** was **sterile**—
for he thought that the one who had made the **promise**
was **trustworthy**.
So it **was** that there came **forth** from one **man**,
himself as good as **dead**,
descendants as **numerous** as the **stars** in the **sky**
and as **countless** as the **sands** on the **seashore**.]

Even emphasis on "All these died" and "faith."

All these died in **faith**.
They did not **receive** what had been **promised**
but **saw** it and **greeted** it from **afar**
and **acknowledged** themselves to be **strangers** and **aliens**
on **earth**,
for **those** who speak thus **show** that they are **seeking**
a **homeland**. »

unseen." He explains that by faith we understand that the *visible* universe was ordered by the word of the invisible yet real God (Hebrews 11:3).

Abraham and Sarah are examples par excellence of people who live by faith. Abraham trusted God's word that he would have countless descendants and receive a heavenly inheritance—things that only God could give. At God's command, he left his homeland and lived the rest of his life as a resident alien in a strange land. (In the United States, he would have a green card.) Circumstances could have eroded Abraham

and Sarah's faith and convinced them either to return home or to fit into the culture around them. They, however, chose not to look back and trusted that God would give them a family. Because of their deep faith, God is "not ashamed" to be called their God. What a tribute!

The challenges to the couple's faith seemed endless. Their childbearing years pass by, and still they have no son. And then, when at long last Isaac came forth from Abraham, who was "as good as dead," God further tests his faith by asking him to give Isaac back. By this time, however,

Abraham trusts that God will in some unexpected and unimaginable way be faithful, that God can raise his son from the dead. The author of Hebrews interprets God's sparing of Isaac as a symbol of the resurrection of Christ, the act that makes the ultimate fulfilment of all divine promises possible—for those who believe.

GOSPEL In the passage preceding today's Gospel, Jesus assures his disciples that the Father knows and provides for all their needs. Now he tells them to stop being afraid, for the

If they had been **thinking** of the land from which they had **come**,
 they would have had **opportunity** to **return**.
But **now** they desire a better **homeland**, a **heavenly** one.
Therefore, God is not **ashamed** to be called their **God**,
 for he has prepared a **city** for them.

By **faith** Abraham, when **put** to the **test**, offered up **Isaac**,
 and he who had received the **promises** was ready
  to offer his **only** son,
 of **whom** it was **said**,
 "Through **Isaac** descendants shall bear your **name**."
He reasoned that **God** was able to raise even from the **dead**,
 and he received **Isaac** back as a **symbol**.

[Shorter: Hebrews 11:1–2, 8–12 (see brackets)]

GOSPEL   Luke 12:32–48

A reading from the holy Gospel according to Luke

[**Jesus** said to his **disciples**:]
 "**Do not** be **afraid** any **longer**, little flock,
  for your **Father** is pleased to give you the **kingdom**.
 Sell your **belongings** and give **alms**.
 Provide **money bags** for yourselves that do not **wear out**,
  an inexhaustible **treasure** in **heaven**
  that no **thief** can reach nor **moth** destroy.
 For where your **treasure** is, there also will your **heart** be.

["**Gird** your loins and **light** your lamps
  and be like **servants** who **await** their master's **return**
   from a **wedding**,
  ready to open **immediately** when he **comes** and **knocks**.
 Blessed are those **servants**
  whom the master finds **vigilant** on his **arrival**.
 Amen, I say to you, he will **gird** himself,
  have them **recline** at table, and **proceed** to **wait** on them.

Side notes:

"Therefore" suggests the argument is coming to its conclusion. However, it's not.

This final use of "by faith" signals the conclusion of this argument, returning to the example of Abraham.

A largely didactic reading embedded in a narrative and that begins with elements of an exhortation. In addition to a parable, the reading includes an explanation of the parable with a difficult example. Best to embrace the difficulty.
The reading begins with helpful advice.

And then shifts into a parable of sorts, emphasizing preparation.

gird = gerd

Father is also pleased to give them the kingdom. Jesus turns the thoughts of his hearers to the value of this great gift by contrasting its riches with the possessions that people acquire and then fret about maintaining and keeping safe. He tells his disciples to sell their stuff, give alms, and then work for lasting heavenly riches. When he says, "where your treasure is, there also will your heart be," he means that whatever preoccupies us, sustains our emotions, and engages our will indicates what is truly most important to us.

The rest of the Gospel shows disciples what they should be afraid of, namely, that when Jesus returns, he will find them going about their business instead of his. In this passage, faithful servants are those who are ready for action. They "gird their loins," a phrase that means to bind up excess clothing so that one can move more freely and go to work. By extension, the phrase means to prepare oneself to do God's will each day by removing whatever thoughts or excuses hinder their doing so. Faithful servants also keep their lamps lit to light the way for Jesus' return. They are ready to open the door the moment he knocks. What a surprise they will get when Jesus exchanges roles and immediately becomes their servant, when he "girds" himself, has *them* recline at table, and waits on *them*.

Jesus answers Peter's question indirectly, making it applicable to both community leaders and to all his disciples. All are in some way responsible for taking care of the needs of someone else, a responsibility which in modern times extends to the global community. All, like the master of the

And should he **come** in the second or third **watch**
and find them **prepared** in this **way**,
blessed are those **servants**.
Be sure of **this**:
if the **master** of the house had known the **hour**
when the thief was **coming**,
he would not have let his **house** be broken **into**.
You also must be **prepared**, for at an hour you do not **expect**,
the **Son** of **Man** will **come**."]

Then Peter said,
"**Lord**, is this parable meant for **us** or for **everyone**?"
And the Lord replied,
"**Who**, then, is the faithful and prudent **steward**
whom the **master** will put in charge of his **servants**
to distribute the **food allowance** at the proper **time**?
Blessed is that **servant** whom his **master** on arrival finds **doing** so.
Truly, I say to you, the **master** will put the **servant**
in **charge** of all his **property**.
But if that **servant** says to **himself**,
'My **master** is delayed in **coming**,'
and begins to **beat** the menservants and the maidservants,
to **eat** and **drink** and get **drunk**,
then that servant's **master** will come
on an **unexpected day** and at an **unknown hour**
and will **punish** the servant **severely**
and **assign** him a place with the **unfaithful**.
That **servant** who knew his master's **will**
but did not make **preparations** nor act in **accord** with his **will**
shall be beaten **severely**;
and the servant who was **ignorant** of his master's **will**
but acted in a way **deserving** of a severe **beating**
shall be beaten only **lightly**.
Much will be required of the person **entrusted** with **much**,
and still **more** will be demanded of the person **entrusted**
with **more**."

[Shorter: Luke 12:35–40 (see brackets)]

The tone shifts when Peter asks the meaning of the parable.

Here the tone turns ugly when Jesus recommends that an underprepared servant be severely beaten. A sincere question to ask as you proclaim is "How is the Kingdom of Heaven like this?"

household in Jesus' parable, serve and must one day answer to the household's lord.

Like the second reading, this Gospel shows how the delayed fulfillment of divine promises—here that Jesus will return—can wear down disciples' faith and weaken their dedication to the mission that he gives them. Some, for example, begin to mistreat other members of the Lord's household, or are sidetracked by human pleasures. They "eat and drink and get drunk." Such actions display a lack both of

faith in Jesus and of conviction that he is alive and will indeed return.

Jesus warns his disciples that those who live as if this world were all there is, who seek its treasures and pleasures instead of heavenly ones, will be shocked when he shows up and judges them, removing all delusions that they are his disciples. He will assign them an unchangeable and eternal place with the unfaithful. Their punishment will be harsher than that of other wrongdoers who were ignorant of Jesus' will.

Jesus reminds us today that discipleship is extremely demanding and that the kingdom is a gift whose value exceeds all others. More is demanded of Jesus' disciples than of other people—more service, more "slavery." Blessed are they whom he finds ready to work and with their lamps lit when he returns. E.N.

TWENTIETH SUNDAY IN ORDINARY TIME

LECTIONARY #120

READING I   Jeremiah 38:4–6, 8–10

A reading from the Book of the Prophet Jeremiah

In **those** days, the princes said to the **king:**
"**Jeremiah** ought to be put to **death;**
   he is **demoralizing** the **soldiers** who are **left** in this **city,**
   and all the **people,** by **speaking** such **things** to them;
   he is not **interested** in the **welfare** of our **people,**
   but in their **ruin.**"
King **Zedekiah** answered: "He is in **your** power";
   for the **king** could do **nothing** with them.
And so they **took Jeremiah**
   and **threw** him into the **cistern** of Prince **Malchiah,**
   which was in the **quarters** of the **guard,**
   letting him **down** with **ropes.**
There was no **water** in the **cistern,** only **mud,**
   and Jeremiah **sank** into the **mud.**

Ebed-melech, a court official,
   went there from the **palace** and said to him:
   "My lord king,
   these **men** have been at **fault**
   in **all** they have **done** to the **prophet Jeremiah,**
   casting him into the **cistern.**
He will **die** of **famine** on the **spot,**
   for there is **no more food** in the **city.**"

Jeremiah = jayr-uh-MĪ-uh

A narrative reading consisting of four parts in which a decision is made to throw the prophet Jeremiah into a cistern (where he will die), and then the decision is reversed.

demoralizing = dih-MOHR-uhl-iz-ing

Zedekiah = zed-uh-KĪ-uh
King Zedekiah's words are at the core of the reading. Emphasize "your."

Malchiah = mal-KĪ-uh

cistern = SIS-tehrn

Ebed-melech = ee-bihd-MEE-lihk

Even emphasis, "My lord king."

famine = FAM-ihn

READING I Today's Scriptures spotlight the struggles that come to those who choose to live by God's word rather than by traditional human advice and practice. The first reading shows the prophet Jeremiah suffering for relaying an unpopular message from the Lord to his contemporaries in Jerusalem. He is telling them that they should submit to the Babylonians (Jeremiah 38:1–3), who have conquered but not yet destroyed the city. Jerusalem is under siege. Food and water supplies are dwindling.

Zedekiah is a weak king who vacillates between submitting to and trying to throw off Babylonian rule. Here, he heeds his royal counsellors who complain that Jeremiah's preaching submission to the Babylonians "makes the hands of the soldiers grow slack" (the text says literally in Hebrew) and lowers the people's morale, that the prophet is unpatriotic and a traitor (Jeremiah 38:13–15). The king puts the prophet's fate in the hands of his royal advisers.

They take Jeremiah and throw him into a cistern, a "jail cell" of the biblical world.

The author's words, like a camera, zoom in on Jeremiah's miserable situation. We watch his enemies lower him by ropes down into the pit that no longer contains water. Only filthy sediment covers its floor toward the end of the dry season. We watch the prophet slowly sink into the mire.

The Lord comes to Jeremiah's aid through a Cushite who serves in Zedekiah's court. When this foreigner reports that the king's other counsellors are endangering the prophet's life, the king reverses their orders. The gifted narrator leaves us with

Cushite = KOOSH-ĭt

Slight pause between "Jeremiah" and "out."

Then the **king** ordered **Ebed-melech** the **Cushite**
  to take **three men** along with him,
    and draw the **prophet Jeremiah out** of the **cistern**
      before he should **die.**

For meditation and context:

TO KEEP IN MIND
Read the Scripture passage and its commentary in *Workbook*. Then read it from your Bible, including what comes before and after it, so that you understand the context.

RESPONSORIAL PSALM   Psalm 40:2, 3, 4, 18 (14b)

R. Lord, come to my aid!

I have waited, waited for the LORD,
  and he stooped toward me.

The LORD heard my cry.
He drew me out of the pit of destruction,
  out of the mud of the swamp;
he set my feet upon a crag;
  he made firm my steps.

And he put a new song into my mouth,
  a hymn to our God.
Many shall look on in awe
  and trust in the LORD.

Though I am afflicted and poor,
  yet the LORD thinks of me.
You are my help and my deliverer;
  O my God, hold not back!

Hebrews = HEE-brooz

An exhortatory reading whose message is encouragement.

READING II   Hebrews 12:1–4

A reading from the letter to the Hebrews

Brothers and **sisters**:
Since we are **surrounded** by so great a cloud of **witnesses**,
  let us **rid** ourselves of every **burden** and **sin** that **clings** to us
  and **persevere** in running the **race** that **lies before** us
  while keeping our **eyes fixed** on **Jesus**,
    the **leader** and **perfecter** of **faith**.
For the **sake** of the **joy** that lay **before** him
  he **endured** the cross, **despising** its **shame**,
    and has **taken** his seat at the **right** of the **throne** of God.
Consider how he endured such **opposition** from **sinners**,
  in order that you may not grow **weary** and lose **heart**.
In your **struggle** against **sin**
  you have not yet **resisted** to the **point** of shedding **blood**.

Endurance leads to joy. Emphasize "endured."

An encouraging tone at the end—the struggle against sin continues.

---

the poignant image of Jeremiah's rescue, four men drawing up the Lord's prophet out of that dark, dank hole.

<table><tr><td>READING II</td></tr></table> The author of Hebrews reminds the baptized that committing their life to Jesus will entail suffering, but also that no one suffers alone. He draws our attention to that great cloud of witnesses who surround us at all times and inspire us to "rid ourselves of every burden and sin that clings to us." We must persevere in the unique course that God assigns us. The Greek for "race," *agōna*,

denotes a contest that demands all one's physical and mental resources. It is a race toward a prize that a person wants more than anything else. We keep our eyes on Christ Jesus at the finish line—Christ who persevered, enduring even the cross *for the sake of the joy* that lay before him, despising its shame.

In this passage, the baptized follow Jesus' example by enduring the opposition of those who rely on human wisdom and ways rather than God's word. Hard as our struggle might be, the author points out that few have yet to resist (Greek *antagōnizomai,*

a verb form of *agōna*) sin to the point of shedding blood—as Jesus did.

<table><tr><td>GOSPEL</td></tr></table> In this Gospel, Jesus does not aim to comfort but rather to jar the crowds out of their tepid interest in him and in his mission to change their life forever. As Jesus approaches Jerusalem, he speaks for the third time of his coming passion. In the Greek, the sentences in Jesus' prediction begin with—and thus emphasize—the nouns "fire" and "baptism." He says literally: "*Fire*, I came to throw upon the earth. . . . [And] *a baptism,* I have

GOSPEL   Luke 12:49–53

A reading from the holy Gospel according to Luke

Jesus said to his **disciples**:
    "I have **come** to set the **earth** on **fire**,
        and how I **wish** it were **already blazing**!
There is a **baptism** with which I must be **baptized**,
        and how **great** is my **anguish** until it is **accomplished**!
Do you **think** that I have come to establish **peace** on the **earth**?
No, I tell you, but rather **division**.
From **now on** a household of **five** will be **divided**,
        three against **two** and **two** against **three**;
        a **father** will be divided against his **son**
        and a **son** against his **father**,
        a **mother** against her **daughter**
        and a **daughter** against her **mother**,
        a **mother-in-law** against her **daughter-in-law**
        and a **daughter-in-law** against her **mother-in-law**."

An exhortatory reading consisting entirely of Jesus' speech and that includes a challenging, even vexing, teaching. Proclaiming this Gospel reading requires some care. It begins with one of Jesus' most mysterious declarations.

Allow a harshness and exasperation to color your tone as you ask this question.

These divisions and oppositions: There is no harmonious way to proclaim them.

---

to be baptized with." The evangelist Luke associates fire with divine judgment (Luke 3:9; 3:17; 9:54) and the Holy Spirit (Luke 3:16; Acts 2:3). Baptism refers to Jesus' coming ordeal. He realizes that his death is "in the cards," that his enemies plan to get rid of him. He is in anguish until they put their plot into action, until he sets ablaze that cleansing fire that will open the way to life in God's kingdom. "Fire" and "baptism" are the images that Jesus uses to break through the crowd's casual attention and skepticism that he is who he claims and can do what he promises.

Jesus' coming in the flesh forever disrupted traditional societal patterns and practices. The crowds are not getting this, so Jesus (I imagine in exasperation) asks, "Did you think *peace* I came to give the earth? No, . . . rather division." Jesus seems desperate that his disciples understand that he does not call them to a tranquil life, but one like his own. He seeks bold followers who do not put out fires but keep the fire that he set ablaze, who do not shy away from the interpersonal conflicts that attend his presence and work, but trust that his Spirit is working with them.

The detailed list of ruptured family relationships immerses hearers in the wrenching personal consequences that can accompany living one's life with the Lord. Disciples must expect that commitment to Jesus can change even their most cherished relationships. E.N.

THE ASSUMPTION OF THE BLESSED VIRGIN MARY: VIGIL

LECTIONARY #621

Chronicles = KRAH-nih-k*ls

A narrative reading in which the Ark of the Covenant is presented to the Israelites. There is a solemn and supernatural quality to this presentation.

Aaron = AYR-uhn
Levites = LEE-vĭts

lyres = lĭrz
cymbals = SIM-buhlz
Give even emphasis to all of the musical instruments listed.

Ritual solemnity characterizes the conclusion to this reading.

TO KEEP IN MIND
Pause after you announce the book of the Bible at the beginning of the reading. Pause again after the reading, before you proclaim the concluding statement ("The Word of the Lord" or "The Gospel of the Lord").

READING I   1 Chronicles 15:3–4, 15–16; 16:1–2

A reading from the first Book of Chronicles

David assembled **all Israel** in **Jerusalem** to bring the
    ark of the L ORD
    to the **place** that he had **prepared** for it.
David also called together the sons of **Aaron** and the **Levites**.

The **Levites** bore the ark of **God** on their **shoulders** with **poles**,
    as **Moses** had ordained according to the **word** of the L ORD.

David commanded the **chiefs** of the **Levites**
    to appoint their **kinsmen** as **chanters**,
    to play on musical **instruments**, **harps**, **lyres**, and **cymbals**,
    to make a **loud sound** of **rejoicing**.

They brought **in** the ark of **God** and **set** it within the **tent**
    which **David** had **pitched** for it.
Then they offered up **burnt offerings** and **peace offerings** to God.
When **David** had finished offering up the **burnt offerings** and
    peace offerings,
    he blessed the **people** in the **name** of the L ORD.

READING I   Today's reading from 1 Chronicles continues the story of the transfer of the Ark of the Covenant to its final permanent place in the Temple in Jerusalem. We should recall the encounter between God and David in 2 Samuel, in which God told David that only God could build a house suitable for his dwelling (2 Samuel 7:1–16). The major difference between the transfer of the Ark in 2 Samuel and here in 1 Chronicles is that in the latter story, God has fully formed the Israelites into his own household. After many trials and tribulations, as well as bat-

tles with troublesome neighbors, the Israelites have proven themselves worthy for God to dwell in their midst.

David spares no expense in welcoming God's presence in the Ark to its resting place in Jerusalem. First, he assembles the entire tribe of Israel together for the event. He instructs the Levites to bear the Ark upon their shoulders. And he fills the city with every sound from musical instruments, chanting, and the "loud sound of rejoicing." Offerings are made before the tent that covers the Ark, and finally, David blesses the people in God's name. David

provides well for a liturgy filled with hope and joy, as God takes his rightful place at the head of his people.

READING II   Paul is writing to a community that has begun to question the truth of resurrection and to engage in debate as to what will happen to our earthly bodies after death. For Paul, death simply loses its meaning in light of Christ's triumph. In answering Hosea's question "Where, O death, is your sting?" Paul states that "the sting of death is sin." Paul understands sin to be spiritual separation

For meditation and context:

RESPONSORIAL PSALM   Psalm 132:6–7, 9–10, 13–14 (8)

R. Lord, go up to the place of your rest, you and the ark of your holiness.

Behold, we heard of it in Ephrathah;
  we found it in the fields of Jaar.
Let us enter into his dwelling,
  let us worship at his footstool.

May your priests be clothed with justice;
  let your faithful ones shout merrily for joy.

For the sake of David your servant,
  reject not the plea of your anointed.

For the LORD has chosen Zion;
  he prefers her for his dwelling.
"Zion is my resting place forever;
  in her will I dwell, for I prefer her."

READING II   1 Corinthians 15:54b–57

Corinthians = kohr-IN-thee-uhnz
A didactic reading, the core of which is a question likely very familiar to your assembly. Don't overdramatize your proclamation. Treat the questions and their interpretation evenly.
immortality = ihm-ohr-TAL-ih-tee

Don't overdo these questions. Allow them to sound out to your assembly.

A reading from the first Letter of Saint Paul to the Corinthians

Brothers and **sisters**:
When **that** which is **mortal clothes** itself with **immortality**,
  then the **word** that is **written** shall come **about**:

> **Death** *is swallowed up in* **victory**.
> **Where**, *O death, is your* **victory**?
> **Where**, *O death, is your* **sting**?

Recite these interpretations like the explanations they are.

The **sting** of **death** is **sin**,
  and the **power** of **sin** is the **law**.
But **thanks** be to **God** who **gives** us the **victory**
  through our **Lord Jesus Christ**.

GOSPEL   Luke 11:27–28

A very short narrative reading—perhaps the shortest in all of Year C. It consists of a statement of setting, followed by something a woman in the crowd says, and concludes with Jesus contradicting and extending the woman's claim. It has the rhythm of a joke—though with a very different intent.

A reading from the holy Gospel according to Luke

While **Jesus** was **speaking**,
  a **woman** from the crowd called out and **said** to him,
  "**Blessed** is the **womb** that **carried** you
  and the **breasts** at **which** you **nursed**."
He replied,
  "**Rather**, blessed are **those**
  who hear the **word** of **God** and **observe** it."

---

from God. But Christ has united that which was formerly separated by his death and resurrection. Because sin has been destroyed by Christ's display of love and obedience to the Father, all believers experience the reversal of the age-old curse of Adam and Eve. We are once again able to live fully with God.

  Paul's teaching on the resurrection turns to thanksgiving in the final verse. Those who participate in Christ's victory through the gift of faith experience the defeat of three opponents to eternal life: death, sin, and the law. Christians who abide by the law of Christ know true freedom from sin and death, directing their ceaseless thanks to God.

GOSPEL   On his way to Jerusalem, Jesus has been discovered as having the power to expel demons. Some question where it comes from. However, one woman in the crowd yells out words of blessing for Jesus. She recognizes the source: a mother who sacrificed for her child both in the womb and in infancy.

  Jesus' reply is not a rejection of the woman's blessing but a teaching the nature of power and authority in God's kingdom. Those who hear the word of God and act according to it are the ones who are truly blessed. Jesus knows that although he may have succeeded in casting evil out from the hearts of those possessed by demons, the far greater strength is to respond to God's mercy by living a life of discipleship. Mary is the first among disciples: she heard the word of God and internalized it through her life of obedience to God's will. S.W.

THE ASSUMPTION OF THE BLESSED VIRGIN MARY: DAY

LECTIONARY #622

READING I   Revelation 11:19a; 12:1–6a, 10ab

A reading from the Book of Revelation

God's **temple** in **heaven** was **opened**,
   and the **ark** of his **covenant** could be **seen** in the **temple**.

A great **sign** appeared in the **sky**, a woman **clothed** with the **sun**,
   with the **moon** under her **feet**,
and on her **head** a crown of **twelve stars**.
She was with **child** and wailed **aloud** in **pain** as she **labored** to
      give **birth**.
Then **another sign** appeared in the **sky**;
   it was a **huge red dragon**, with **seven heads** and **ten horns**,
   and on its **heads** were **seven diadems**.
Its **tail** swept away a **third** of the **stars** in the **sky**
   and **hurled** them **down** to the **earth**.
Then the **dragon** stood before the **woman about** to give **birth**,
   to devour her **child** when she **gave birth**.
She gave **birth** to a **son**, a **male child**,
   destined to **rule** all the **nations** with an **iron rod**.
Her **child** was caught up to **God** and his **throne**.
The woman **herself** fled into the **desert**
   where she had a **place prepared** by **God**. »

A powerful and visionary narrative reading filled with signs, heavenly voices, and mythical beasts. Much is compressed in this reading; proclaim it straightforwardly, in an even, authoritative tone.
covenant = KUHV-eh-n*nt

The first sign—the pregnant woman who appears in the sky. She represents Mary, in part.

The second sign—the huge red dragon. The dragon represents Satan, in part.

diadems = DĪ-uh-dems

Slight pause between "woman" and "about."
devour = dih-VOWR
The signs converge—the dragon interferes with the woman, whose child represents Christ, in part.

Slight pause between "place" and "prepared."

READING I   The Book of Revelation was composed toward the end of the first century AD. Nearly seventy years have passed since the death of Jesus; Christians who witnessed his death and heard the first proclamation of his Resurrection have died; and the Church has begun to experience persecution at the hands of the Roman Empire. Revelation thus depicts a cosmic conflict between the powers of this world and the authority of God.

Three figures serve as the focal points of this apocalyptic story: the woman, the child, and the dragon. The dragon repre- sents the evil of the age as he stands ready to devour the woman's newborn child. Both the woman and the child can be seen as significant to Hebrew history as well as to Christians of the new age. The woman takes on the characteristics of Israel itself, for it is Israel as a nation that would bring the Messiah into the world. Just as the woman fled into the desert, so Israel went down to Egypt to recover from famine and to discover God's protection. While Christians might want to designate Mary as the unnamed woman, it is more likely that the author intended the character to repre- sent the Church. The Church becomes the new Israel who is destined to see the salva- tion and power that comes from God's Anointed One.

Certainly, the child must be seen as the Messiah born into this world. Imme- diately God demonstrates his protection and care for the child as he carries him to heaven. While the evangelists Matthew and Luke wrote infancy narratives detailing the birth of the Messiah in lowly environs, the Revelation account portrays God's victory in combating the world from the start of the child's birth. There can be no doubting

Conclude with a slightly elevated authoritative tone.

Then I heard a **loud voice** in **heaven** say:
"**Now** have **salvation** and **power** come,
    and the **Kingdom** of our **God**
    and the **authority** of his **Anointed** One."

For meditation and context:

RESPONSORIAL PSALM   Psalm 45:10, 11, 12, 16 (10bc)

R. The queen stands at your right hand, arrayed in gold.

The queen takes her place at your
    right hand in gold of Ophir.

Hear, O daughter, and see; turn your ear,
    forget your people and your father's house.

So shall the king desire your beauty;
    for he is your lord.

They are borne in with gladness and joy;
    they enter the palace of the king.

READING II   1 Corinthians 15:20–27

Corinthians = kohr-IN-thee-uhnz

A reading from the first Letter of Saint Paul to the Corinthians

A didactic reading in which St. Paul makes a subtle but forceful argument about Christ's reign over death.

Brothers and **sisters**:
Christ has been **raised** from the **dead**,
    the **firstfruits** of **those** who have fallen **asleep**.
For since **death** came through **man**,
    the resurrection of the **dead** came **also** through man.
For **just** as in **Adam** all die,
    so **too** in **Christ** shall all be brought to **life**,
    but **each one** in proper **order**:
Christ the firstfruits;
then, at his **coming**, those who **belong** to Christ;
then comes the **end**,
    when he hands **over** the **Kingdom** to his **God** and **Father**,
    when he has **destroyed** every **sovereignty**
    and every **authority** and **power**.
For he must **reign** until he has put all his
        enemies under his **feet**.
The last **enemy** to be **destroyed** is **death**,
    for "he subjected **everything** under his **feet**."

Beginning here, Paul's argument is elaborated in a sequence that begins with Adam, proceeds to Christ, and then eventually to the Kingdom of God. Lay each statement like a plank for a dock you are constructing.

sovereignty = SOV-ehr-uhn-tee *or* SOV-ruhn-tee

Slight emphasis on "death."

---

the authority of this one who has come into the world. Similarly, since Christ's authority has been passed over to the Church, the Christian community has the power and authority to withstand any persecution and evil that the world wishes to inflict upon it.

READING II   Paul devotes the fifteenth chapter of his letter to the Christians at Corinth to teachings on the nature of the resurrection. He was deeply troubled at the discovery that some Christians were beginning to depart from following Christ because his return seemed

delayed and his resurrection was beginning to be held suspect. What was at stake was the misunderstanding that Christ's reign may have come to an end with his death rather than continuing until the final resurrection of the just, which would prove definitively the power of God's kingdom. Here, in the context of that teaching on the resurrection, Paul discusses three primary actors in the history of salvation: Christ, Adam, and death. Each has a very important role in the saga of redemption.

By rising from the dead, Christ becomes the "firstfruits" of all those who

have gone before him. He sets the pattern for where the dead are to go. In a sense, Christ initiates a great offering of souls to the Father, even though he alone has risen while the dead still await the day. Where Christ has gone, we hope to follow. Christ's selfless death has broken our allegiance to the sin of Adam, who failed to listen to the Lord's voice, to be obedient, and to resist the temptation to be just like God himself.

When the day comes for Christ to return in glory, he will complete the resurrection in proper order. Christ himself will be the first to return to his Father, then all

GOSPEL   Luke 1:39–56

A reading from the holy Gospel according to Luke

Mary set **out**
    and **traveled** to the **hill country** in **haste**
    to a **town** of **Judah**,
    where she **entered** the **house** of **Zechariah**
    and greeted **Elizabeth**.
When **Elizabeth** heard Mary's **greeting**,
    the **infant leaped** in her **womb**,
    and **Elizabeth**, **filled** with the Holy **Spirit**,
    cried **out** in a **loud voice** and **said**,
    "**Blessed** are **you** among **women**,
    and **blessed** is the **fruit** of your **womb**.
And **how** does this **happen** to me,
    that the **mother** of my **Lord** should come to **me**?
For at the **moment** the **sound** of your **greeting** reached my **ears**,
    the **infant** in my **womb** leaped for **joy**.
Blessed are **you** who **believed**
    that what was **spoken** to **you** by the **Lord**
    would be **fulfilled**."

And Mary said:

    "My **soul** proclaims the **greatness** of the **Lord**;
        my **spirit rejoices** in God my **Savior**
        for he has **looked** with **favor** on his **lowly servant**.
    From **this day** all **generations** will call me **blessed**:
        the **Almighty** has done **great things** for me
        and **holy** is his **Name**.
    He has **mercy** on those who **fear** him
        in **every generation**.
    He has shown the **strength** of his **arm**,
        and has scattered the **proud** in their **conceit**. »

A narrative reading of sublime beauty from St. Luke's nativity story.

Zechariah = zek-uh-RĪ-uh

Slight pause between "infant" and "leaped."

The words of the "Hail Mary." Proclaim them as if saying these words for the first time.

Here Elizabeth extends the words of her praise of Mary.

The words of the "Magnificat." As with the words of the "Hail Mary" above, proclaim them as if saying these words for the first time.

conceit = kuhn-SEET

---

those who have been grafted onto the life of Christ, and finally, Christ will destroy "every sovereignty and every authority and power." In the end there can be no supreme being or institution able to compete with God's final implementation of the kingdom. This includes the third personified character in Paul's story, death, "the last enemy to be destroyed." This will complete the mission for which Christ was sent into the world. He will have successfully destroyed the one thing that keeps us from perpetual union with our God, a punishment inflicted upon the human race as a curse for their

disobedience. Fully united with the "first-fruits," Christians will be given eternal participation in divine life.

GOSPEL   Mary's visitation to her cousin Elizabeth is really the meeting of two covenants. Each bears in her womb a son who will serve as a seal to a covenant. John will bring an end to the first covenant by being the forerunner of Jesus, who will seal the covenant God makes with creation through his death on the cross and subsequent resurrection. In Mary's greeting of Elizabeth, the two cove-

nants are joined, and the blessing of God's grace can now be detected and proclaimed.

Elizabeth raises her voice loudly and exclaims: "Blessed are you among women, and blessed is the fruit of your womb." John leaps for joy in his mother's womb, as the lesser meets the greater. What is it that makes Mary "blessed" in the eyes of Elizabeth? Surely it is the fullness of the Holy Spirit, who also filled the heart of Mary, making it possible for her to reply to the angel, "may it be done to me according to your word." It is the Holy Spirit that opens eyes

Note that as the reading concludes, in a hymn-like way, each line ends with an emphasized word. Let that rhythm carry your proclamation.

He has cast down the **mighty** from their **thrones**,
  and has **lifted up** the **lowly**.
He has filled the **hungry** with good **things**,
  and the **rich** he has sent away **empty**.
He has come to the **help** of his servant **Israel**
  for he has **remembered** his promise of **mercy**,
  the **promise** he made to our **fathers**,
  to **Abraham** and his children **forever**."

Mary remained with her about **three months**
  and then **returned** to her **home**.

and changes hearts, creating the desire to be fully responsive to the will of God.

Elizabeth's prayer of blessing now turns to Mary's song of thanksgiving. The Magnificat is Mary's affirmation of her commitment to being God's servant and her prophetic announcement of how God will overturn the ways of this world: the proud will be scattered, the mighty will be brought down, the rich will hunger, and the poor will be lifted up and filled "with good things." Surely the presence of God's Son growing within her causes Mary to see the world in a whole new light. She is blessed to provide a dwelling place for the means of the world's salvation. She is the ark of the New Covenant. Mary remains with Elizabeth for about three months, just enough time to witness the birth of John, who will herald the coming of the Lord. S.W.

TWENTY-FIRST SUNDAY IN ORDINARY TIME

LECTIONARY #123

READING I   Isaiah 66:18–21

A reading from the Book of the Prophet Isaiah

Thus says the LORD:
I know their **works** and their **thoughts**,
    and I come to gather **nations** of every **language**;
    they shall **come** and see my **glory**.
I will set a **sign among** them;
    from **them** I will send **fugitives** to the **nations**:
    to **Tarshish**, **Put** and **Lud**, **Mosoch**, **Tubal** and **Javan**,
    to the **distant coastlands**
    that have never **heard** of my **fame**, or **seen** my **glory**;
    and they shall **proclaim** my **glory** among the **nations**.
They shall bring **all** your **brothers** and **sisters** from **all** the nations
    as an **offering** to the LORD,
    on **horses** and in **chariots**, in **carts**, upon **mules**
        and **dromedaries**,
    to **Jerusalem**, my holy **mountain**, says the LORD,
    just as the **Israelites** bring their **offering**
    to the **house** of the LORD in clean **vessels**.
Some of these I will take as **priests** and **Levites**, says the LORD.

Isaiah = ī-ZAY-uh

An exhortatory reading of rich poetic power. The words of God announced in this reading are in the future tense. A mood of anticipation pervades.

Slight pause between "sign" and "among."
fugitives = FYOO-jih-tihvz
Tarshish = TAHR-shihsh
Put = poot
Lud = luhd
Mosoch = MOH-sok
Tubal = TOO-buhl
Javan = JAY-vuhn
Proclaim all these names slowly; savor them.
Slight pause between "distant" and "coastlands."

Dromedaries = DROM-eh-dayr-eez = camels

The reading concludes on a note of anticipation that hangs in the air.

READING I This passage echoes a central theme of the book of Isaiah, namely, that Israel's God is the Lord of all nations. The Lord knows how all people think and act, and uses this knowledge to accomplish divine plans. In this reading, Israelites and people from other nations—all of whom survived Babylon's temporary domination of their world—travel to Jerusalem. This gathering of diverse peoples on the Lord's holy mountain is a sign of the divine involvement in international affairs and a manifestation of the Lord's "glory" (Hebrew *kabod*).

Isaiah compares the animals and vehicles that will transport Israel's new brothers and sisters to Jerusalem to the purified vessels that carry the Israelites' offerings to the temple—a comparison that presents the foreigners' journey as a sacred procession into the Lord's presence. After experiencing the divine glory, the survivors proclaim it to other nations.

READING II The author of Hebrews reminds us that life in Christ does not come naturally, but requires life-long training. One element of this train-ing is the sufferings that are part of every life. Christ's followers need to accept this "discipline," here emphasized by the thrice-repeated Greek noun *paideia*, which can also denote "training," "correction," or "guidance." The author's use of *paideia* presents the spiritual life as a continuous workout. Divine training sessions—all the struggles that arise in one's daily routines and human interactions—correct bad habits and activate the unique charisms that every person receives in baptism.

The opening verse urges us not to disdain or disregard the Lord's discipline or

For meditation and context:

An exhortatory reading—"exhortation" appears in the first line!—that also makes a complex argument that takes some care to express.
Exhortation = ehg-zohr-TAY-shuhn

The argument circles around an expression of "discipline," which is used four times in a short space. Since it doesn't always mean exactly the same thing each time it is spoken, take some time to register its subtleties.

Slight pause between "peaceful" and "fruit."

Slight pause between "straight" and "paths."

RESPONSORIAL PSALM   Psalm 117:1, 2 (Mark 16:15)

R. Go out to all the world and tell the Good News.
or R. Alleluia.

Praise the LORD, all you nations;
    glorify him, all you peoples!

For steadfast is his kindness toward us,
    and the fidelity of the LORD
    endures forever.

READING II   Hebrews 12:5–7, 11–13

A reading from the Letter to the Hebrews

Brothers and **sisters**,
You have **forgotten** the **exhortation** addressed to you as
        children:
    "My **son**, do not disdain the **discipline** of the **Lord**
        or lose **heart** when **reproved** by him;
    for **whom** the Lord **loves**, he **disciplines**;
        he **scourges** every **son** he **acknowledges**."
Endure your **trials** as "**discipline**";
    God treats you as **sons**.
For what "**son**" is there whom his **father** does not **discipline**?
At the **time**,
    all **discipline** seems a cause not for **joy** but for **pain**,
    yet **later** it brings the **peaceful fruit** of **righteousness**
    to **those** who are **trained** by it.

So **strengthen** your drooping **hands** and your weak **knees**.
Make straight paths for your **feet**,
    that what is **lame** may not be **disjointed** but **healed**.

---

training, and not "to lose heart" (the Greek for this phrase denotes not "to slack off, give out, lose courage") when reproved. For the Lord disciplines (Greek verb *paideuo*) beloved disciples and "scourges" (Greek *mastigoō*) them. The Christian's role in the face of these trials is to "endure"—in Greek *hupomenete*, which denotes to "hold out" or "last" till one's mission is completed as they draw their final breath.

Christ's followers learn to reinterpret what causes pain as a cause for eventual joy. They take the long view and trust that temporary trials will bear the peaceful fruit

borne by doing the right thing. Disciples get with their trainer's program. To endure, they must exercise their weak hands and weak or disabled knees so that these can be restored to health before they become irreparably useless.

GOSPEL   Someone asks Jesus, "Lord, will only a few people be saved?" (literally, "Are only a few being saved?"). Jesus does not give a direct answer, perhaps because preoccupation with the issue distracts from or becomes an excuse for not carrying out one's unique

mission for the Lord, for not entering through the narrow gate. This entrance requires strenuous effort. The Greek for "strive," *agōnizomai*, denotes "to struggle, to strain every nerve and muscle till the winning moment of an athletic contest." Jesus declares that many will not be strong enough to do this.

Jesus warns his disciples and us that one day, the master will rise up and lock the narrow door, and they will gather outside and beg him to open it. Jesus, who was previously compassionate and forgiving, will say to them, "I do not know where

GOSPEL   Luke 13:22–30

A reading from the holy Gospel according to Luke

Jesus passed through **towns** and **villages**,
　　teaching as he went and **making** his **way** to **Jerusalem**.
Someone asked him,
　　"**Lord**, will only a **few** people be **saved?**"
He answered them,
　　"**Strive** to enter through the **narrow gate**,
　　for **many**, I tell you, will attempt to **enter**
　　but will **not** be **strong** enough.
After the **master** of the **house** has **arisen** and locked the **door**,
　　then will you stand **outside knocking** and **saying**,
　　'**Lord**, open the **door** for us.'
He will **say** to you in **reply**,
　　'I do not **know** where you are **from**.'
And you will **say**,
　　'We **ate** and **drank** in your **company** and you **taught**
　　　in our **streets**.'
Then he will **say** to you,
　　'I do not **know** where you are **from**.
Depart from me, all you **evildoers!**'
And there will be **wailing** and **grinding** of **teeth**
　　when you see **Abraham**, **Isaac**, and **Jacob**
　　and all the **prophets** in the kingdom of **God**
　　and you **yourselves** cast **out**.
And people will **come** from the **east** and the **west**
　　and from the **north** and the **south**
　　and will **recline** at table in the **kingdom** of **God**.
For **behold**, some are **last** who will be **first**,
　　and some are **first** who will be **last**."

A narrative reading that contains a parable whose story intensifies as it moves along. The parable seems to function, in part, to get to its concluding teaching, which is well known. But the parable itself is strange and disturbing.

Here starts the parable, which involves a petition.

Slight pause between "outside" and "knocking."

Here the parable intensifies, becoming stranger as it goes. You can pick up your pace at this point.

The teaching: Proclaim it directly and emphatically.

---

you are from." Shocked, those who call themselves his disciples rattle off activities that they thought guaranteed their salvation: they shared meals with Jesus and heard his teachings (as we do at every Eucharist).

Jesus calls these nominal disciples "evildoers"—in Greek *ergatai adikias,* which denotes "those who work for injustice." He then declares that at the end of time there will be wailing and grinding of teeth. Those who are Jesus' disciples in name only will experience eternal anxiety and regret when they see Abraham, Isaac, Jacob, all the prophets, and foreigners from all corners of the earth reclining at table in the kingdom of God—and no place reserved for them.

Like Isaiah, Jesus pushes his hearers outside the comfort of their little local community by reminding them that he has stellar faithful disciples around the globe. His final saying warns us that when he returns, we could find ourselves standing outside the narrow gate, watching a diverse group of other people pass into the kingdom of God. E.N.

TWENTY-SECOND SUNDAY IN ORDINARY TIME

LECTIONARY #126

READING I   Sirach 3:17–18, 20, 28–29

A reading from the Book of Sirach

Sirach = SEER-ak or SĪ-ruhk

A highly poetic exhortatory reading that uses the organizational element of parallelism. There are five statements in the reading. Each begins with a claim, which is then added to or completed in its second half. Use the rhythm of these statements to pace your proclamation.

My **child**, conduct your **affairs** with **humility**,
    and you will be **loved** more than a **giver** of **gifts**.
Humble yourself the **more**, the **greater** you **are**,
    and you will find **favor** with **God**.
What is too **sublime** for you, seek **not**,
    into things beyond your **strength** search **not**.
The **mind** of a **sage** appreciates **proverbs**,
    and an attentive **ear** is the **joy** of the **wise**.
Water quenches a flaming **fire**,
    and **alms** atone for **sins**.

For meditation and context:

RESPONSORIAL PSALM   Psalm 68:4–5, 6–7, 10–11 (see 11b)

R. God, in your goodness, you have made a home for the poor.

The just rejoice and exult before God;
    they are glad and rejoice.
Sing to God, chant praise to his name,
    whose name is the LORD.

The father of orphans and the defender
    of widows
    is God in his holy dwelling.
God gives a home to the forsaken;
    he leads forth prisoners to prosperity.

A bountiful rain you showered down, O God,
    upon your inheritance;
    you restored the land when it languished;
your flock settled in it;
    in your goodness, O God, you provided it
    for the needy.

TO KEEP IN MIND

Make eye contact with the assembly. This helps keep the assembly engaged with the reading.

READING I   The Jewish wisdom teacher Sirach writes around 180 BC to Jews who, in their search for a full life, are turning to the newer Greek philosophies of their day. Sirach urges them to rely instead on the wisdom that Israel learned from its long relationship with God and passes down in its Scriptures.

In this reading, the sage stresses the essential role that humility plays in the life of people who seek true greatness. He tells them to conduct all their affairs with "humility," the Greek for which, *prautaes*, also denotes gentleness, courtesy, and considerateness. The more they "humble" or "lower" themselves (Greek *tapeinoō*), the more they find favor with God. Also, the truly great are not busybodies (Sirach 3:22) who meddle in matters beyond their understanding, like the affairs of others. They are too busy learning about God's ways and looking for them in the world around them. They ponder proverbs, pithy sayings that place two statements side by side in order to stimulate thought about how God's views and ways apply to a particular "slice of life." For example, the proverb "Water quenches a flaming fire, and alms atone for sins."

READING II   This reading contrasts Israel's experience of entering God's covenant at the foot of Mount Sinai (in Exodus) or Horeb (in Deuteronomy) to Christian baptism. For Israel, signing up was a scary event. Gloom and stormy darkness shroud the mountain, which, like a volcano, spews fire into the heart of heaven. Sounding like claps of thunder, God's voice speaks from the fire. The people beg to hear that voice no more. Any person or beast that touches the mountain must be stoned to death. Even Moses is terrified and trembles (see Exodus 19—20; Deuteronomy 4—5).

Hebrews = HEE-brooz
A potent, exhortatory reading constructed in two parts. In the first part, in vivid language, the Hebrews are told what they have *not* done. In the second part, in equally vivid language, the Hebrews are told what they *have* done.

The first part begins with "You." The word "and" holds the list together.

Zion = ZĪ-uhn *or* ZĪ-ahn
festal = FES-tuhl
The second part begins with "No." Despite that word, this part is filled with things of splendor and awe. Once again, "and" holds things together. You can quicken the pace of your proclamation slightly.

mediator = MEE-dee-ay-tehr

eloquently = EL-uh-kwent-lee

READING II   Hebrews 12:18–19, 22–24a

A reading from the Letter to the Hebrews

Brothers and **sisters**:
You have not **approached** that which could be **touched**
    and a blazing **fire** and gloomy **darkness**
    and **storm** and a **trumpet blast**
    and a **voice** speaking **words** such that those who **heard**
    begged that no **message** be further **addressed** to them.
No, you have approached **Mount Zion**
    and the **city** of the living **God**, the heavenly **Jerusalem**,
    and countless **angels** in festal **gathering**,
    and the **assembly** of the firstborn enrolled in **heaven**,
    and **God** the judge of **all**,
    and the **spirits** of the **just** made **perfect**,
    and **Jesus**, the **mediator** of a new **covenant**,
    and the sprinkled **blood** that speaks more **eloquently**
        than that of **Abel**.

sabbath = SAB-uhth
Pharisees = FAYR-uh-seez
A narrative reading whose focus is didactic. Even though Luke calls it a parable, it's really a pointed lesson broken into two examples. The words after "when" contain the example. The words after "rather" contain the teaching.

parable = PAYR-uh-b*l

Here begins the first example.

GOSPEL   Luke 14:1, 7–14

A reading from the holy Gospel according to Luke

On a **sabbath** Jesus went to **dine**
    at the home of one of the leading **Pharisees**,
    and the **people there** were observing him **carefully**.

He told a **parable** to those who had been **invited**,
    noticing how they were choosing the places of **honor**
        at the **table**.
"When you are **invited** by someone to a **wedding** banquet,
    do not **recline** at table in the **place** of **honor**. »

In contrast, Christian baptism is a jubilant event. In it, the people of the new covenant draw near to (the Greek perfect verb form conveys that they *continue* to approach) an unending party on Mount Zion. For Jews, Mount Zion or Jerusalem is the place to which all nations will stream to worship Israel's God. For Christians, Mount Zion becomes the site where God is fully revealed in Jesus. It is "the city of the living God, the heavenly [or spiritual] Jerusalem."

Alive and celebrating together in God's city are countless angels; the assembly of people who at baptism were enrolled in heaven; God, the judge of all; the spirits of the just made perfect; and Jesus who, by becoming human, suffering, and dying, mediated the new covenant that made this joyful assembly possible.

GOSPEL A leading Pharisee invites Jesus to his home and is "observing him carefully," trying to catch him off guard. Meanwhile, Jesus is watching how the guests are choosing places of honor at the banquet table. The verb "recline" suggests that this table is a low, three-sided, u-shaped "triclinium" at which each guest reclines on his side with his feet away from the table.

Even emphasis on "more distinguished guest."

A **more distinguished guest** than you may have been
   invited by him,
and the **host** who invited **both** of you may **approach** you
   and say,
'Give your **place** to this **man**,'
and then you would **proceed** with **embarrassment**
to take the lowest **place**.

Here begins the first teaching, which corrects the first example, directed at the guests.

Rather, when you are **invited**,
   go and take the **lowest place**
so that when the **host** comes to **you** he may **say**,
'My **friend**, move **up** to a higher **position**.'
Then you will **enjoy** the **esteem** of your **companions** at
   the **table**.

exalts = ehg-ZAHLTs

For every one who **exalts** himself will be **humbled**,
   but the one who **humbles** himself will be **exalted**."

Here begins the second example.

Then he said to the **host** who invited him,
   "When you hold a **lunch** or a **dinner**,
   do not invite your **friends** or your **brothers**
   or your **relatives** or your wealthy **neighbors**,
   in **case** they may invite you **back** and you have **repayment**.

And here the lesson concludes with the second teaching, directed at the host.

Rather, when you hold a **banquet**,
   invite the **poor**, the **crippled**, the **lame**, the **blind**;
   blessed **indeed** will you **be** because of their **inability**
      to **repay** you.

righteous = RĪ-chuhs

For you will be **repaid** at the **resurrection** of the **righteous**."

Drawing on Proverbs 25:6–7, Jesus imagines for his listeners a scene in which a guest chooses a place of honor near his host. Then, the host walks over to him and tells him that the spot he's in belongs to a more distinguished person whom the host also invited. Red-faced, the self-important guest must stand up and, under the stares of his dinner companions, walk to the lowest place (the place that Jesus' disciples always choose).

Then Jesus describes the opposite scenario of a guest who chooses the place farthest from the head table. The host surprises this guest by approaching him and inviting him to move to a higher place. In both scenes, the rationale that Jesus gives for choosing a place is what other people think—here expressed by the esteem or the disdain of the other guests. However, the verbs in the reversal saying, "will be humbled" and "will be exalted," are theological passives that remind Jesus' hearers that God, who is always present at human gatherings, is also the One who orchestrates the humbling or exalting.

Jesus' advice to the host is another crazy (that is, divine) teaching about how his disciples can experience life in the kingdom more deeply. He tells his host that he should not invite the people he normally does but instead those who, perhaps for physical or financial reasons, are unable to repay him. If he does this, Jesus declares that he "will be repaid" (a theological passive) by God in ways beyond human imagining. What a great family or small-group project: to take Jesus literally and then experience together God's "repayment"! E.N.

TWENTY-THIRD SUNDAY IN ORDINARY TIME

LECTIONARY #129

READING I   Wisdom 9:13–18b

A reading from the Book of Wisdom

> **Who** can know God's **counsel**,
>   or **who** can conceive what the LORD **intends**?
> For the **deliberations** of **mortals** are **timid**,
>   and **unsure** are our **plans**.
> For the **corruptible body burdens** the **soul**
>   and the **earthen shelter** weighs **down** the mind
>   that has **many concerns**.
> And **scarce** do we **guess** the **things** on **earth**,
>   and what is within our **grasp** we find with **difficulty**;
>   but when **things** are in **heaven**, who can search them **out**?
> Or who ever **knew** your **counsel**, except you had given **wisdom**
>   and sent your holy **spirit** from on **high**?
> And thus were the **paths** of those on earth made **straight**.

An exhortatory reading whose power lies in the plaintive questions the speaker asks. The reading opens with a question. Use it to set your tone.

deliberations = dih-lihb-uh-RAY-shuhnz

Note the rhythm: Proclaim this line slowly. corruptible = kohr-RUPT-uh-b*l

Again, note the rhythm: Proclaim this line slowly as well.

These final two questions prepare for the conclusion.

> **TO KEEP IN MIND**
> The words in bold are suggestions for ways to express the meaning of the reading. Consider using them as you practice the reading, then choose to stress them or to find your own way of proclaiming.

READING I This passage is part of a beautiful prayer, which the author places on the lips of King Solomon. The king asks the Creator to give him wisdom to rule with holiness and righteousness and to judge people fairly (Wisdom 9:1–3). This Wisdom "knows your works and was present when you made the world; . . . understands what is pleasing in your eyes and what is conformable with your commands." The king begs God, "Send her forth from your holy heavens and from your glorious throne dispatch her that she may be with me and work with me, that I may know what is pleasing to you" (Wisdom 9:9–10).

Solomon realizes that he is "a man weak and short-lived and lacking in comprehension of judgment and of laws" (9:5). His thoughts, like all human deliberations, are too cowardly or timid (Greek *deilos*) to comprehend God's bold ways. His intentions are "unsure" and can even be "dangerous" (Greek *episphalaes*). Why? Because the corruptible or perishable body is a high-maintenance organism. Its constant needs and wants encumber the soul. With difficulty, people can figure out a few earthly matters, but they are incapable of understanding heavenly ones. The wise person simply lives with the conviction that, within every single circumstance, happening, and encounter of their day, God's holy spirit is straightening their path.

READING II There is much that is unclear about this letter, including who Philemon and Onesimus are and why they are separated. What is clear, however, is Paul's concern that the master Philemon treat the slave Onesimus not as a valuable piece of property (Onesimus is a

For meditation and context:

RESPONSORIAL PSALM   Psalm 90:3–4, 5–6, 12–13, 14 and 17 (1)

R. In every age, O Lord, you have been our refuge.

You turn man back to dust,
saying, "Return, O children of men."
For a thousand years in your sight
are as yesterday, now that it is past,
or as a watch of the night.

You make an end of them in their sleep;
the next morning they are like the
changing grass,
which at dawn springs up anew,
but by evening wilts and fades.

Teach us to number our days aright,
that we may gain wisdom of heart.
Return, O LORD! How long?
Have pity on your servants!

Fill us at daybreak with your kindness,
that we may shout for joy and gladness all
our days.
And may the gracious care of the LORD our
God be ours;
prosper the work of our hands for us!
Prosper the work of our hands!

Philemon = fi-LEE-muhn
Onesimus = oh-NES-ih-muhs

A rare reading from one of the letters of St. Paul to an individual rather than to a community. The intimate quality of the address should set your tone.

imprisonment = ihm-PRIZ-uhn-m*nt
Note the plaintive rhythm. There's a slight pause at the comma between "heart" and "back."

At "Perhaps," this letter takes on a very personal tone.

Even emphasis on "welcome him as you would me.'

READING II   Philemon 9–10, 12–17

A reading from the Letter of Saint Paul to Philemon

I, **Paul**, an old **man**,
and now also a **prisoner** for Christ **Jesus**,
urge you on behalf of my child **Onesimus**,
whose **father** I have become in my **imprisonment**;
I am **sending** him, that is, my **own heart**, **back** to you.
I should have **liked** to retain him for **myself**,
so that he might **serve** me on your **behalf**
in my **imprisonment** for the **gospel**,
but I did not want to do **anything** without your **consent**,
so that the **good** you do might not be **forced** but **voluntary**.
Perhaps this is why he was **away** from you for a **while**,
that you might have him **back forever**,
no longer as a **slave**
but **more** than a slave, a **brother**,
beloved especially to **me**, but even **more so** to **you**,
as a **man** and in the **Lord**.
So if you **regard** me as a **partner**, welcome him as you would me.

---

common slave name which means "useful" or "profitable"), but as a person of equal status because of their relationship in Christ. Once again, Paul preaches that baptism removes the distinctions that society insists on making. He urges Christians to live by Christ's standards.

To stress his point, Paul refers to Onesimus, whom he apparently met in prison, as "my *own* heart." He suggests to Philemon that the (divine) purpose for his separation from Onesimus was that he might have him back forever—"no longer as a slave but more than a slave, a brother"

who is especially beloved by Paul and even more beloved to Philemon "as a man and in the Lord."

GOSPEL   As Jesus journeys on to Jerusalem, he turns to the great crowds that are traveling with him and speaks plainly about the costs of discipleship. His threefold repetition of the declaration "cannot be my disciple" suggests that the crowds fail to grasp how much they will have to change if they follow him.

Jesus' first statement, that his disciples must "hate" father, mother, wife, chil-

dren, brothers, sisters, and even their own life, is shocking. His hearers depended for security on their family (not, for example, on money, insurance policies, or the like). "Hate" is part of a word-pair, "love / hate," that belongs to the language of international treaties in the biblical world. In covenant contexts (like discipleship), the terms denote not deep-seated feelings but rather actions which demonstrate respectively one's loyalty or disloyalty to an overlord. The person who "loves" his lord is faithful to him, while the one who "hates" his lord rebels against him. In this Gospel, Jesus'

GOSPEL   Luke 14:25–33

A reading from the holy Gospel according to Luke

Great crowds were **traveling** with **Jesus**,
    and he **turned** and **addressed** them,
    "If **anyone** comes to me without hating his **father** and
        mother,
    wife and **children**, **brothers** and **sisters**,
    and even his **own life**,
    he **cannot** be my **disciple**.
Whoever does not **carry** his own **cross** and come **after** me
    cannot be my **disciple**.
Which of you wishing to construct a **tower**
    does not **first** sit down and **calculate** the **cost**
    to see if there is **enough** for its **completion**?
Otherwise, after **laying** the **foundation**
    and finding himself **unable** to finish the **work**
    the **onlookers** should **laugh** at him and **say**,
    '**This one** began to **build** but did not have the **resources**
        to **finish**.'
Or what **king** marching into **battle** would not **first** sit down
    and decide whether with **ten thousand troops**
    he can successfully **oppose** another **king**
    advancing upon him with **twenty thousand troops**?
But if **not**, while he is still far **away**,
    he will send a **delegation** to ask for **peace** terms.
In the **same way**,
    anyone of you who does not **renounce** all his **possessions**
    cannot be my **disciple**."

A narrative reading with a strong didactic emphasis. Jesus makes a harsh demand of his followers. He elaborates with two examples to explain the harshness of his demand, which he comes back to and repeats explicitly in the end. There is no way to sugarcoat this reading.

Here is the harsh demand: you have to give up and hate your family to follow Christ.

Here is the first example.

And here is the second example.

Jesus concludes by revisiting his harsh claim but qualifying it: You have to give up all of your possessions.

---

saying warns his disciples that situations will arise that will test where their greater loyalty lies: with him or with the members of their family.

Scholars note that the evangelists Matthew and Luke use different verbs in Jesus' next saying about the cross. In Matthew 10:38, a disciple must "receive" or "accept" his or her cross, while in Luke the disciple must "carry" it. Luke shifts the focus from initially accepting one's mission to the day-by-day fulfilling of the responsibilities that come with it. Luke also stresses the uniqueness of each disciple's task, his

or her *own*—and therefore often lonely—cross that only Jesus understands fully and helps carry.

Jesus' scenarios of the man who would build a tower and a king who might go to war depict discipleship as an enormously expensive undertaking. Following Jesus will demand all that a person is and has. The man must "first sit down" and determine the cost of the tower, lest he fail to complete it and look like a fool. The king must "first sit down" and calculate his chances of success, lest he lose his kingdom and even his life.

Jesus' final declaration, that anyone who does not renounce their material possessions "cannot be my disciple," seems to take an odd turn. In context, however, the saying suggests that one's attachment to or freedom from possessions provides an instant read on one's understanding of how much discipleship can cost him or her. E.N.

TWENTY-FOURTH SUNDAY IN ORDINARY TIME

LECTIONARY #132

Exodus = EK-suh-duhs

A narrative reading that relates a conversation between God and Moses. God is irate, but Moses convinces God to relinquish his anger.

Molten = MOHL-t*n = made of melted and casted gold or other metal

God's anger at the Israelites explodes in this threat.

The tone of the reading shifts here when Moses begins to try to persuade the Lord. No need to plead; Moses is making a sensible case to God.

TO KEEP IN MIND
Be careful not to swallow your words. Articulate carefully, especially at the end of lines.

READING I Exodus 32:7–11, 13–14

A reading from the Book of Exodus

The **LORD** said to **Moses**,
  "Go **down** at once to your **people**,
  whom you brought **out** of the land of **Egypt**,
  for they have become **depraved**.
They have **soon turned aside** from the way I pointed **out**
    to them,
  making for themselves a molten **calf** and **worshiping** it,
  sacrificing to it and crying out,
  '**This** is your **God**, O **Israel**,
  who brought you **out** of the **land** of **Egypt**!'
I see how **stiff-necked** this people is," continued the LORD
    to Moses.
"Let me **alone**, then,
  that my **wrath** may blaze up **against** them to **consume** them.
Then I will make of you a great **nation**."

But **Moses** implored the LORD, his **God**, saying,
"**Why**, O LORD, should your **wrath** blaze up
    against your own **people**,
  whom you brought **out** of the **land** of **Egypt**
  with such **great power** and with so **strong** a hand?
Remember your servants **Abraham**, **Isaac**, and **Israel**,
  and how you **swore** to them by your own self, saying,

READING I This exchange between the Lord and Moses takes place on top of the covenant mountain while down below the Israelites pray and offer sacrifices to the work of their hands, the golden calf. Especially rankling to the Lord is the people's chant that credits the calf with delivering them from bondage in Egypt. They say, "*This* is your God, O Israel." (The Hebrew *elohim* is a plural form which can be translated either as a "plural of majesty" or "honorific," that is, as "God," or as the regular grammatical plural, "gods.") The Israelites are "stiff-necked," a posture seen in children and adults who refuse to change their mind or behavior. Here it conveys the people's determination to go their own way rather than follow the Lord. So soon after the spectacular deliverance at the Red Sea, they doubt that their invisible God is with them. Are we so different? How often do our own actions "say," "This ____ is your God, O John or O Jane, who rescued you from ____."

The Lord, depicted as acting like a human would, decides to destroy Israel and start over again with Moses. No doubt, the idea of leaving behind those stubborn, complicated, unbelieving companions would appeal to Moses. Instead, he pleads on their behalf, pointing out that the Lord's oath to Abraham, Isaac, and Israel would go unfulfilled if the Israelites were annihilated. The Lord heeded Moses' words and relented.

READING II This letter portrays Paul the great evangelist as Paul the great sinner. The author calls himself a blasphemer, for he vilified Jesus and persecuted his followers. He describes himself as violent and filled with arrogance, or

Perpetual = pehr-PECH-oo-uhl

A storm has passed.

'I will make your **descendants** as **numerous** as the **stars**
    in the **sky**;
and **all this land** that I **promised**,
I will give your **descendants** as their perpetual **heritage**.'"
So the LORD relented in the **punishment**
    he had **threatened** to inflict on his **people**.

For meditation and context:

RESPONSORIAL PSALM   Psalm 51:3–4, 12–13, 17, 19 (Luke 15:18)

R. I will rise and go to my father.

Have mercy on me, O God, in your goodness;
    in the greatness of your compassion wipe
      out my offense.
Thoroughly wash me from my guilt
    and of my sin cleanse me.

A clean heart create for me, O God,
    and a steadfast spirit renew within me.

Cast me not out from your presence,
    and your Holy Spirit take not from me.

O Lord, open my lips,
    and my mouth shall proclaim your praise.
My sacrifice, O God, is a contrite spirit;
    a heart contrite and humbled, O God, you
      will not spurn.

READING II   1 Timothy 1:12–17

An exhortatory reading, which relates unusually personal details of St. Paul's life to his disciple Timothy.

A reading from the first Letter of Saint Paul to Timothy

Beloved:
I am **grateful** to **him** who has **strengthened** me, **Christ Jesus**
    our **Lord**,
    because he **considered** me **trustworthy**
    in **appointing** me to the **ministry**.
I was once a **blasphemer** and a **persecutor** and **arrogant**,
    but I have been **mercifully treated**
    because I **acted** out of **ignorance** in my **unbelief**.
Indeed, the **grace** of our Lord has been **abundant**,
    along with the **faith** and **love** that are in **Christ Jesus**.
This **saying** is trustworthy and deserves **full** acceptance:
    Christ Jesus came into the **world** to save **sinners**.
Of **these** I am the **foremost**.
But for that **reason** I was mercifully **treated**,
    so that **in** me, as the **foremost**, **»**

blasphemer = blas-FEEM-er

Here Paul lays bare the life he lived before his conversion. These labels are harsh.

The core of the reading.

---

hubris (Greek *hubristaes*). This egregious portrayal accentuates the power that changed Paul, the power that flows into the world through Christ's redemptive work.

    Because Paul acted out of ignorance in his unbelief, Christ treated him mercifully. He exhibited great patience toward Paul, in effect incarnating the slowness to anger for which the God of Israel became famous. For this, and because Christ Jesus strengthened him and gave him a ministry (*diakonia*), Paul was most grateful.

    This letter presents Paul's conversion and subsequent dedicated service as evidence of the superabundant grace, faith, and self-giving love of Christ that sustain and work through him—as they do through all the baptized. Paul's experiences led him to find "trustworthy" the early Christological confession that "Christ came into the world to save sinners." The Greek for "save," *sōzō*, denotes a variety of experiences, among them those of rescuing, setting free, healing, and protecting sinners from harm.

    The closing doxology acknowledges God as *the* king of every age, as incorruptible, unseen, and the only God (Greek *monōtheō*). To this God alone belongs honor and glory.

GOSPEL   This Gospel displays God's ardent desire to be with sinners. In it, Jesus addresses two groups—the tax collectors and sinners who draw near to listen to him, and the Pharisees and scribes who complain that he welcomes sinners and eats with them. The religious

incorruptible = ihn-koh-RUHP-tuh-b*l
The reading concludes with uplift, a triumphant tone.

A long narrative reading that, in its longer form, includes three whole parables! One of them, in fact, is repeated from the Fourth Sunday of Lent. Aside from the Gospel readings during Holy Week, this is the longest reading in Year C.
Pharisees = FAYR-uh-seez

This first parable is as straightforward as it is perplexing. Its strangeness is overshadowed by the familiarity of the Prodigal Son parable that follows it. Linger slightly on its details to highlight its strangeness.

Jesus provides an interpretation of his own parable.

This second parable repeats the themes of the first and is comparatively brief. In a compressed way, it follows the same formula as the first parable.

Christ Jesus might display all his **patience** as an **example**
for **those** who would come to **believe** in him for
   everlasting life.
To the king of **ages**, **incorruptible**, **invisible**, the only **God**,
   honor and **glory forever** and **ever**. Amen.

GOSPEL   Luke 15:1–32

A reading from the holy Gospel according to Luke

[**Tax** collectors and **sinners** were all drawing **near** to **listen**
      to **Jesus**,
   but the **Pharisees** and **scribes** began to **complain**, saying,
   "**This man** welcomes **sinners** and **eats** with them."
So to **them** he addressed this **parable**.
"What **man** among you having a hundred **sheep**
      and **losing** one of them
   would not **leave** the **ninety-nine** in the **desert**
   and go after the **lost one** until he **finds** it?
And when he **does** find it,
   he **sets** it on his **shoulders** with **great joy**
   and, upon his **arrival home**,
   he **calls** together his **friends** and **neighbors** and **says** to them,
   '**Rejoice** with me because I have **found** my lost **sheep**.'
I **tell** you, in **just** the same **way**
   there will be **more joy** in heaven over **one sinner** who **repents**
   than over **ninety-nine righteous** people
   who have no **need** of **repentance**.

"Or what **woman** having **ten coins** and losing **one**
   would not **light** a **lamp** and **sweep** the **house**,
   searching **carefully** until she **finds** it?
And when she **does** find it,
   she calls together her **friends** and **neighbors**
   and **says** to them,
   '**Rejoice** with me because I have **found** the **coin** that I **lost**.'

leaders seem annoyed that Jesus is not content merely to point his finger at sinners but instead goes looking for them and when he finds them, hangs out with them. Sinners for their part are attracted to Jesus, no doubt surprised and moved that he does not shun them. In Luke, Jesus spends so much time with social outcasts that he earns the epithet "the friend of sinners," the friend of those who are temporarily lost. In contrast, his opponents choose not to associate with such public offenders for

fear that doing so might tarnish their own reputation for holiness.

Jesus' three parables explain his actions to the religious leaders. Like the shepherd who searches for one of ninety-nine lost sheep, and the woman who searches for one of ten lost coins, he searches for lost people *because* God loves them and wants to share life with them. The shepherd's joy at finding his sheep and the tenderness he demonstrates after all the trouble that sheep caused him reflect

God's contentment at being reunited with one who was lost. Unable to contain his elation, the shepherd calls his "friends and neighbors" to celebrate with him. Their rejoicing reaches the heavens, where there is more joy over one sinner who changes his or her mind and ways (*metanoeō*) than over the rest who are faithful to their covenant with God.

In the second parable, Jesus depicts God as a woman who looks for a lost coin until she finds it. She too calls her "friends

Once again, Jesus provides an interpretation.

In **just** the **same way**, I **tell** you,
    there will be **rejoicing** among the **angels** of God
    over **one sinner** who **repents**."]

The third parable is the parable of the Prodigal Son, as cinematic as a great film.

Then he said,
    "A **man** had two sons, and the **younger son** said to his father,
    '**Father** give me the **share** of your estate that should come
        to **me**.'
So the father **divided** the property **between** them.
After a **few days**, the younger son collected **all** his belongings
    and set **off** to a distant **country**
    where he **squandered** his inheritance on a **life** of **dissipation**.

Slight emphasis on "dissipation."
dissipation = dihs-ih-PAY-shuhn

famine = FAM-ihn

When he had **freely spent** everything,
    a severe **famine** struck that country,
    and he found himself in **dire need**.
So he **hired** himself **out** to one of the local **citizens**
    who sent him to his **farm** to tend the **swine**.

Emphasis on "swine fed."

And he **longed** to eat his **fill** of the **pods** on which the **swine fed**,
    but **nobody** gave him **any**.
Coming to his **senses** he thought,
    'How **many** of my father's **hired workers**
    have **more** than enough **food** to **eat**,
    but **here** am I, **dying** from **hunger**.
I shall get **up** and go to my **father** and I shall **say** to him,
    "**Father**, I have **sinned** against **heaven** and against **you**.

Speech within a speech; make sure it's clear to your assembly.

I no longer **deserve** to be called your **son**;
    treat me as you would treat one of your **hired** workers."'
So he got **up** and went **back** to his **father**.
While he was **still** a long way **off**,
    his **father** caught **sight** of him,
    and was **filled** with **compassion**.
He ran to his **son**, **embraced** him and **kissed** him.
His son **said** to him,

Direct repetition of the speech above.

    '**Father**, I have **sinned** against **heaven** and against **you**;
    I no longer **deserve** to be called your **son**.' ❯❯

and neighbors" to rejoice with her. And again, the celebration of God's reunion with one sinner merges the heavenly and earthly realms. Jesus declares, "there will be rejoicing among the angels of God over one sinner who repents [*metanoeō*]."

In the third parable, Jesus describes God as a father who loses one of two sons. When the younger asks for his share of the estate, the father gives him his portion (perhaps one third of the father's wealth since, according to Deuteronomy 21:17, the eldest receives a double portion). Unlike the shep-

herd and the woman, the father does not go looking for the son but waits at home until the son comes to his senses. One day, while feeding pigs in a foreign land, it dawns on young man that the slaves in his father's house are better off than he is.

When the waiting father sees his son from a long way off, he is moved with compassion (the Greek *splagchnizomai* denotes "to be moved in the depths of one's being"). The ensuing scene draws one of the most poignant portraits of the loving God in all of Scripture. Seeing not a sinner but a son, the

father runs to him, throws his arms around him, and kisses him. The father says nothing about the son's loss of his hard-earned wealth. He treats the son as if he has done nothing wrong.

Neither does the father comment on the son's confession. His actions, however, show what he thinks about the son's sense of unworthiness. The father immediately orders his servants to bring the symbols and clothing that will show to all that he reinstates the prodigal as a son in his household —the fine clothes, a ring (perhaps one with

It's appropriate to add a little excitement and tenderness to your proclamation in the words of the father.

Note the rhythm: "COME to LIFE aGAIN."

Slight pause between "celebration" and "began."

The perspective shifts to the older son. Allow for a slight change to a more sober tone.

Slight pause between "back" and "safe."

The son's tone can express justified exasperation.

Repetition of the rhythm above: "COME to LIFE aGAIN."

But his **father** ordered his **servants**,
  '**Quickly** bring the **finest robe** and put it **on** him;
  put a **ring** on his **finger** and **sandals** on his **feet**.
Take the fattened **calf** and **slaughter** it.
Then let us **celebrate** with a **feast**,
  because this **son** of **mine** was **dead**, and has **come** to
    life again;
  he was **lost**, and has been **found**.'
Then the **celebration began**.
Now the **older** son had been **out** in the **field**
  and, on his way **back**, as he neared the **house**,
  he heard the sound of **music** and **dancing**.
He **called** one of the **servants** and asked what this might mean.
The servant **said** to him,
  '**Your brother** has **returned**
  and your **father** has **slaughtered** the **fattened calf**
  because he has him **back safe** and **sound**.'
He became **angry**,
  and when he **refused** to enter the **house**,
  his **father** came out and **pleaded** with him.
He said to his **father** in **reply**,
  '**Look**, all these years I **served** you
  and not **once** did I disobey your **orders**;
  yet you **never** gave me even a young **goat** to **feast on**
    with my **friends**.
But when your **son** returns,
  who swallowed up your **property** with **prostitutes**,
  for **him** you **slaughter** the fattened **calf**.'
He **said** to him,
  '**My son**, you are **here** with me **always**;
  everything I **have** is **yours**.
But **now** we must **celebrate** and **rejoice**,
  because your **brother** was **dead** and has **come** to **life again**;
  he was **lost** and has been **found**.'"

[Shorter: Luke 15:1–10 (see brackets)]

a seal that gives the bearer authority to transact business in his father's name, like a modern-day credit card), and sandals. But all this is not enough to express the father's profound joy at being with his son again. He calls for a feast of the best he has "because this son of mine was dead and has come to life again; he was lost and has been found. Meanwhile, the older son returns home after a day's work. When a servant explains why there is music and dancing, the son becomes angry. This reaction and his words reflect those of the Pharisees and scribes

and, indeed, of most people who resent Jesus' teaching that God is outrageously merciful to sinners. The older son rages. Doesn't the father realize that his youngest son squandered a third of the family fortune on prostitutes? Doesn't the father appreciate that his oldest son "slaves" daily for him and never disobeys a single command? His father never gave him even a young goat to celebrate with his friends and yet now slaughters the fattened calf—held in reserve for the biggest family

celebrations—because one ordinary day his disgraceful son shows up broke.

  To this son, the father responds: "My son, you are here with me always, *everything* I have is yours." The son (like all disciples) enjoys an indescribably rich life daily in his father's house. And the return to life and to that father's house of one who is lost and dead cannot go uncelebrated. E.N.

TWENTY-FIFTH SUNDAY IN ORDINARY TIME

LECTIONARY #135

READING I Amos 8:4–7

A reading from the Book of the Prophet Amos

> Hear this, **you** who **trample** upon the **needy**
>   and **destroy** the poor of the **land**!
> "**When** will the **new** moon be **over**," you ask,
>   "that we may **sell** our **grain**,
>   and the **sabbath**, that we may **display** the **wheat**?
> We will **diminish** the **ephah**,
>   **add** to the **shekel**,
>   and **fix** our **scales** for **cheating**!
> We will buy the **lowly** for **silver**,
>   and the **poor** for a pair of **sandals**;
>   even the **refuse** of the **wheat** we will **sell**!"
> The LORD has **sworn** by the **pride** of Jacob:
>   **Never** will I forget a **thing** they have **done**!

RESPONSORIAL PSALM Psalm 113:1–2, 4–6, 7–8 (see 1a, 7b)

**R. Praise the Lord who lifts up the poor.
or Alleluia.**

Praise, you servants of the LORD,
  praise the name of the LORD.
Blessed be the name of the LORD
  both now and forever.

High above all nations is the LORD;
  above the heavens is his glory.
Who is like the LORD, our God, who is
  enthroned on high
  and looks upon the heavens
  and the earth below?

He raises up the lowly from the dust;
  from the dunghill he lifts up the poor
to seat them with princes,
  with the princes of his own people.

Amos = AY-m*s

An exhortatory reading from one of the minor prophets, not heard from very often in the liturgical repertoire.

Sabbath = SAB-uhth
Take care with the unusual language.
ephah = EE-fuh
shekel = SHEK-*l

The Lord's promise is tinged with pride.

For meditation and context:

READING I The prophet Amos declares that—in the Lord's view—people who profit by taking advantage of those who are less well off "trample on the needy" and ruin the God-given lives of the poor. The prophet puts words on the lips of merchants—words which they probably never said but which display their inner thoughts and greed. The question "when will the new moon be over that we may sell our grain, and our sabbath that we my display the wheat?" expresses sellers' frustration that religious customs curtail their profits.

Amos also attacks their sneaky business practices. They "diminish the ephah and add to the shekel," or as another translation clearly puts it, "They measure out less and charge more." They also tamper with the scales. The poor have no recourse against such cheating, but the Lord does. Amos warns that the Lord, who sees everything, will never forget a single fraudulent transaction that diminished the well-being of another, no matter how slightly. The negative "never forget" denotes more than "keeping in mind." It entails concrete action; the Lord will deal personally with anyone

who takes advantage of the poor. Dishonest, scheming people can count on that.

READING II Every baptized person is called to pray not only for themselves, their family, community, and country, but for the entire human race. The author of this letter reminds Christians that they are not an elite group of "the saved," but people who are called to carry on Christ's redemptive work. Regardless of their position, health, age, or any other condition, they can do this by offering supplications, intercessions, and thanksgiving

READING II   1 Timothy 2:1–8

A reading from the first Letter of Saint Paul to Timothy

Beloved:
First of all, I **ask** that **supplications**, **prayers**,
   petitions, and **thanksgivings** be **offered** for **everyone**,
   for **kings** and for **all** in **authority**,
   that we may **lead** a **quiet** and tranquil **life**
   in all **devotion** and **dignity**.
This is **good** and **pleasing** to **God** our **savior**,
   who wills **everyone** to be **saved**
   and to come to **knowledge** of the **truth**.
      For there is **one** God.
      There is also **one** mediator between **God** and **men**,
      the man **Christ Jesus**,
      who gave **himself** as **ransom** for **all**.
This was the **testimony** at the proper **time**.
For **this** I was appointed **preacher** and **apostle**
   —I am speaking the **truth**, I am not **lying**—,
   teacher of the **Gentiles** in **faith** and **truth**.

It is my **wish**, then, that in **every place** the men should **pray**,
   lifting up **holy hands**, without **anger** or **argument**.

A didactic reading whose tone is personal, because St. Paul is writing to an individual disciple.

supplications = sup-lih-KAY-shuhnz

The teaching of the reading is contained in this main, longer section of the reading. Take care to proclaim these verses clearly.

mediator = MEE-dee-ay-tehr

Here, Paul declares his purpose.

The reading concludes with his wish. Use a hopeful tone.

---

to God for others. Prayer for those in charge is especially important. In the Judeo-Christian tradition, the primary responsibility of rulers is to work for the common good by maintaining justice for all. They are in a position to influence change. They have the power to fight the systemic injustices that ultimately lead to social strife.

In this passage, "being saved" brings people to knowledge of the truth. In other words, they are saved from ignorance. The truth is that there is one God and one mediator between God and humankind—"the

man Christ Jesus." Christ sent Paul to spread this truth, which entered the world through Judaism, to the rest of humankind.

The closing verse shows Christians at prayer around the world. Raising hands in prayer is a liturgical practice of both Jewish and early Christian assemblies. "Holy hands" are those of people who strive to do things God's way. Especially when at prayer, they shut off angry thoughts, for example, the tapes of upsetting interactions with others that the mind constantly replays.

GOSPEL Drawing ever nearer to Jerusalem and to his death, Jesus seems desperate for his hearers to understand that commitment to him requires rearranging their views on everything. Today, he addresses the touchy subject of the place of wealth in the lives of believers. His parable, like most parables, does not accuse anyone, but rather prompts everyone to think about how they regard and use material possessions. Neither does his parable dictate a moral so much as tell a tale that draws its listeners in so that

GOSPEL Luke 16:1–13

A reading from the holy Gospel according to Luke

[Jesus **said** to his **disciples**,]
   "A **rich man** had a **steward**
   who was **reported** to him for squandering his **property**.
He **summoned** him and said,
   'What is this I **hear** about you?
Prepare a **full account** of your **stewardship**,
   because you can no **longer** be my **steward**.'
The steward said to himself, 'What shall I **do**,
      now that my **master** is taking the position of **steward**
         away from me?
I am not **strong** enough to **dig** and I am **ashamed** to **beg**.
I **know** what I shall **do** so that,
      when I am **removed** from the stewardship,
      they may **welcome** me into their **homes**.'
He called in his **master's debtors** one by one.
To the **first** he said,
   'How much do you owe my **master**?'
He replied, 'One **hundred** measures of **olive oil**.'
He said to him, '**Here** is your **promissory** note.
Sit down and quickly write one for **fifty**.'
Then to **another** the steward said, 'And **you**,
      how much do **you** owe?'
He replied, 'One **hundred** kors of **wheat**.'
The steward said to him, '**Here** is your **promissory** note;
   write one for **eighty**.'
And the master **commended** that dishonest **steward**
      for acting **prudently**.

"For the **children** of this **world**
      are more **prudent** in dealing with their own **generation**
      than **are** the children of **light**. »

---

steward = STOO-erd
squandering = SKWAHN-dehr-ing

A long narrative reading of a parable and its explanation, which gives it a didactic quality as well. While the parable appears to be about forgiveness, it reveals itself in Jesus' explanation to be about devotion. Lead your assembly to its well-known conclusion as you proclaim it.

The steward's anxiety is palpable.

The steward quickly comes up with a solution to his perilous problem.

The tone shifts at Jesus begins his explanation.

---

they can hear Jesus speak to them personally about their unique situation.

Jesus tells us that a rich man (God) had a steward or business manager who squandered the possessions that the master entrusted to him. So, the master fires him for mishandling his property and demands that the steward show him the accounts. This triggers a crisis for the steward. What will he do now? He weighs his options and decides that he will take advantage of the short time left to him by doing favors for people who will in turn owe him a favor when he is unemployed. In the context of Luke's Gospel, the steward's "solution" seems to represent almsgiving, using one's assets to provide for others' needs (Luke 12:33; Acts 4:34; 2:44–45).

The master praises the steward for acting prudently (the Greek *phronimos* connotes practical wisdom). This unexpected commendation shifts attention from the steward's questionable morality to his response to his dire situation. Jesus declares that the steward acts like a child of this world who is "more prudent in dealing with their own generation than are the children of light."

Then the parable moves to that moment at the end of time when the "master" will demand from every individual an account of how he or she managed the possessions that God entrusted to their care. Jesus says to use them to "make friends for yourselves with dishonest wealth [mammon]" (*mamōna* is an Aramaic word for wealth or property) "so that when it fails [at death] you will be welcomed into eternal dwellings."

The sayings that follow Jesus' parable present wealth as a "small matter" and divine riches as a "greater matter." Jesus

The explanation focuses on forms of trustworthiness. It's a straightforward explanation, but it involves a lot of parallelisms. Don't rush.

Give this conclusion its appropriate due.

mammon = MAM-uhn

I tell you, make **friends** for **yourselves** with dishonest **wealth**,
    so that when it **fails**, you will be **welcomed**
        into eternal **dwellings**.
[The **person** who is **trustworthy** in very small **matters**
    is also **trustworthy** in **great** ones;
    and the **person** who is **dishonest** in very small **matters**
    is also **dishonest** in **great** ones.
If, therefore, you are not **trustworthy** with **dishonest wealth**,
    who will **trust** you with **true wealth**?
If you are not **trustworthy** with what belongs to **another**,
    who will **give** you what is **yours**?
No **servant** can **serve** two **masters**.
He will either **hate** one and **love** the other,
    or be **devoted** to one and **despise** the other.
You cannot **serve** both **God** and **mammon**."]

[Shorter: Luke 16:10–13 (see brackets)]

insists that how people deal with small matters demonstrates how they will deal with greater ones. Those who show God that they are trustworthy with material possessions will be entrusted with the valuables of God's kingdom. These are the gifts that God destines for everyone and that only God can give—possessions that Jesus' disciples can take with them at death.

The final saying, "You cannot serve both God and mammon," should provoke a crisis for Jesus' disciples. There is no middle ground here, no moderate option. To compromise is to choose one or the other. At every moment, a disciple is hating and despising *either* wealth *or* God, loving and being devoted *either* to wealth *or* to God. Some scholars capitalize and personify "*mammon*," making the choice between "God" and "Mammon" a personal one.

The verse following this passage shows that the religious leaders apparently overhear Jesus teaching his disciples, for Luke notes, "The religious pharisees, who loved money (*philaguroi*, literally "the lovers of money") heard all these things and sneered at him [Jesus]"! And what is our response? Does how we manage our possessions show that we are sneering at him too? E.N.

TWENTY-SIXTH SUNDAY IN ORDINARY TIME

LECTIONARY #138

READING I   Amos 6:1a, 4–7

A reading from the Book of the Prophet Amos

> **Thus** says the LORD, the **God** of **hosts**:
> **Woe** to the complacent in **Zion**!
> **Lying** upon beds of **ivory**,
>   stretched **comfortably** on their **couches**,
> they eat **lambs** taken from the **flock**,
>   and **calves** from the **stall**!
> **Improvising** to the music of the **harp**,
>   like **David**, they **devise** their own **accompaniment**.
> They drink **wine** from **bowls**
>   and **anoint** themselves with the best **oils**;
>   yet they are **not** made **ill** by the **collapse** of **Joseph**!
> **Therefore**, now they shall be the **first** to go into **exile**,
>   and their **wanton revelry** shall be done **away** with.

RESPONSORIAL PSALM   Psalm 146:7, 8–9, 9–10 (1b)

R. Praise the Lord, my soul!
or R. Alleluia.

Blessed is he who keeps faith forever,
    secures justice for the oppressed,
    gives food to the hungry.
The LORD sets captives free.

The LORD gives sight to the blind;
    the LORD raises up those who were
    bowed down.
The LORD loves the just;
    the LORD protects strangers.

The fatherless and the widow he sustains,
    but the way of the wicked he thwarts.
The LORD shall reign forever;
    your God, O Zion, through all generations.
    Alleluia.

Amos = AY-m*s

An exhortatory reading from one of the minor prophets, Amos. It offers lyrically charged accusations toward the hedonists in Zion.

complacent = kuhm-PLAY-s*nt

accompaniment = uh-KUHM-p*-nee-m*nt

anoint = uh-NOYNT
wanton = WAHN-tuhn
revelry = REV-uhl-ree
The reading concludes with the Lord's intention to punish these sinners for their excesses.

For meditation and context:

READING I   In the first half of the eighth century BC, Israel enjoyed a period of unusual prosperity because the powerful nations of Assyria to the north and Egypt to the south were too preoccupied with internal problems to expand their territory. But in the second half of the century, this situation changes as the Assyrian armies move toward Israel. In this passage, Amos declares that they will conquer God's people because Israel's leaders indulge themselves and ignore their covenant responsibility to care for the needy.

The prophet calls those in charge "complacent," in Hebrew, *sha'anan*. The word describes people who are "at ease" or "feel secure" and fall into careless, intemperate habits. They lie around on expensive furniture and dine on the costliest meats, lamb and veal. They "stretch comfortably" (Hebrew *seruchim)* on couches that are inlaid with fine ivory carvings. The picturesque participle, *seruchim*, depicts them "sprawled"—like a piece of material draped over a couch or like the dangling branches of a wild vine. Making up songs, they fancy themselves to be musicians like David.

They drink wine from "bowls" (Hebrew *miz-raqim*)—probably not ordinary bowls but vessels normally used in sacred rituals (see Numbers 4:14; 7:13, 19, 37, for example). They anoint themselves with the best oils. In biblical times, olive oil was used to cleanse the skin. Expensive brands of it were scented.

Especially egregious in the Lord's view is that Israel's leaders are not sickened by or grieving for the fall of "Joseph"—a name for the areas of northern Israel that were settled by Joseph's sons and are now threatened by the Assyrians. Because the

READING II   1 Timothy 6:11–16

A reading from the first Letter of Saint Paul to Timothy

But **you**, man of **God**, pursue **righteousness**,
    devotion, **faith**, **love**, **patience**, and **gentleness**.
Compete **well** for the **faith**.
Lay **hold** of eternal **life**, to which you were **called**
    when you made the **noble confession** in the **presence**
        of many **witnesses**.
I charge you before **God**, who gives **life** to all **things**,
    and **before Christ Jesus**,
    who gave **testimony** under Pontius **Pilate**
        for the **noble confession**,
    to keep the **commandment** without **stain** or **reproach**
    until the **appearance** of our **Lord** Jesus **Christ**
    that the **blessed** and only **ruler**
    will make **manifest** at the proper **time**,
    the King of **kings** and Lord of **lords**,
    who **alone** has **immortality**, who **dwells**
        in unapproachable **light**,
    and whom **no human being** has **seen** or can **see**.
To **him** be **honor** and eternal **power**. Amen.

GOSPEL   Luke 16:19–31

A reading from the holy Gospel according to Luke

Jesus said to the **Pharisees**:
"There was a **rich man** who dressed in **purple garments**
        and **fine linen**
    and dined **sumptuously** each day.
And **lying** at his **door** was a **poor man** named **Lazarus**,
        covered with **sores**,
    who would **gladly** have **eaten** his **fill** of the **scraps**
        that **fell** from the rich man's **table**.

leaders always had to be "first," the Lord declares they shall be the "first" to go into exile. Their party is over.

READING II This reading reminds Timothy, a "man of God," of the noble confession that he made before many witnesses. As a pastor, he is especially bound to model a virtuous life. His mission is to "Compete well for the faith" or literally, "fight (*agōnizomai*) the good fight (*agōna*) of the faith." The Greek for both the verb and the noun "fight" here conveys the

constant struggle to act justly, patiently, gently—in a godly manner—in situations that demand all of one's mental and physical energy. Those who stay in the fight are laying hold of eternal life to which all the baptized are called.

GOSPEL Jesus' parable pairs a stereotypical rich man and Lazarus, a poor man whose name is the Greek version of the Hebrew Eliezar, which means "my God helps." The rich man sports the finest fashions and dines on sumptuous

meals "every day." And Lazarus lies, always hungry, at his door while the dogs lick his sore-covered body.

The death of both men precipitates the main issue of the parable, namely, a person's post-death, irreversible, everlasting destiny. Lazarus, who was probably carried daily to the rich man's gate, dies and is carried by God's angels to the bosom of Abraham. The rich man died and "was buried." How shocked those who mourn him would be to see his changed circumstances! Now in torment, he raises his eyes from the

bosom = BOO-zuhm *or* BOO-zuhm

netherworld = NETH-ehr-wehrld

Here the dialogue begins between the rich man and Abraham. There's a pitiful extravagance in the rich man's request.

Abraham's rebuke is sober in tone.

The rich man quickly grasps the nature of his situation and, surprisingly, shows a change of heart.

Abraham once again rebukes the rich man, more quietly this time.

The rich man pleads again. He is in dead earnest.

Abraham elaborates on his previous response.

Dogs even used to come and **lick** his **sores**.
When the **poor** man died,
   he was carried **away** by **angels** to the **bosom** of **Abraham**.
The **rich** man also died and was **buried**,
   and from the **netherworld**, where he was in **torment**,
   he raised his **eyes** and saw **Abraham** far off
   and **Lazarus** at his side.
And he cried out, 'Father **Abraham**, have **pity** on me.
Send Lazarus to dip the **tip** of his **finger** in **water** and **cool**
     my **tongue**,
   for I am suffering **torment** in these **flames**.'
Abraham **replied**,
   'My **child**, **remember** that you **received**
   what was **good** during your **lifetime**
   while **Lazarus likewise received** what was **bad**;
   but **now** he is **comforted** here, whereas **you** are **tormented**.
Moreover, between **us** and **you** a great **chasm** is **established**
   to prevent **anyone** from **crossing** who might wish to go
   from **our** side to **yours** or from **your side** to **ours**.'
He said, 'Then I **beg** you, father,
   send him to my father's **house**, for I have **five brothers**,
   so that he may **warn** them,
   lest **they too** come to this **place** of **torment**.'
But **Abraham** replied, 'They have **Moses** and the **prophets**.
Let them **listen** to **them**.'
He said, 'Oh no, father **Abraham**,
   but if **someone** from the **dead** goes to them, they will **repent**.'
Then **Abraham** said, 'If they will not **listen** to **Moses**
     and the **prophets**,
   neither will they be **persuaded** if someone should **rise**
     from the **dead**.'"

---

other side of a great gaping chasm and sees Abraham—and *Lazarus (of all people)* at his side.

Still not grasping his changed status, he begs "Father Abraham" to have pity on him (Greek *eleeison me*) and orders Lazarus to dampen and cool his parched tongue. The rich man is like the "crowd of vipers" whom the prophet John the Baptist tells: "Produce good fruit as evidence of your repentance [Greek *metanoia*; in other words, prove that you've changed your thinking and thus your ways] and do not begin to say to yourselves, 'We have

Abraham as our father.'" John also tells them that to avoid the wrath to come, "Whoever has two tunics should share with the person who has none. And whoever has food should do likewise" (Luke 3:8, 11). The rich man now suffers the consequences of doing neither. For him, the wrath has come.

His worry about his five brothers reflects Luke's concern to persuade second- or third-generation Christians, who (like us) never saw Jesus, to take Scripture seriously. When they fail to do so and follow instead the advice of the countless "experts" of

their day, their discipleship becomes a cushy caricature of the life that Jesus calls them to live.

Today's parable haunts us with the possibility that after death, like the self-absorbed rich man, we too could find ourselves on the wrong side of an uncrossable chasm. Stuck there and suffering one torment after another, we raise our eyes to see the Lord comforting the needy whom we ignored. It finally dawns on us that, like the rich man, we cannot improve our situation. E.N.

TWENTY-SEVENTH SUNDAY IN ORDINARY TIME

LECTIONARY #141

Habakkuk = huh-BAK-kuhk *or* HAB-uh-kuhk

An exhortatory reading from one of the minor prophets we don't often hear from in the lectionary. In this one, Habakkuk voices timely frustration and receives encouraging counsel from the Lord.

intervene = ihn-tehr-VEEN

This question focuses the first half of the reading, which voices Habakkuk's plea.

clamorous = KLAM-ehr-uhs

The Lord's answer is succinct. A tone of clarity and reassurance carries through.

This ends on a good note.

READING I   Habakkuk 1:2–3; 2:2–4

A reading from the Book of the Prophet Habakkuk

How **long**, O LORD? I **cry** for **help**
   but you do not **listen!**
I cry **out** to you, "**Violence!**"
   but you **do** not **intervene.**
Why do you let me see **ruin;**
   why must I look at **misery?**
Destruction and **violence** are **before** me;
   there is **strife**, and clamorous **discord.**
Then the LORD **answered** me and said:
   Write down the vision **clearly** upon the **tablets,**
   so that one can **read** it readily.
For the **vision** still has its **time,**
   presses **on** to **fulfillment**, and will **not** disappoint;
if it **delays, wait** for it,
   it will **surely** come, it will **not** be late.
The **rash** one has no **integrity;**
   but the **just** one, because of his **faith**, shall **live.**

READING I Oppressed people of every age ask Habakkuk's question, "How long, O Lord, [will] I cry for help, but you do not listen?" How long before the Lord intervenes and stops the "violence." This violence, in Hebrew *chamas*, denotes the calculated actions of arrogant and greedy people who take advantage of others and diminish their chances for a full and peaceful life. The prophet sees *chamas* everywhere: destruction, accusation and litigation, clamorous debate, and misery. Even people with only slight control over

the lives of others too often wield their bit of power for harm rather than for good.

The Lord does not answer Habakkuk's question, "How long?", but tells him to write down clearly the vision that announces the downfall of tyrants of every ilk and the Lord's coming reign over all the earth. As these events unfold, the long-suffering will realize that the Lord heard their cries. In the meantime, the task of the just is to live with integrity and thus to display their faith that the Lord is dependable and at work.

Despite appearances to the contrary, the divine vision is pressing on to fulfillment.

READING II In the verse that precedes this reading, Paul expresses his confidence that the faith that dwelt in Timothy's grandmother Lois and in his mother, Eunice, now dwells in Timothy. Timothy, however, needs to live this faith more resolutely. He needs to "stir into flame the gift [Greek, *charisma*] of God," that is, the unique talents he received when Paul laid hands on him. To bear wit-

For meditation and context:

RESPONSORIAL PSALM   Psalm 95:1–2, 6–7, 8–9 (8)

R. If today you hear his voice, harden not your hearts.

Come, let us sing joyfully to the LORD;
  let us acclaim the Rock of our salvation.
Let us come into his presence with
    thanksgiving;
  let us joyfully sing psalms to him.

Come, let us bow down in worship;
  let us kneel before the LORD who made us.
For he is our God,
  and we are the people he shepherds, the
    flock he guides.

Oh, that today you would hear his voice:
  "Harden not your hearts as at Meribah,
    as in the day of Massah in the desert,
where your fathers tempted me;
  they tested me though they had seen
   my works."

TO KEEP IN MIND

The responsorial psalm "has great liturgical and pastoral importance, since it fosters meditation on the Word of God," the *General Instruction of the Roman Missal* says. Pray it as you prepare.

READING II   2 Timothy 1:6–8, 13–14

An exhortatory reading from St. Paul to his disciple Timothy that is laced with intimate encouragement.

A reading from the second Letter of Saint Paul to Timothy

Beloved:
I **remind** you to stir into **flame**
  the gift of **God** that you **have** through the **imposition**
    of my **hands**.

cowardice = KOW-ehr-dihs

For **God** did not give us a **spirit** of **cowardice**
  but rather of **power** and **love** and **self-control**.

Paul uses the rhetorical device of setting up his encouragement by stating something in the negative. Emphasis on "do not."

So **do not** be **ashamed** of your **testimony** to our **Lord**,
  nor of **me**, a **prisoner** for his **sake**;
  but **bear** your share of **hardship** for the **gospel**
    with the **strength** that comes from **God**.

With "Take," Paul really moves to reinforce his encouragement. Emphasis on "within."

Take as your norm the **sound words** that you **heard** from me,
  in the **faith** and **love** that are in Christ **Jesus**.
Guard this **rich trust** with the **help** of the Holy **Spirit**
  that dwells **within** us.

---

ness to the Lord effectively, Timothy must practice and develop pastoral skills.

   The main gift that Timothy (and every baptized person) received is the Holy Spirit. This is not a spineless or fainthearted spirit, but rather a spirit of power (Greek *dunamis*, from which derive the English words "dynamite," "dynamic"). The imprisoned, Spirit-filled Paul is Timothy's model. This intrepid apostle was never embarrassed to speak out. He never hesitated to counter the world's beliefs and opinions with the sound words of the Gospel. His courage, love, and self-discipline in the face of harsh treatment

and countless dangers both validated his teaching and persuaded many to live for the Lord alone. Now it is Timothy's turn to boldly bear his "share of hardship for the Gospel," relying on the strength (*dunamis*) that comes from God.

GOSPEL   In the first of two teachings, Luke suggests that the apostles are not convinced that Jesus is trustworthy. They hesitate to place their life completely in his hands, and so ask him to increase their faith.

   In response, Jesus points to a mulberry tree and tells them that if they (in Greek, "you" is plural) have faith the size of the tiniest seed, they could command the mulberry tree to "be uprooted and planted in the sea." And it would obey them! Picture it: this land-loving tree wriggles free its extensive, long-tentacled root system and then, with no apparent assistance, plants itself *in the sea*—an environment that is foreign and hostile to its makeup. Likewise, even a little faith in Jesus can achieve unimaginable outcomes.

GOSPEL   Luke 17:5–10

A reading from the holy Gospel according to Luke

The **apostles** said to the **Lord**, "**Increase** our **faith**."
The Lord replied,
>   "If you have **faith** the size of a **mustard** seed,
>   you would **say** to this mulberry tree,
>   'Be **uprooted** and **planted** in the **sea**,' and it would **obey** you.

>   "Who **among** you would **say** to your **servant**
>   who has just come **in** from plowing or tending **sheep**
>   in the **field**,
>   'Come here **immediately** and take your **place** at **table**'?
>   Would he **not** rather **say** to him,
>   '**Prepare** something for **me** to **eat**.
>   Put on your **apron** and **wait** on me while I **eat** and **drink**.
>   You may **eat** and **drink** when I am **finished**'?
>   Is he **grateful** to that **servant** because he **did** what
>   was **commanded**?
>   **So should** it **be** with **you**.
>   When you have **done** all you have been **commanded**,
>   say, '**We are unprofitable servants**;
>   we have **done** what we were **obliged** to **do**.'"

A didactic reading with a genuinely puzzling message. A straightforward, direct, and uncomplicated delivery will serve this reading best.

mulberry = MUL-bayr-ee *or* MUL-buh-ree

The example Jesus gives here is challenging. Emphasize the details of the scenario he offers: the field, the table, the apron.

Note the rhythm: "SO SHOULD it BE with YOU."

Again, note the rhythm: "WE ARE unPROFitable SERVants."

Jesus' second saying equates the life of his disciples to that of a slave in the biblical world. These servants are on call 24/7. Their master gives them a daily "to-do" list, an agenda which may not include any personal time. Jesus could have made his point about the demands of discipleship by simply asking the hypothetical question: Who among you would say to a servant who comes in after completing a task, "Come here, sit down, and eat"? In the biblical world, the obvious answer would be "Not me! No way!" But Jesus draws out the scene to give more time for his point to sink in. He

has the master command his servant to prepare a meal for him, put on an apron, and stand by waiting on (Greek *diakoneō*) him while he eats and drinks. Only after the master is satisfied can the servant, who is no doubt quite exhausted and hungry by now, take care of his own needs.

Again, Jesus could have stopped his teaching at this point, but he adds another detail to the master's already harsh portrait. He asks, "Is the master grateful?" i.e., does he thank his servant who did only what he was obliged to do? The form of Jesus'

question in the Greek expects a resounding "No! The master is not grateful."

Jesus' teaching shocks part-time disciples, but also forces us to assess if we are truly bearing "our share of hardship for the Gospel." Do we take on tasks that both eat up our free time and necessitate "the strength that comes from God"? Or are we settled, useless servants who do the bare minimum that we are required to do? E.N.

TWENTY-EIGHTH SUNDAY IN ORDINARY TIME

LECTIONARY #144

READING I   2 Kings 5:14–17

A reading from the second Book of Kings

Naaman went **down** and **plunged** into the Jordan **seven times**
    at the word of **Elisha**, the man of **God**.
His **flesh** became again like the **flesh** of a little **child**,
    and he was **clean** of his **leprosy**.

Naaman **returned** with his whole **retinue** to the man of **God**.
On his **arrival** he stood before **Elisha** and said,
    "Now I **know** that there is **no God** in **all** the earth,
    except in **Israel**.
Please accept a **gift** from your **servant**."

Elisha replied, "As the LORD **lives** whom I **serve**, I will not
    take it";
    and despite Naaman's **urging**, he still **refused**.
Naaman said: "If you will **not accept**,
    please let me, your **servant**, have **two mule-loads** of **earth**,
    for I will no **longer** offer **holocaust** or **sacrifice**
    to any other **god** except to the LORD."

A narrative reading of healing, devotion, and sacrifice. Naaman, who suffered from leprosy and was healed, is the focus of the reading. Use his name to focus your proclamation.

leprosy = LEP-ruh-see
Naaman = NAY-uh-muhn
retinue = RET-*n-oo *or* RET-*n-yoo
Elisha = ee-LI-shuh
There's an urgency to Naaman's return after he's healed.

Elisha's reply to Naaman has a tricky rhythm. Practice it a few times.

Naaman's reply indicates his newfound devotion.

Holocaust =
HAHL-uh-kawst *or* HOH-luh-kawst

READING I Naaman is a successful commander of the king of Aram's army. But he is also a "leper"—one who, in biblical times, suffers from some kind of skin disorder. This reading pares a long story down to the moment of Naaman's cure and his deep gratitude to Elisha's God. The sudden transformation of his "leprous" skin to that of a "young man" convinces him that the God of Israel is the only God.

Naaman's request that Elisha allow him to take two mule-loads of earth from Israel reflects the belief in his day that gods are associated with a certain territory.

Naaman wants to take some of Lord's territory with him so that, when he returns home, he can build an altar on it and there continue to thank and worship the Lord who healed him.

The omitted sections of this story emphasize the new relationship with the Lord that begins with Naaman's healing. In one scene, when Naaman offers Elisha a gift for his healing, Elisha swears by the Lord that he will not take it. Though Naaman keeps pressing him to accept expensive gifts, the "man of God" insists on redirecting the Aramean's attention and

gratitude to God. Elisha persists in his refusal until, finally, Naaman gives up.

In the concluding scenes of the story (2 Kings 5:19b–27), Elisha's servant Gehazi provides a counterexample to the "man of God." For selfish reasons, he directs Naaman's thoughts away from the Lord, back to the Elisha who is the Lord's human agent. He does this for a selfish reason; he cannot resist benefitting personally from what the Lord did for Naaman. He goes to the commander with a tale that needy guild-prophets showed up and that to care for them Elisha now needs some of the

For meditation and context:

RESPONSORIAL PSALM Psalm 98:1, 2–3, 3–4 (see 2b)

R. The Lord has revealed to the nations his saving power.

Sing to the LORD a new song,
   for he has done wondrous deeds;
his right hand has won victory for him,
   his holy arm.

The LORD has made his salvation known:
   in the sight of the nations he has
     revealed his justice.

He has remembered his kindness and
   his faithfulness
   toward the house of Israel.

All the ends of the earth have seen
   the salvation by our God.
Sing joyfully to the LORD, all you lands:
   break into song; sing praise.

READING II 2 Timothy 2:8–13

An exhortatory reading from St. Paul's second letter to his disciple Timothy. The personal quality of this letter yields in this reading to an impassioned exhortation.

A reading from the second Letter of Saint Paul to Timothy

Beloved:
Remember Jesus Christ, raised from the dead,
   a **descendant** of **David**:
  such is my gospel, for which I am **suffering**,
  even to the point of **chains**, like a **criminal**.
But the **word** of **God** is not **chained**.

With "Therefore," Paul is revving his rhetorical engines, getting ready to make a powerful statement.

Therefore, I bear with **everything** for the **sake** of those
   who are **chosen**,
  so that **they too** may obtain the **salvation** that is
   in **Christ Jesus**,
  together with eternal **glory**.
This saying is **trustworthy**:

The reading concludes with a series of rhythmical statements of reinforcing intensity, concluding with "cannot deny himself."

  If we have **died** with him
   we shall also **live** with him;
  if we **persevere**
   we shall also **reign** with him
  But if we **deny** him
   he will **deny** us.
  If we are **unfaithful**
   he remains **faithful**,
   for he **cannot deny himself**.

> **TO KEEP IN MIND**
> When you proclaim of the Word you participate in catechizing the faithful and those coming to faith. Understand what you proclaim so those hearing you may also understand.

---

offered gifts. Naaman graciously complies, giving him money and clothing. Elisha witnesses the exchange "in spirit" and, in the end, Gehazi walks away with the gifts he craved but also with Naaman's leprosy.

READING II Paul sits in prison because he never stopped preaching the Gospel that Jesus Christ was raised from the dead. He reflects that, though *he* is locked up and in chains, "the word of God" that he preaches is not—indeed cannot be—chained.

Paul endures (Greek *hupomenō*) every situation for the sake of the people he encounters. He considers each one a unique person whom God is drawing into a relationship with Christ. Paul's experiences convinced him that, if in baptism we have *died with* Christ, we shall also *live with* him, and if we persevere (*hupomenō*) to the end of our mission we shall also *reign with* him. "Died *with*," "live *with*," "reign *with*"—the Greek prefix *sun* ("with") in each verb form emphasizes the intimate companionship that Christ offers every believer. Their union is so real that even if the baptized are

unfaithful, Christ remains faithful to them because he cannot deny himself.

GOSPEL As Jesus continues his journey to Jerusalem, he enters a village and hears voices crying out to him, "Have mercy [Greek *eleeison*] on us." Seeing ten lepers standing at a distance, he commands them to go show themselves to the priests who can declare them "clean" and therefore able to rejoin community life. As the lepers go off, they are cleansed. After this brief recounting of the healing, the rest of the Gospel develops the Samaritan's

GOSPEL Luke 17:11–19

A reading from the holy Gospel according to Luke

As **Jesus** continued his **journey** to **Jerusalem**,
 he traveled through **Samaria** and **Galilee**.
As he was entering a **village**, **ten lepers met** him.
They **stood** at a **distance** from him and raised
  their **voices**, saying,
 "**Jesus, Master!** Have **pity** on us!"
And when he **saw** them, he said,
 "Go **show** yourselves to the **priests**."
As they were **going** they were **cleansed**.
And **one** of them, realizing he had been **healed**,
 returned, glorifying **God** in a **loud voice**;
 and he fell at the feet of **Jesus** and **thanked** him.
He was a **Samaritan**.
Jesus said in reply,
 "**Ten** were cleansed, were they **not**?
Where are the other **nine**?
Has **none** but this **foreigner returned** to give **thanks** to God?"
Then he said to him, "Stand **up** and **go**;
 your **faith** has **saved** you."

A narrative reading about healing and thankfulness whose message could not be any clearer. Let the expression of numbers in this reading guide your proclamation.
 Slight pause between "village" and "ten."
Samaria = suh-MAYR-ee-uh
Galilee = GAL-ih-lee
lepers = LEP-ehrz

Emphasis on "one."

Emphasis on "ten," "nine," and then "none."

reaction to his sudden cure and his encounter with Jesus.

Unlike his companions, the Samaritan does not rush on his way to get the official declaration that will allow him to return to his old life. The extraordinary and sudden reversal of his condition stops him in his tracks. As to a magnet, he is drawn back to Jesus, to the *person* who healed him and removed the stigma that kept him separated from others. This return of the one leper who is not a Jew sparks Jesus' question about the majority of his co-religionists who went their way. He asks, "Where are the other nine?" Seemingly, once Jesus answered their cry for mercy, they have no further interest in him.

Jesus tells the Samaritan that his faith "saved" him. In this passage, it is clear that faith entails more than verbal assent to a collection of religious teachings. Accompanying the Samaritan's belief in Jesus is an overwhelming desire to continue a relationship with him.

Lastly, this anecdote shows that the proof of each person's faith is the thanksgiving that he or she directs to God. There is nothing restrained or rote about this gratitude. The Samaritan, for example, is not content merely to offer a quiet prayer or recite formulas or a creed. His faith constrains him to put the rest of his life on hold and express his gratitude by glorifying God loudly and falling to his knees at the feet of Jesus. E.N.

TWENTY-NINTH SUNDAY IN ORDINARY TIME

LECTIONARY #147

READING I Exodus 17:8–13

Exodus = EK-suh-duhs
A narrative reading whose details are as peculiar as they are magical and whose outcome is grim. It's as much a myth or fable as it is an instruction.
Amalek = AM-uh-lehk
Joshua = JOSH-oo-uh *or* JOSH-yoo-uh

Joshua's compliance suggests he understands what Moses is offering him: supernatural aid in battle.

Aaron = AYR-uhn
Hur = her
These details are peculiar and compelling. Don't rush through this passage.

The conclusion is grim: Amalek and his people are destroyed by Joshua because of Moses' jerry-rigged supernatural aid.

A reading from the Book of Exodus

In **those days, Amalek** came and waged **war** against **Israel**.
Moses, therefore, said to **Joshua**,
    "**Pick out** certain **men**,
    and **tomorrow** go **out** and engage **Amalek** in **battle**.
I will be **standing** on top of the **hill**
    with the **staff** of **God** in my **hand**."
So **Joshua** did as Moses **told** him:
    he engaged **Amalek** in **battle**
    after **Moses** had climbed to the top of the **hill**
        with **Aaron** and **Hur**.
As long as **Moses** kept his **hands** raised **up**,
    Israel had the better of the **fight**,
    but when he let his **hands rest**,
    Amalek had the better of the **fight**.
Moses' hands, however, grew **tired**;
    so they put a **rock** in place for him to **sit** on.
Meanwhile Aaron and **Hur** supported his **hands**,
    one on **one** side and **one** on the **other**,
    so that his **hands** remained **steady** till **sunset**.
And Joshua **mowed down Amalek** and his **people**
    with the **edge** of the **sword**.

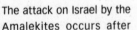 **READING I** The attack on Israel by the Amalekites occurs after the Lord brings the people through the Red Sea, during their wandering in the wilderness. One aim of this attack, like all the trials and dangers that confront Israel on their journey to the promised land, is to teach the people to trust that the Lord is always active on their behalf.

Joshua engages the Amalekites in battle while Moses, Aaron, and Hur go to the top of a hill overlooking the scene. However, the main participant in this encounter is "the staff of God." This is the staff with which Moses struck the Nile river and turned it to blood, which made frogs overrun the land of Egypt, turned all the dust of Egypt into gnats, and brought the hail and the locusts. It is also the staff that split the Red Sea in two, opening an escape route for Israel where none existed.

As long as Moses holds high the staff of God, the tide of the battle with the Amalekites favors the Israelites. But when his hand grows heavy and he lowers the staff, the Amalekites begin to win. Eventually, Moses tires and needs to sit down on a rock while Aaron and Hur support his arms to keep aloft the staff. All these details show that the victory at sundown is clearly the result of God's fighting on Israel's side.

READING II In this passage, Scripture refers to the Jewish writings that trace the relationship that developed between God and Israel up to the time of Christ. Paul urged Timothy, a pastor, to be faithful to these writings, to recall how they lead people to appreciate the salvation that Christ Jesus—God incarnate—offers to those who believe in him. The

For meditation and context:

RESPONSORIAL PSALM Psalm 121:1–2, 3–4, 5–6, 7–8 (see 2)

R. Our help is from the Lord, who made heaven and earth.

I lift up my eyes toward the mountains;
   whence shall help come to me?
My help is from the LORD,
   who made heaven and earth.

May he not suffer your foot to slip;
   may he slumber not who guards you:
indeed he neither slumbers nor sleeps,
   the guardian of Israel.

The LORD is your guardian; the LORD is
   your shade;
   he is beside you at your right hand.
The sun shall not harm you by day,
   nor the moon by night.

The LORD will guard you from all evil;
   he will guard your life.
The LORD will guard your coming and
   your going,
   both now and forever.

READING II 2 Timothy 3:14—4:2

An exhortatory reading from St. Paul to his disciple Timothy in which he is urged to be true to Scripture. The tone is one of encouragement and urgency.

A reading from the second Letter of Saint Paul to Timothy

Beloved:

Remain **faithful** to what you have **learned** and **believed**,
   because you **know** from whom you **learned** it,
   and that from **infancy** you have known the **sacred Scriptures**,
   which are **capable** of giving you **wisdom** for **salvation**
   through **faith** in Christ **Jesus**.
All Scripture is inspired by **God**
   and is **useful** for **teaching**, for **refutation**, for **correction**,
   and for **training** in **righteousness**,
   so that one who **belongs** to God may be **competent**,
   equipped for every good **work**.

With "All Scripture," Paul is orienting Timothy to Scripture for support.

> **TO KEEP IN MIND**
> Recognize how important your proclamation of the Word of God is. Prepare well and take joy in your ministry.

I **charge** you in the presence of **God** and of Christ **Jesus**,
   who will judge the **living** and the **dead**,
   and by his **appearing** and his kingly **power**:
   proclaim the **word**;
   be **persistent** whether it is **convenient** or **inconvenient**;
   convince, **reprimand**, **encourage** through all **patience**
      and **teaching**.

Paul shifts into the imperative voice. The urgency mounts. Emphasize "proclaim" and "word."
All the verbs in this concluding verse are in the imperative.

---

declaration that all Scripture is "inspired by God" (Greek *theopneustos*, "breathed into by God") is the basis for the Church's confidence in the Bible's preeminent suitability for "teaching, refutation, correction, and for training in righteousness."

In the presence of God and Christ Jesus, who is the final judge of all, Paul solemnly charges Timothy to proclaim the word continually and urgently—whether it is convenient or not. Paul insists that it is not enough to recite Scripture. With unfailing patience, Timothy must convincingly teach those he pastors that God, who acts

on behalf of Israel in the first reading, came in Christ and is now working through the baptized. Timothy must teach them how God uses the incidents of daily life to increase their faith, to build their competence, and to equip them for the unique work that God gives them to do.

| GOSPEL | Jesus' parable stresses that his disciples must pray always without becoming weary, without losing heart. He insists that their prayers, like "the staff of God" that Moses and his helpers held high, channel God's saving

power into earthly situations. Today, he pairs a local judge and a widow who is taken advantage of because she has no man to speak for her.

The judge does not "fear" God, that is, he does not consider God to be a real player in earthly events. Nor does this judge respect other people's opinions. A law unto himself, he goes his own way in the world and does what he pleases. The unjustly treated widow comes to him time after time, begging him to take legal action against her adversary. But the judge repeatedly refuses to give the justice due

GOSPEL   Luke 18:1–8

A reading from the holy Gospel according to Luke

Jesus told his **disciples** a **parable**
   about the **necessity** for them to pray **always**
      without becoming **weary**.
He said, "There was a **judge** in a certain **town**
   who neither feared **God** nor respected **any human being**.
And a **widow** in that town used to come to him and say,
   '**Render** a **just decision** for me against my **adversary**.'
For a **long time** the judge was **unwilling**, but eventually
     he thought,
   'While it is **true** that I neither **fear God** nor respect
     any human being,
   because this **widow** keeps **bothering** me
   I shall deliver a **just** decision for her
   lest she finally come and **strike** me.'"
The Lord said, "**Pay attention** to what the **dishonest** judge says.
Will not **God** then secure the **rights** of his **chosen ones**
   who call **out** to him **day** and **night**?
Will he be slow to **answer** them?
I **tell** you, he will **see** to it that **justice** is **done** for them **speedily**.
But when the Son of **Man** comes, will he find **faith** on **earth**?"

A narrative reading that consists largely of a parable, one that Jesus offers along with a series of questions, rather than an interpretation. The questions suggest that the teaching of the parable is not obvious but something more subtle.

The character of this dishonest judge is at the center of this parable.

adversary = AD-vehr-sayr-ee

His character is reemphasized in the judge's own words.

Emphasis on "bothering" (The widow is a bother).

Jesus concludes with these questions. Best to ask them in earnest.

---

her because, as the Greek puts it, "he didn't want to."

The widow, however, does not lose heart. Her persistence moves the judge to act. Jesus focuses, not on the judge's abuse of his position, but on why he finally does the right thing for the widow. Namely, he worries that she might "strike" him. The Greek, *hupōpiazō*, means literally "to strike in the face / under the eye," leading some scholars to translate it "to give a black eye." *Hupōpiazō* can figuratively convey "to wear down, torment, or browbeat."

Jesus sums up: if the widow's prayers can move such a judge, will not the prayers of God's chosen ones secure justice for them? The word pair "day and night" expresses "all the time." If God's people pray continually, Jesus assures them that God will suddenly or quickly act.

Scholars note the plaintive or doubtful tone of Jesus' final question—a tone that is injected by the Greek interrogative particle (*ara*). Difficult to translate, *ara* can convey worry or impatience, in which case Jesus says something like "Will the Son of Man

actually find any faith on earth when he returns?" Will he find any disciples praying —holding high the "staff of God"—over the dangers that assail them? Will the risen Christ find any people through whom he can send his saving grace into the world? E.N.

THIRTIETH SUNDAY IN ORDINARY TIME

LECTIONARY #150

READING I   Sirach 35:12–14, 16–18

A reading from the Book of Sirach

> The LORD is a God of **justice**,
>   who **knows** no **favorites**.
> Though **not** unduly **partial** toward the **weak**,
>   yet he **hears** the **cry** of the **oppressed**.
> The **Lord** is not deaf to the **wail** of the **orphan**,
>   nor to the **widow** when she pours **out** her **complaint**.
> The one who serves God **willingly** is **heard**;
>   his **petition** reaches the **heavens**.
> The prayer of the **lowly** pierces the **clouds**;
>   it does not **rest** till it reaches its **goal**,
> nor will it **withdraw** till the **Most High responds**,
>   judges **justly** and affirms the **right**,
> and the **Lord** will **not delay**.

RESPONSORIAL PSALM   Psalm 34:2–3, 17–18, 19, 23 (7a)

R. The Lord hears the cry of the poor.

I will bless the LORD at all times;
    his praise shall be ever in my mouth.
Let my soul glory in the LORD;
    the lowly will hear me and be glad.

The LORD confronts the evildoers,
    to destroy remembrance of them
        from the earth.

When the just cry out, the LORD hears them,
    and from all their distress he rescues them.

The LORD is close to the brokenhearted;
    and those who are crushed in spirit
        he saves.
The LORD redeems the lives of his servants;
    no one incurs guilt who takes refuge
        in him.

Sidebar notes:

Sirach = SEER-ak or SĪ-ruhk

An exhortatory reading with a focus on justice and petition. The tone is emphatic and forceful.

Emphasis on "out," even though this might seem unusual.

Slight pause between "Most High" and "responds."

Note the rhythm: "and the LORD will NOT deLAY."

For meditation and context:

TO KEEP IN MIND

As you prepare your proclamation, make choices about what emotions need to be expressed. Some choices are evident from the text, but some are harder to discern. Understanding the context of the Scripture passage will help you decide.

READING I   The wisdom teacher Sirach declares that the Lord is a just God who shows no partiality to either the weak or their oppressors. Nevertheless, he also teaches that God is especially attentive to those who have little power and are easily taken advantage of—like widows and orphans.

Sirach assures his readers that the Lord hears the prayers of every person who serves God willingly. In this passage, the sage imagines these prayers shooting heavenward through the clouds and travelling as personal envoys who do not rest until they reach their destination. Once there, they do not leave until the Most High responds by executing justice for those in the right.

READING II   This reading invites each of us who are baptized to evaluate our commitment to Christ. In other words, if we were to die today, could we honestly say what Paul says to Timothy? First, Paul declares that he is already being poured out like a "libation," the drink offering that is poured out at the end of some Jewish sacrificial rituals. The sacrifice that Paul offers is his life, which is drawing to a close. He sees all his personal experiences and trials as elements of a ritual that, over time, fused his life with Christ until he no longer sensed any separation between them.

Looking back, Paul can also say, "I have competed well," literally "I have fought the good fight" (see the commentary for the Twenty-Sixth Sunday in Ordinary Time). The physical scars from shipwrecks and beatings and his worn-down body bear witness to his resolute devotion to his Lord.

READING II   2 Timothy 4:6–8, 16–18

A reading from the second Letter of Saint Paul to Timothy

Beloved:
I am **already** being poured **out** like a **libation**,
　　and the **time** of my **departure** is at **hand**.
I have competed **well**; I have finished the **race**;
　　I have kept the **faith**.
From **now on** the **crown** of **righteousness awaits** me,
　　which the **Lord**, the just **judge**,
　　will **award** to me on that **day**, and not **only** to **me**,
　　but to **all** who have **longed** for his **appearance**.

At my **first defense** no one **appeared** on my **behalf**,
　　but **everyone deserted** me.
May it **not** be **held against** them!
But the **Lord** stood by me and gave me **strength**,
　　so that **through** me the **proclamation** might be **completed**
　　and all the **Gentiles** might **hear** it.
And I was **rescued** from the lion's **mouth**.
The Lord will **rescue** me from **every evil threat**
　　and will bring me **safe** to his heavenly **kingdom**.
To **him** be **glory forever** and **ever**. Amen.

An exhortatory reading in which St. Paul encourages his disciple Timothy. It begins with the genuinely striking image that Paul is being "poured out like a libation."
libation = li-BAY-shuhn

Slight pause between "everyone" and "deserted."

Note the rhythm: "May it NOT be HELD aGAINST them."

Despite the emphasis on "every evil threat," the tone of this conclusion is uplifting.

Paul never retired. He finished "the race," the unique life-long mission that Christ gave him. And now, he knows that "the crown of righteousness" awaits him, as it awaits all who live for Christ and long for his return. Paul imagines the moment when the Lord himself will place that crown on his head.

Concerning those who failed to stand up for him and deserted him (see 2 Timothy 4:10, 14), Paul says, "May it not be held against them." For him, the Lord's loyalty and companionship far, far outweigh and

overshadow the hurt and aftermath of human betrayals.

He can honestly say that he never passed up a chance to spread "the proclamation" (Greek *kaerugma* / English *kerygma*). He sought, by word and action, to convince every person he encountered that Christ is alive and with him or her.

The context for Paul's image of rescue "from the lion's mouth" is a shepherd's life. For example, in 1 Samuel 17:34–35, David boasts when a lion would take a sheep from his father's flock, he would chase after it and "snatch the prey from its mouth."

Paul found—as every deeply committed Christian will find—that deliverance from dangerous situations is a standard feature of life in Christ. Paul's various rescues convince him that until his last breath, he can trust the Lord to save him from every possible evil and bring him safely into his heavenly kingdom.

GOSPEL   Luke tells us that Jesus addresses this parable to people who are both self-righteous and enjoy looking down on everyone else. Two men go up to the temple area to pray. One

GOSPEL Luke 18:9–14

A reading from the holy Gospel according to Luke

Jesus addressed this **parable**
to **those** who were convinced of their own **righteousness**
and **despised** everyone **else.**
"**Two people** went **up** to the temple area to **pray;**
one was a **Pharisee** and the **other** was a **tax** collector.
The **Pharisee** took up his **position** and **spoke** this prayer
to **himself,**
'O **God**, I **thank** you that I am **not like** the **rest** of **humanity**—
greedy, dishonest, adulterous—or **even** like this **tax** collector.
I fast **twice** a week, and I pay **tithes** on my **whole income.**'
But the **tax** collector stood off at a **distance**
and would not even raise his **eyes** to heaven
but beat his **breast** and **prayed,**
'O **God**, be **merciful** to me a **sinner.**'
I **tell** you, the **latter** went home **justified**, not the **former;**
for whoever **exalts** himself will be **humbled,**
and the one who **humbles** himself will be **exalted.**"

A narrative reading in which Jesus tells a short parable with a straightforward message he presents at its end.

Pharisee = FAYR-uh-seez

The pace here is important. Be sure to emphasize "not like," even if it doesn't feel like the obvious rhythm.
Even emphasis on all these qualities: "greedy," "dishonest," "adulterous."
tithes = tīths

justified = JUHS-tuh-fīd

The parable concludes with Jesus' message about it, expressed in the form of a classic inversion. For Jesus, this is an obvious truth.

---

is a religious leader, a Pharisee, to whom people look up; the other is an irreligious, unprincipled businessman, a tax collector whom people despise because he overcharges them to increase his personal profit.

The Pharisee goes to his usual place, his "pew" as it were, and immediately begins to pray "to himself." This last phrase does not appear in the description of the tax-collector, perhaps intimating that the Pharisee, though he "prays" to God, speaks only to himself. He is thankful that he is not a sinner like everyone else. Nor is he greedy or dishonest. He is trustworthy and

does not cheat on his wife. Because he fasts, he considers himself "religious." And rather than donate an arbitrary amount that he decides is adequate, he donates a full ten percent of his income.

In contrast, the tax collector positions himself at a distance from the temple and does not immediately start talking to God. He does not even presume to raise his eyes, but with head bowed he beats his breast. He is painfully aware that he is a sinner and asks only that God "be merciful." The Greek here is not the usual *eleison*, but *ilasthaeti*, which denotes "to expiate" or

"make atonement" for someone. The tax collector realizes that he cannot undo the chain reaction of harm that his greed and dishonesty set off in the lives of others.

The tax collector walks away from the temple justified in the only eyes that matter —God's. The Pharisee, who cultivates and cherishes an exalted opinion of his piety, does not. E.N.

THIRTY-FIRST SUNDAY IN ORDINARY TIME

LECTIONARY #153

READING I Wisdom 11:22—12:2

A reading from the Book of Wisdom

An exhortatory reading with strong language emphatically spilled out. Because it involves some complex phrasing, test out the stresses to suit your style of proclamation.

Slow your pace as you move through these phrases and into the question.
loathe = lohth

imperishable = ihm-PAYR-ih-shuh-b*l
rebuke = rih-BYOOK
Again, slow your pace slightly as you develop this conclusion.

Before the LORD the whole **universe** is as a **grain**
    from a **balance**
or a **drop** of morning **dew** come **down** upon the **earth**.
But you have **mercy** on **all**, because you can **do** all things;
    and you overlook people's **sins** that they may **repent**.
For you **love** all things that are
    and loathe **nothing** that you have **made**;
    for what you **hated**, you would not have **fashioned**.
And **how** could a thing **remain**, unless you **willed** it;
    or be **preserved**, had it **not** been called **forth** by **you**?
But you **spare** all things, because they are **yours**,
    O LORD and **lover** of **souls**,
    for your **imperishable spirit** is **in all things**!
Therefore you **rebuke** offenders **little** by **little**,
    warn them and **remind** them of the **sins**
        they are **committing**,
    that they may **abandon** their wickedness and **believe**
        in **you**, O LORD!

> **TO KEEP IN MIND**
> The words in bold are suggestions for ways to express the meaning of the reading. Consider using them as you practice the reading, then choose to stress them or to find your own way of proclaiming.

READING I This passage focuses on the relationship between the Lord's power and mercy. It first reminds us that, compared to the Lord, we have a very shallow knowledge of creation. We see only a small section of the universe and stand in awe before the power of its natural phenomena. To the Lord, however, the entire cosmos is like a grain from a balance or a single drop of morning dew come down upon the earth.

Even more awesome than the Lord's power, however, is the loving mercy that the Lord extends to all creation. The author calls the Lord a "lover of souls" (Greek *philo* + *psuchos*, a "lover of the living, of people"). Lest we miss his point that the Lord cares for every person and thing, the author elaborates: "you loathe nothing that you have made"; and again, "for what you hated, you would not have fashioned."

In short, every person exists because the Lord created them and keeps them alive. The Lord fashioned all people with the unique personality and traits that they would need to play their role in the divine plan for the cosmos. The Lord's imperishable spirit, which is in all things, moves creation along this divine path.

Though humans constantly fall short of the role they are given, the merciful Lord loves them too much to give up on them. Here, the author defines mercy as the Lord's "overlooking" human failings to allow time for people to repent and change. "Little by little," the Lord opens their eyes to their shortcomings in the hope that they will abandon their wickedness and cooperate with the Lord's spirit at work in their life and in the world around them.

For meditation and context:

RESPONSORIAL PSALM   Psalm 145:1–2, 8–9, 10–11, 13, 14 (see 1)

R. I will praise your name for ever, my king and my God.

I will extol you, O my God and King,
    and I will bless your name forever
        and ever.
Every day will I bless you,
    and I will praise your name forever
        and ever.

The LORD is gracious and merciful,
    slow to anger and of great kindness.
The LORD is good to all
    and compassionate toward all his works.

Let all your works give you thanks, O LORD,
    and let your faithful ones bless you.
Let them discourse of the glory of
        your kingdom
    and speak of your might.

The LORD is faithful in all his words
    and holy in all his works.
The LORD lifts up all who are falling
    and raises up all who are bowed down.

Thessalonians thes-uh-LOH-nee-uhnz

An exhortatory reading that also concludes a request of the members of the early Church in Thessalonica, one that might seem a little strange. St. Paul is asking the letter's recipients to ignore rumors that the day of the Lord is at hand, which suggests that such rumors were circulating. Emphasis on "every good purpose."

READING II   2 Thessalonians 1:11—2:2

A reading from the second Letter of Saint Paul to the Thessalonians

Brothers and **sisters**:
We **always pray** for you,
    that our **God** may make you **worthy** of his **calling**
    and powerfully bring to **fulfillment every good purpose**
    and every **effort** of **faith**,
    that the **name** of our Lord **Jesus** may be **glorified** in **you**,
    and **you** in **him**,
    in **accord** with the **grace** of our **God** and **Lord** Jesus **Christ**.

We **ask** you, **brothers** and **sisters**,
    with **regard** to the coming of our **Lord Jesus Christ**
    and our **assembling** with him,
    not to be shaken **out** of your **minds suddenly**, or to be **alarmed**
    either by a "**spirit**," or by an oral **statement**,
    or by a **letter allegedly** from **us**
    to the **effect** that the **day** of the **Lord** is at **hand**.

The second half of this reading consists of Paul's advice to the Thessalonians to ignore rumors. Your tone should be corrective and a little urgent.

READING II Paul and his coworkers pray constantly that God will make the baptized worthy of their unique calling. Specifically, they pray that God may *powerfully* bring to fulfillment every good purpose and every effort that they undertake because of their faith in the risen Lord. These early Church leaders also pray that Jesus "may be glorified" in every Christian and every Christian in him. The full reality of this glorified union, this astonishing divine-human partnership, will be manifested only when all are gathered before the Lord at his return. In the mean-

time, the evidence for it is a community of believers who follow Jesus' teachings and clearly continue his work on earth.

By the time that this second letter to the Thessalonians was written, it had become apparent that the Lord was not immediately coming back to earth. This frustrated some of Jesus' disciples so much that they interpreted current events as signs of his imminent return. The final verses of this reading urge Jesus' followers to ignore all such predictions about the end of the world, whether these come by "a spirit," or "an oral statement," or a letter

allegedly from a Church authority (like Paul). Jesus himself taught that no one, not even he, knows when the end of time will come. *Only* the Father knows this. Paul sees identifying signs of Jesus' impending return as a waste of time because it sidetracks disciples from the work they need to be doing for the Lord.

GOSPEL Luke presents Jesus as the incarnation of Wisdom's omnipotent God and merciful "lover of people." This Gospel opens with a man, Zacchaeus, "seeking to see Jesus." But as it

GOSPEL   Luke 19:1–10

A reading from the holy Gospel according to Luke

At that time, Jesus came to **Jericho** and intended
    to **pass** through the **town**.
Now a **man there** named **Zacchaeus**,
    who was a **chief tax collector** and also a **wealthy** man,
    was **seeking** to see who **Jesus** was;
    but he could not **see** him because of the **crowd**,
    for he was **short** in **stature**.
So he ran **ahead** and climbed a **sycamore** tree
    in **order** to see **Jesus**,
    who was about to **pass** that way.
When he **reached** the place, Jesus looked up and said,
    "**Zacchaeus**, come down **quickly**,
    for **today** I must **stay** at your **house**."
And he came down **quickly** and **received** him with **joy**.
When they all **saw** this, they began to **grumble**, saying,
    "He has **gone** to stay at the house of a **sinner**."
But Zacchaeus **stood** there and said to the **Lord**,
    "**Behold**, **half** of my possessions, Lord, I shall **give** to the **poor**,
    and if I have extorted **anything** from **anyone**
    I shall **repay** it four times **over**."
And Jesus **said** to him,
    "**Today salvation** has **come** to this **house**
    because **this man too** is a **descendant** of **Abraham**.
For the Son of **Man** has come to **seek**
    and to **save** what was **lost**."

A narrative reading about Zacchaeus the tax collector. It begins with a phrase, "at that time," that functions in Scripture like "Once upon a time," immersing its audience in scriptural time.
Jericho = JAYR-ih-koh
Zacchaeus = zuh-KEE-uhs

stature = STACH-ehr
The detail about Zacchaeus' short stature is notable; we don't often hear explicitly about people's appearance in the Gospels.
sycamore = SIK-uh-mohr

This grumbling is as predictable as it is accusatory.

Zacchaeus' mood, on the other hand, is one of excitement.

extorted = ehk-STOHR-t*d

Jesus concludes this reading with words expressing his satisfaction.

---

ends, we realize that Jesus is "seeking" Zacchaeus and, by overlooking his failings, "saving" him.

Zacchaeus is a chief tax collector. This office allows him to profit not only from the taxes that he personally collects but also from the money collected by those he supervises. It is not surprising that most of Zacchaeus' contemporaries despise him. His abuse of his powerful station makes it easy for them to forget that God created Zacchaeus, loves him, and keeps him in existence *so that* he might become the man God created him to be. Jesus, however, does not forget and reaches out publicly to the despised tax collector.

Zacchaeus' short stature—a divinely bestowed genetic trait—leads him to climb that sycamore tree. This impulsive strategy so moves Jesus that he changes his own plan to pass through Jericho and instead invites himself to Zacchaeus' home. Zacchaeus is thrilled, climbs down quickly, and welcomes Jesus. Not so thrilled, Jesus' followers grumble because he looks past Zacchaeus' failings and socializes with him.

Jesus' openness moves Zacchaeus to change. *Half* of his possessions Zacchaeus will give to the poor. *All* the money he made by overcharging people, he will repay *four* times. This Gospel invites Jesus' disciples to evaluate what drastic changes *they* made because they believe that, in Jesus, salvation "comes" or literally, "happens" to them. E.N.

ALL SAINTS

LECTIONARY #667

READING I   Revelation 7:2–4, 9–14

A reading from the Book of Revelation

I, John, saw **another angel** come up from the **East**,
　　holding the **seal** of the living **God**.
He cried **out** in a **loud voice** to the **four angels**
　　who were given **power** to **damage** the **land** and the **sea**,
　　"Do not **damage** the **land** or the **sea** or the **trees**
　　until we put the **seal** on the **foreheads** of the **servants**
　　　　of our **God**."
I heard the **number** of those who had been **marked** with the **seal**,
　　one hundred and **forty-four thousand** marked
　　from **every tribe** of the **children** of Israel.

After **this** I had a **vision** of a **great multitude**,
　　which **no one** could **count**,
　　from every **nation**, **race**, **people**, and **tongue**.
They **stood** before the **throne** and before the **Lamb**,
　　wearing **white robes** and holding **palm branches** in
　　　　their **hands**.
They cried **out** in a loud **voice**:

　　"**Salvation** comes from our **God**, who is **seated** on the **throne**,
　　and from the **Lamb**."

All the angels **stood** around the **throne**
　　and around the **elders** and the **four living creatures**.
They **prostrated** themselves before the **throne**,
　　worshiped **God**, and **exclaimed**: »

Revelation = rev-uh-LAY-shuhn

A narrative reading of visionary power and enticing detail. Revelation has inherent drama in its language and imagery. You only need to proclaim the passage with clarity and directness; its power will express itself through your voice.
Note the repetitions: "damage, land, sea."

Even stresses on the words in this line.

Emphasis on "Lamb," which will be repeated at the end of the passage.

READING I The vision that John receives foreshadows the eschatological Church, when the earthly liturgy will be united with the heavenly, uninterrupted praise of the Almighty. Until that day comes, the Church is to wait in vigilant hope. John's vision begins with an angel arriving from the east—the direction of salvation—who bears the seal that will mark the elect for eternal life. This angel commands the four angels that govern the four corners of the earth to withhold their destructive powers until all of God's servants are properly designated and sealed.

John is precise regarding the number of those who are to be so labelled: 144,000, a number meant to be as great but not as complete as the number John beholds before the heavenly throne.

Thus, John's vision turns from the salvation of God's servants on earth to the eternal liturgy in heaven. Here John reports seeing a "great multitude, which no one could count, from every nation, race, people, and tongue." They are dressed in white baptismal garments and carry palm branches in their hands, suggesting that they have embraced the suffering of Christ

and have been grafted onto his life. They have endured persecution on earth in order to participate in Christ's triumph in heaven. They recognize that the one seated upon the throne is responsible for their salvation and that their new life comes from the Lamb.

The vision concludes with an elder asking John the identity and the origin of those wearing the white robes. John acknowledges that the heavenly elder knows the answer to his own question. This is knowledge that belongs to heaven alone: They are the ones who have survived great suffering

Note the heavy emphases on the words in this exclamation.

"**Amen. Blessing** and **glory**, **wisdom** and **thanksgiving**,
    honor, **power**, and **might**
        be to our **God forever** and **ever**. Amen."

Then one of the **elders** spoke up and **said** to me,
    "**Who** are these wearing **white robes**, and **where** did they
        come from?"
I said to him, "My **lord, you** are the one who **knows**."
He **said** to me,
    "**These** are the **ones** who have **survived** the time
        of **great distress**;
    they have **washed** their **robes**
    and made them **white** in the **Blood** of the **Lamb**."

Allow this image to expand in your proclamation of it. Emphasis on "Lamb."

For meditation and context:

RESPONSORIAL PSALM   Psalm 24:1bc–2, 3–4ab, 5–6 (see 6)

R. Lord, this is the people that longs to see your face.

The LORD's are the earth and its fullness;
    the world and those who dwell in it.
For he founded it upon the seas
    and established it upon the rivers.

Who can ascend the mountain of the LORD?
    or who may stand in his holy place?
One whose hands are sinless, whose heart
    is clean,
    who desires not what is vain.

He shall receive a blessing from the LORD,
    a reward from God his savior.
Such is the race that seeks him,
    that seeks the face of the God of Jacob.

READING II   1 John 3:1–3

A reading from the first Letter of Saint John

Beloved:
See what love the **Father** has **bestowed** on us
    that we may be **called** the **children** of **God**.
Yet **so** we **are**.
The **reason** the world does not **know** us
    is that it **did not know him**.
Beloved, we are **God's** children now;
    what we shall **be** has not yet been **revealed**.

An exhortatory reading proclaiming the mysterious nature of God's revelation.

Emphasis on "know." In the next line, on "him."

---

and who were strong enough to wash their robes in the Blood of the Lamb.

READING II   When John addresses the recipients of his letter as "children of God," he underscores the relationship of love that God has established with his people. Certainly, God had made this desire known when he took the Israelites out of Egypt and made them a chosen people. John employs the term "children" to suggest that those who have been brought into relationship with the Father through Christ are part of one family.

This is precisely the relationship that the world fails to recognize. John could have launched into a variety of reasons why the world cannot comprehend the family comprised by God's children. He could certainly point to examples of greed and self-centeredness that suggest a lack of cohesiveness in the Church. Instead, he states that it is because the world failed to recognize God. The "world" is portrayed as the opposite of the "love" that the Father bestows upon his children. For those who are still in the world and who are confronted with its evils and distress, the understanding of our full identity remains a mystery.

For this reason, John speaks of a "hope" that is to be lived out by every child of God, the hope that we will be like him, pure. The promise to those who have maintained purity in Christ is that they will behold the fullness of God's glory. The children of God have already begun to share in the outcome of this hope, as Christ, "the firstborn from the dead" (Colossians 1:18), has gone before us to begin the promise of our transformation.

Note the interplay between "revealed" and "see."

We **do know** that when it is **revealed** we shall be **like** him,
  for we shall **see** him as he is.
Everyone who has this hope **based** on him makes himself **pure**,
  as **he** is **pure**.

GOSPEL   Matthew 5:1–12a

A reading from the holy Gospel according to Matthew

When **Jesus** saw the **crowds**, he **went** up the **mountain**,
  and after he had sat **down**, his disciples **came** to him.
He began to **teach** them, saying:

An exhortatory reading whose expressions are familiar but whose specifics are helpfully reintroduced to your assembly. This Gospel reading is an opportunity to teach the Beatitudes anew.

Blessed = BLES-uhd
Note the rhythmical emphases. The first word in each beatitude is stressed, as is the last word in each line. Let that rhythm guide your proclamation.

  "**Blessed** are the poor in **spirit**,
    for **theirs** is the **Kingdom** of **heaven**.
  Blessed are they who **mourn**,
    for **they** will be **comforted**.
  Blessed are the **meek**,
    for **they** will inherit the **land**.
  Blessed are they who **hunger** and **thirst** for **righteousness**,
    for **they** will be **satisfied**.
  Blessed are the **merciful**,
    for **they** will be shown **mercy**.
  Blessed are the clean of **heart**,
    for **they** will see **God**.
  Blessed are the **peacemakers**,
    for **they** will be called **children** of **God**.
  Blessed are they who are **persecuted** for the sake
      of **righteousness**,
    for **theirs** is the **Kingdom** of **heaven**.
  Blessed are you when they **insult** you and **persecute** you
    and utter every kind of evil **against** you falsely **because**
      of me.
  Rejoice and be glad,
    for your reward will be great in heaven."

GOSPEL The Beatitudes, the opening section of Jesus' inaugural sermon, serve as a spiritual checklist for the disciples. Those who hold to attitudes founded on right relationship with God, others, and all of material creation are deemed "blessed." Unlike the Beatitudes that are found in Luke 6:20–23, which are economic in nature and centered on reward provided in this life, Matthew's Beatitudes are eschatological in nature and look forward to a great reward provided for the disciples in heaven.

Matthew's spiritual adaptation of the Beatitudes serves to expand the scope of those who might be blessed. For example, the first Beatitude in Luke reads, "How happy are you who are poor," but Matthew begins his list of blessings with the words "Blessed are the poor in spirit." Rather than being strictly a blessing for those who are materially poor, Matthew's account suggests a wide range of possibilities for those who are "poor in spirit." The same can be said for the category of hunger. Luke states: "happy you who are hungry now,"

but Matthew's understanding of hunger is not a physical state but rather a yearning for a world that is just: "Blessed are they who hunger and thirst for righteousness." Simply stated, Matthew's Beatitudes represent a proactive approach to the coming reign of God. Proclaiming this particular Gospel passage on the Feast of All Saints is particularly significant. Saints are those who recognize that the Kingdom of God is at hand and respond by living its attitudes fully in this life. S.W.

THE COMMEMORATION OF ALL THE FAITHFUL DEPARTED (ALL SOULS' DAY)

LECTIONARY #668

READING I   Wisdom 3:1–9

An exhortatory and poetic reading that reassures about the fate of the souls of the dead. The language is rich and effective.

A reading from the Book of Wisdom

The **souls** of the **just** are in the **hand** of God,
  and no **torment** shall **touch** them.
They **seemed**, in the view of the **foolish**, to be **dead**;
  and their passing **away** was thought an **affliction**
  and their going **forth** from us, utter **destruction**.
But **they** are in **peace**.
For if before men, indeed, they be **punished**,
  yet is their hope full of **immortality**;
chastised a little, they shall be greatly **blessed**,
  because God **tried** them
  and found them **worthy** of **himself**.
As **gold** in the **furnace**, he **proved** them,
  and as sacrificial **offerings** he took them to **himself**.
In the **time** of their **visitation** they shall **shine**,
  and shall dart **about** as sparks through **stubble**;
they shall judge **nations** and rule over **peoples**,
  and the LORD shall be their **King forever**.
Those who **trust** in him shall understand **truth**,
  and the **faithful** shall **abide** with him in **love**:
because **grace** and **mercy** are with his **holy** ones,
  and his **care** is **with** his **elect**.

The solemn core of the reading. Note the unusual phrasing, "in peace" rather than "at peace," which would be more common.

"Gold" anticipates "shine" below. From this point, the reading shifts into a more emphatically uplifting tone.

Note the concluding rhythm: "and his CARE is WITH his eLECT".

There are options for today's readings. Contact your parish staff to learn which readings will be used.

READING I This passage from the Book of Wisdom is a popular choice for funeral liturgies. Wisdom presents life in this age as a sort of test, in which being "chastised a little," those who persevere with justice and righteousness will be judged favorably and receive the reward of new life with God. From the outset, Wisdom testifies that "the souls of the just are in the hand of God," where no torment shall afflict them. Who are the just? Those who imitate the justice of God, by which every aspect of creation is allowed to fulfill its purpose, and in which all things are in perfect relationship with God and each other.

Wisdom suggests that only the foolish would imagine that those who live justly in this life come to an end in death. For believers, death is not a curse nor an "affliction" nor "utter destruction." Instead, the just ones who have died are in peace; their souls have returned to God as an offering. Through the struggles of this life, they have been purified like gold and they will shine with radiance before God. Their lives of true justice will be the pattern by which the Lord will come to judge the nations. In fact, Wisdom goes so far as to suggest that the just souls will participate in God's final judgement of the world: "they shall judge nations and rule over peoples."

In opposition to the foolish, who see nothing beyond death, the just souls are those who trust in God and labor to understand the mystery of his ways. This is so because God has treated them with "grace and mercy, . . . and his care is with his

For meditation and context:

RESPONSORIAL PSALM   Psalm 27:1, 4, 7, 8b, 9a, 13–14 (1) (13)

R. The Lord is my light and my salvation.
or R. I believe that I shall see the good things of the Lord in the land of the living.

The LORD is my light and my salvation;
  whom should I fear?
The LORD is my life's refuge;
  of whom should I afraid?

One thing I ask of the LORD;
  this I seek:
To dwell in the house of the LORD
  all the days of my life,
That I may gaze on the loveliness of the LORD
  and contemplate his temple.

Hear, O LORD, the sound of my call;
  have pity on me and answer me.
Your presence, O LORD, I seek.
  Hide not your face from me.

I believe that I shall see the bounty of
    the LORD
  in the land of the living.
Wait for the LORD with courage;
  be stouthearted, and wait for the LORD!

READING II   Romans 5:5–11

A reading from the Letter of Saint Paul to the Romans

A cunningly and persuasively argued didactic reading from St. Paul. There's real pleasure in listening to Paul build up his argument.

Brothers and **sisters**:
Hope does not **disappoint**,
  because the **love** of **God** has been poured **out** into our **hearts**
  through the Holy **Spirit** that has been **given** to us.
For **Christ**, while we were still **helpless**,
  died at the appointed **time** for the **ungodly**.
Indeed, only with **difficulty** does one **die** for a just **person**,
  though perhaps for a good **person**
  one might even find **courage** to **die**.
But **God** proves his **love** for **us**
  in that while we were still **sinners Christ died** for us.
How much **more** then, since we are now **justified** by his **Blood**,
  will we be **saved** through **him** from the **wrath**.
Indeed, if, while we were **enemies**,
  we were **reconciled** to **God** through the **death** of his **Son**,
  how much **more**, once **reconciled**,
  will we be **saved** by his **life**.
Not only **that**,
  but we also **boast** of **God** through our **Lord** Jesus **Christ**,
  through whom we have now **received reconciliation**.

Slight pause between "sinners" and "Christ."

Note the repetition of "how much more," which Paul uses to move towards the point he is making.

Here, Paul uses the rhetorical strategy of using "not only" to indicate the triumph of faith in Jesus on top of all that he has said before his conclusion.

---

elect." Without providing an exact blueprint, Wisdom presents rich imagery to help the believer imagine the beautiful gift of immortality.

READING II   **Romans 5.** Paul's logic in defense of hope follows this simple course: first, all of us were estranged from God due to sin and therefore made completely "helpless." Then, Christ, "at the appointed time" came into the world to destroy this helplessness through his death on the cross. Paul suggests that someone may choose to die for

another if they are just, but Christ died for the unjust, those who knew the law but continued to sin. This, Paul suggests, demonstrates the depths of God's love for us: that Christ died for us even "while we were still sinners."

After establishing the grounds for hope—a love stronger than anything humanly imaginable—Paul distinguishes the ideas of "justification" and "salvation." Justification applies to those who participate in the death of Jesus and the outpouring of the Spirit, those made members of the Church. Salvation refers to the escha-

ton, the end of time, or "the wrath," as Paul calls it, when God will attempt a final reconciliation with the powers of this world. Thus, for those who maintain faith in the death of the Lord, the issue of salvation should not lead to despair of any sort. If as sinners we were justified, our salvation is assured. The state of being reconciled with God is all the hope that we could possibly need. Christians must "boast" in the power of God, for hope in our future is the cause of our rejoicing.

Romans 6. The baptismal font is often described as both the womb and the tomb

Or:

READING II   Romans 6:3–9

A didactic reading from St. Paul in which he meditates on the meaning and purpose of death.

Key terms in Paul's reading are "death," "baptism," "life," "union." Use these words and their variations to orient your proclamation.

A reading from the Letter of Saint Paul to the Romans

Brothers and **sisters:**
Are you **unaware** that we who were **baptized** into Christ **Jesus**
    were **baptized** into his **death**?
We were indeed **buried** with him through **baptism** into **death**,
    so that, just as **Christ** was raised from the **dead**
    by the **glory** of the **Father**,
    we too might live in **newness** of **life**.

For if we have **grown** into **union** with **him** through a death
        like his,
we shall also be **united** with **him** in the **resurrection**.
We **know** that our **old self** was **crucified** with him,
    so that our **sinful body** might be done **away** with,
    that we might **no longer** be in **slavery** to **sin**.
For a **dead person** has been **absolved** from sin.
If, then, we have **died** with **Christ**,
    we believe that we shall also **live** with him.
We know that **Christ**, **raised** from the **dead**, **dies** no more;
    death no **longer** has **power** over him.

The contrast between "died" and "live" is important.

Paul uses negatives just so in the conclusion of this reading: "dies no more and death no longer."

---

of the Church. In the waters of baptism, life in Christ begins; a new creation takes shape, while a person dies to self to be freed from sin and live anew as a follower of Christ. Just as Jesus died before he rose to new life, so too must Christians enter into a real death in order to be raised to life in Christ. Thus, Paul directly asks the Romans: "Are you unaware that we who were baptized into Christ Jesus were baptized into his death?" Evidently, many Christians at Rome failed to let go of their past lives and sinful ways. But this cannot be so for Christians. Those who have professed Jesus

as Lord must die to sin through incorporation into Christ's death, in order to be raised and live with him "in newness of life."

In the second half of this passage, Paul states that if believers are truly united with Christ in his death, then their resurrection is equally assured. The death of Christ is a complete victory; for Christians who are grafted tightly onto him, nothing can strip away the promise of resurrection. This permanent incorporation into Christ does not mean that Christians are protected without effort on their part. They must work to refrain from turning back to sinful ways.

Paul ends with the statement that death has no more power over the risen Lord. Because we are still in the world, we must be vigilant to avoid the things that baptism works to put to death in us.

GOSPEL   Each day Christians around the world pray the Lord's Prayer, asking that the will of the Father be done both in heaven and on earth. But what is the will of the Father? The four verses that we read from John's Gospel today provide a concrete and concise answer: The will of the Father is that Christ

An exhortatory and poetic reading that reassures about the fate of the souls of the dead. The language is rich and effective.

When Jesus speaks of the "will of the one who sent me," he can sound cryptic. Proclaim this passage a little slowly.

Good news concludes the reading.

GOSPEL   John 6:37–40

A reading from the holy Gospel according to John

Jesus said to the **crowds**:
"**Everything** that the Father **gives** me will **come** to me,
   and I will **not reject anyone** who **comes** to me,
   because I came **down** from **heaven** not to do my **own will**
   but the **will** of the **one** who **sent** me.
And **this** is the **will** of the **one** who **sent** me,
   that I should **not lose anything** of what he **gave** me,
   but that I should **raise** it on the **last day**.
For **this** is the **will** of my **Father**,
   that **everyone** who sees the **Son** and **believes** in him
   may **have** eternal **life**,
   and I shall **raise** him on the **last day**."

should not let us turn from him that we might share eternal life. He must not lose any of his followers: seeing and believing in him is the key to their being raised up on the last day.

   This teaching on the Father's will to save all those who have come to see and believe in his beloved Son follows upon the heels of Jesus feeding the five thousand. Just as Jesus ordered the disciples to collect the leftover pieces of bread "so that nothing gets wasted" (John 6:12), so is it God's plan for all who believe: none will be lost. All will be collected on the final day. Jesus tells the

crowds at the beginning of today's reading that he will not reject anyone who comes to him; seeing and believing in Jesus is fulfillment for our deepest hungers in this life and assurance that we will be raised to new and eternal life on the last day. S.W.

THIRTY-SECOND SUNDAY IN ORDINARY TIME

LECTIONARY #156

READING I   2 Maccabees 7:1–2, 9–14

Maccabees = MAK-uh-beez

A narrative reading depicting a tale of torture and martyrdom from the Book of Maccabees. The details in this reading are lurid and violent. Don't play them up; rather, let the language of the reading itself do the work of depicting these troubling scenes.

scourges = SKER-j*z

transgress = trans-GRES

A reading from the second Book of Maccabees

It **happened** that **seven brothers** with their **mother** were **arrested**
 and **tortured** with **whips** and **scourges** by the **king**,
 to force them to eat **pork** in **violation** of **God's law**.
One of the **brothers**, **speaking** for the **others**, said:
 "**What** do you expect to **achieve** by **questioning** us?
We are **ready** to **die** rather than **transgress** the **laws**
 of our **ancestors**."

accursed = uh-KERST *or* uh-KER-sihd

Emphasis on "live again forever."

At the **point** of death he said:
 "**You accursed fiend**, you are **depriving** us of this present **life**,
 but the **King** of the **world** will raise us **up** to **live again forever**.
It is for **his laws** that we are **dying**."

disdain = dihs-DAYN

Slight pause between "attendants" and "marveled."

After him the **third** suffered their **cruel sport**.
He put **out** his tongue at **once** when told to **do** so,
 and **bravely** held out his **hands**, as he **spoke** these noble **words**:
 "It was from **Heaven** that I **received** these;
 for the **sake** of his laws I **disdain** them;
 from **him** I hope to **receive** them **again**."
Even the king and his **attendants marveled**
 at the young man's **courage**,
 because he **regarded** his **sufferings** as **nothing**.

READING I Today's readings challenge us to evaluate the sincerity of our personal belief that we will be raised up after death to a new kind of life. They do this by showing how the human values and preoccupations that dominate our earthly life and determine our daily choices often contradict this belief. The first reading focuses on the conviction that people need a sound body to live a full and meaningful life, and that, as far as possible they should avoid all pain and suffering. The Gospel looks at one of the most universal and respected traditions, marriage, in the light of the resurrection.

The Second Book of Maccabees was written during a time when the Greeks dominated the biblical world. In order to control and unite conquered populations, these rulers forced people to abandon their religious culture and values and adopt Greek ones. To counter this program and to inspire Jews to remain faithful to their religious practices, the author of 2 Maccabees presents stories about courageous ancestors who chose to die rather than appear disloyal to their God. These martyrs trusted so unwaveringly in the divine plan for their life—a plan revealed to Israel through their more than millennium-long journey with God—that they preferred to die rather than deny the true "King of the world."

Today's story is about a mother who watches her seven sons being tortured and killed because they refuse to violate God's law by eating pork. The sons proclaim that their life will not end with physical death. Nothing their torturers can say will persuade them otherwise. One declares: "the

maltreated = mal-TREET-ed

After he had **died**,
> they **tortured** and **maltreated** the **fourth brother**
>> in the same way.
When he was **near death**, he said,
> "It is **my** choice to **die** at the **hands** of **men**
> with the **hope God gives** of being **raised up** by him;
> but for **you**, there will be **no resurrection** to **life**."

Emphasis on "hope God gives."

For meditation and context:

RESPONSORIAL PSALM   Psalm 17:1, 5–6, 8, 15 (15b)

R. Lord, when your glory appears, my joy will be full.

Hear, O LORD, a just suit;
> attend to my outcry;
> hearken to my prayer from lips
>> without deceit.

My steps have been steadfast in your paths,
> my feet have not faltered.
I call upon you, for you will answer me,
> O God;
> incline your ear to me; hear my word.

Keep me as the apple of your eye,
> hide me in the shadow of your wings.
But I in justice shall behold your face;
> on waking I shall be content in
>> your presence.

Thessalonians = thes-uh-LOH-nee-uhnz

An exhortatory reading in which St. Paul insists on God's love to encourage the members of the early Church in Thessalonica.

READING II   2 Thessalonians 2:16 — 3:5

A reading from the second Letter of Saint Paul to the Thessalonians

Brothers and **sisters**:
May our **Lord Jesus Christ himself** and **God** our **Father**,
> who has **loved** us and given us everlasting **encouragement**
> and **good hope** through his **grace**,
> encourage your **hearts** and **strengthen** them
>> in **every good deed** and **word**.

Paul uses "Finally" to request the prayers of the Thessalonians for himself and his community.

perverse = pehr-VERS

Finally, brothers and **sisters**, **pray** for us,
> so that the **word** of the **Lord** may speed **forward** and be **glorified**,
> as it did **among** you,
> and that we may be **delivered** from **perverse** and **wicked people**,
> for not **all** have **faith**. **»**

King of the world will raise us up to live forever." This son takes the long view and sides, not with men who have the power to kill him, but with God, whose greater power can raise him from the dead. For this man, dying is a temporary condition, like sleep or a passing illness.

Another son, when told by his torturers to stick out his tongue so that they can cut it off, holds out his hands to be cut off as well. Even the king and his court marvel at his courage. They are astounded by his absolute indifference to horrendous suffering and its life-changing consequences. The

author hopes that his readers too will marvel at such bravery and be inspired to overcome natural fears and bear bolder witness to the King of the world's sovereignty. He urges all who hear this reading to live no longer like spineless, unenlightened unbelievers but like God's courageous people, who plan to live forever.

READING II There are two prayers in this reading. In the first, community leaders pray that the gracious Lord Jesus and God the Father will encourage and strengthen the hearts of each of

the baptized in every good word and deed. They pray that the faithful will always speak and act in ways that benefit others and shed light on the risen Lord's active presence in their midst.

The second prayer is that the leaders of Christian communities will be delivered from wicked people. In this passage, the "wicked" are those whose actions show that they do not truly believe that the Lord was raised from the dead and now works on earth in the baptized. The lives of wicked people are clearly earthbound. For example, their fears cause them to bend

The tone of encouragement intensifies in the conclusion of this reading.

But the **Lord** is **faithful**;
>he will **strengthen** you and **guard** you from the **evil** one.

We are **confident** of you in the **Lord** that what we **instruct** you,
>you are **doing** and will **continue** to do.

May the **Lord** direct your **hearts** to the **love** of **God**
>and to the **endurance** of **Christ**.

GOSPEL Luke 20:27–38

Sadducees = SAD-yoo-seez

A narrative reading that depicts a disputation between the Sadducees and Jesus. The subject is the levirate, the custom by which a man might be obliged to marry his brother's widow in order to sire the dead brother's heir. Jesus' response defies this custom altogether.

A reading from the holy Gospel according to Luke

[Some **Sadducees**, **those** who **deny** that there is a **resurrection**,
>came **forward**] and put this **question** to **Jesus**, saying,
>"**Teacher, Moses wrote** for us,
>If *someone's* ***brother dies*** leaving a **wife** but no **child**,
>his **brother** *must take the* **wife**
>and **raise up descendants** *for his* **brother**.

Now there were **seven brothers**;
>the **first** married a **woman** but died **childless**.

Slight pause between "third" and "married."

Then the **second** and the **third married** her,
>and **likewise** all the **seven** died **childless**.

Finally the woman also **died**.

Now at the **resurrection whose wife** will that **woman** be?

For all **seven** had been **married** to her."

Here begins Jesus' defiant response. It's much more cosmic than legalistic; don't overdo it.

[Jesus **said** to them,
>"The **children** of this age **marry** and **remarry**;
>but **those** who are deemed **worthy** to attain to the coming **age**
>and to the **resurrection** of the **dead**
>neither **marry** nor are **given** in **marriage**.

They can **no longer die**,
>for they are like **angels**;
>and they are the **children** of **God**
>because **they** are the ones who will **rise**.

---

under the influence of earthly powers and live by merely human standards rather than God's. The wicked spend their days unburdened by their promise to represent God boldly and to reject human views and ways. Their speech and actions loudly declare that, for them, this life is all that there is.

GOSPEL Once again, a group of Jewish religious authorities tries to discredit the layman Jesus' teachings. This time it is the Sadducees, who, because they do not believe in resurrection from the dead, promote traditions that

focus on earthly blessings like prosperity and posterity. A corollary of these is that parents "live on" in their children—an idea attested to by the biblical concerns about a woman's barrenness and a man's failure to beget a son. In contrast to the Sadducees, the Pharisees taught that there would be a general resurrection of all people at the last judgment. It is not clear, however, whether they expected this to be a spiritual or a bodily resurrection.

Since the Sadducees give authority only to the teachings of Moses found in the Torah (Genesis through Deuteronomy), they

base their debate with Jesus on the levirate law (Deuteronomy 25:5). This law states that if a man dies without a son, his brother must marry his widow so that she can bear an heir for her first husband. After the Sadducees concoct the elaborate case of a woman who loses seven husbands, they ask Jesus, "At the Resurrection whose wife will that woman be?" They intend to embarrass Jesus by showing that his teaching is absurd and contradicts the Torah.

Jesus' response would have frustrated the Sadducees. He does not identify one of the seven men as the woman's resurrected

Slight pause between "him" and "all."

That the dead will rise
 even Moses made known in the passage about the bush,
 when he called out 'Lord,'
 the God of Abraham, the God of Isaac, and the God of Jacob;
 and he is not God of the dead, but of the living,
 for to him all are alive."]

[Shorter: Luke 20:27, 34–38 (see brackets)]

husband but uses the custom of marriage as a springboard to teach about life in God's kingdom. His next words clarify that he is talking about resurrection, not immortality. Resurrection is not merely the continuation of life as we know it. One difference will be that in the coming age people will neither marry nor be given in marriage. They will not need to worry about living on in their children because they themselves will be raised up and live forever. In Jesus' view, the sacred shared life of a married couple is a mere foreshadowing of the intimacy that the children of God will enjoy together in the age to come.

Jesus elaborates that resurrected human beings will leave behind this-worldly fixations like avoiding pain and having a sound body. They will be "like angels," another jibe at the Sadducees who do not believe in the existence of these spiritual beings.

Jesus concludes his argument by again citing the Sadducees,' favorite authority, Moses. He points out that, in Exodus 3:6, Moses hears God say, "I am"—not "I was"— "the God of Abraham, the God of Isaac, and the God of Jacob." God not only *was* the God of Israel's ancestors—and of our ancestors—while they lived on earth, God *is* their God now because they are with him. E.N.

THIRTY-THIRD SUNDAY IN ORDINARY TIME

LECTIONARY #159

Malachi = MAL-uh-kī

A short but very potent exhortatory reading filled with vivid language and poetic intensity. In fact, it reads like a short, inspired poem.

READING I   Malachi 3:19–20a

A reading from the Book of the Prophet Malachi

Lo, the day is **coming**, **blazing** like an **oven**,
  when all the **proud** and all **evildoers** will be **stubble**,
and the **day** that is **coming** will **set** them on **fire**,
  leaving them neither **root** nor **branch**,
  says the LORD of **hosts**.
But for **you** who fear my **name**, there will **arise**
  the **sun** of **justice** with its **healing rays**.

For meditation and context:

RESPONSORIAL PSALM   Psalm 98:5–6, 7–8, 9 (see 9)

R. The Lord comes to rule the earth with justice.

Sing praise to the LORD with the harp,
  with the harp and melodious song.
With trumpets and the sound of the horn
  sing joyfully before the King, the LORD.

Let the sea and what fills it resound,
  the world and those who dwell in it;
let the rivers clap their hands,
  the mountains shout with them for joy.

Before the LORD, for he comes,
  for he comes to rule the earth;
he will rule the world with justice
  and the peoples with equity.

READING I The context for this reading is the people's complaint that it is useless to serve God (Malachi 3:14–15). It seems to them that, even though the arrogant and the evildoers insult and test God, they continue to enjoy the promised blessings of success and prosperity. In the face of this apparent divine unfairness, the faithful ask, "What do we gain by keeping the Lord's commands?"

In response, Malachi assures them that the "day" is coming when the Lord of Hosts will rectify this situation. The prophet imagines "the day" as a blazing hot oven whose heat will set on fire and destroy those who are proud and who do evil. Nothing—"neither root nor branch"—will be left of them.

On that same day, for those "who fear my name, there will arise the sun of justice with its healing rays." To fear or reverence the Lord's name entails following the Lord's instructions, even when these seem naïve and purposeless.

The image of the "sun of justice" references a winged solar disk, which was a widespread symbol in the biblical world. Given the Middle Eastern climate (and the absence of air conditioning), these images of a sun with wings hovering over the earth aptly convey divine omnipresence and uncontested power. Here (as in Psalms 17:8–9; 36:8; 61:5; 91:4; among others), the faithful take refuge in the shadow of the Lord's "wings," where they are protected from all manner of harm and enjoy continuous blessings.

READING II The delay in Jesus' return weakens the Thessalonians' commitment to living a Christian life. In this passage, Paul urges them to imitate him

Thessalonians = thes-uh-LOH-nee-uhnz

A didactic reading from St. Paul about the discipline and virtue of work.

Slight pause between "way" and "among."

With "Rather," Paul moves more fully into his didactic mode.

The reading concludes with direct advice. Emphasis on "urge" and "quietly."

A prophetic, visionary reading presented in the context of a narrative of Jesus speaking to his disciples. The content of this reading is striking and alarming, even as it moves toward its end into hopefulness. Keep this sense of alarm—and Jesus' certainty of it—near at hand as you proclaim.

Jesus is surveying future history as well as what he sees in front of him.

READING II   2 Thessalonians 3:7–12

A reading from the second Letter of Saint Paul to the Thessalonians

Brothers and **sisters**:
You **know** how one must **imitate** us.
For we did not **act** in a disorderly **way among** you,
   nor did we eat **food** received **free** from **anyone**.
On the **contrary**, in **toil** and **drudgery**, **night** and **day**
   we **worked**, so as **not** to burden **any** of you.
Not that we do not have the **right**.
Rather, we wanted to **present** ourselves as a **model** for you,
   so that you might **imitate** us.
In **fact**, when we were **with** you,
   we **instructed** you that if **anyone** was unwilling to **work**,
   neither should that one **eat**.
We **hear** that some are **conducting** themselves among you
      in a **disorderly** way,
   by **not** keeping **busy** but **minding** the business of **others**.
Such **people** we **instruct** and **urge** in the **Lord Jesus** Christ
      to work quietly
   and to **eat** their own **food**.

GOSPEL   Luke 21:5–19

A reading from the holy Gospel according to Luke

While some **people** were speaking about
   how the **temple** was adorned with costly **stones**
      and **votive offerings**,
   Jesus said, "**All** that you **see** here—
   the **days** will **come** when there will **not** be **left**
   a **stone** upon another **stone** that will **not** be **thrown down**." ❯❯

and his team, specifically, to stop acting in disorderly or inappropriate ways (the Greek verb *atakteō* can also mean "to be idle or lazy"). Paul and his coworkers pass their nights and days in "toil and drudgery" so as not to burden anyone. "Toil" denotes demanding and often exasperating effort, and "drudgery" a daily grind that saps all one's energy but produces little apparent result.

Paul and his team decide not to accept food from the community without paying for it. Though Paul has the "right" (Greek *exousia*, "authority") to expect people to

provide for his needs, he makes a pastoral choice not to do so. In effect, he teaches by example that if anyone does not work, he or she is not entitled to the care and providence of those who do.

Paul concludes by specifying the disorderly behavior or manifestation of idleness that he alluded to above. The Greek is terse: some people are not *ergazomenous alla peri-ergazomenous*—translated in our reading today as "not *keeping busy but minding the business of others*." In short, some are not toiling to spread the Gospel by word and deed but instead are con-

stantly meddling in other people's concerns. What these people need to do, Paul says, is simply to "*work* quietly [stop talking about other people] and to eat their own food."

GOSPEL   The evangelist Luke writes to a community who is trying to live by faith that Jesus was raised up and will shortly return. As time passes, however, doubts assail them and challenge their beliefs. They want to know exactly when Jesus will return. "What sign will there be" that things foretold but unimaginable (like the destruction of the Jerusalem

insurrections = ihn-suh-REK-shuhnz
These are alarming signs of the end of things.

famines = FAM-ihnz
plagues = playgz

With "Before," Jesus offers stark advice for preparation.
synagogues = SIN-uh-gogs

The mixture of terror and hope in this conclusion is chaotic, which is probably the point.

Then they **asked** him,
    "**Teacher**, **when** will this **happen**?
And what **sign** will there **be** when all these **things**
        are about to **happen**?"
He answered,
"**See** that you not be **deceived**,
    for **many** will come in my **name**, saying,
    'I am **he**,' and 'The time has **come**.'
Do not follow them!
When you hear of **wars** and **insurrections**,
    do **not** be **terrified**; for such **things** must happen **first**,
    but it will not **immediately** be the **end**."
Then he **said** to them,
    "**Nation** will rise against **nation**, and **kingdom**
        against **kingdom**.
There will be powerful **earthquakes**, **famines**, and **plagues**
    from **place** to **place**;
    and awesome **sights** and mighty **signs** will **come**
        from the **sky**.

"**Before** all this **happens**, however,
    they will **seize** and **persecute** you,
    they will hand you **over** to the **synagogues** and to **prisons**,
    and they will have you **led** before **kings** and **governors**
    because of my **name**.
It will **lead** to your giving **testimony**.
Remember, you are **not** to prepare your defense **beforehand**,
    for **I myself** shall give you a **wisdom** in **speaking**
    that **all** your **adversaries** will be **powerless** to **resist** or **refute**.
You will **even** be handed **over** by **parents**, **brothers**,
        relatives, and **friends**,
    and they will put **some** of you to death.
You will be **hated** by **all because** of my **name**,
    but not a **hair** on your **head** will be **destroyed**.
By your **perseverance** you will **secure** your **lives**."

temple) are about to take place? Jesus' words today redirect their concerns from the future to their mission in the present. They must persevere in living in a way that bears witness that Malachi's Lord of Hosts came in Jesus, and that with Jesus' resurrection Malachi's "day" dawned.

For some of the baptized, this is simply too difficult. They need Jesus to come back *now*, so they latch onto the pronouncements of false prophets who identify current international conflicts and natural disasters—events that recur in every era of every age—as *the* signs of Jesus' imminent return. To them and to us, Jesus says "do not be fooled" by such phonies, by self-inflated charlatans who claim to be privy to God's plans.

Jesus also teaches that if his disciples remain faithful to him and his mission, they must expect to be hated—even by relatives and friends—and to be handed over to religious authorities. These painful experiences, Jesus says, are the vehicles that bring disciples into the presence of people that God wants to hear about Jesus' resurrection and reign. Disciples must never worry about what they will say when they bear witness, for the Spirit will give them "wisdom in speaking," literally, "a mouth and words" of divine wisdom. E.N.

OUR LORD JESUS CHRIST, KING OF THE UNIVERSE

LECTIONARY #162

READING I   2 Samuel 5:1–3

A narrative reading about the anointing of David as king of Israel. Its feel is heraldic and mytho-historic.

Hebron = HEB-ruhn

Israelites = IZ-ree-uh-līts *or* IZ-ray-uh-līt

Emphasis on "shepherd" and "Israel" as well as "commander" and "Israel."

A reading from the second Book of Samuel

In **those days**, all the tribes of **Israel** came to **David**
    in **Hebron** and said:
  "**Here we are**, your bone and your **flesh**.
In days **past**, when **Saul** was our **king**,
  it was **you** who led the Israelites **out** and brought them **back**.
And the LORD **said** to you,
  'You shall **shepherd** my people **Israel**
  and shall be **commander** of **Israel**.'"
When all the **elders** of **Israel** came to **David** in **Hebron**,
  King **David** made an **agreement** with them **there**
    before the LORD,
  and they **anointed** him **king** of **Israel**.

For meditation and context:

RESPONSORIAL PSALM   Psalm 122:1–2, 3–4, 4–5 (see 1)

R. Let us go rejoicing to the house of the Lord.

I rejoiced because they said to me,
  "We will go up to the house of the LORD."
And now we have set foot
  within your gates, O Jerusalem.

Jerusalem, built as a city
  with compact unity.

To it the tribes go up,
  the tribes of the LORD.

According to the decree for Israel,
  to give thanks to the name of the LORD.
In it are set up judgment seats,
  seats for the house of David.

READING I Even while King Saul lived, David ruled over some of the tribes of Israel. Then, when Saul died all the tribes came to David and asked him to be their king. They say, "Here we are, your bone and flesh"—an idiom that expresses their feeling of kinship with David. The idiom also appears in Genesis 2:23 when Adam says that Eve is "bone of my bones and flesh of my flesh," that is, a human being just like himself.

The Israelite tribes want David to rule over them because they recognize that they have an affinity with him that they did not have with Saul. Perhaps this is because, though Saul had the title of king, it was David who truly shepherded the people. He was the one who "led the Israelites out [to battle] and brought them back"—the leader who was by their side in life-threatening situations.

READING II This reading praises Jesus, who became bone of our bones and flesh of our flesh, and describes the consequences of his doing so. Paul urges us to give thanks (Greek *eucharisteō*) that through baptism God made us "fit to share" (Greek *hikanoō*, "qualified to share, or given the ability to share") in the inheritance that Jesus made available to humankind, namely, the life enjoyed by the holy ones. This is a life freed from the power of darkness, that is, from evils without and within us and from the fears that keep us from committing totally to God's beloved Son and the standards of his kingdom.

The reading concludes with a hymn to Christ that praises his rule over the cosmos. He—no other created person or thing—is the image of the invisible God. In Jesus, God came to share our life and to

Colossians = kuh-LOSH-uhnz

A didactic reading of powerful and poetic assertions about God that resonate into all of Christian belief.

As Paul begins to characterize God in several phrases beginning "He is," you will notice the emphases on the prepositions. Let the prepositions (of, in, on, through, for, before, through, from) do the work of guiding your proclamation—they point towards the image of the invisible God and allow your assembly to visualize it.

These are traditional names of angels. Add a note of reverence.
dominions = doh-MIN-yuhns
principalities = prihn-suh-PAL-uh-teez
Slight pause between "things" and "hold."

preeminent = pree-EHM-ih-nuhnt

reconcile = REK-uhn-sīl

READING II   Colossians 1:12–20

A reading from the Letter of Saint Paul to the Colossians

Brothers and **sisters**:
Let us give **thanks** to the **Father**,
　who has made you **fit** to **share**
　in the **inheritance** of the **holy ones** in **light**.
He **delivered** us from the **power** of **darkness**
　and **transferred** us to the **kingdom** of his beloved Son,
　in whom we have **redemption**, the **forgiveness** of **sins**.

He is the **image** of the invisible **God**,
　the **firstborn** of all **creation**.
For **in** him were created **all things** in **heaven** and on **earth**,
　the **visible** and the **invisible**,
　whether **thrones** or **dominions** or **principalities** or **powers**;
　all things were created **through** him and **for** him.
He is **before** all things,
　and **in** him **all things hold** together.
He is the **head** of the **body**, the **church**.
He is the **beginning**, the **firstborn** from the **dead**,
　that in **all things** he **himself** might be **preeminent**.
For in him all the **fullness** was **pleased** to dwell,
　and **through** him to **reconcile** all things **for** him,
　making **peace** by the **blood** of his **cross**
　through him, whether those on **earth** or those
　　in **heaven**.

reveal its purpose. Jesus is the firstborn of creation: he existed before *all* other things. And all things visible and invisible—*all* things that exist in the spiritual and worldly realms—were created through him and for him. In him alone "*all* things hold together."

Jesus was also the firstborn of the dead—the first to be raised up from the dead so "that in *all* things he himself might be preeminent." In Jesus' bones and flesh, "*all* the fullness" (Greek *plerōma*) of God, that is, everything that makes God God, was pleased to dwell. And when Jesus will-

ingly shed his lifeblood on the cross, he reconciled *all* things on heaven and earth with God and made their peace with God. One consequence of this peace is that God recognizes in every person one who is kin of the beloved Son, who is bone of Jesus' bones and flesh of his flesh.

GOSPEL   The scene in this Gospel displays just how different Christ our king is from all earthly rulers. As he faces the great human battle with death, he does not declare his innocence or

flaunt his power. Rather, he submits to the limited power of human rulers. He allows them to hang him on a cross between two criminals and to place a sarcastic inscription over his head that reads, "This is the King of the Jews." The rulers, soldiers, and one of the criminals mock Jesus' apparent weakness. If he is the Christ of God, they jeer, why does he not save himself and come down off the cross?

But one person in this scene sees a power in Jesus that the mockers miss. The other criminal who suffers by his side sees

GOSPEL   Luke 23:35–43

A reading from the holy Gospel according to Luke

The **rulers** sneered at **Jesus** and **said**,
　　"He saved **others**, let him **save** himself
　　if he is the **chosen** one, the **Christ** of **God**."
Even the **soldiers** jeered at him.
As they **approached** to offer him **wine** they called **out**,
　　"If you are **King** of the **Jews**, **save** yourself."
Above him there was an **inscription** that read,
　　"**This** is the **King** of the **Jews**."

Now one of the **criminals hanging** there **reviled Jesus**, saying,
　　"Are you **not** the **Christ**?
Save yourself and **us**."
The **other**, however, **rebuking** him, said in **reply**,
　　"Have you **no fear** of **God**,
　　for you are **subject** to the **same condemnation**?
And **indeed**, we have been **condemned justly**,
　　for the **sentence** we **received corresponds** to our **crimes**,
　　but **this man** has done **nothing criminal**."
Then he said,
　　"**Jesus**, **remember** me when you **come** into your **kingdom**."
He **replied** to him,
　　"**Amen**, I **say** to **you**,
　　today you will be **with** me in **Paradise**."

The final reading for Year C from Luke's Gospel, taken from the Passion. This Gospel reading is included in the long Passion reading on Palm Sunday.

reviled = rih-VĪLD

Slight pause between "criminals" and "hanging."

rebuking = rih-BYOOK-ing

Slight pause between "received" and "corresponds."

This moving exchange between St. Dismas and Jesus is as clear a sign of his full humanity and his full divinity as found in the Gospels. Don't rush through it. Proclaim these words to the assembly as if to the whole Church.

that Jesus, though innocent, does not try to change his fate. He realizes that Jesus, by staying on his cross, stays also with him in his suffering. The criminal is so stirred by Jesus' loyal companionship that his desire to be with him supersedes his fear of death. He acknowledges Jesus' kingship and asks Jesus to remember him when he comes into his kingdom. And Jesus, seeing in that criminal a person worthy of the life he offers, grants his final desire: that very day he will be with Jesus in Paradise. What a surprising end of that condemned man's day! He began it facing a death sentence and ended it beside the King of the universe!

This scene raises questions that the evangelist Luke expects us to answer. When we suffer on our cross, do we side with the mockers or the second criminal? Do we scorn Jesus' kingship and doubt his power? Do we expect him to save us by taking us off our own cross? Or, like that criminal, do we recognize Jesus' kinship with us? Do we appreciate that he became bone of our bones and flesh of our flesh so that he could experience with us the trials that are part of every human life, especially the battle with death? Do we see in him what the second criminal saw, a king who offers us life in his eternal kingdom? Does our desire to be with him override our fear of death? Are we living and will we die in ways that show us to be worthy of his companionship and his kingdom? E.N.